HEGEMONY AND WORLD ORDER

Hegemony and World Order explores a key question for our tumultuous times of multiple global crises. Does hegemony – that is, legitimated rule by dominant power – have a role in ordering world politics of the twenty-first century? If so, what form does that hegemony take: does it lie with a leading state or with some other force? How does contemporary world hegemony operate: what tools does it use and what outcomes does it bring?

This volume addresses these questions by assembling perspectives from various regions across the world, including Canada, Central Asia, China, Europe, India, Russia and the USA. The contributions in this book span diverse theoretical perspectives from realism to postcolonialism, as well as multiple issue areas such as finance, the Internet, migration and warfare. By exploring the role of non-state actors, transnational networks and norms, this collection covers various standpoints and moves beyond traditional concepts of state-based hierarchies centred on material power. The result is a wealth of novel insights on today's changing dynamics of world politics.

Hegemony and World Order is critical reading for policymakers and advanced students of International Relations, Global Governance, Development, and International Political Economy.

Piotr Dutkiewicz is Professor of Political Science and the Director of the Centre for Governance and Public Management, Carleton University, Ottawa, Canada.

Tom Casier is Jean Monnet Chair and Reader in International Relations at the University of Kent's Brussels School of International Studies (BSIS), Belgium.

Jan Aart Scholte is Professor of Global Transformations and Governance Challenges at Leiden University, Netherlands and Co-Director of the Centre for Global Cooperation Research at the University of Duisburg-Essen, Germany.

ROUTLEDGE GLOBAL COOPERATION SERIES

The *Routledge Global Cooperation* series develops innovative approaches to one of the most pressing questions of our time – how to achieve cooperation in a culturally diverse and politically contested global world?

Many key contemporary problems such as climate change and forced migration require intensified cooperation on a global scale. Accelerated globalisation processes have led to an ever-growing interconnectedness of markets, states, societies and individuals. Many of today's problems cannot be solved by nation states alone and require intensified cooperation at the local, national, regional and global level to tackle current and looming global crises.

Series Editors:

Tobias Debiel, Dirk Messner, Sigrid Quack and Jan Aart Scholte are Co-Directors of the Käte Hamburger Kolleg / Centre for Global Cooperation Research, University of Duisburg-Essen, Germany. Their research areas include climate change and sustainable development, global governance, internet governance and peacebuilding. Tobias Debiel is Professor of International Relations and Development Policy at the University of Duisburg-Essen and Director of the Institute for Development and Peace in Duisburg, Germany. Dirk Messner is President of the German Environment Agency (Umweltbundesamt – UBA). Sigrid Quack is Professor of Sociology at the University of Duisburg-Essen, Germany. Jan Aart Scholte is Professor of Peace and Development at the School of Global Studies, University of Gothenburg, Sweden.

Patricia Rinck is editorial manager of the series at the Centre for Global Cooperation Research.

https://www.routledge.com/Routledge-Global-Cooperation-Series/book-series/RGC

Titles:

Global Cooperation and the Human Factor in International Relations
Edited by Dirk Messner and Silke Weinlich

Peacebuilding in Crisis
Rethinking paradigms and practices of transnational cooperation
Edited by Tobias Debiel, Thomas Held and Ulrich Schneckener

Humanitarianism and Challenges of Global Cooperation
Edited by Volker M. Heins, Kai Koddenbrock and Christine Unrau

Gifts of Cooperation, Mauss and Pragmatism
Frank Adloff

Democratization and Memories of Violence
Ethnic minority rights movements in Mexico, Turkey, and El Salvador
Mneesha Gellman

Knowledge Production, Area Studies and Global Cooperation
Claudia Derichs

Democracy and Climate Change
Frederic Hanusch

World Politics in Translation
Power, Relationality, and Difference in Global Cooperation
Edited by Tobias Berger and Alejandro Esguerra

Integrating Sustainable Development in International Investment Law
Normative Incompatibility, System Integration and Governance Implications
Manjiao Chi

American Hegemony and the Rise of Emerging Powers
Cooperation or Conflict
Edited by Salvador Santino F. Regilme Jr. and James Parisot

Moral Agency and the Politics of Responsibility
Challenging Complexity
Edited by Cornelia Ulbert, Peter Finkenbusch, Elena Sondermann and Tobias Debiel

Public Participation in African Constitutionalism
Edited by Tania Abbiate, Markus Böckenförde and Veronica Federico

The Globalization of Foreign Aid
Developing Consensus
Liam Swiss

Region-Making and Cross-Border Cooperation
New Evidence from Four Continents
Edited by Elisabetta Nadalutti and Otto Kallscheuer

Trust in International Relations
Rationalist, constructivist, and psychological approaches
Edited by Hiski Haukkala, Carina van de Wetering and Johanna Vuorelma

The Justification of Responsibility in the UN Security Council
Practices of Normative Ordering in International Relations
Holger Niemann

Mapping and Politics in the Digital Age
Edited by Pol Bargués-Pedreny, David Chandler and Elena Simon

Refugee Governance, State and Politics in the Middle East
Zeynep Şahin Mencütek

Rethinking Governance in Europe and Northeast Asia
Multilateralism and Nationalism in International Society
Uwe Wissenbach

China's New Role in African Politics
From Non-Intervention towards Stabilization?
Edited by Christof Hartmann and Nele Noesselt

Hegemony and World Order
Reimagining Power in Global Politics
Edited by Piotr Dutkiewicz, Tom Casier, Jan Aart Scholte

HEGEMONY AND WORLD ORDER

Reimagining Power in Global Politics

Edited by Piotr Dutkiewicz, Tom Casier and Jan Aart Scholte

Centre for
**Global
Cooperation
Research**

SPONSORED BY THE

Federal Ministry
of Education
and Research

Routledge
Taylor & Francis Group

LONDON AND NEW YORK

First published 2021
by Routledge
2 Park Square, Milton Park, Abingdon, Oxon OX14 4RN

and by Routledge
52 Vanderbilt Avenue, New York, NY 10017

Routledge is an imprint of the Taylor & Francis Group, an informa business

British Library Cataloguing in Publication Data
A catalogue record for this book is available from the British Library

Library of Congress Cataloging-in-Publication Data
Names: Dutkiewicz, Piotr, editor. | Casier, Tom, editor. | Scholte, Jan
Aart, editor.
Title: Hegemony and world order : reimagining power in global politics /
edited by Piotr Dutkiewicz, Tom Casier and Jan Aart Scholte.
Description: Abingdon, Oxon ; New York, NY : Routledge, 2021. | Includes
bibliographical references.
Identifiers: LCCN 2020017050 (print) | LCCN 2020017051 (ebook) | ISBN
9780367479015 (hardback) | ISBN 9780367457242 (paperback) | ISBN
9781003037231 (ebook)
Subjects: LCSH: Hegemony. | World politics–21st century.
Classification: LCC JZ1312 .H46 2021 (print) | LCC JZ1312 (ebook) | DDC
327.1/14–dc23
LC record available at https://lccn.loc.gov/2020017050
LC ebook record available at https://lccn.loc.gov/2020017051

ISBN: 978-0-367-47901-5 (hbk)
ISBN: 978-0-367-45724-2 (pbk)
ISBN: 978-1-003-03723-1 (ebk)

Typeset in Bembo
by Taylor & Francis Books

This work and its open access publication has been supported by the Federal
Ministry of Education and Research (BMBF) in the context of its funding of the
Käte Hamburger Kolleg/Centre for Global Cooperation Research at the
University of Duisburg-Essen (grant number 01UK1810).

CONTENTS

ILLUSTRATIONS

Figures

Tables

ACKNOWLEDGEMENTS

The editors owe a gratitude to many people who gave their time and efforts to help this volume to materialise. First of all, we are grateful to the Dialogue of Civilizations Research Institute (DOC) Berlin for providing a strategic grant for this three-year project and very effective organisational support for its duration. DOC is an independent platform for dialogue that brings together diverse perspectives in a non-confrontational and constructive spirit. Our thanks go to the Carleton University Centre for Governance and Public Management (CGPM) for co-sponsoring two conferences (Warsaw, 2018 and Shanghai, 2019) and Mr Justin Li, Director of the Confucius Institute at Carleton University, for the partial funding of Carleton's participants in the conference in Shanghai (2019). We are grateful to Warsaw University for assisting in organising a project conference in May 2018. We are thankful to the Shanghai School of Advanced International Area Studies of East China Normal University (and its Dean, Professor Liu Jun) for co-hosting a conference to discuss final drafts of our book. We are most grateful to all contributors for the very effective and stimulating collaboration during the last three years. Piotr Dutkiewicz is grateful to Ewa Hebda-Dutkiewicz for her time and encouragement. It is also our pleasure to acknowledge the great support we received from Routledge Publishing.

CONTRIBUTORS

Viktoria Akchurina is an Assistant Professor at the Dauphine University in Paris. She is an author of academic publications on the incomplete state (Palgrave Macmillan, 2018), security and radicalisation (Routledge, 2015), and border and water management in central Eurasia (Lexington, 2018). She also co-edited a Special Section on 'Power and Competing Regionalism in a Wider Europe' in the *Journal of Europe-Asia Studies* (2018). In her previous capacity as a Researcher at TRENDS Consulting in Abu Dhabi, she published a number of policy papers on the Belt and Road Initiative in the Middle East and conducted research on European Union and Russian foreign policy in the Middle East, among other projects. Viktoria received her PhD in International Politics from the University of Trento (Italy), with a dissertation titled 'State as Social Practice: Sources, Resources, and Forces in Central Asia', which examines state-building processes comparatively in Uzbekistan, Tajikistan and Kyrgyzstan.

Ravi Dutt Bajpai is a China and India watcher who has published social and political commentaries in various Hindi and English media outlets in India and Australia. After two decades of experience in the IT industry, he decided to pursue his academic interests. He is currently a doctoral researcher in International Relations at Deakin University, Melbourne, Australia. He was a Fellow with the Australia India Institute in Delhi. His research is focused on civilisational exchanges in contemporary China–India relations. He is the co-author (with Harivansh) of *Chandra Shekhar: The Last Icon of Ideological Politics*, published by Rupa, New Delhi.

Tom Casier (Co-Editor) is Jean Monnet Chair and Reader in International Relations at the University of Kent's 'Brussels School of International Studies' (BSIS). He led BSIS as Academic Director from 2014 to 2017 and is currently Director of the Global Europe Centre. Tom Casier's research focuses mainly on

Russian foreign policy and EU–Russia relations, with a particular interest in power and identity. An edited volume (with Joan DeBardeleben) entitled *EU–Russia Relations in Crisis: Understanding Diverging Perceptions* was published with Routledge in 2018. Recent articles have appeared in *Cooperation and Conflict, Geopolitics, International Politics, Contemporary Politics, Europe-Asia Studies* and others. He led a Jean Monnet project on EU–Russia relations with three other Jean Monnet chairs, resulting in the policy report: 'EU–Russia relations: which way forward?' (2016). He has also provided policy advice for different institutions and organisations, including the European Parliament, the House of Lords and the US State Department.

Elena Chebankova is a Research Fellow at the Centre for Governance and Public Management, Carleton University. Previously she was a Reader in Politics at the University of Lincoln, UK. She holds a PhD in social and political sciences from King's College, Cambridge and is the author of numerous articles and books on Russian politics.

Piotr Dutkiewicz (Co-Editor) is Professor of Political Science and the Director of the Centre for Governance and Public Management, Carleton University, Ottawa, Canada. He was Editor-in-Chief of a 17-volume series on Local and Regional Development in Poland (1986–1989). Most recent books include Piotr Dutkiewicz, Richard Sakwa and Fyodor Lukyanov (eds), *Eurasia on the Edge: Managing Complexity* (Rowman US, 2018); Vladimir Popov and Piotr Dutkiewicz (eds), *Mapping a New World Order: The Rest beyond the West* (Edgar Edward Publishing, 2017); Piotr Dutkiewicz, Richard Sakwa and Vladimir Kulikov (eds), *Social History of Post-Communist Russia* (Routledge, 2016); Piotr Dutkiewicz and Richard Sakwa (eds), *Eurasian Integration: The View from Within* (Routledge, 2015); Piotr Dutkiewicz and Richard Sakwa (eds), *22 Ideas to Fix the World* (NYU Press, 2013); Piotr Dutkiewicz and Vladislav Inozemtsev (eds), *Democracy versus Modernisation: A Dilemma for Russia and for the World* (Routledge, 2012); Piotr Dutkiewicz and Dmitri Trenin (eds), *Russia: The Challenges of Transformation* (NYU Press, 2011). He has received two doctorates *honoris causa* (2006 and 2007), and is a Member of the Valdai Club.

Martin Geiger is Associate Professor of Politics of Migration and Mobility at Carleton University, Ottawa. He is a Member of the International Steering Committee of Metropolis (a global network of academics, practitioners and government representatives on migration), a Corresponding Member of the Institute for Migration Research and Intercultural Studies at University of Osnabrück (Germany), and a Senior Non-Resident Research Fellow at the Center for China and Globalization (Beijing). Dr Geiger founded and co-edits the Palgrave Macmillan series 'Mobility & Politics'. His research focuses on global migration governance and the politics of migration and other forms of mobility. He is particularly interested in the role of intergovernmental agencies, non-state actors and private corporations in managing global mobility and migration. Recent contributions have been published in the *Journal of Ethnic Migration Studies* and the series International Political Economy (Palgrave Macmillan).

Randall Germain is Professor of Political Science at Carleton University, Canada. His teaching and research focus on the political economy of global finance, issues and themes associated with economic and financial governance, and theoretical debates within the field of international political economy (IPE). His work has been published in journals such as *International Studies Quarterly, Review of International Political Economy, Review of International Studies, Global Governance*, and *European Journal of International Relations*. He is the author of *The International Organization of Credit* (Cambridge University Press, 1997) and *Global Politics and Financial Governance* (Palgrave, 2010). Most recently he edited *Susan Strange and the Future of Global Political Economy* (Routledge, 2016). He is currently working on a manuscript that explores the use of the idea of history in IPE.

Leslie A. Pal is Founding Dean of the College of Public Policy at Hamad Bin Khalifa University, Doha, Qatar, and Chancellor's Professor of Public Policy and Administration at Carleton University, Ottawa, Canada. He is the author, co-author or editor of over 30 books, the most recent of which are *Beyond Policy Analysis: Public Issue Management in Turbulent Times* (6th edn, 2020), *Global Governance and Muslim Organizations* (2019), *Public Policy Transfer: Micro-Dynamics and Macro-Effects* (2017), and *Policy Making in a Transformative State: The Case of Qatar* (2016). He has published over 90 articles and book chapters in a wide variety of areas of public policy and administration, international human rights, and international public management reform. He has also served as a consultant to several international organisations including the World Bank and the OECD.

Swati Parashar is Associate Professor in Peace and Development at the School of Global Studies, University of Gothenburg, Sweden. She is also a Research Associate with the Centre for International Studies and Diplomacy (CISD) at the School of Oriental and African Studies (SOAS), University of London and a Visiting Faculty at the Malaviya Centre for Peace Research, Banaras Hindu University, Varanasi, India. Her research engages with the intersections between feminism and postcolonialism, focused on conflict and development issues in South Asia. She is the author of *Women and Militant Wars: The Politics of Injury* (Routledge, 2014), co-editor (with Ann Tickner and Jacqui True) of *Revisiting Gendered States: Feminist Imaginings of the State in International Relations* (Oxford University Press, 2018), and co-editor (with Jane Parpart) of *Gender, Silence and Agency in Contested Terrains* (Routledge, 2019).

Corey R. Payne is a PhD student in the Department of Sociology and the Arrighi Center for Global Studies at Johns Hopkins University. He studies the dynamics of historical capitalism, war-making, class struggle and geopolitics.

Ivan Safranchuk is Senior Fellow with the Institute for International Studies at MGIMO University (Moscow) and Associate Professor at the National Research University Higher School of Economics (Moscow). He is also non-resident Fellow at the Center for Strategic and International Studies (Washington). As Visiting Professor he has lectured at Yale University and Beijing University. He has published on international relations and security, US–Russian relations, Central Asia and Afghanistan. His work has been published inter alia in *Strategic Analysis, India Quarterly, Russia in Global Affairs*, and *Russian Politics and Law*, as well as several edited volumes in English.

Brian C. Schmidt is Associate Professor in the Department of Political Science at Carleton University, Ottawa, Canada. His primary research interest is the disciplinary history of the academic field of International Relations. He is also interested in international relations theory, especially the theory of realism. Professor Schmidt has published widely in academic journals such as *International Studies Quarterly, Review of International Studies, Security Studies*, and *Millennium: Journal of International Studies*. He is the author of *The Political Discourse of Anarchy: A Disciplinary History of International Relations* (SUNY Press, 1998), which received the *Choice* outstanding book award. He is the editor, with David Long, of *Imperialism and Internationalism in the Discipline of International Relations* (SUNY Press, 2005), *International Relations and the First Great Debate* (Routledge, 2012), and with Nicolas Guilhot, *Historiographical Investigations in International Relations* (Palgrave Macmillan, 2019). He is the co-editor, with David Long, of the Palgrave Macmillan History of International Thought Series.

Jan Aart Scholte (Co-Editor) is Professor of Global Transformations and Governance Challenges at Leiden University and Co-Director of the Centre for Global Cooperation Research at the University of Duisburg-Essen. Previous positions were at the University of Sussex, the Institute of Social Studies, the University of Warwick, the London School of Economics (Centennial Professor), and the University of Gothenburg. He has (co-)coordinated various projects and programmes on global governance and is a former lead editor of the academic journal *Global Governance*. Books include *Contesting Global Governance* (co-author, Cambridge University Press, 2000); *Globalization: A Critical Introduction* (author, Palgrave Macmillan, 2005), *Building Global Democracy? Civil Society and Accountable Global Governance* (editor, Cambridge University Press, 2011), *New Rules for Global Justice* (lead editor, Rowman & Littlefield International, 2016), and *Legitimacy in Global Governance* (co-editor, Oxford University Press, 2018). Recent articles have appeared in *European Journal of International Relations, Global Governance, Globalizations, International Theory*, and *Review of International Studies*.

Beverly J. Silver is Professor and Chair of the Department of Sociology, as well as Director, Arrighi Center for Global Studies at the Johns Hopkins University. Her many publications include: Beverly J. Silver and Sahan Savas Karatasli, 'Historical

Dynamics of Capitalism and Labor Movements' in *The Oxford Handbook of Social Movements* (Oxford University Press, 2015); Beverly Silver, 'Labour, War and World Politics: Contemporary Dynamics in World-Historical Perspective', in *Handbook of International Political Economy of Production* (Edward Elgar, 2015); Beverly Silver, 'Theorising the Working Class in Twenty-First-Century Capitalism', in *Workers and Labour in a Globalised Capitalism: Contemporary Themes and Theoretical Issues* (Palgrave Macmillan, 2013); Beverly J. Silver and Giovanni Arrighi, 'End of the Long Twentieth Century', in *Business as Usual: The Roots of the Global Financial Meltdown* (New York University Press, 2011); Beverly J. Silver and Lu Zhang, 'China as an Emerging Epicenter of World Labor Unrest', in *China and the Transformation of Global Capitalism* (Johns Hopkins University Press, 2009); Giovanni Arrighi, Beverly J. Silver and Benjamin D. Brewer, 'Industrial Convergence and the Persistence of the North-South Divide: A Rejoinder to Firebaugh', *Studies in Comparative International Development*, 40, 1, 2005.

Elinor Sloan is Professor of International Relations and Chair of the Department of Political Science at Carleton University, Ottawa where she specialises in Canadian, US and Allied security and defence policy. A graduate of the Royal Military College of Canada, she holds an MA from the Norman Paterson School of International Affairs at Carleton University and a PhD from the Fletcher School of Law and Diplomacy at Tufts University in Boston. Prior to joining academia, she was a regular forces officer in the Canadian Armed Forces and a defence analyst in Ottawa's National Defence Headquarters. Professor Sloan is author of five books in the field of international security studies as well as two second editions, most recently *Modern Military Strategy* (Routledge, 2017).

Yong Wang is a Director of the Center for International Political Economy and Professor at the School of International Studies at Peking University. Yong received his BA and MA in law and international politics and PhD in law from Peking University. He joined the faculty of the School of International Studies at Peking University in 1990. He studied at the Hopkins-Nanjing Center and was also a visiting scholar at the University of California San Diego and a joint visiting fellow at the Pacific Council on International Policy and the University of Southern California. His major authored books include *International Political Economy in China: The Global Conversation* (co-edited with Greg Chin and Margaret Pearson, Routledge, 2015), *Political Economy of International Trade* (China Market Press, 2008) and *Political Economy of China–U.S. Trade Relations* (China Market Press, 2007), which was awarded the first prize for Excellent Social Sciences Works by the Beijing Municipal Government and the Beijing Confederation of Social Scientists in 2008.

Xin Zhang is an Associate Professor at the School of Advanced International and Area Studies, East China Normal University in Shanghai. He holds a PhD in political science from UCLA and has taught at Reed College (Oregon), Fudan

University (Shanghai), and the Higher School of Economics (Moscow and St. Petersburg). His major fields of expertise are comparative and international political economy, political sociology, critical geopolitics, and Russian and Eurasian politics. His academic and policy research has appeared in multiple languages in *Review of International Political Economy, Geopolitics, Osteuropa, China Journal,* and *Russia in Global Affairs,* etc. An active public commentator on global affairs, he has also written commissioned policy reports for the Ministry of Foreign Affairs of China, the China Development Bank, and the Valdai Club.

HEGEMONY IN WORLD POLITICS

An introduction

Jan Aart Scholte, Tom Casier and Piotr Dutkiewicz

Two features stand out in world politics today: pressing global challenges and shifting power constellations. On the one hand, the contemporary world faces unprecedented demands for global cooperation around problems such as digital networks, disease control, ecological changes, finance capital, heritage preservation, migration, military security and much more. On the other hand, the current political situation is highly volatile, with transformations around the distribution of state power, technological developments, the nature of capitalism, intercultural relations and so on. What are the prospects of world order in these uncertain times?

Important answers to this question may lie with hegemony, understood as legitimated rule by dominant power. Under conditions of hegemony, superior forces in world politics deploy their concentrations of resources to sponsor ordering arrangements for world society. Importantly, hegemonically generated rules and regulatory institutions enjoy substantial legitimacy. That is, although hegemony largely imposes its ordering framework on the world, many or most of the affected actors endorse the hegemonic power as being appropriate and rightful.

This quality of legitimacy makes hegemony a special kind of supremacy. Subjects believe that the dominant force, and the order that it upholds, offer a good situation. Thus, with hegemony, it is possible to obtain order in world politics without (so much) overt coercion and covert trickery. Of course, normative theorists can ask whether actors make correct judgements when they approve and trust the hegemonic force; however, the sociological point is to observe that subjects do accord such legitimacy. The social research challenge is to explain how and why hegemony happens, and based on that analysis to consider what sort of world order this hegemony could generate today and in the future.

Where might hegemony lie in contemporary world politics? As is elaborated later in this introduction, and indeed throughout this book, rival accounts locate hegemony in different places. For some, hegemony emanates from a dominant

DOI: 10.4324/9781003037231-16

state or group of states. For others, hegemony resides with dominant non-state actors, such as leading business corporations or civil society associations. For still others, hegemony lies not so much with actors (whether state or non-state), but with structural forces. Examples could include a structural hegemony of capitalism (on Gramscian accounts), Western imperialism (on postcolonial accounts), certain knowledge structures (on constructivist accounts), or anthropocentrism (on political ecology accounts). These various competing conceptions of hegemony will occupy us at greater length later. For now, at the outset, it should be underlined that the character of hegemony sparks intense debate.

Long-reigning conventional wisdom has it that the United States Government (USG) played a hegemonic role in world politics during the middle and late twentieth century (Aron 1974; Gilpin 1987; Brilmayer 1994; O'Brien and Clesse 2002; Foot et al. 2003; Reus-Smit 2004; Bromley 2008; Schake 2009; Norrlof 2010). On this account, the USG (with the support of strong internationalist wings of business and civil society in the USA) grasped a moment of heavy resource concentration following the Second World War to underwrite a world order framework based on principles of liberal multilateralism. The so-called *Pax Americana* (Cox 1981; Hippler 1994; Parchami 2009) or 'American world order' (Acharya 2018) was successfully hegemonic inasmuch as, outside the communist orbit, large swathes of elites and general publics around the world approved of this US global leadership. Indeed, the collapse of the communist challenge gave US hegemony a 'unipolar moment' in the 1990s (Ikenberry 2004; Brands 2016).

But what of hegemony in world politics today, facing the twenty-first century? The USG no longer has the degree of resource primacy that it held in the 1940s and the 1990s. Moreover, contested military interventions (in Vietnam, Iraq, etc.) as well as rising economic protectionism have today undercut the moral authority of US power in the wider world. Although some observers might still dismiss US decline as a myth (Strange 1987; Germain, Chapter 7 this volume), most analysts see the era of US world hegemony as passing (Chari 2008; Zakaria 2011; Desai 2013; Reich and Lebow 2014; Acharya 2018). What, if any, other hegemony then could come in its place?

At the moment, no individual state would appear to hold a hegemonic capacity. Some commentators suggest that China could eventually move into such a world-ordering role (Ross and Zhu 2008; Robinson 2011; Lee 2017). However, it seems unlikely that, whatever one makes of assertive steps like the current Belt and Road Initiative, China can for the foreseeable future obtain either singular resource supremacy in the world or widely legitimated leadership in global regime construction.

Might we then instead expect contemporary hegemony to come from a collection of major states, such as the Group of Seven (G7) or the Group of Twenty (G20) (Bailin 2005; Donnelly 2009)? Or might there emerge a 'multi-order world' with several co-existing regional hegemonies (Flockhart 2016)? Or do we enter a non-hegemonic era where legitimated rules of world order do not depend on any dominant state or states (Brem and Stiles 2009)?

Or should one let go of the preoccupation with states and look for contemporary hegemony elsewhere? Indeed, did even US hegemony of the twentieth century more fundamentally emanate from large global corporations rather than the USG itself (Gill 1990; Rupert 1995)? Or does contemporary hegemony lie with one or the other social structure, such as transnational capitalism or securitisation discourses (Agnew 2005; Balzacq 2011; Peoples and Vaughan-Williams 2015; Taylor 2017)? Or has hegemony become 'complex', with a diffusion of legitimated dominant power across multiple actors and structures (Williams 2019; Scholte, Chapter 5 this volume)?

This book explores these issues to discover what, if any, kind of hegemony might play out in our present world of proliferating global challenges and profound systemic shifts. The title speaks of 'reimagining power', since ongoing global transformations may require us radically to reconsider how hegemony operates. Indeed, we ought perhaps to place 'hegemonies' in the plural in order to designate: (a) that, in theory, scholars have multiple understandings of the concept; and (b) that, in practice, contemporary hegemony may operate from several quarters at once.

Contributions of this volume

As this book's lengthy bibliography indicates, researchers have over the years spilt much ink on the question of hegemony in world politics. A sceptical reader might therefore well ask why one should produce yet another publication on the subject. We would underline four distinctive contributions of this volume.

First, *Hegemony and World Order* is special for assembling analyses from a range of theoretical perspectives. In contrast to many other works, we do not limit ideas of hegemony to a single definitional and disciplinary lens. The chapters span constructivist, liberal, Gramscian, postcolonial, realist and world-systems theories. In terms of academic discipline, the authors stem from comparative politics, global studies, international relations, political economy and sociology. The book thereby presents readers with the latest innovative thinking across the conceptual spectrum, in an ongoing debate about the character of hegemony.

Second, *Hegemony and World Order* is exceptional for assembling in one volume studies on hegemony from different parts of the world. The authors herald from Canada, Central Asia, China, Europe, India, Russia and the USA. Indeed, the chapters often explicitly underline how different geopolitical locations understand and practice hegemony differently. The book therefore departs from the Western-centrism that has marked most previous academic discussions of hegemony.

Third, unlike most other work on the subject, *Hegemony and World Order* examines a range of policy fields. The chapters variously consider hegemony as it plays out in respect of armaments, finance, ideology, the Internet, knowledge, labour, migration and money. The book also mixes more macro analyses of encompassing structures of hegemony with more micro analyses of everyday practices of hegemony. The reader thereby obtains both theoretical and substantive breadth.

Finally, *Hegemony and World Order* reaps distinctive benefit from extended exchanges across the aforementioned diversities. The authors have had the rare privilege to meet together in 4 workshops spread across 16 months between May 2018 and September 2019. Thus constructivists, liberals, Gramscians, post-colonialists, realists and world-systems theorists have sat together and learned from each other. Likewise, authors from the different regions of the world have met – and been changed by – new colleagues. In addition, specialists on different issue-areas have compared notes across the same table.

In short, this book addresses one of the most consequential and hotly debated issues in contemporary world politics: how might hegemony operate today, and with what implications for major – even existential – global challenges? The volume makes a distinctive and important contribution to knowledge of world order by (a) focusing on the question of hegemony; (b) encompassing a broad range of divergent theoretical perspectives; (c) assembling authors from around the world; (d) including a broad set of empirical studies; and (e) bringing these diverse perspectives into conversation with each other.

Hegemony: What is it?

Like most key concepts, hegemony can be interpreted in various ways (Haugaard and Lentner 2006; Anderson 2017). Here we understand hegemony to entail *legitimated rule by dominant power*. Hegemony prevails when a supreme force governs society 'top-down' – and does so in ways that a preponderance of affected actors positively endorse. Hegemony therefore combines (a) concentrated control of material resources; (b) leadership in setting societal rules and regulatory processes; and (c) prevailing perceptions among subjects that the dominant power rules appropriately.

So, crucially, hegemony involves legitimacy. Hegemonic legitimacy is not democratic legitimacy, where people have confidence and trust in a regime because they themselves control the governing process. Rather, hegemonic legitimacy prevails when (decisive portions of) a dominated population embrace their domination and positively approve of the dominating force. So, in a hege-monic situation, prevailing opinion might believe in an autocratic government. Or most workers might endorse a capitalist order that subordinates them. Or colonised elites might positively sanction an imperial order. Thus hegemony is different from overt suppression and involuntary dominion. In a situation of hegemony, supreme forces can for the most part avoid active coercion and devious manipulation, since their domination has the consent of (crucial quarters of) the dominated.

To be sure, most situations of hegemony also include some counter-hegemonic resistance. However, when hegemony is robust this opposition constitutes only a fringe force. Thus, for example, protesters periodically took to the streets against USG interventions in Vietnam, Iraq and elsewhere, but overall the legitimacy of *Pax Americana* prevailed. Likewise, a counter-hegemony of liberalism has operated in China and Russia, but a preponderance of citizens still endorse the hegemonic authoritarian state in those two countries. That said, now and again counter-hegemony can substantially weaken or even overturn an existing hegemony, as seen with the collapse of many communist regimes in 1989–91 and feminist resistance against patriarchy in various parts of the world. At present, populist forces seek to undo a hegemony of neoliberal globalisation, and time will tell if they succeed.

To observe and study hegemony is of course not necessarily, as a researcher, to adopt a normative position towards it. Hence this book does not per se advocate or oppose hegemony, either as a general phenomenon or in any particular manifestation. In this respect it is important to distinguish between *sociological* legitimacy and *normative* legitimacy. Sociological investigations of legitimacy, as in this volume, seek to understand how and why people perceive that a regime exercises appropriate authority (Weber 1922; Tallberg et al. 2018). In contrast, normative studies of legitimacy seek to develop and apply philosophical principles for judging the appropriateness or otherwise of a regime (Caney 2005; Buchanan and Keohane 2006). Thus researchers can study hegemony as a sociological phenomenon without themselves morally endorsing that hegemony. Indeed, many sociological accounts of hegemony – including various chapters in this book – also regard it sceptically. For example, a critical theorist might argue that people who endorse a particular hegemony are mistaken to do so and suffer from 'false consciousness'.

Hegemony can operate within a territorial unit. In this case, an authoritarian government might use a concentrated command of resources within a country to set the rules and regulatory processes for its national society – and do so with the general confidence and approval of the resident population. Another reading might say that hegemony in a country lies not so much with the state per se as with a power elite that controls the government, the economic apparatus, and the cultural sphere (Mills 1956). In either case, the key point with domestic hegemony is that citizens broadly endorse their domination by superior forces in the country.

Hegemony can also extend beyond national arenas to operate in world politics. It is world-scale hegemony that most concerns this book. As we shall see shortly, some accounts understand world hegemony in terms of one or several territorial governments having legitimated dominance in an international society of states. Other accounts understand world hegemony in terms of one or more social forces having legitimated dominance in a global society of peoples. Whichever approach one adopts, both cases focus on hegemony as a condition of world affairs rather than domestic politics.

The issue of hegemony in world politics is particularly intriguing given the absence of a world state – and little prospect of one emerging in the foreseeable future. How can dominant power create legitimated rules and regulatory institutions for world affairs without a centralised planetary government? In this anarchical situation, does world hegemony function through informal arrangements, such as the Concert of Europe in the nineteenth century and the G20 today? Or does world hegemony operate through formal international law and international organisation, such as the United Nations (UN) system on a global scale and the European Union (EU) on a regional scale? Or does world hegemony work through non-state channels, including private regulatory mechanisms such as the Forest Stewardship Council (FSC) and deliberative assemblies such as the World Economic Forum (WEF)? Or does world hegemony encompass some combination of these various institutional forms? And what deeper structural forces might lie behind these institutional expressions of hegemony in world politics?

Hegemony in world politics: Contending perspectives

As underlined earlier, different theories offer different propositions about what kind of dominant power can achieve hegemony in world politics. The next paragraphs first review various perspectives that locate world hegemony in a state or group of states. Thereafter we survey a range of approaches that place world hegemony in non-state quarters. Needless to say, this rough overview simplifies a complicated picture. We brush over some of the diversity within the various schools of thought, and we accentuate some of the differences between analytical frameworks. The aim is not to give a comprehensive fine-grained account of theories so much as to distinguish general contrasting ways to understand world hegemony.

Liberal theories of world politics have argued that hegemony arises when a dominant state uses its supreme control of resources to sponsor international regimes that provide collectively beneficial international cooperation. This approach was prominently expounded in the 1970s by the economic historian Charles Kindleberger (1973), who ascribed international disorder of the 1930s to the absence of a hegemonic state. Lacking hegemonically underwritten rules and regulatory institutions, so Kindleberger affirmed, the world tumbled into extended depression and eventual major war. Liberal theorists in the field of International Relations (IR) have highlighted (and with varying degrees of explicitness applauded) the role of the USG in leading multilateral cooperation after 1945 (Keohane 1984; Nye 1990; Ikenberry 2001). Similarly, the English School scholar Ian Clark (2011) has enquired into the possibilities of a 'good' hegemonic state whose leadership is acceptable to the rest of international society.

The liberal suggestion is that, without the internationalist hegemony of the USG, the second half of the twentieth century would have seen less economic prosperity, more military conflict, less representative democracy and greater human rights violations around the world. Looking at contemporary circumstances, liberals are principally concerned whether the USG is able and willing to continue its (purportedly benevolent) hegemonic leadership. Absent a US hegemon, liberal theorists worry for the future of multilateral cooperation through international law and international organisation – and the consequences in turn for economic stability, human rights, democracy and peace in the world. Possible future hegemony of the Chinese state does not appeal to liberals in this regard. Alternatively, according to the 'regime theory' variant of liberalism, the frameworks of international cooperation that were established under USG predominance may be sufficiently embedded to persist without the continued sponsorship of a hegemonic state (Keohane 1984).

Like liberal approaches, realist theories of world politics have located hegemony in a dominant state. (Note here that 'political realism' in IR is distinct from 'critical realism' in social theory – see Joseph 2002.) However, whereas liberal accounts focus on the readiness of a leading state to sponsor collectively beneficial international cooperation, realist arguments explain hegemony in terms of conflict and an ongoing interstate competition for power. For realists, hegemony arises in world politics when a particular state defies the usual balance of power among states and becomes singularly predominant. The hegemonic state then uses its resource supremacy (especially superior military capabilities) to create instruments of world order that are intended to sustain its primacy. As and when these arrangements do not advance the hegemon's national interest and power, it will abandon them. Thus, for example, in realist eyes the USG hegemon established and supported multilateral institutions after 1945 as an extension of its self-serving foreign policy. Realists chart the rise and fall of hegemonic states in history, usually giving war a major role in both the ascendance and the decline (Gilpin 1987, 1988; Kennedy 1988; Webb and Krasner 1989; Mearsheimer 2001).

Whereas liberal theorists generally applaud the 'good' hegemon that promotes universal liberal values, realists tend to examine hegemony without a driving normative concern about the kind of world order that the dominant state should promote. Realists generally seek to understand why hegemonic states arise and how they operate rather than to judge whether the resulting hegemonic order is desirable. That said, several prominent realists have had moral concerns at the core of their analysis and publicly criticised certain policies of the USG hegemon (Niebuhr 1932; Murray 1996).

The rise and fall of hegemonic states has also concerned world-system theory and other analyses of world political economy in long-term perspective. These accounts have suggested that cycles of world hegemony are a key feature of modern (and sometimes also older) history. Authors in this stream variously identify hegemonic states to include Portugal in the sixteenth century, the United Provinces (today's Netherlands) in the seventeenth century, Britain in the nineteenth century, the USA in the twentieth century and (possibly) China in the twenty-first century. Whereas realist theories explain the rise and fall of hegemons solely in terms of a perpetual interstate struggle for power, world-system perspectives focus on an interplay between cycles of interstate relations on the one hand and long cycles of capitalist development on the other. Thus hegemony goes through historical phases in connection with the dynamics of surplus accumulation and associated social conflicts (Wallerstein 1983; Arrighi and Silver 1999; Friedman and Chase-Dunn 2005; also relatedly Modelski 1987). While world-systems theorists undertake a sociological analysis of hegemony, they often express explicit normative sympathies with counter-hegemonic social movements of workers and other structurally disadvantaged groups (Arrighi et al. 1989; Smith and Wiest 2012).

In this respect, world-systems accounts of hegemony share common ground with other critical theories.

Capitalism is an even more focal driver of hegemony for neo-Gramscian theory (Cox 1983; Gill and Law 1989; Burnham 1991; Gill 1993; Overbeek 1993; Kiely 2005; Morton 2007; McNally and Schwarsmantel 2009; Worth 2015). In a Marxist vein, neo-Gramscians explain world politics in terms of surplus accumulation processes and accompanying (transnational) class relations. Thus, for neo-Gramscians, the state and its international relations are not a dynamic in their own right (as per the previously described theories) so much as a regulatory adjunct of the capitalist mode of production. Thus, while world hegemony may manifest itself in a leading state – such as the USG in the twentieth century – the deeper hegemony for Gramscians lies with capitalism and its (transnational) ruling class. Capitalism is the dominant (structural) power that governs in ways that a preponderance of opinion finds legitimate (even if most people may not be fully conscious that capitalism is the ultimate ruler of their society).

Neo-Gramscians are therefore more interested in governance (i.e. regulation in whatever form) than in the state as such. To be sure, capitalist hegemony may at some junctures use a dominant state to generate enabling regulation for surplus accumulation on a world scale. However, capitalist world order could also be achieved through a collective of states such as the G7, or through regional apparatuses such as the EU, or through global multilateralism such as the Bretton Woods institutions, or through private regulatory mechanisms such as International Accounting Standards Board (IASB). Thus, whereas liberal, realist and world-system approaches presume that hegemony emanates from a leading state, neo-Gramscian theory looks for any governance arrangement (state, interstate, or non-state) that secures the structural power of surplus accumulation and the capitalist class. As capitalism globalises in contemporary history, its ruling class also acquires an increasingly transnational character (Van der Pijl 1998; Sklair 2001).

Legitimacy in a neo-Gramscian account of world hegemony arises when subordinated classes consent to the reigning capitalist order. Whereas non-hegemonic capitalism depends on coercion and manipulation to sustain its exploitation, with successful hegemony the exploited classes largely believe that the rules which sustain surplus accumulation also serve their interests. Consumerism and mass media – nowadays operating on a global scale – could play a pivotal role in generating such 'false consciousness'. However, other people may see through this obfuscation and mobilise in counter-hegemonic resistance against the world capitalist order. Neo-Gramscians often celebrate the purported emancipatory potential of these underclass movements that assemble, for example, landless peasants and the urban poor (Gill 2008).

Resistance to arbitrary social inequality is also a motivating concern for postcolonial theories of hegemony (Krishna 2009; Rao 2010; Seth 2013; Anievas et al. 2014). In this perspective, the structural roots of world hegemony lie not so much in the state system or capitalism as in the Western modernity of which the nation-state and capitalism are a part. Originally centred in Europe, the modern social order has spread, via imperialism, to dominate world society as a whole. In that sense, 'the West' as a social structure is now quite pervasive, including in much of the so-called 'Third World' or 'Global South'. In earlier times, imperialism mainly took form as direct colonialism, while the contemporary empire of Western modernity is usually more informal and subtle, operating for example through the UN, global corporations, and nongovernmental organisations (NGOs).

Legitimacy figures in postcolonial conceptions of hegemony inasmuch as subjects – the 'colonised' as well as the 'colonisers' – tend to endorse Western modernity and its hierarchies as a good and 'natural' order of things. Even many marginalised subjects have embraced the modern promise of progress (so-called 'development') toward (Western understandings of) freedom, prosperity and peace. At the same time, however, counter-hegemonic resistance surfaces in what postcolonial theory characterises as 'subaltern' movements: i.e. among people 'below the altar' of Western modernity, such as aboriginals, persons of colour, Dalits and non-Western religions. From a critical theory perspective that looks for social transformation – in this case to create worlds beyond Western imperialism – postcolonial theories usually have normative sympathies with subaltern counter-hegemonic struggles.

Some postcolonial approaches to hegemony, picking up on certain strands of feminist theory, conceive of world power in terms of intersecting social stratifications. Whereas neo-Gramscian theories focus on class as the one – allegedly overriding – structural hierarchy in world politics, intersectional analyses stress a multiplicity of embedded inequalities, including on lines of age, caste, class, (dis) ability, gender, language, nationality, race, religion, sexuality and more. In an intersectional perspective, none of these axes of subordination has primacy over the others. Rather, dominance and subordination in world politics occurs through intricate and varying combinations – i.e. 'intersections' – of the multiple stratifications. Thus, resources and power tend to flow most to people who sit atop several hierarchies at once: e.g. white, middle-aged, propertied, heterosexual men. Conversely, contemporary world order tends to silence 'the Other': people identified inter alia as black, Dalits, disabled, indigenous, LGBTQ+, proletarian, women and youth. Marginalisation is all the more intense for people who are located at the intersection of several subordinations. This structural subjection extends to the regulatory sphere, where the rules of world order are generally made by – and reinforce the predominance of – people at the top end of (combined) social stratifications. This dominance also acquires a hegemonic quality when people, including those in the subordinated positions, endorse the rules that produce the various axes of structural subordination.

For constructivist theories, hegemony in world politics resides with a ruling knowledge frame. Whereas neo-Gramscian approaches understand hegemony in terms of a mode of production, constructivist perspectives look first of all at ideational structure. In this case hegemony – the dominant power that exercises legitimate rule in world politics – resides in certain ways of knowing. In constructivist notions of hegemony, certain ideational structures control a predominance of resources in world society, construct rules and regulatory institutions for the globe, and attract widespread legitimacy.

For example, there could be a world hegemony of economic growth ideology (Schmelzer 2016) or security discourse (Pasha 1996; Hansen 2006). In the first case, ideas of economic growth, which mainly spread from the 1930s, are seen to reign supreme in world politics, guiding governance on scales local-to-global. With hegemony, growth mindsets moreover have legitimacy, in that prevailing opinion regards this paradigm as an appropriate ordering principle for world society (even if it could generate ecological catastrophe). A similar constructivist argument could apply to security, a discourse that initially rose to prominence in the Cold War and progressively spread to all areas of social life. Today ideas of 'security' constitute a structure of world order, as manifested in airport security, cybersecurity, environmental security, food security, military security and so on. Security as a dominant knowledge frame is moreover hegemonically legitimate, in that most people most of the time believe that preoccupations with security are appropriate and serve their interests. Other constructivists have highlighted the discursive power in world politics of 'human rights' (Keck and Sikkink 1998), 'sustainable development' (Bernstein 2001), 'markets' (Plehwe et al. 2006), 'humanitarianism' (Barnett 2011), and certain understandings of 'masculinity' (Messerschmidt 2016).

Constructivist approaches vary in their critical stance toward ideational hegemonies. Some constructivists are principally interested to explain how certain ideas become and remain ruling norms in world politics, without seeking through their analysis to undermine the power of those ideas. In contrast, constructivists with a 'deconstruction' bent – in the vein of postmodernism and poststructuralism – emphasise the historical relativity of reigning discourses and the political consequences of hegemonic ideas in empowering some ways of being and, especially, marginalising others (Larner and Walters 2004; Bonditti et al. 2017). Academic deconstruction might in this sense be viewed as a counter-hegemonic move.

A survey of theoretical approaches to hegemony in world politics can also include notions of structural anthropocentrism from political ecology. Anthropocentrism refers here to a social order – our modern world – in which existence is human-centred and the lives of other species are subordinated to human will (Boddice 2011; Kopnina et al. 2018; Wapner 2020). Theories of political ecology regard anthropocentrism as hegemonic to the extent that: (a) resources of the planet are concentrated on humans and human ends; (b) rules and regulatory processes in world society serve this human-centredness; and (c) prevailing human opinion regards this order of things as appropriate. Indeed, the hegemony of anthropocentrism is so strong – perhaps still more powerful than that of the state or capitalism – that most people are not even aware of this world-order structure and can imagine no alternative mode of ecology. Yet, so political ecologists would warn, this hegemony could put at risk the future of life on earth. The answer, for these critics, is a counter-hegemonic 'posthumanism' in world politics (Cudworth and Hobden 2011, 2018).

In sum, multiple and widely varying understandings of hegemony in world politics are available. Liberals, realists, world-systems theorists, neo-Gramscians, postcolonialists, intersectionalists, constructivists and political ecologists understand hegemony in very different ways. That said, individual authors may combine several strands of thinking. For example, many critical theories invoke Gramscian ideas of counter-hegemony without adopting a Marxist analysis of the nature of that counter-hegemony. In addition, a complexity approach (as exemplified by Scholte, Chapter 5 this volume) may locate hegemony in an interrelation of forces that other theories treat separately, so that, for example, hegemony might lie in a combination of state, capital, social stratification and discourse.

The rest of this volume reflects this theoretical diversity. Chapters by Schmidt, Sloan, Wang and Zhang develop realist conceptions of hegemony. Silver and Payne take forward earlier work in a world-systems vein. Casier, Germain and Safranchuk take broadly neo-Gramscian routes. Achkurina, Bajpai and Parashar elaborate postcolonial perspectives. Chebankova, Geiger and Pal take constructivist paths. Scholte experiments with complexity thinking. Having in this introduction mapped the overall terrain, we can now turn to the individual chapters for more detailed enquiries. In the book's conclusion we assess what these chapters collectively suggest about our overarching questions concerning the character and consequences of hegemony in contemporary world politics.

References

Acharya, A. (2018) *The End of American World Order*, 2nd edn. Cambridge: Polity Press.

Agnew, J. (2005) *Hegemony: The New Shape of Global Power*. Philadelphia, PA: Temple University Press.

Anderson, P. (2017) *The H-Word: The Peripeteia of Hegemony*. London: Verso.

Anievas, A., Manchanda, N. and Shilliam, R. (eds) (2014) *Race and Racism in International Relations: Confronting the Global Colour Line*. Abingdon: Routledge.

Aron, R. (1974) *The Imperial Republic: The United States and the World, 1945–1973*. London: Weidenfeld & Nicolson.

Arrighi, G., Hopkins, T.K. and Wallerstein, I. (1989) *Anti-Systemic Movements*. London: Verso.

Arrighi, G. and Silver, B.J. (1999) *Chaos and Governance in the Modern World System*. Minneapolis: University of Minnesota Press.

Bailin, A. (2005) *From Traditional to Group Hegemony: The G7, the Liberal Economic Order and the Core-Periphery Gap*. Aldershot: Ashgate.

Balzacq, T. (ed.) (2011) *Securitization Theory: How Security Problems Emerge and Dissolve*. Abingdon: Routledge.

Barnett, M. (2011) *Empire of Humanity: A History of Humanitarianism*. Ithaca, NY: Cornell University Press.

Bernstein, S. (2001) *The Compromise of Liberal Environmentalism*. New York: Columbia University Press.

Boddice, R. (ed.) (2011) *Anthropocentrism: Humans, Animals, Environments*. Leiden: Brill.

Bonditti, P., Bigo, D. and Gros, F. (eds) (2017) *Foucault and the Modern International: Silences and Legacies for the Study of World Politics*. New York: Palgrave Macmillan.

Brands, H. (2016) *Making the Unipolar Moment: U.S. Foreign Policy and the Rise of the Post-Cold War Order*. Ithaca, NY: Cornell University Press.

Brem, S. and Stiles, K. (eds) (2009) *Cooperating without America: Theories and Case Studies of Non-Hegemonic Regimes*. Abingdon: Routledge.

Brilmayer, L. (1994) *American Hegemony: Political Morality in a One-Superpower World*. New Haven, CT: Yale University Press.

Bromley, S. (2008) *American Power and the Prospects for International Order*. Cambridge: Polity.

Buchanan, A. and Keohane, R.O. (2006) 'The Legitimacy of Global Governance Institutions', *Ethics and International Affairs*, 20(4): 405–437.

Burnham, P. (1991) 'Neo-Gramscian Hegemony and the International Order', *Capital & Class*, 15(3): 73–92.

Caney, S. (2005) *Justice beyond Borders: A Global Political Theory*. Oxford: Oxford University Press.

Chari, C. (ed.) (2008) *War, Peace and Hegemony in a Globalized World: The Changing Balance of Power in the Twenty-First Century*. Abingdon: Routledge.

Clark, I. (2011) *Hegemony in International Society*. Oxford: Oxford University Press.

Cox, R.W. (1981) 'Social Forces, States and World Orders: Beyond International Relations Theory', *Millennium*, 10(2): 126–155.

Cox, R.W. (1983) 'Gramsci, Hegemony and International Relations: An Essay in Method', *Millennium*, 12(2): 162–175.

Cudworth, E. and Hobden, S. (2011) *Posthuman International Relations: Complexity, Ecologism and Global Politics*. London: Zed.

Cudworth, E. and Hobden, S. (2018) *The Emancipatory Project of Posthumanism*. Abingdon: Routledge.

Desai, R. (2013) *Geopolitical Economy: After US Hegemony, Globalization and Empire*. London: Pluto.

Donnelly, J. (2009) 'Rethinking Political Structures: From "Ordering Principles" to "Vertical Differentiation"', *International Theory*, 1(1): 49–86.

Flockhart, T. (2016) 'The Coming Multi-Order World', *Contemporary Security Policy*, 37(1): 3–30.

Foot, R., MacFarlane, S.N. and Mastanduno, M. (eds) (2003) *US Hegemony and International Organizations*. Oxford: Oxford University Press.

Friedman, J. and Chase-Dunn, C. (eds) (2005) *Hegemonic Declines: Present and Past*. Boulder, CO: Paradigm.

Gill, S. (1990) *American Hegemony and the Trilateral Commission*. Cambridge: Cambridge University Press.

Gill, S. (ed.) (1993) *Gramsci, Historical Materialism and International Relations*. Cambridge: Cambridge University Press.

Gill, S. (2008) *Power and Resistance in the New World Order*, 2nd edn. Basingstoke: Palgrave Macmillan.

Gill, S. and Law, D. (1989) 'Global Hegemony and the Structural Power of Capital', *International Studies Quarterly*, 33(4): 475–499.

Gilpin, R. (1987) *The Political Economy of International Relations*. Princeton, NJ: Princeton University Press.

Gilpin, R. (1988). 'The Theory of Hegemonic War', *Journal of Interdisciplinary History*, 18(4): 591–613.

Hansen, L. (2006) *Security as Practice: Discourse Analysis and the Bosnian War*. Abingdon: Routledge.

Haugaard, M. and Lentner, H.H. (eds) (2006) *Hegemony and Power: Consensus and Coercion in Contemporary Politics*. Lanham, MD: Lexington Books.

Hippler, J. (1994) *Pax Americana? Hegemony or Decline*. London: Pluto.

Ikenberry, G.J. (2001) *After Victory: Institutions, Strategic Restraint, and the Rebuilding of Order after Major Wars*. Princeton, NJ: Princeton University Press.

Ikenberry, G.J. (2004) 'Liberalism and Empire: Logics of Order in the American Unipolar Age', *Review of International Studies*, 30(4): 609–630.

Joseph, J. (2002) *Hegemony: A Realist Analysis*. Abingdon: Routledge.

Keck, M.E. and Sikkink, K. (1998) *Activists beyond Borders: Advocacy Networks in International Politics*. Ithaca, NY: Cornell University Press.

Kennedy, P. (1988) *The Rise and Fall of the Great Powers: Economic Change and Military Conflict from 1500 to 2000*. London: Unwin Hyman.

Keohane, R.O. (1984) *After Hegemony: Cooperation and Discord in the World Political Economy*. Princeton, NJ: Princeton University Press.

Kiely, R. (2005) *Empire in the Age of Globalization: US Hegemony and Neoliberal Disorder*. London: Pluto.

Kindleberger, C.P. (1973) *The World in Depression 1929–1939*. Berkeley, CA: University of California Press.

Kopnina, H., Washington, H., Taylor, B. and Piccolo, J.J. (2018) 'Anthropocentrism: More than Just a Misunderstood Problem', *Journal of Agricultural Environmental Ethics*, 31: 109–127.

Krishna, S. (2009) *Globalization & Postcolonialism: Hegemony and Resistance in the Twenty-First Century*. Lanham, MD: Rowman & Littlefield.

Larner, W. and Walters, W. (eds) (2004) *Global Governmentality: Governing International Spaces*. Abingdon: Routledge.

Lee, J.-Y. (2017) *China's Hegemony: Four Hundred Years of East Asian Domination*. New York: Columbia University Press.

McNally, M. and Schwarzmantel, J. (eds) (2009) *Gramsci and Global Politics: Hegemony and Resistance*. Abingdon: Routledge.

Mearsheimer, J.J. (2001) *The Tragedy of Great Power Politics*. New York: W.W. Norton.

Messerschmidt, J.W. (2016) *Masculinities in the Making: From the Local to the Global*. Lanham, MD: Rowman & Littlefield.

Mills, C.W. (1956) *The Power Elite*. New York: Oxford University Press.

Modelski, G. (1987) *Long Cycles in World Politics*. Seattle, WA: University of Washington Press.

Morton, A.D. (2007) *Unravelling Gramsci: Hegemony and Passive Revolution in the Global Economy*. London: Pluto.

Murray, A.J.H. (1996) 'The Moral Politics of Hans Morgenthau', *Review of Politics*, 58(1): 81–107.

Niebuhr, R. (1932) *Moral Man and Immoral Society: A Study of Ethics and Politics*. New York: Scribner.

Norrlof, C. (2010) *America's Global Advantage: US Hegemony and International Cooperation*. Cambridge: Cambridge University Press.

Nye, J.S. (1990) *Bound to Lead: The Changing Nature of American Power*. New York: Basic Books.

O'Brien, P.K. and Clesse, A. (eds) (2002) *Two Hegemonies: Britain 1846–1914 and the United States 1941–2001*. Aldershot: Ashgate.

Overbeek, H. (ed.) (1993) *Restructuring Hegemony in the Global Political Economy: The Rise of Transnational Neo-Liberalism in the 1980s*. London: Routledge.

Parchami, A. (2009) *Hegemonic Peace and Empire: The Pax Romana, Britannica, and Americana*. Abingdon: Routledge.

Pasha, M.K. (1996) 'Security as Hegemony', *Alternatives*, 21(3): 283–302.

Peoples, C. and Vaughan-Williams, N. (2015) *Critical Security Studies: An Introduction*. Abingdon: Routledge.

Plehwe, D., Walpen, B. and Neuenhöffer, G. (eds) (2006) *Neoliberal Hegemony: A Global Critique*. Abingdon: Routledge.

Rao, R. (2010) *Third World Protest: Between Home and the World*. Oxford: Oxford University Press.

Reich, S., and Lebow, R.N. (2014) *Good-Bye Hegemony! Power and Influence in the Global System*. Princeton, NJ: Princeton University Press.

Reus-Smit, C. (2004) *American Power and World Order*. Cambridge: Polity.

Robinson, W.I. (2011) 'Giovanni Arrighi: Systemic Cycles of Accumulation, Hegemonic Transitions, and the Rise of China', *New Political Economy*, 16(2): 267–280.

Ross, R.S., and Feng, Z. (eds) (2008) *China's Ascent: Power, Security, and the Future of International Politics*. Ithaca, NY: Cornell University Press.

Rupert, M. (1995) *Producing Hegemony: The Politics of Mass Production and American Global Power*. Cambridge: Cambridge University Press.

Schake, K.N. (2009) *Managing American Hegemony: Essays on Power in a Time of Dominance*. Stanford, CA: Hoover Institution Press.

Schmelzer, M. (2016) *The Hegemony of Growth: The OECD and the Making of the Economic Growth Paradigm*. Cambridge: Cambridge University Press.

Seth, S. (ed.) (2013) *Postcolonial Theory and International Relations: A Critical Introduction*. Abingdon: Routledge.

Sklair, L. (2001) *The Transnational Capitalist Class*. Oxford: Blackwell.

Smith, J. and Wiest, D. (2012) *Social Movements in the World-System: The Politics of Crisis and Transformation*. New York: Russell Sage Foundation.

Strange, S. (1987) 'The Persistent Myth of Lost Hegemony', *International Organization*, 41(4): 551–574.

Tallberg, J., Bäckstrand, K. and Scholte, J.A. (eds) (2018) *Legitimacy in Global Governance: Sources, Processes, and Consequences*. Oxford: Oxford University Press.

Taylor, I. (2017) *Global Governance and Transnationalizing Capitalist Hegemony: The Myth of the 'Emerging Powers'*. Abingdon: Routledge.

Van der Pijl, K. (1998) *Transnational Classes and International Relations*. London: Routledge.

Wallerstein, I. (1983) 'The Three Instances of Hegemony in the History of the Capitalist World-Economy', *International Journal of Comparative Sociology*, 24(1–2): 100–108.

Wapner, P. (2020) *Is Wildness Over?* Cambridge: Polity.

Watson, A. (2007) *Hegemony & History*. Abingdon: Routledge.

Webb, M.C. and Krasner, S.D. (1989) 'Hegemonic Stability Theory: An Empirical Assessment', *Review of International Studies*, 15(2): 183–198.

Weber, M. (1922) *Economy and Society*. Berkeley, CA: University of California Press, 1978.

Williams, A. (2019) *Political Hegemony and Social Complexity: Mechanisms of Power after Gramsci*. London: Palgrave Macmillan.

Worth, O. (2015) *Rethinking Hegemony*. Basingstoke: Palgrave Macmillan.

Zakaria, F. (2011) *The Post-American World: And the Rise of the Rest*. London: Penguin.

PART 1

Hegemony as conceptual map

1

CRISES OF WORLD HEGEMONY AND THE SPEEDING UP OF SOCIAL HISTORY

Beverly J. Silver and Corey R. Payne

A new period of global systemic chaos?

Escalating geopolitical tensions and deep internal divisions within the United States, culminating in the election of Donald Trump, are among the indicators that we are living through the *terminal crisis* of United States world hegemony – a crisis that began with the bursting of the New Economy stock market bubble in 2000–1 and that deepened with the ongoing blowback from the Bush Administration's failed Project for a New American Century and 2003 invasion of Iraq. Whereas in the 1990s, the United States was almost universally viewed as the world's sole and unshakable superpower, by the time of the 2008 financial meltdown, the notion that US hegemony was in a deep and potentially terminal crisis moved from the fringes into the mainstream. Since 2016, the view that we are in the midst of an irremediable breakdown of US hegemony has gained even wider adherence with the intended and unintended consequences of Trump's movement to 'Make America Great Again'.

The current moment is now widely perceived both as a crisis of US hegemony and a deep crisis for global capitalism on a scale not witnessed since the 1930s. When historians look back on 2019–2020, two major signs of deep systemic crisis will stand out. First, the worldwide wave of social protest that swept the globe following the 2008 financial meltdown, reaching a first peak around 2011 and then escalating toward a crescendo in 2019. Second, the failure of Western states to respond in a competent manner to the COVID-19 global pandemic, undermining the credibility of the West (and especially the United States) in the eyes of both their own citizens and citizens of the world.

Toward the end of 2019 – before the scale of the COVID-19 crisis was apparent – it looked like the rising wave of global social protest would turn out to be the story of the decade, given the 'tsunami of protests that swept across six continents and engulfed both liberal democracies and ruthless autocracies' (Wright

DOI: 10.4324/9781003037231-1

2019). As unrest inundated cities from Paris and La Paz to Hong Kong and Santiago, declarations of 'a global year of protest' or 'the year of the street protester' lined the pages of newsstands worldwide (e.g. Diehl 2019; Johnson 2019; Rachman 2019; Walsh and Fisher 2019). Mass protest waves came to define the entire decade. Already in 2011, *Time* magazine had declared 'The Protester' to be their 'Person of the Year' (Andersen 2011) as popular unrest spread across the globe from Occupy Wall Street and anti-austerity movements in Europe to the Arab Spring and waves of workers' strikes in China. Two decades into the twenty-first century, it has become clear that popular discontent with the current social setup is both wide and deep.

This explosion of social protest around the world is a clear sign that *the social foundations* of the global order are crumbling. If we conceptualise hegemony as 'legitimated rule by dominant power' (following the introduction to this volume), then the breadth and depth of social protest is a clear sign that the legitimacy of dominant power(s) has been badly shaken. These twin processes – global protest and global pandemic – were laying bare a stunning incapacity of the world's ruling groups to envision, much less implement, changes that could adequately address the grievances from below or satisfy the growing demands for safety and security.

The major waves of global social protest and the incapacity of the declining hegemonic power to satisfy demands from below are clear signs that we are in the midst of a period of world-hegemonic breakdown. Indeed, as argued elsewhere (Arrighi and Silver 1999, chapter 3), past periods of world-hegemonic breakdown – that is, the late eighteenth/early nineteenth century transition from Dutch to British hegemony and the early twentieth century transition from British to US hegemony – were also characterised by both mass protest from below in the form of strikes, revolts, rebellions and revolutions *and* by a failure of leadership on the part of the declining hegemonic power.

A new world hegemony – if one is to emerge – would require two conditions. First, it would require that a new power bloc 'collectively rise up to the task of providing system-level solutions to the system-level problems left behind by U.S. hegemony', Second, if a new world hegemony is to emerge in a *non-catastrophic* fashion, it would require that 'the main centers of Western civilization [especially the United States] adjust to a less exalted status' as the balance of power on a world-scale shifts away from the United States and the West (Arrighi and Silver 1999: 286).

Seen from 2020, it would appear that the second condition – the graceful adjustment by the United States (specifically) and Western powers (more generally) to a more equal distribution of power among states – has failed to materialise in a spectacular fashion. If the second condition depends mainly on the behaviour of the declining hegemonic power, the first condition – the development of system-level solutions to system-level problems – depends on the capacity of a new power bloc to meet the demands emerging from below.

In the past, a new hegemonic power could lead the system away from chaos only by fundamentally reorganising the world system in ways that at least partially met the demands for livelihood and protection emanating from mass movements.

Put differently, they could become hegemonic only by providing reformist solutions to the revolutionary challenges from below. In this sense, world hegemony requires the capacity (and vision) to provide system-level solutions.

Hegemony and world-systems analysis

This chapter takes a *world-systems* approach to 'hegemony', as we focus on the interrelationship between historical capitalism and successive world hegemonies. Moreover, we argue that world hegemonies cannot be understood without examining their *evolving social and political foundations*. As such, our work is part of a tradition within the world-systems school that builds out from Antonio Gramsci's conceptualisation of hegemony (see especially Arrighi 1994 [2010], chapter 1).

A series of what might be called *non-debates* (or talking at cross-purposes) has emerged in the literature on *hegemony* as a result of the divergent ways in which the term is understood.[1] Different definitional starting points exist even *within* schools of thought, including *within the world-systems perspective*. Thus, Immanuel Wallerstein (1984: 38–9) defined hegemony as synonymous with domination or supremacy – that is, as a 'situation in which the ongoing rivalry between the so-called "great powers" is so unbalanced that one power is truly *primus inter pares; that is,* one power can largely *impose its rules and its wishes* ... in the economic, political, military, diplomatic, and even cultural arenas'. Economic supremacy provided the material basis for a series of hegemonic states – the United Provinces in the seventeenth century, the United Kingdom in the nineteenth century, the United States in the twentieth century – to 'impose its rules and its wishes' in all spheres.

Instead, we start from the work of Giovanni Arrighi (1982, 1994 [2010]: 28–9) – exponent of another major theoretical strand within the world-systems literature – who defines world hegemony as '*leadership or governance* over a system of sovereign states', Building on Gramsci's writings, Arrighi conceptualises world hegemony as something 'more and different from "domination" pure-and-simple'. It is rather 'the power associated with dominance expanded by the exercise of "intellectual and moral leadership"'. Whereas dominance rests primarily on coercion, hegemony is 'the *additional* power that accrues to a dominant group by virtue of its capacity to place all issues around which conflicts rage on a "universal" plane',[2]

Hegemonic rule, in practice, combines two elements: consent (leadership) and coercion (domination). However, the targets of consent and coercion are different. As Gramsci put it:

> the supremacy of a social group manifests itself in two ways, as 'domination' and as intellectual and moral leadership'. A social group dominates antagonistic groups, which it tends to 'liquidate' or to subjugate perhaps by armed force; it leads kindred or allied groups (Gramsci 1971: 57).

In situations of stable world hegemony, the element of consent is strong – its reach is relatively wide (geographically) and deep (socially). Social protest is relatively infrequent and tends to be normative in nature (for example, legal strikes within the confines of institutionalised collective bargaining). In situations of world-hegemonic crisis or breakdown (like the present period), the overall balance between consent and coercion tilts increasingly toward the latter. Social protest tends to escalate and take on increasingly non-normative forms, while the response from above takes on increasingly coercive forms (Arrighi and Silver 1999, chapter 3; Silver 2003, chapter 4).

Periods of stable world hegemony are characterised by a situation in which the dominant power makes a credible claim to be leading the world system in a direction that not only serves the dominant group's interests but is also perceived as serving a more general interest, thereby fostering consent (Arrighi and Silver 1999: 26–8). As Gramsci put it, with reference to hegemony at the national level:

> It is true that the [hegemon] is seen as the organ of one particular group, destined to create favorable conditions for the latter's maximum expansion. But the development and expansion of the particular group are conceived of, and presented, as being *the motor force of a universal expansion* … (Gramsci 1971: 181–2, emphasis added).

To be sure, the claim of the dominant power to represent the general interest is always more or less fraudulent. Even in situations of stable hegemony, those excluded from the hegemonic bloc – Gramsci's 'antagonistic groups' – are predominately ruled by force. However, in periods of hegemonic breakdown, like the present, claims by the dominant power to be acting in the general interest look increasingly hollow and self-serving, *even in the eyes of the 'kindred or allied groups'.* Such claims lose their credibility and/or are abandoned entirely from above.

Nevertheless, in situations of world hegemony, the claim of the dominant power to represent the general interest must have a significant degree of credibility in the eyes of allied groups. Thus, for example, in the high period of global Keynesianism and Developmentalism,[3] the United States was able to credibly claim that an expansion of US world power was in a broader (if not universal) interest, by establishing global institutional arrangements that fostered employment and welfare (immediately in the case of the First World; and as the promised fruit of 'development' in the case of the Third World); thus, addressing the demands coming from the mass labour, socialist and national liberation mobilisations of the early and mid-twentieth century.

Arrighi argues that the willingness of subordinate groups and states to accept a new hegemon (or even purely dominant power) becomes especially widespread and strong in periods of 'systemic chaos' – that is, in 'situations of total and apparently irremediable lack of organization'.

> As systemic chaos increases, the demand for 'order' - the old order, a new order, any order! - tends to become more and more general among rulers, or among subjects, or both. Whichever state or group of states is in a position to

satisfy this system-wide demand for order is thus presented with the opportunity of becoming world hegemonic (Arrighi 1994 [2010], 31).[4]

As the early twenty-first century progresses, there is mounting evidence that the world has entered into another 'period of systemic chaos - analogous *but not identical* to the systemic chaos of the first half of the twentieth century' (Silver and Arrighi 2011, 68). Moreover, there is mounting evidence of increasingly coercive responses from above (cf. Robinson 2014). On both theoretical and historical grounds, however, there is every reason to expect that power exercised through increasingly coercive means will only succeed in deepening the systemic chaos.

Instead, a move toward world hegemony and away from systemic chaos would require an aspiring hegemonic power to be able to, one, recognise the grievances of classes and status groups *beyond* the dominant group/state and, two, be able to lead the world system through a set of transformative actions that (at least in part) successfully address those grievances. Transformative actions that succeed in widening and deepening consent transform 'domination pure-and-simple' into hegemony.[5]

Put differently, the establishment of a new world-hegemonic order has both a 'supply' side and a 'demand' side. The supply side of the problem refers to the capacity of the would-be hegemonic power to implement system-level solutions to system-level problems. In other words, hegemony is not strictly a matter of ideology; it has a material base. The final section of this chapter will return to the 'supply' side of the problem. The next section will focus on elucidating the 'demand side' of world hegemony in the early twenty-first century.

Global social protest and the demand for world hegemony

The crumbling social foundations of US world hegemony

The concept of the 'speeding up of social history' in this chapter's title refers to the fact that the waves of global social protest that have characterised periods of hegemonic transition – and the challenges that they pose for declining and aspiring hegemons – have become wider and deeper over the *longue durée* of historical capitalism. Relatedly, the social contradictions of each successive hegemony – Dutch, British, US – have emerged more quickly from one hegemony to the next; thus, periods of relatively stable world hegemony have become shorter and shorter.[6] In sum, we can observe an evolutionary pattern of increasing *social complexity* from one world hegemony to the next, as each successive hegemonic power has had to accommodate demands from a wider and deeper array of social movements (see Arrighi and Silver 1999, chapters 3, 4 and 5).

This speeding up of social history and increasing social complexity can be seen when we compare the trajectory of US world hegemony to previous world hegemonies. As was the case for both Dutch and British world hegemonies, the firm establishment of US hegemony did not just depend on the country's preponderance in military and economic power. Rather it also depended on the capacity of the rising hegemons to offer reformist solutions to a string of revolutionary challenges, ranging (in crude short-hand) from the American Revolution to the French and Haitian Revolutions in the case of British hegemony, and from the Russian through the Chinese Revolutions in the case of US hegemony. But the social compact that would undergird US hegemony following the Second World War – the mass consumption social contract for workers in the Global North and decolonisation and the promise of development for the Global South – was *broader in geographical scope and reached deeper into the class structure* than the social compacts upon which either Dutch or British hegemony stood (Arrighi and Silver 1999, chapters 3 and 5).

Relatedly, US hegemony was also the most short-lived since the US-led solutions to the revolutionary challenges of the twentieth century were unsustainable in the context of global capitalism. Fully implementing the hegemonic promises of mass consumption for the core working class and of 'catching-up' development for the Third World would quickly bring about a squeeze on profits, given their substantial redistributive effects (Wallerstein 1995: 25; Silver 2019). Indeed, the initial crisis of US hegemony in the late 1960s and 1970s was an intertwined crisis of profitability for capital, on the one hand, and a legitimacy crisis, on the other hand. A variety of movements – from militant strike waves in the First World to the efforts to establish a New International Economic Order emanating from the Third World – were in essence demanding a quicker and more complete fulfilment of the implicit and explicit promises of US hegemony.

The financial expansion and neoliberal counter-revolution that began in the 1980s temporarily resolved these intertwined crises. Financialisation – the massive withdrawal of capital out of trade and production and into financial speculation and intermediation – had a debilitating effect on social movements worldwide, most notably via the mechanism of the debt crisis in the Global South and mass layoffs at the heart of the labour movement in the Global North. The result was a US *belle époque* in the 1990s as power and profits were restored; however, as in the case of the Dutch and British *belles époques*, this resurgence of power and profitability turned out, in the words of Braudel (1984), to be a sign of 'autumn' rather than a new spring for these hegemonies.[7]

Financialisation and the neoliberal project marked a shift from hegemony toward domination, a tilt away from consent and towards coercion. At the same time, however, the process of *creative destruction* (to use Schumpeter's term) has been fuelling a political backlash amongst those who had been incorporated as junior partners into the mid-twentieth century hegemonic social compact (and were now being ejected from it) – most notably male mass production workers in core countries. At the same time, new (and increasingly militant) groups and classes are being 'created' that cannot be easily accommodated in the decaying hegemonic order – most notably, an expanding but precariously employed working class in the Global South and immigrant working class in the Global North.

The social foundations of a twenty-first century world hegemony

We have argued that the exercise of world hegemony requires an aspiring hege-monic power to be able to, one, recognise the grievances of classes and status groups *beyond* the dominant group/state and, two, be able to lead the world system through a set of transformative actions that (at least in part) successfully address those grievances. In more general terms, we have argued that a precondition for world hegemony in the twenty-first century is the emergence of a new power bloc that would 'collectively rise up to the task of providing system-level solutions to the system-level problems left behind by U.S. hegemony'.

The remainder of this section examines actors and grievances in the early twenty-first century wave of global social protest from 2011 to 2019 as a window onto the system-level problems that an aspiring hegemon would need to address in order to transform domination (coercion) into hegemony (consent), and thus meet the 'demand' side conditions necessary to bring to a close the phase of deepening systemic chaos into which we have now fallen. We pay particular attention to new system-level challenges that have emerged over the past half-century – challenges that would make a simple return to the US-led postwar social compact inadequate to the task at hand.

Contesting inequality between countries

A first fundamental difference between the social-political conditions to be accommodated within any twenty-first century world hegemony and all previous world hegemonies is the significant change in the balance of power between the West and 'The Rest' (Popov and Dutkiewicz 2017). All previous hegemonies were Western hegemonies in a double sense. First, the West had amassed an over-whelming preponderance of economic and military power vis-à-vis the rest of the world. Second, consent (hegemony) applied to allied classes and groups within Western states, whereas force (domination) prevailed with few exceptions in the non-Western world.

To be sure, faced with rising national liberation movements in the first half of the twentieth century, the United States led a transformation of the world system that fostered decolonisation and normalised *de jure*[8] national sovereignty. Never-theless, the main levers of economic and military power remained firmly controlled by the US and Western allies. With the increasing economic power of the non-West in the twenty-first century, especially but not limited to China, a stable Western-dominated world order is no longer possible. Collective action by states in the Global South, reflected in institutional innovations such as BRICS and ALBA, further signals this impossibility. A new world hegemony (whether led by a single state, a coalition of states, or a world state) would have to accommodate this greater equality between the Global North and Global South. This changing bal-ance of power is, in turn, the context in which the search for solutions to major system-level problems – such as stark class inequalities within countries, environmental degradation and climate change, and guarantees for physical safety and human dignity – will play out in the coming decades.

Protesting inequality within countries

One recurrent theme that has animated protest movements over the past decade is extreme social inequality. For the Occupy Wall Street movement, which spread from Zucotti Park near Wall Street to 951 cities in 82 countries in 2011 (Milkman, Luce, and Lewis 2013), a key grievance of the protestors was stark inequality – encapsulated in the slogan of the 99% against the 1%. In the years following the Occupy Wall Street movement, class inequality became even more extreme in most countries, sparking yet another worldwide upheaval in 2019. Protests erupted in Hong Kong, India, Chile, Colombia, Bolivia, Lebanon, Iran and Iraq, leaving commentators struggling to identify their common theme. 'But there is one', writes Michael Massing (2020): 'rage at being left behind. In each instance, the match may differ, but the kindling has (in most cases) been furnished by the gross inequality produced by global capitalism'. While the 'matches' were varied and 'seemingly modest' – a subway fare hike in Chile, a tax on WhatsApp calls in Lebanon, cuts to fuel subsidies in Iran and Ecuador, and price increases on bread and onions in Sudan and India (respectively) – 'these uprising aren't just about a few dimes here and there. They're about an ever-growing majority of the global populace that has become fed up with cost of living increases, low wages, [and] the erosion of public trusts' (Silk 2019).

The early twenty-first century has also seen a return of labour unrest, but in new industrial and geographical sites. There were major strike waves featuring new working classes – particularly in East and South Asia – that had been 'formed' in the process of the neoliberal restructuring of the world economy (Karatasli et al. 2015, 191). China, especially, emerged as a new epicentre of world labour unrest. As Friedman (2012) notes: 'While there are no official statistics, it is certain that thousands, if not tens of thousands, of strikes take place each year … with many strikers capturing large wage increases above and beyond any legal requirements' (see also Silver and Zhang 2009).

Even in the Global North, we have seen a rise of labour militancy among the sectors of the working class that have grown in size and centrality in the course of the past several decades, most notably immigrant workers and workers of colour. The majority of these workers are 'concentrated in low-wage, precarious work in such industries as domestic service, agriculture, food and garment manufacturing, hotel and restaurant jobs, and construction'. In the process, the struggle for immigrant rights is intertwining with the struggle for labour rights (Milkman 2011); for example, with US unions being driven to fight on behalf of their members against deportation raids in the Trump era (Elk 2018).

The rise of new working classes in the Global North and Global South has gone hand-in-hand with the 'unmaking' of the unionized, well-paid and overwhelmingly white industrial working classes that were junior partners in the twentieth-century world-hegemonic order. Abandoned by capital for cheaper locales or, in the case of public sectors workers, seeing their welfare eroded by the hollowing out of government functions, these workers have waged defensive struggles. The post-2008 protests against austerity in Europe are particularly noteworthy, but far from the only examples of such defensive struggles (Karatasli et al. 2015, 190–1). At the same time, we have seen an increase in protests by the unemployed and irregularly employed (or to use Marx's term, the 'stagnant relative surplus population'). This part of the working class played a prominent (and often overlooked) role in Egypt, Tunisia, Bahrain, and Yemen in the 2011 Arab Spring (see Karatasli et al. 2015, 192–3) and beyond.

A radical new vision for the twenty-first century is required to meet these challenges from below. The US hegemonic promise of mass consumption and development was never credible within the context of historical capitalism. Wallerstein's (1995) claim that capitalism could not accommodate the 'combined demands of the Third World (for relatively little per person but for a lot of people) and [of] the Western working class (for relatively few people but for a lot per person)', remains true today. The challenge for the twenty-first century is to credibly incorporate the widening and deepening array of working classes and movements that are demanding greater equality, both between and within countries. Needless to say, this precludes a simple return to the twentieth-century US world-hegemonic model.

The fight against environmental degradation and climate change

All previous world hegemonies of historical capitalism have been based on the *externalisation* of the costs of reproduction of labour and of nature. The natural world was treated as a no-cost input, while profitability at the system-level depended on paying the vast majority of the world's workers below the full cost of the reproduction of their labour power. The externalisation of the costs of reproduction of labour and nature were taken to an extreme with the highly resource-intensive and wasteful model associated with the 'American way of life',

Almost a century ago, Mohandas Gandhi recognised the unsustainability of the Western capitalist model of development. He wrote:

> The economic imperialism of a single tiny island nation [England] is today [1928] keeping the world in chains. If an entire nation of 300 million [India's population at the time] took to similar economic exploitation, it would strip the world like locusts (quoted in Guha 2000).

The existential threat posed by the hegemonic promise to universalise the American way of life – fundamentally an updated version of Gandhi's critique – has been taken up by environmental and climate change activists, whose movement has gained momentum over the past decade, culminating in the September 2019 worldwide climate strike of students and young people. As reported by *The New*

York Times, in cities around the world – from Berlin to Melbourne, in Manila, Kampala, Nairobi, Mumbai and Rio – the number of strikers was easily in the tens of thousands, with many cities seeing hundreds of thousands. 'Rarely, if ever, has the modern world witnessed a youth movement so large and wide, spanning across societies rich and poor, tied together by a common if inchoate sense of rage' (Sengupta 2019).

Demands for physical safety and dignity

Speaking at the 2019 climate strike in New York, youth climate activist Greta Thunberg declared: 'We demand a safe future. Is that really too much to ask?'

Indeed, the credible promise of safety is fundamental to all world hegemonies. Today, the threats to safety are multiple, growing and interconnected. Constant, if relatively low-intensity, conflicts rage around the world, precipitating the greatest refugee crisis since the Second World War. In turn, neo-fascist and far right movements have been in resurgence, blaming refugees and immigrants for the (real and imagined) insecurities of populations in host countries (e.g. Schultheis 2019; Becker 2019). Climate change, militarism, and the refugee crisis are all intertwined in a vicious circle that fuels the dynamics of twenty-first century systemic chaos.

All these processes are playing out in the context of the huge inequalities that have grown together with the decay of the US hegemonic world order. The global COVID-19 pandemic is bringing this social inequality into stark relief for those who did not already have eyes to see (Fisher and Bubola 2020). Meagan Day aptly compared the relationship between the pandemic and inequality to analysing waterflows with dye tracing:

> A river just looks like a river until the dye is added, and the dye reveals how the structural features of the riverbed send the water coursing in specific patterns. A pandemic is like that ... [it] shows how the shape of our [social] systems send people careening in particular directions depending on their location upstream. *It was happening before, but now it's a bright color for all to see.* (Day 2020, emphasis added)

Likewise, the global pandemic highlighted the pre-existing fault lines in the world order – rising inequality, insecurity of employment and livelihoods, the refugee crisis and the looming threat of climate change – making these fault lines now clear 'for all to see'. As borders closed and the world economy shut down, the collateral damage from the pandemic in the form of surging unemployment and the evaporation of (already) precarious means of livelihood was breathtaking in scale and scope.

As global systemic chaos deepens, there is, in Arrighi's words, a growing 'demand for order - 'the old order, a new order, any order!' (1994 [2010: 31]). The initial response from above has been to accelerate an already ongoing global shift toward increasingly coercive forms of rule. As we enter the third decade of the twenty-first century, the proliferation of emergency executive powers, police-enforced shelter-in-place orders, and the domestic deployment of military forces to manage the fallout from the pandemic – including anticipated waves of social protest – were among the signs of this trend. Nonetheless, such shifts toward coercion and away from consent, as argued above, are only likely to further deepen the global systemic chaos.

The supply of world hegemony in the twenty-first century

'What, if any, kind of hegemony might play out in our present world of proliferating global challenges and profound systemic shifts?' – this is the central question posed in the Introduction to this volume (Scholte et al., this volume, page 3).

The argument put forward in this chapter leads us to a set of interconnected answers. We agree with the claim, implicit in the volume's title, that answering this question requires 'reimagining power in global politics'. However, we also argue that this re-imagining is not a new phenomenon; rather, each successive world hegemony of historical capitalism has involved an analogous re-imagining of power in global politics. Successive hegemonic powers have responded to global challenges by promoting the 'recurrent fundamental restructuring [of the modern world system]' (Arrighi 1994 [2010]: 31–2).

We have argued that a central driving force behind the successive restructuring of global capitalism – and re-imagining of world hegemonies – has been the challenges posed by major world-scale waves of social protest. The Haitian Revolution and mass revolts by enslaved people in the Americas in the late eighteenth century forced the rising hegemonic power (the UK) to 're-imagine' global capitalism without one of its fundamental pillars – plantation slavery. The upsurge of labour movements, socialist revolutions and national liberation movements in the first half of the twentieth century forced the rising hegemonic power (the US) to 're-imagine' global capitalism without the fundamental pillars of formal colonialism and the restriction of the democratic franchise to property owners. The latest wave of global social protest in the early twenty-first century will also require any aspiring hegemonic power to re-imagine hegemony in fundamental ways (Arrighi and Silver 1999, chapter 3).

The question that we must pose here, however, is whether we've reached the limits of 're-imagining' hegemony within a capitalist world system. One common feature of all past world hegemonies – Dutch, British, US – is that they succeeded in finding *reformist* solutions to the *revolutionary* challenges posed by mass movements from below. In other words, each successive hegemony managed to lay the foundations for a major new expansion of the capitalist world system. They were, *for a time*, able to resolve the fundamental contradiction between profitability and legitimacy that has characterised historical capitalism.

With the further 'speeding up of social history' – with protest today emanating from an even wider and deeper array of social movements – the question arises as to whether another world hegemony can be imagined, much less successfully implemented, *within the context of global capitalism*. Put differently, is it possible to find a credible reformist solution to the challenges posed by today's mass movements?

Until recently any such reformist efforts were not on the agenda of most global governmental and business elites; instead coercive measures and doubling down on the neoliberal project were the order of the day (Silver 2019). However, the fallout from the global pandemic (itself coming on the heels of a decade of escalating worldwide social protest) may have finally shaken the confidence of those in power. Thus, for example, the Financial Times' Editorial Board (2020) opined that: 'Radical reforms [analogous to those pursued in the decades following the Second World War] will need to be put on the table' in order to 'offer a social contract that benefits everyone', In essence, they are proposing a return to the mid-twentieth-century social compacts that undergird US-led world hegemony.

Regardless of whether such calls for 'radical reforms' from global elites fade or grow over time, a return to the mid-twentieth-century solution is not sustainable. Indeed, as argued above, the US hegemonic project – which proclaimed its goal to be the universalisation of the American way of life – fell into a combined crisis of profitability and legitimacy just two decades after its launch.

As Gramsci noted in another context:

> Hegemony (under capitalism) presupposes that *'the leading group should make sacrifices of an economic-corporate kind*. But there is also no doubt that *such sacrifices and such a compromise cannot touch the essential*; for though hegemony is ethical-political, it must also be economic, must necessarily be based on the decisive function exercised by the leading group in the decisive nucleus of economic activity.' (Gramsci 1971: 161, emphasis added).

Thus, without a clear commitment to prioritise the protection of humans and nature over the pursuit of profitability, as soon as the social contract begins to threaten profitability (as it did in the 1960s and 1970s), it would once again be abandoned from above (Silver 2019). A new world hegemony would instead require a radical re-imagining of world power and global politics. Social movements will no doubt play a key role in this process, either directly, or by generating transformative pressures on aspiring hegemonic powers. Either way, a serious 're-imagining' of movement 'strategies, organizational structures and ideologies' including 'internationalism' is required (Karatasli 2019) if we are to collectively rise up to the task of providing system-level solutions to the system-level problems left behind by US world hegemony.

Notes

1 For a comprehensive review of the use of the term hegemony – from the ancient Greeks through to Barack Obama – see Anderson (2017).
2 In transporting Gramsci's concept of social hegemony from intrastate relations to interstate relations, Arrighi (1982, 1994 [2010]) takes a similar path as IPE School Gramscians such as Cox (1983, 1987), Keohane (1984), Gill (1986, 1993), Gill and Law (1988).

3 See, for example, McMichael (2012).
4 'Historically, the states that have successfully seized this opportunity did so by reconstituting the world system on new and enlarged foundations thereby restoring some measure of interstate cooperation' (Arrighi 1994 [2010], 31–2).
5 In emphasizing the transformative nature of hegemony, Arrighi puts forward an *evolutionary* theory of the *longue durée* of historical capitalism, which is another key contrast between his approach within the world-systems school and that of Wallerstein. For Arrighi, the 'fundamental transformations carried out by successive hegemonic powers" means that "world hegemonies have not "risen" and "declined" in a world system that expanded independently on the basis of an invariant structure... Rather, the modern world system itself has been formed by, and has expanded on the basis of, *recurrent fundamental restructuring led and governed by successive hegemonic states*' (Arrighi 1994 [2010]: 31–2, emphasis added).
6 'While the governmental and business organizations leading each [systemic cycle of accumulation] have become more powerful and complex, the life-cycles of the regimes of accumulation have become shorter. The time it has taken for each regime to emerge out of the crisis of the preceding dominant regime, to become itself dominant, and to attain its limits (as signaled by the beginning of a new financial expansion) was less than half, both in the case of the British regime relative to the Genoese and in the case of the US regime relative to the Dutch' (Arrighi 1994 [2010]: 225).
7 The three periods of financial expansion discussed by Braudel each led to a dramatic resurgence of power and prosperity for the leading capitalist country of the time (e.g. a second golden age for the Dutch; the Victorian *belle epoque* for Britain). Yet in each case, the resurgence of world power and prosperity was short-lived. For Braudel, the successive shifts by Genoese, Dutch, and British capitalists away from trade and industry and into finance were each a sign that the material expansion had reached 'maturity'. Financialisation turned out to be a prelude to a terminal crisis of world hegemony and to the rise of a new geographical centre of world economic and military power (Braudel 1984; Arrighi 1994 [2010]).
8 The extension of legal sovereignty to former colonies was not matched by an equivalent extension of *de facto* sovereignty or effective national self-determination.

References

Andersen, K. (2011) 'The Protester', *Time*, 14 December.

Anderson, P. (2017) *The H-Word: The Peripeteia of Hegemony*. London: Verso.

Arrighi, G. (1982) 'A Crisis of Hegemony', in S. Amin, G. Arrighi, A.G. Frank and I. Wallerstein (eds), *Dynamics of Global Crisis*, New York: Monthly Review Press, 55–108.

Arrighi, G. (1994 [2010]) *The Long Twentieth Century: Money, Power, and the Origins of Our Times*. London: Verso.

Arrighi, G. and Silver, B.J. (1999) *Chaos and Governance in the Modern World-System*. Minneapolis: University of Minnesota Press.

Becker, J. (2019) 'The Global Machine behind the Rise of Far-Right Nationalism', *The New York Times*, 10 August.

Braudel, F. (1984) *Civilization and Capitalism, 15th–18th Century*, Vol. 3: *The Perspective of the World*. New York: Harper and Row.

Cox, R. (1983) 'Gramsci, Hegemony, and International Relations: An Essay in Method', *Millennium Journal of International Studies* 12(2): 162–175.

Cox, R. (1987) *Production, Power, and World Order: Social Forces in the Making of History*. New York: Columbia University Press.

Day, M. (2020) *Twitter*, 16 March. Available at: https://twitter.com/meaganmday/status/1239657773765255168

Diehl, J. (2019) 'From Hong Kong to Chile, 2019 Is the Year of the Street Protester. But Why?', *The Washington Post*, 27 October.

Elk, M. (2018) 'Undocumented Workers Find New Ally as Unions Act to Halt Deportation', *The Guardian*, 22 March.

Financial Times Editorial Board (2020) 'Virus Lays Bare the Frailty of the Social Contract', *Financial Times*, 3 April.

Fisher, M. and Bubola, E. (2020) 'As Coronavirus Deepens Inequality, Inequality Worsens Its Spread', *The New York Times*, 16 March.

Friedman, E. (2012) 'China in Revolt', *Jacobin Magazine*, 1 August.

Gill, S. (1986) 'Hegemony, Consensus and Trilateralism', *Review of International Studies*, 12: 205–221.

Gill, S. (ed.) (1993) *Gramsci, Historical Materialism and International Relations*. Cambridge: Cambridge University Press.

Gill, S. and Law, D. (1988) *The Global Political Economy: Perspectives, Problems and Policies*. Baltimore, MD: The Johns Hopkins University Press.

Gramsci, A. (1971) *Selections from the Prison Notebooks*. New York: International Publishers.

Guha, R. (2000) *Environmentalism: A Global History*. New York: Longman.

Johnson, K. (2019) '2019: A Year of Global Protest', *Foreign Policy*, 23 December.

Karataslı, S.S. (2019) 'The Twenty-First Century Revolutions and Internationalism: A World Historical Perspective'. *Globalizations*, 16(7): 985–997. doi:10.1080/14747731.2019.1651525

Karataslı, S.S., Kumral, S., Scully, B. and Upadhyay, S. (2015) 'Class, Crisis, and the 2011 Protest Wave: Cyclical and Secular Trends in Global Labor Unrest', in I. Wallerstein, C. Chase-Dunn, and C. Suter (eds), *Overcoming Global Inequalities*, London: Paradigm Publishers, 184–200.

Keohane, R. (1984) *After Hegemony: Cooperation and Discord in the World Political Economy*. Princeton, NJ: Princeton University Press.

Massing, M. (2020) 'Most Political Unrest Has One Big Root Cause: Soaring Inequality', *The Guardian*, 24 January.

McMichael, P. (2012) *Development and Social Change: A Global Perspective*. Los Angeles: Sage.

Milkman, R. (2011) 'Immigrant Workers, Precarious Work, and the US Labor Movement', *Globalizations*, 8(3): 361–372.

Milkman, R., Luce, S. and Lewis, P. (2013) 'Changing the Subject: A Bottom-Up Account of Occupy Wall Street in New York City'. Available at: https://portside.org/2013-01-30/changing-subject-bottom-account-occupy-wall-street-new-york-city

Polanyi, K. (2001 [1944]) *The Great Transformation*. Boston: Beacon Press.

Popov, V. and Dutkiewicz, P. (eds) (2017) *Mapping a New World Order: The Rest beyond the West*. Northhampton, MA: Edward Elgar Publishing.

Rachman, G. (2019) '2019: The Year of Street Protest', *The Financial Times*, 23 December.

Robinson, W. (2014) *Global Capitalism and the Crisis of Humanity*. Cambridge: Cambridge University Press.

Schmalz, S., Sommer, B. and Xu, H. (2016) 'The Yue Yuen Strike: Industrial Transformation and Labour Unrest in the Pearl River Delta', *Globalizations*, 14(2): 285–297.

Schultheis, E. (2019) 'The Small-Town Disputes that Fuel Germany's Far Right', *The Atlantic*, 2 September.

Sengupta, S. (2019) 'Protesting Climate Change, Young People Take to Streets in a Global Strike', *The New York Times*, 21 September.

Silk, Z. (2019) 'Protests in Chile around Subway Fare Price Hikes are just Another Example of How Economic Inequality Has Become a Global Crisis', *Business Insider*, 20 December.

Silver, B.J. (2003) *Forces of Labor: Workers' Movements and Globalization since 1870*. Cambridge: Cambridge University Press.

Silver, B.J. (2019) '"Plunges into Utter Destruction" and the Limits of Historical Capitalism', in R. Atzmuller, B. Aulenbacher, U. Brand, F. Decieux, K. Fischer and B. Sauer (eds), *Capitalism in Transformation: Movements and Countermovements in the 21st Century*, North-hampton, MA: Edward Elgar Publishing, 35–45.

Silver, B.J. and Arrighi, G. (2011) 'The End of the Long Twentieth Century', in C. Calhoun and G. Derluguian (eds), *Business as Usual: The Roots of the Global Financial Meltdown*, New York: New York University Press, 53–68.

Silver, B.J. and Zhang, L. (2009) 'China as an Emerging Epicenter of World Labor Unrest' in Ho-fung Hung (ed.), *China and the Transformation of Global Capitalism*, Baltimore, MD: Johns Hopkins University Press, 174–187.

Wallerstein, I. (1984) *The Politics of the World-Economy: The States, the Movements, and the Civilizations*. Cambridge: Cambridge University Press.

Wallerstein, I. (1995) 'Response: Declining States, Declining Rights?' *International Labor and Working-Class History*, 47: 24–27.

Walsh, D. and Fisher, M. (2019) 'From Chile to Lebanon, Protests Flare over Wallet Issues', *The New York Times*, 23 October.

Wright, R. (2019) 'The Story of 2019: Protests in Every Corner of the Globe', *The New Yorker*, 30 December.

2

HEGEMONY

A conceptual and theoretical analysis and its application to the debate on American hegemony

Brian C. Schmidt

The primary aim of this chapter is to provide some conceptual and theoretical clarity on the diverse manner in which the field of International Relations (IR) understands the concept of hegemony. A secondary aim is to consider what these different theoretical accounts have to say about the debate on American hegemony. While there are a multiplicity of debates involving the concept of hegemony, a case can certainly be made that the debate on whether or not American hegemony is in decline is a central issue for understanding world politics in the twenty-first century. Although the concept of hegemony is frequently employed in the IR literature, it is quite apparent that different meanings are attributed to it. This is not necessarily surprising because the field itself is divided into different theoretical perspectives that offer contrasting accounts of key concepts including hegemony. Even though some have called for a 'cross-fertilisation between the different theories of hegemony in IR', the mainstream view is that this is difficult to accomplish (Antoniades 2018, 596). It is difficult to deal with the concept of hegemony in the abstract without linking it to specific schools of thought such as realism, liberalism and constructivism. Nevertheless, I begin the chapter by providing a few definitions of hegemony. In this brief section, I aim to establish that two main ideas can be derived from the various definitions of hegemony. The first is the notion that hegemony entails overwhelming or preponderant material power. The second is the idea that hegemony involves the exercise of some form of leadership. The second section of the chapter examines how different theoretical approaches in the field comprehend the concept of hegemony. Here I focus primarily on the two main rival theories of realism and liberalism. After discussing realist and liberal theories of hegemony, I next consider how neo-Gramscians, constructivists and members of the English School grasp the concept of hegemony. In the conclusion, I consider what the different theoretical accounts offer to understanding the current debate about US hegemony.

DOI: 10.4324/9781003037231-2

The *Oxford English Dictionary* defines hegemony in the following manner: 'leadership, predominance, preponderance; especially the leadership or predominant authority of one state of a confederacy or union over others'. Here we can already see how the definition of hegemony embodies the twin propositions of overwhelming power (capabilities) and the exercise of leadership. The latter attribute of hegemony is emphasised in the definition provided by *The International Studies Encyclopedia*:

> The concept of hegemony refers to international leadership by one political subject, be it the state or a 'historical bloc' of particular social groupings, whereby the reproduction of dominance involves the enrollment of other, weaker, less powerful parties (states/classes) constituted by varying degrees of consensus, persuasion and, consequently, political legitimacy.[1]

The *Cambridge Dictionary* defines hegemony as 'the position of being the strongest and most powerful and therefore able to control others'.[2] This definition accentuates the notion of hegemony as encompassing overwhelming power while at the same time assuming that this automatically entails the ability of the hegemon to exercise control over others. In this manner, hegemony involves a relationship between actors whether it be people or states. This relational aspect of hegemony is important for those who conceptualise hegemony as the exercise of some form of leadership. This leadership can be consensual or dominating, but the important point is the idea that hegemony entails a relationship between a preponderant state or social group and others. As we will see in the next section, those who emphasise domination largely associate hegemony with preponderant material capabilities while those who emphasise the leadership dimension argue that this is an insufficient basis for understanding the concept of hegemony.

Realism and hegemony

There is no monolithic theory of realism; instead, there is a diverse family of realist theories. Nevertheless, despite some exceptions, realists generally define hegemony in terms of first, overwhelming power and second, the ability to use this power to dominate others. The predominant tendency among realists, however, is to equate hegemony with overwhelming material power. Yet simply equating hegemony with a preponderance of power is problematic because power is also a contested term.[3] Yet this has not stopped realists from labelling the most powerful state in the international system as the hegemon. Here the hegemon is identified as a state that possesses vastly superior capabilities. Power, according to this view, is synonymous with capabilities, and the capabilities of a state represent nothing more than the sum total of a number of loosely identified national attributes including 'size of population and territory, resource endowment, economic capability, military strength, political stability and competence' (Waltz 1979, 131). Because realists believe that violent conflict is always a possibility in the anarchical international system, military power is usually considered the most important foundation of hegemony. Barry Posen (2003), for example, argues that the military foundation of United States' hegemony is provided by its command of the commons: the sea, space and air.

Closely connected to the idea that hegemony entails the concentration of material capabilities in one state is the related idea that this preponderant state is able to dominate all of the subordinate states.[4] John Mearsheimer, for example, defines a hegemon as a 'state that is so powerful that it dominates all the other states in the system'. He adds, 'no other state has the military wherewithal to put up a serious fight against it'. Hegemony, for Mearsheimer 'means domination of the system, which is usually interpreted to mean the entire world' (Mearsheimer 2001, 40). With this definition, we can begin to see how the concept of hegemony becomes less an attribute of a single state and more a property of what is termed the international system. This is clearly apparent in the work of Robert Gilpin, who considers hegemony to be a particular structure that has periodically char- acterised the international system. For Gilpin, a hegemonic structure exists when 'a single powerful state controls or dominates the lesser states in the system' (Gilpin 1981, 29).

Christopher Layne largely concurs with Gilpin and argues that 'hegemony is about structural change, because if one state achieves hegemony, the system ceases to be anarchic and becomes hierarchic' (Layne 2006, 4). Layne posits that there are four features of hegemony. First, and most importantly, is that it entails hard power. Like Mearsheimer, Layne argues that hegemons have the most powerful military. They also possess economic supremacy to support its pre-eminent military capabilities. Second, hegemony is about the dominant power's ambitions; namely, 'a hegemon acts self-interestedly to create a stable international order that will safeguard its security and its economic and ideological interests'. Third, 'hegemony is about polarity', because if one state (the hegemon) has more power than anyone else, the system is by definition unipolar. Finally, 'hegemony is about will'. Layne writes 'not only must a hegemon possess overwhelming power, it must purposefully exercise that power to impose order on the international system' (Layne 2006, 4).

Within the realist literature on hegemony, there is a tendency to conflate hegemony with unipolarity. Unipolar systems are by definition those with only one predominant state. As William Wohlforth explains 'unipolarity is a structure in which one state's capabilities are too great to be counterbalanced'. According to Wohlforth, 'once capabilities are so concentrated, a structure arises that is funda- mentally distinct from either multipolarity (a structure comprising three or more especially powerful states) or bipolarity (a structure produced when two states are substantially more powerful than all others)' (1999, 9). While both multipolar and bipolar systems are characterised by active counterbalancing, unipolar systems, according to Wohlforth, do not exhibit any counterbalancing efforts at all. Brooks and Wohlforth explain that 'the balancing constraint may well work on the leading state up to a threshold of hegemony or unipolarity'. They continue 'once a state passes this threshold, however, the causal arrows reverse: the stronger the leading state is and the more entrenched its dominance, the more improbable and thus less constraining counterbalancing dynamics are' (Brooks and Wohlforth 2008, 48).

Those who equate hegemony with unipolarity accentuate the overwhelming material power dimension of the hegemon and ignore, or discount, the wilful exercise of leadership component of the concept. According to this formula, hegemony and unipolarity are essentially synonymous with preponderant material power. Many theorists who do not adhere to realist theory reject this formula. Instead, these theorists make a distinction between hegemony and unipolarity; they are different concepts. As Cornelia Beyer explains, '"Hegemony" implies more than just having preponderant material capabilities at one's disposal; additional factors also play a role, such as the capacity to exercise power based on material capabilities, and "soft power" or ideological power, meaning the capability to change others' behaviour by influencing their belief system, their way of thinking, and even their rationality' (Beyer 2009, 413). According to this alternative formulation, 'polarity is a description of the distribution of power across the system, while hegemony is the outcome of an active attempt to create and sustain a set of rules' (Fettweis 2017, 432). Thus, whereas unipolarity is characterised by an international system with one predominant power, hegemony entails the active exercise of some form of leadership to achieve certain ends. According to this conceptualisation, it is certainly possible to have a unipolar system without anyone exercising hegemony.[5]

The realist variant of hegemonic stability theory does make an attempt to marry the dual components of preponderant power and the exercise of leadership. David Lake (1993) argues that the theory of hegemonic stability is not a single theory, but a research programme composed of two, analytically distinct theories: leadership theory and hegemony theory. The starting point of hegemonic stability theory is the presence of a single dominant state. In addition to preponderant power, hegemonic stability theory argues that one of the roles of the hegemon is to ensure international order by creating international institutions and norms that facilitate international cooperation. Hegemonic stability theory is basically a realist prescription of how to achieve international stability in an anarchical international system. As Gilpin explains, 'according to the theory of hegemonic stability as set forth initially by Charles Kindleberger an open and liberal world economy requires the existence of a hegemonic or dominant power' (1987, 72). The hegemon, according to this theory, provides public goods out of self-interest to achieve an open, liberal economic order. The creation of regimes, 'defined as sets of implicit or explicit principles, norms, rules, and decision-making procedures around which actors' expectations converge in a given area of international relations', is a function of the presence of a hegemon who is willing to act in a collectively beneficial manner (Krasner 1983, 2). Hegemonic stability theory, according to Keohane, 'holds that hegemonic structures of power, dominated by a single country, are most conducive to the development of strong international regimes whose rules are relatively precise and well obeyed' (Keohane 1980, 132). The functioning of a liberal economic order is contingent upon the existence of a hegemon who is willing to exercise the necessary leadership to maintain the system. The liberal variant of hegemonic stability theory underscores the importance of a hegemon in establishing a liberal economic order. As Gilpin explains, hegemonic stability theory 'argues that a particular type of international economic order, a liberal one, could not flourish and reach its full development other than in the presence of such as hegemonic power' (Gilpin 1987, 72). When the power of the hegemon begins to erode, hegemonic stability theory predicts that there will be a corresponding weakening of the liberal economic order. According to the theory, 'the decline of hegemonic structures of power can be expected to presage a decline in the strength of corresponding international economic regimes' (Keohane 1980, 132). This is a point that many liberal critics of hegemonic stability theory contest. Keohane, for example, believes that cooperation and the perpetuation of international regimes is certainly possible once a hegemon declines.[6]

Liberalism and hegemony

Liberal theories of hegemony emphasise the particular type of leadership that is exercised by the hegemon. Liberals do not completely discount the importance of preponderant material power, but they argue that this alone is insufficient for understanding the concept of hegemony. Liberal theorists are interested in the mechanisms and processes through which hegemony is exercised. This is also the case with other schools of thought including constructivism, neo-Gramscianism and the English School. For liberals, hegemony refers less to brute power and domination and more to consensus and political leadership. This is certainly the view of those who subscribe to liberal conceptions of hegemony. Liberal hegemony, according to John Ikenberry, 'refers to rule and regime-based order created by a leading state'. He continues that 'like empire, it is a form of hierarchical order—but in contrast, it is infused with liberal characteristics' (2011, 70). Ikenberry argues that there are three institutional features of liberal hegemony: one, 'the leading state sponsors and operates within a system of negotiated rules and institutions;' two, 'the lead state provides some array of public goods;' and third, 'the hegemonic order provides channels and networks for reciprocal communication and influence' (2011, 71–2). According to Ikenberry, 'in a liberal hegemonic order, order is also established and maintained through the exercise of power by the leading state, but power is used to create a system of rule that weaker and secondary states agree to join' (2011, 74). Unlike hierarchically organised political orders based on command, whereby 'superordinate and subordinate relations are established between the leading state and weaker and secondary political entities that are arrayed around it', liberal hegemonic order 'relies on shared interests and the rule of law' (Ikenberry 2011, 55, 61).

Ikenberry argues that liberal hegemonic order is based on consensus and is characterised by a high degree of constitutionalism: 'that is, state power is embedded in a system of rules and institutions that restrain and circumscribe its exercise. States enter international order out of enlightened self-interest, engaging in self-restraint and binding themselves to agreed-upon rules and institutions. In this way, order is based on consent' (Ikenberry 2011, 61). In essence, a grand bargain is made between the hegemonic state and the secondary states to create a liberal hegemonic order. The latter willingly agree to participate within the order and the dominant state agrees to place limits on the exercise of its power.[7] The power that is exercised by the hegemon is based on the rule of law. In this manner, Ikenberry argues that 'political authority within the order flows from its legal-constitutional foundation rather than from power capabilities'. Thus, 'in this situation, hegemony is manifest essentially as rule-based leadership' (Ikenberry 2011, 83). This, in turn, helps to legitimate hegemonic liberal order. Gilpin argues that 'hegemony or leadership is based on a general belief in its legitimacy at the same time that it is constrained by the need to maintain it; other states accept the rule of the hegemon because of its prestige and status in the international political system' (1987, 73). For Ikenberry, the maintenance of liberal international order, as well as its legitimacy, is contingent upon the hegemon abiding by the rules and institutions that it helped to create in the first place.

In addition to the exercise of hegemonic power via rules and institutions, which is the foundation of liberal hegemonic order, Ikenberry and Charles Kupchan argue that there are two other ways, besides for outright imperial domination, by which a hegemonic state can exercise power and gain the acquiescence of other states. The first way is by 'manipulating material incentives' in such a way that acquiescence is gained through coercion. The second way is by 'altering the substantive beliefs of leaders in other nations'. Ikenberry and Kupchan explain that 'hegemonic control emerges when foreign elites buy into the hegemon's vision of international order and accept it as their own-that is, when they internalise the norms and value orientations espoused by the hegemon and accept its normative claims about the nature of the international system' (1990, 285). They identify this second way as exercising power through socialisation. Unlike coercive forms of hegemony that rely solely on the hegemons preponderant material resources and ability to dominate others, hegemony through socialisation enables the hegemon to get others to acquiesce without the use of coercive power. In this manner, hegemony is achieved more cheaply as other states voluntarily agree to comply with the hegemon on the basis of shared interests and a sense of legitimacy. In relation to hegemonic power, Ikenberry and Kupchan 'conceptualize it as the process through which national leaders internalize the norms and value orientations espoused by the hegemon and, as a consequence, become socialized into the community formed by the hegemon and other nations accepting its leadership position' (1990, 289).

Neo-Gramscianism, constructivism, the English School and hegemony

The neo-Gramscian approach to hegemony also accepts the view that hegemony is about more than just raw material power and domination. For Robert Cox, one of the leading neo-Gramscians, 'dominance by a powerful state may be a necessary but not a sufficient condition of hegemony'. According to Cox, the concept of hegemony 'is based on a coherent conjunction or fit between a configuration of material power, the prevalent collective image of world order (including certain norms) and a set of institutions which administer the order with a certain semblance of universality' (1981, 139). Cox combines material power, ideas and institutions into a comprehensive theory of hegemony. Drawing from the work of Antonio Gramsci, Cox argues that hegemony incorporates two elements: force and consent. Thus for Cox, hegemony cannot be reduced to pure material domination. Hegemony, for Cox, 'means dominance of a particular kind where the dominant state creates an order based ideologically on a broad measure of consent, functioning according to general principles that in fact ensure the continuing supremacy of the leading state or states and leading social classes but at the same time offer some measure or prospect of satisfaction to the less powerful' (Cox 1987, 7).

By conceptualising hegemony as a fit between material power, ideas and institutions, it is difficult to privilege one set of factors over another. Nevertheless, it is possible to argue that international institutions and the process of institutionalisation are key components of the neo-Gramscian conception of hegemony. Similar to liberal conceptions of hegemony, Cox argues that international institutions help to mitigate conflict and reduce the necessity of resorting to force. Crucially, while international institutions embody the material interests of the hegemon, they also, according to Cox, perform an ideological function in that they help to legitimate the norms of world order. By casting its interests as universal, rather than parochial, the hegemon is more likely to get secondary states to acquiesce to the existing order and accept it as legitimate. This is what Gramsci meant by hegemony. By recognising that there is a close connection between institutionalisation and hegemony, Cox underlined the importance of ideology in helping to maintain consent with minimum recourse to force. Institutions, as well as formal international organisations, are, for Cox, a key anchor of the hegemons ruling strategy. Cox identifies five features of international organisation that express its hegemonic role: '(1) they embody the rules which facilitate the expansion of hegemonic world orders; (2) they are themselves the product of the hegemonic world order; (3) they ideologically legitimate the norms of the world order: (4) they co-opt the elites from the peripheral countries and (5) they absorb counter-hegemonic ideas' (Cox 1983, 172). As important as institutions are for Cox, he argues that they are only one pillar of a hegemonic order and need to be considered together with material capabilities and ideas.

By emphasising the role of ideas, and recognising that the social world is composed of both material and ideational forces, social constructivist conceptions of hegemony are not dissimilar to those put forward by Cox and neo-Gramscians. Constructivists, however, are more inclined to emphasise the ideational aspects of hegemony over the material. According to Ted Hopf, Cox's account is still too materialistic in the sense that ideas continue to be a manifestation of the dominant power's political economic interests. Yet for Hopf, the importance of Gramsci's conception of hegemony is that it helps us understand why the masses go along with and accept a given order. It is not just the ideology of elites that matter, but also how dominant ideas percolate downward and become accepted as taken for granted by the broader public. This is what Gramsci meant by 'common sense'. What Hopf attempts to do is provide a 'neo-Gramscian constructivist account of hegemony that restores common sense to a more central theoretical role, a role as a structural variable in world politics, akin to distributions of material power or national identities' (2013, 318). He argues that hegemonic power is exercised when dominant ideas are embraced by the people in general. Hopf writes that 'hegemonic power is maximized to the extent that these ideas become taken for granted by the dominated population'. He explains that 'a taken-for-granted truth is one that people assume to be so without questioning its empirical or normative validity' (2013, 321). The degree to which there is a discursive fit between the ideas propounded by the elites and the 'common sense' of the masses is a key indicator of the exercise of hegemony.

Qingxin Wang applauds constructivists for the attention they pay to the ideational dimension of hegemony, but, like Hopf, argues that too much of the focus has been placed on the ideas of the ruling elites and not enough on mass public opinion. Hegemony, Wang argues, entails more than just gaining the acquiescence of elites in secondary states, but the mass public as well. According to Wang, constructivists conceptualise hegemony as 'a type of hierarchical international order whereby the dominant state in the international system exercises transnational authority over secondary states' (Wang 2003, 101). While admitting that the emphasis that constructivists place on the ideational dimension of hegemony is a significant improvement over purely materialist accounts, Wang, like Hopf, believes that the mass public's attitudes toward hegemony deserves serious attention.

The English School approach to international relations emphasises yet another aspect of hegemony: social recognition. According to this view, hegemony is not equivalent to predominant material power. Neither is it solely an attribute of the dominant state itself. Rather it is, as Ian Clark puts it, 'a status bestowed by others, and rests on recognition by them'. Clark defines hegemony as 'an institutionalized practice of special rights and responsibilities conferred on a state with the resources to lead' (2009, 24). In reviewing the English School literature, Clark finds that there has been a general reluctance among its members to engage the concept of hegemony. Yet given the pre-eminence of the United States since the end of the Cold War, Clark argues that it is necessary for the English School to engage seriously the concept of hegemony. Building on the work of Hedley Bull, Clark proposes that we consider hegemony as an institution of international society. His book *Hegemony in International Society* 'is intended as an exploration of the role of international legitimacy in a context, not of equilibrium, but of considerable concentration and preponderance of material power'. Clark's core claim is 'that this is best approached conceptually through hegemony, and theoretically by regarding that hegemony as a putative institution of international society' (2011, 5). Clark finds that it is possible for international order to be compatible with a concentration of power in one actor.

Clark does insist that a distinction be made between primacy, as conceptualised in terms of preponderant material resources, and hegemony as the exercise of some form of legitimate leadership. He is quite clear that primacy and hegemony are different concepts: 'hegemony is than an institutionalized practice, legitimated within international society, whereas primacy depicts nothing beyond a distribution of power in which one state enjoys predominance' (Clark 2011, 34). Clark draws on the work that the English School, especially Bull, devoted to the institution of the great powers in facilitating international order. The great powers were defined not simply in terms of their material capabilities but also by the special managerial functions they performed as one of the key institutions of international society. Just as the great powers helped to make anarchy compatible with international society, Clark, by extension, finds this to be true with the institution of hegemony. For Clark, 'it is this institutional dimension that marks a clear separation between hegemony and primacy; hegemony is then an institutionalized practice, legitimated within international society, whereas primacy depicts nothing beyond a distribution of power in which one state enjoys predominance' (2011, 34). It is only by conceptualising hegemony as an institutionalised practice that can help the English School to overcome their belief that hegemony is incompatible with an anarchical society.

Reasoning by analogy, Clark finds that the institution of hegemony functions in a manner similar to that of the great powers. This is one of the reasons that he argues that social recognition is a key component of hegemony. The institution of the great powers was not reducible to a set of material assets, but instead rested on a shared normative framework in which others bestowed status and recognition on those who performed a managerial function in international society. Clark explains that 'what hegemony adds to primacy then is not just some further supplement to the resources of the leading state, but instead the social capital needed to pursue collective interests' (2011, 242). As with the case of the institution of the great powers, Clark argues that legitimacy is a core component of hegemony. Reiterating one of his main points that hegemony cannot be simply assessed in terms of material power alone, Clark argues that it needs to be assessed 'just as importantly in terms of the distinctive legitimacy dynamics that come into play between the hegemon and its various constituencies' (2011, 51).

US hegemony

Given the diversity that exists among how the different theories comprehend the concept of hegemony, it is not surprising that there have been endless debates about the character and durability of US hegemony. Two questions about US hegemony have become fundamental today: one, does the maintenance of hegemony continue to serve American interests; and two, is American hegemony in decline? The answers to these two questions are actually interrelated. If one believes that hegemony is beneficial for the United States, as both proponents of primacy and liberalism assert, then every effort should be made to preserve it.

Conversely, if one does not believe that hegemony serves American interests, which is the position of balance of power realists and offensive realists, then instead of pursuing policies to maintain it, the United States should begin adjusting to the reality of inevitable hegemonic decline. The debate about the decline of US hegemony has a long history stretching back to the 1970s, but it has recently intensified because of the rise of China.[8] And while support for a liberal international order underwritten by US hegemony has been a cornerstone of American foreign policy since 1945, it has greatly weakened under the presidency of Donald Trump.

One of the advantages of the realist conception of hegemony is its focus on the material basis of hegemony: military and economic strength. Yet even while agreeing that material capabilities are the cornerstone of hegemony, there are a number of contending views on the relative power position of the United States today. A key point of contention among realists is the degree to which the United States continues to have unrivalled capabilities.

In Layne's terminology, 'unipolar optimists believe that American hegemony will last for a very long time and that it is beneficial for the United States and for the international system as a whole' (2006, 134). The best representatives of this view are William Wohlforth and Stephen Brooks. They dispute the popular view that China's rise represents a challenge to US hegemony insisting that the United States continues to have unrivalled material capabilities that are vastly greater than any other state.[9] According to Brookes and Wohlforth, American hegemony is beneficial to both the United States and the world primarily because it greatly reduces security competition by rendering the balance of power inoperable and continues to confer significant benefits to the United States. This view is consistent with what Doug Stokes terms the 'the structurally advantaged hegemon, whereby 'leadership gives the hegemon the capacity to shape world order in ways that confer upon it advantages that will enable it not only to recover the costs of supplying public goods, but to accrue other positional advantages' (Stokes 2018, 141). While recognising the need for US leadership, primarily in terms of maintaining security commitments to key allies, Wohlforth and Brookes accentuate the material advantages that continue to place the United States as the predominant power in the current international system. For Brookes and Wohlforth, it is of vital important that the United States continue to pursue a grand strategy of primacy or 'deep engagement' in order to prevent a return of balance of power politics, which they argue is not possible in a unipolar system.[10] In addition to the problems of conflating hegemony with unipolarity and of accentuating material factors over all others, plenty of critics challenge the notion that America's power is not declining as well as the idea that unipolarity under American primacy is conducive to peace.[11]

This leads to a second position that Layne terms 'unipolar pessimists', who not only believe that the United States' relative power position is declining but also see the grand strategy of primacy to be antithetical to American interests. Most structural realists believe that global hegemony is either impossible to achieve or fleeting. There are various reasons for this belief. One reason stems from the manner in which structural realists conceptualise hegemony in terms of domination. It is difficult to dominate the entire globe. A second reason is specific to Mearsheimer's theory of offensive realism; namely his claim about the 'stopping power of water' (Mearsheimer 2001, 40–2). He argues that it is impossible to project power across large bodies of water to dominate distant territories. The best a state can achieve, according to Mearsheimer, is a position of regional hegemony. The third, and most fundamental, reason is that most structural realists adhere to balance of power theory. The core claim of balance of power theory is that states will engage in balancing behaviour to prevent anyone state from achieving a preponderant position. Contrary to unipolar optimists such as Brookes and Wohlforth, structural realists do not believe that balancing has failed to take place since the dawn of the unipolar moment following the end of the Cold War.

It is for the very reason that active balancing is taking place, especially on the part of China and Russia, that many structural realists argue that the United States needs to abandon the grand strategy of primacy and adopt a grand strategy of restraint or offshore balancing.[12] This is certainly the case for scholars who argue that American power is declining relative to rising powers such as China. The argument is that unipolarity was an aberration and the distribution of power is shifting in the direction of multipolarity. Proponents of an offshore balancing grand strategy argue that unlike the current hegemonic grand strategy of perpetuating unipolarity, offshore balancing is for a multipolar world 'and therefore it would accommodate the rise of new great powers while simultaneously shifting, or devolving, to Eurasia's major powers the primary responsibility for their own defense' (Layne 2006, 160). Offshore balancing is only committed to maintaining the United States position as a regional hegemon and therefore seeks to preserve America's relative power position by shifting the burden of providing defence to other states and distancing itself from the power struggles taking place in Europe and Asia.

Liberal conceptions of hegemony have much to offer on the debate about US hegemony. Instead of simply emphasising material capabilities, proponents of liberal hegemony accentuate the leadership and institutionalised components of hegemony. However, like unipolar optimists, those adhering to liberal versions of hegemonic stability theory argue that American hegemony is beneficial to both the United Sates and the world. The prevailing view among liberals is that it was American hegemony after World War Two that led to the creation and maintenance of the current liberal international order. An advantage of liberal conceptions of hegemony is the equal emphasis placed on both power and leadership. Like primacists, liberal internationalists agree that it is in the United States' interest to preserve its pre-eminent position in the world and are not in favour of retrenchment.[13] The argument is that the United States is better able to pursue a liberal grand strategy – democracy promotion, free trade, interdependence and multilateral institutionalism—when it has unrivalled capabilities.[14] With respect to whether or not the United States can maintain its hegemonic position indefinitely, liberals are, in Layne's terminology, unipolar agnostics. The issue of the durability of American hegemony is not simply about trends in the relative distribution of power, but about the character of American leadership.

According to liberal conceptions of hegemonic stability theory, US power is not used to dominate others, but rather to provide the leadership that is necessary for an open, liberal international order to exist. This is the crux of Ikenberry's story of how the United States built and maintained a liberal hegemonic order that has produced peace and prosperity for the world. According to Ikenberry, the United States did not use its preponderant power after World War Two to dominate the world and create an empire. Instead, American hegemonic leadership was wisely used to strike a grand bargain and establish the foundations of a liberal international order. Ikenberry explains: 'The United States would open itself up and bind itself to its partners; in return, European and East states would accept American leadership and operate within the liberal hegemonic order.' He continues 'the order would remain hierarchical, but it would be made more consensual, cooperative, and integrative than coercive' (Ikenberry 2011, 213). While Ikenberry argues that American hegemony is benevolent and its power rendered safe for the world, plenty of critics challenge this conception.[15]

With the rise of new powers, the growth of right-wing populism, the turn to authoritarianism, and the election of Donald Trump, the durability of the liberal international order is being called into question (Norrlof 2018). Yet most liberals remain confident that the liberal international order will endure, even if the current US president does not believe it any longer serves American interests. As both Keohane and Ikenberry explain, the institutionalised aspect of the American liberal hegemonic order means that it can survive even if American hegemony is declining. The argument is that the institutions that the United States helped build under *Pax Americana* will persist making it difficult for revisionist states to change fundamentally the liberal international order. Ikenberry, for example, argues 'that although America's hegemonic position may be declining, the liberal international characteristics of order—openness, rules, multilateral cooperation—are deeply rooted and likely to persist' (2018, 18).[16] This, of course, is an open question that only can be answered in time.

The English School and constructivism's advantage, as well as that of Cox's neo-Gramscian perspective, in thinking about the character of American hegemony is the emphasis that they all place on the ideational aspect of hegemony in general and the role of legitimacy in particular. For the English School and constructivism, relative material capabilities are less important than how those capabilities are utilised to legitimise the exercise of American hegemony. This is also true of Cox who conceptualises hegemony as a fit between power, ideas and institutions. Sometimes these three elements come together, such as during the Pax Britannica in the mid-nineteenth century and Pax Americana in the mid-twentieth century, and other times they do not. In terms of the debate about the durability of American hegemony, Cox takes a distinctive position arguing that it essentially ended in the mid-1970s. Given the preponderant military and economic power of the United States, especially after the end of the Cold War, it is clearly apparent that hegemony, for Cox, means more than the dominance of single world power. As noted above, dominance is of a particular kind for Cox, whereby the dominant state relies less on coercion and more an ideology to create an international order based on consent. When that consent is waning, which appears to be the case today, it opens up the possibility of both a non-hegemonic or post-hegemonic world, which several chapters in this volume discuss.

The English School and social constructivism move the discussion of American hegemony away from raw material capabilities to the dynamics of legitimacy. Instead of engaging in the endless debate about China's rise and the future of US power, the English School and constructivism emphasise the role of legitimacy in maintaining any given hegemonic order. After all, even hegemon have to act in a legitimate manner in order for their power to be seen as consensual rather than dominating, and here is another area where under the Trump administration, the future of American hegemony is in trouble.[17] While Ikenberry and others might be correct to argue that this was the case when US policymakers set out to build a liberal hegemonic order after World War Two, legitimacy has been much more difficult to achieve in the unipolar era and especially under an administration that pursues an American first agenda. Only time will tell if future US presidents will be able to reclaim a legitimate liberal order or if China is able to provide the legitimacy necessary either to take over leadership of the liberal international order or offer an alternative vision.[18]

Conclusion

As evidenced by the review of the literature, hegemony is a multifaceted and complex concept. Different theories of international relations offer competing conceptions of hegemony. All of the theories, however, emphasise two elements of hegemony: preponderant material power and the exercise of some form of leadership. Although some theories simply accentuate the preponderant power component of hegemony most theories emphasise, in different degrees, both components. Realist theories of hegemony are notorious for their tendency to conflate hegemony with overwhelming material power. Realist inspired hegemonic stability theory does bring the leadership component of hegemony back into the picture. While the starting point of hegemonic stability theory is the presence of a materially preponderant state, the crux of the theory centres on the leadership function the hegemon provides to establish and maintain an international order. This is especially the case with liberal versions of hegemonic stability theory that argue that liberal hegemons exercise a particular form of leadership to ensure an open, liberal economic order. This is why liberal theorists emphasise the leadership functions that successful hegemons fulfil in establishing a liberal international order. The other theories surveyed in this chapter, especially the English School and constructivism, highlighted the role of legitimacy in the exercise of hegemony.

This is why many are asking whether the liberal international order is in trouble today. It is not simply a question of how the relative distribution of power is changing today, but about the role of the United States in continuing to the play the leading role in upholding the liberal international order and exercising its power in a legitimate manner. The second half of this chapter has attempted to illustrate how the different theories of hegemony contribute to the debate on American hegemony. Questions about the character and durability of American hegemony cannot be answered in the abstract; they are beholden to a particular theoretical framework. The theoretical debate about the meaning of hegemony is directly related to the foreign policy debate about how the United State should act in a world undergoing shifts in the distribution of power. I would conclude by arguing that we need theory to help sort out the different positions that both academics and politicians are taking on this fundamental question.

Notes

1 See www.oxfordreference.com/view/10.1093/acref/9780191842665.001.0001/acref-9780191842665-e-0176?rskey=IvSGTJ&result=197
2 See https://dictionary.cambridge.org/us/dictionary/english/hegemony
3 For a good overview of the realist concept of power in IR, see Schmidt, B.C. (2005) 'Competing Realist Conceptions of Power', *Millennium: Journal of International Studies*, 33 (1): 523–49.
4 See Levy, J.S. and Thompson, W.R. (2005) 'Hegemonic Threats and Great-Power Balancing in Europe, 1495–1999', *Security Studies*, 14(1): 1–33.
5 See Wilkinson, D. (1999) 'Unipolarity without Hegemony', *International Studies Review*, 1: 141–72.
6 See Keohane, R.O. (1984) *After Hegemony: Cooperation and Discord in the World Political Economy*, Princeton, NJ: Princeton University Press.
7 See Ikenberry, G.J. (2002) 'Democracy, Institutions, and American Restraint', in G.J. Ikenberry (ed.), *America Unrivaled: The Future of the Balance of Power*, Ithaca, NY: Cornell University Press.
8 See Cox, M. (2002) 'September 11th and U.S. Hegemony—Or Will the 21st Century Be American Too?', *International Studies Perspectives*, 3(1): 53–70.
9 See Brooks and Wohlforth (2008).
10 See Brookes, S.G., Ikenberry, G.J. and Wohlforth, W.C. 'Don't Come Home America: The Case against Retrenchment', *International Security*, 37(3): 7–51.
11 See Layne, C. 'This Time It's Real: The End of Unipolarity and the *Pax Americana*', *International Studies Quarterly*, 55(1): 1–11; and Monteiro, N.P. (2014) *Theory of Unipolar Politics*, Cambridge: Cambridge University Press.
12 See Posen, B.S. (2014) *Restraint: A New Foundation for U.S. Grand Strategy*, Ithaca, NY: Cornell University Press; Layne, 2006; and Schwarz, B. and Layne, C. (January 2002) 'A New Grand Strategy', *The Atlantic Monthly*, 36–42.
13 See Brooks, S.G., Ikenberry, G.J. and Wohlforth, W.C. (2012/13) 'Don't Come Home, America: The Case against Retrenchment', *International Security*, 37(3), 7–51.
14 See Ikenberry, G.J. (2000) 'America's Liberal Grand Strategy: Democracy and National Security in the Post-War Era', in M. Cox, G.J. Ikenberry and T. Inoguchi (eds), *American Democracy Promotion: Impulses, Strategies, and Impacts*, Oxford: Oxford University Press.
15 See Mearsheimer, J.J. (2018) *The Great Delusion: Liberal Dreams and International Realities*, New Haven, CT: Yale University Press.
16 Also see Deudney, D. and Ikenberry, G.J. (2018) 'Liberal World: The Resilient Order', *Foreign Affairs*, 97(4): 16–24.

17 See Clark (2011) and Posen, B.R. (2018) 'The Rise of Illiberal Hegemony: Trump's Surprising Grand Strategy', *Foreign Affairs*, 97(3): 20–27.
18 See Schweller, R.L. and Pu, X. (2011) 'After Unipolarity: China's Visions of International Order in an Era of U.S. Decline', *International Security*, 36(1): 41–72.

References

Antoniades, A. (2018) 'Hegemony and International Relations', *International Politics*, 55(5): 595–611.

Beyer, C. (2009) 'Hegemony, Equilibrium, and Counterpower: A Synthetic Approach', *International Relations*, 23(3): 411–427.

Brooks, S.G. and Wohlforth, W.C. (2008) *World Out of Balance: International Relations and the Challenge of American Primacy*. Princeton, NJ: Princeton University Press.

Clark, I. (2009) 'Bringing Hegemony back In: The United States and International Order', *International Affairs*, 85(1): 23–36.

Clark, I. (2011) *Hegemony in International Society*. Oxford: Oxford University Press.

Cox, R.W. (1981) 'Social Forces, States and World Orders: Beyond International Relations Theory', *Millennium: Journal of International Studies*, 10(2): 126–155.

Cox, R.W. (1983) 'Gramsci, Hegemony and International Relations: An Essay in Method', *Millennium: Journal of International Studies*, 12(2): 162–175.

Cox, R.W. (1987) *Production, Power, and World Order: Social Forces in the Making of History*. New York: Columbia University Press.

Fettweis, C.J. (2017) 'Unipolarity, Hegemony, and the New Peace', *Security Studies*, 26(3): 423–451.

Gilpin, R. (1981) *War and Change in World Politics*. Cambridge: Cambridge University Press.

Gilpin, R. (1987) *The Political Economy of International Relations*. Princeton, NJ: Princeton University Press.

Hopf, T. (2013) 'Common-sense Constructivism and Hegemony in World Politics', *International Organization*, 67(2): 317–354.

Ikenberry, G.J. (2011) *Liberal Leviathan: The Origins, Crisis, and Transformation of the American World Order*. Princeton, NJ: Princeton University Press.

Ikenberry, G.J. (2018) 'Why the Liberal International Order Will Survive', *Ethics & International Affairs*, 32(1): 17–29.

Ikenberry, G.J. and Kupchan, C. (1990) 'Socialization and Hegemonic Power', *International Organization*, 44(3): 283–315.

Keohane, R.O. (1980) 'The Theory of Hegemonic Stability and Changes in International Economic Regimes, 1967–1977', in O.R. Holsti *et al.* (eds), *Change in the International System*, Boulder, CO: Westview Press, 131–162.

Krasner, S.D. (1983) 'Structural Causes and Regime Consequences: Regimes as Intervening Variables', in S.D. Krasner (ed.), *International Regimes*, Ithaca, NY: Cornell University Press, 1–21.

Lake, D.A. (1993) 'Leadership, Hegemony, and the International Economy: Naked Emperor or Tattered Monarch with Potential?', *International Studies Quarterly*, 37(4): 459–489.

Layne, C. (2006) *The Peace of Illusions: American Grand Strategy from 1940 to the Present*. Ithaca, NY: Cornell University Press.

Mearsheimer, J.J. (2001) *The Tragedy of Great Power Politics*. New York: W. W. Norton.

Norrlof, C. (2018) 'Hegemony and Inequality: Trump and the Liberal Playbook', *International Affairs*, 94(1): 63–88.

Posen, B.R. (2003) 'Command of the Commons: The Military Foundation of U.S. Hegemony', *International Security*, 28(1): 5–46.

Stokes, D. (2018) 'Trump, American Hegemony and the Future of the Liberal International Order', *International Affairs*, 94(1): 133–150.

Waltz, K.N. (1979) *Theory of International Politics*. New York: Random House.

Wang, Q.K. (2003) 'Hegemony and Socialisation of the Mass Public: The Case of Postwar Japan's Cooperation with the United States on China Policy', *Review of International Studies*, 29(1): 99–119.

Wohlforth, W.C. (1999) 'The Stability of a Unipolar World', *International Security*, 24(1): 5–41.

3

UNRAVELLING POWER AND HEGEMONY

Why shifting power relations do not equal a change of international order

Tom Casier

Introduction

A profound shift of power relations in the world does not automatically entail a reversal of international order. To grasp how power relations and hegemonic orders are shifting in today's world, it is essential to understand how both concepts differ from and relate to each other. Power is inherently dynamic, fluid and complex. Hegemony is a relatively stable structure based on a close configuration of mutually reinforcing factors. Understanding the relation between both concepts is complicated by the tendency in much of the International Relations literature to reduce the concepts of power and hegemony to a single dimension, central to one particular theoretical approach, for example material capabilities. Yet, both power and hegemony continuously operate along multiple dimensions. To reflect this, power and hegemony are explored in this chapter through two influential and integrative models of power (Barnett and Duvall's taxonomy of power) and hegemony (Robert Cox). Both take a pluralistic approach, looking at power and hegemony as differentiated or multi-dimensional. In other words, both models recognise that power and hegemony have different dimensions, which together produce certain outcomes but cannot be reduced to one single dimension. The chapter seeks to understand fundamental differences and to establish links between the approaches. Surprisingly, bridging hegemony and power is still largely undiscovered terrain. As Mark Haugaard argued, 'there is remarkably little literature which theorises both concepts' (Haugaard 2006, 45).

In the second part of the chapter, both models of power and hegemony are used to compare two main challengers of the current US-led hegemonic order, China and Russia, in terms of their power and their capacity to shape an alternative hegemonic order. It will be argued that China is much better positioned than Russia to do so. Yet – and leaving debates on China's intentions aside – it will be

DOI: 10.4324/9781003037231-3

argued that there may be material and ideational factors that weaken the probability of China to effectively take over the hegemonic position of the US in the future. Finally, two bigger questions are raised about the change of hegemonic structure: first whether the current hegemonic international order could survive even in case of a decline of its traditional hegemon; secondly the possibility of complex 'multi-order' world (Flockhart) is discussed as a potential replacement of a global hegemonic order.[1]

Conceptualising hegemony

Hegemony is typically a concept that covers very diverse meanings in different theoretical approaches. Such approaches share a vague idea of dominance but diverge strongly in terms of what makes up hegemony – material capabilities and/or ideology – and who the actors are – states versus non-state actors.[2] Two influential but highly different concepts of hegemony are used in structural realism and neo-Gramscian theory. For structural realism, hegemony results from the relative distribution of power. It refers to the dominant position of a state due to its relative share of material capabilities. In the Gramscian tradition, hegemony is seen as a combination of coercion and consent. While backed up by the hegemon's material capabilities, a historic bloc guarantees a reproduction of ideas, making them widely accepted by those who are subjugated to the hegemon. This bloc does not consist of states only, but consists equally of non-state actors, such as international institutions or networks of private and public actors (see also Puchala 2005).

This chapter builds on the approach of Robert Cox (1981) and his concept of 'historical structures' (or 'international orders'). Cox uses a historical materialist angle, but the core elements of his model can also be used outside this context, as this analysis will do. For Cox, a historical structure is 'a particular configuration of forces' (Cox 1981, 135), 'in a particular sphere of human activity' (Cox 1981, 137), rather than representing the world as a whole. It does not prescribe players' actions in a deterministic way but provides the context of 'habits, pressures, expectations and constraints within which actions take place'. A historical structure can be resisted or approved but never ignored (Cox 1981, 135). The structure is formed by the interaction of three forces: material capabilities; ideas; and institutions. There is no a priori hierarchy or unilateral determinism among them. The three forces co-determine each other in a reciprocal way.

Material capabilities refer to factors such as technology and organisational capacity, natural resources, industry, infrastructure or military force. They make up the material pillar of power.

Cox defines *ideas* as 'intersubjective meanings' and 'collective images of social order' (Cox 1981, 136). The first category may, for example, refer to the notion that people are organised into states who have the ultimate authority over territories or subjects. In a case of conflict, certain types of behaviour such as diplomatic negotiations or the outbreak of a war can be expected to occur. The second category refers to what we consider to be just or legitimate. Intersubjective meanings are mainly shared during a certain historical structure and provide the basis for social interaction. Collective images on the other hand can be multiple and contested. Clashes of collective images can lead to the rise of alternative or even new historical structures.

Institutions serve the purpose of 'stabilising and perpetuating a particular order' and are a reflection of the power relations at the time of their creation (Cox 1981, 136). They provide a forum for dealing with conflicts and therefore contribute to a reduced use of force.

The three forces interact, reinforce each other, and form a 'framework for action', which 'does not determine actions in any direct, mechanical way but imposes pressures and constraints' (Cox 1981, 135). Hegemony implies 'a fit between power, ideas and institutions' (Cox 1981, 139).

Institutionalisation is particularly important to understand hegemony, but hegemony cannot be reduced to institutions. 'Institutionalisation is a means of stabilising and perpetuating a particular order. Institutions reflect the power relations prevailing at their point of origin and tend, at least initially, to encourage collective images consistent with these power relations ... Institutions are particular amalgams of ideas and material power which in turn influence the development of ideas and material capabilities' (Cox 1981, 136–37). Institutions play an important role in forging consent, so that dominance can be maintained without necessarily resorting to the use of force. Cox argues: 'Institutions may become the anchor of [a] hegemonic strategy since they lend themselves both to the representations of diverse interests and to the universalisation of policy' (Cox 1981, 137). In his dialectical model of historical structures, there needs to be a focus on the emergence of rival (non-hegemonic) historical structures.

A successful international order is thus a relatively stable hegemonic historical structure. It is based on 'a coherent conjunction or fit between a configuration of material power, the prevalent collective image of world order (including certain norms) and a set of institutions which administer the order with a certain semblance of universality' (Cox 1981, 139).

Following Keohane's discussion of hegemonic structure, Cox looks into two examples: the pax Britannica of the mid-nineteenth century and the pax Americana after World War Two. The first was based on Britain's role as a sea power, its economic power, including the liberal economic ideas and institutions sustaining it – for example the Gold Standard, separation of economics and politics – and its capacity to balance power within Europe. The three reinforced each other, guaranteeing the world order a certain longevity, outliving the decline of British power. The pax Americana, in turn, was based on American nuclear power and military alliances, its economic power, the norms and ideas of revised liberalism, and the Bretton Woods institutions. Again, the three forces reinforced each other. The Bretton Woods institutions reproduced liberal ideas, but were also sustained by them. They reflected American power, but also supported it.

Understanding the complexity of power

Hegemony – as a particular configuration of forces – refers to a state of affairs which is assumed to have a certain durability. World orders have 'relative stability' (Cox 1981, 139), even if changing and challenged by rival structures. This assumption of relative stability is not present in Barnett and Duvall's pluralistic concept of power (Barnett and Duvall 2005). In their taxonomy of power, they tried to integrate different approaches to power. They show power in it various guises of 'compulsion, institutional bias, privilege and unequal constraints on action' (Barnett and Duvall 2005 62). With their taxonomy, Barnett and Duvall seek to overcome the classic dichotomies in approaches to power: between power over and power to; and between agent-centred and structural views of power (see Haugaard 2006). What their differentiated model of power teaches us is that power and thus hegemony – which it feeds – can only be understood in terms of its multiple, complex dimensions.

Barnett and Duvall define power as 'the production in and through social relations, of effects that shape the capacities of actors to determine their circumstances and fate' (Barnett and Duvall 2005, 42). They conceptually distinguish forms of power along two dimensions. The first dimension concerns 'the kinds of social relations through which power works' (Barnett and Duvall 2005, 42), taking either the form of interaction or of constitution. In the former case power is an attribute: actors are assumed to be given, pre-constituted. In the case of constitution, power refers to 'a social process of constituting ... their social identities and capacities' (Barnett and Duvall 2005, 42). The second dimension refers to 'the specificity of social relations through which effects on actors' capacities are produced' (Barnett and Duvall 2005, 42), which are either socially specific and direct – assuming an immediate connection – or socially diffuse and indirect.

On the basis of these two dimensions, Barnett and Duvall present a taxonomy with four types of power: compulsory power (referring to the direct capacity to control another actor's action or circumstances, for example through military power or economic dependence), institutional power (referring to indirect control over other actors, for example through institutions or treaties distributing costs and benefits unevenly over states), structural power (derived from social identities produced through interaction, forming relatively stable structures of super- and subordination) and productive power (referring to diffuse networks of social forces shaping each other through the creation of 'systems of signification', p. 55).

An important feature in Barnett and Duvall's approach is that they do not suppose power to be intentional. Power may exist, in different forms, even without the intention to have power. This avoids one of the major issues in International Relations, namely the difficulty in detecting motivations and intentions in actors. Furthermore, perception also plays a crucial role. Power exists if there is a perception of power. In the case of power as an attribute, it is not only the perception of capabilities which matters but also the perception of the willingness to use these capabilities for a particular purpose. This implies that power may play out very differently in diverse contexts, but also that it has a considerably stretchable element, i.e. there may be diverging understandings of power with given capabilities in different contexts, by different actors.

Connecting hegemony and power

If we compare both models, which self-evidently engage in different categorisations, we can summarise the main differences as follows. Hegemony refers to a dominant coherent configuration of forces. What is important is the fit of material capabilities, ideas and institutions. The latter gives hegemony a 'semblance of universality' (Cox). A hegemonic structure is relatively stable, but may be challenged by rival structures. Hegemony in this approach is thus something more static: a given configuration of forces over a certain period of time.

Power refers to the continuous 'effects that shape the capacity of other actors'. These effects result from an omnipresent, non-stop, evolving set of multi-dimensional social relations. This implies power is a complex outcome of many different factors which all undergo continuous changes, but do not per se alter more durable relations of hierarchy and subordination. Power in this approach is thus something dynamic: constantly fluctuating and highly complex.

As a result, hegemony is not an instance of power, as Haugaard (2006) argues, but the three pillars – material capabilities, ideas, institutions – are all three rooted in and fed by the dynamics of power. Continuously evolving, multifaceted power relations ultimately determine the success and relative stability of certain hegemonic structures. In the same way, it is through complex processes of power that these hegemonic structures may be successfully challenged. Yet, a hegemonic historical structure may also come to an end because the mutually reinforcing links between material capabilities, ideas and institutions break. This implies that, while power relations fluctuate constantly, hegemonies may collapse rather suddenly. In sum, power feeds hegemony, but because of the latter's relative autonomy, shifting power relations are not per se a sufficient condition for a change of hegemonic order.

Power, hegemony and counter-hegemony today

The US-dominated hegemonic configuration of forces is seen by many analysts to be under pressure and to be facing increasing resistance. This resistance is coming from rising or aspiring powers, who wish to see their economic power translated into political voice and seek to gain status.[3] The flood of literature about the decline of the West contrasts strongly with the views in the 'rising' countries, where the focus is on rapid rise and development as a tale of mass emancipation from poverty and of return to normality after centuries of exceptional Western domination (see for example Mahbubani 2013).

In what follows, the models of hegemony and power will be used to reflect on the role of two major – but very different – contenders to the current hegemonic order, Russia and China. Reflecting compulsory, institutional and constitutive forms of power, this section compares the evolution of material capabilities between China and Russia, their capacity to set up international institutions and their ability to determine identities and hierarchies among them. The next section explores the strategies of both countries and their potential to develop alternative hegemonic structures.

Comparing material capabilities

Both China and Russia are – in distinctly different ways – challengers of the current US-dominated hegemonic order. Putin has regularly spoken out against the 'unilateral Diktat' the West is seeking to impose. Xi Jinping (2017) referred to the need to replace 'superiority by coexistence' (p. 53). Both countries are unhappy with the current international structures of governance, which they find unrepresentative and unjust. Yet, the power position and counter-hegemonic strategies of both countries diverge strongly. The next section compares capabilities of the relevant actors before turning to institutional and structural aspects of power.

When looking at economic capabilities, the gap between China and Russia is remarkable. It is even more remarkable if we consider the evolution over time (see Table 3.1). Back in 1992, the first year following the collapse of the Soviet Union, China and Russia represented a comparable share of the global economy with a GDP of approximately 5% of the world's total. Twenty-five years later, in 2017, this share has increased for China to 18.22% (at similar levels with the EU-28 and the US) but has fallen for Russia in relative terms to 3.15%.

When looking at military capabilities, Russia's power rests mainly on its nuclear arsenal, which remains on par with that of the US (see Table 3.2). This nuclear deterrence capacity is crucial to uphold the country's claims to great power status. China's nuclear stockpile is much smaller, in the same category as France and the UK. When it comes to military expenditure, however, China has well surpassed Russia (Table 3.3). As the second-highest military spender, China accounts for 13% of global military expenditure compared to 3.8% for Russia.

TABLE 3.1 Gross domestic product based on purchasing power parity (PPP) share of world total (US, EU, Russia and China)

	1992	*2017*
United States	19.89%	15.26%
European Union	24.71%	16.51%
China	4.49%	18.22%
Russia	5.18%	3.15%

Source: International Monetary Fund 2018.

TABLE 3.2 Estimated numbers of nuclear weapons in 2017 (five major nuclear powers)

Russia	7,000
United States	6,800
France	300
China	270
United Kingdom	215

Source: Kile and Kristensen 2017.

TABLE 3.3 Comparison of share of global military expenditure of US, China, and Russia, 2017

United States	35%
China	13%
Russia	3.8%

Source: Stockholm International Peace Research Institute 2018.

Institutional arrangements

China has invested in the construction of sustainable international networks, of which some complement or form possible alternatives for global institutions. This is most notably the case of the Asian Infrastructure Investment Bank (AIIB). It includes 102 members, many of which are European countries. China holds 28.7% of voting rights, implying that power relations within the bank are distributed in a significantly different way than in the World Bank or the International Monetary Fund (IMF), where China holds only 4.59% of the votes. In terms of trade and infrastructure, the Belt and Road Initiative (BRI) has been the flagship. China has also invested in closer economic relations with several neighbours. Overall, it follows a non-alliance policy and regards cooperation as non-exclusionary. Finally, it holds the largest foreign exchange reserves.

Russia, on the other hand, finds itself in a position of relative isolation. It is not part of the main international organisations in Europe and has seen both NATO and the EU extend further to and towards its borders. Its security organisation, the Collective Security Treaty Organisation (CSTO), is incomparable to NATO. The Eurasian Economic Union (EAEU) now includes five members but represents a small share of the global economy overall. Only 5% of Russia's trade is with other EAEU members. Moscow is one of the main promotors of the BRICS consultations (Brazil, Russia, India, China and South Africa), yet this does not represent a close coalition of any sort. The BRICS countries have strongly diverging interests, and the group's future depends on China's willingness to participate. The same holds, to a lesser extent, for the Shanghai Cooperation Organisation, which has increased its visibility but forms all but a platform for a future counter-hegemonic network.

In sum, China is developing global institutional networks that will further enhance its economic power. It may not yet be in a prime position to influence the ideas, norms and rules of today's economy, but the possibility undoubtedly exists for the future. How things develop will depend on many factors, not least the economic conjuncture, investors' trust in the American dollar and the degree to which the US and the EU will seek to diffuse similar norms.

Identities and hierarchies

Both China and Russia are status seekers in the international system. Both believe that the current system is biased in favour of the West and the US specifically and have claimed fairer representation. China, which has long been recognised for its global economic position, strives to see this translated into better political representation. Within an international order they consider inimical, both Moscow and Beijing have logically declared themselves ardent supporters of the principles of sovereignty and non-interference.

China has embraced the free trade norms of the Western hegemonic order and thrived on it as an export-oriented economy. Yet it has done so on the basis of a revised version of the neoliberal model. Some have referred to this as the 'Beijing consensus', suggesting an alternative for the Washington consensus. The term was coined by Joshua Cooper Ramo (2004) to refer to a model of innovation-based development, an emphasis on sustainability and self-determination for China, independently from the US. Others have used this and similar terms to refer to state capitalism and a rejection of political liberalism in creating economic development and export-based growth. The latter implies deviance from the US model where free trade and liberal political principles are traditionally professed as part of one and the same philosophy. In this sense, it could form an attractive alternative development model for other, non-democratic countries.

After the collapse of the Soviet Union, Russia has slowly integrated itself into the world economy. It has done so on the basis of a system of 'bureaucratic capitalism' (Sakwa 2010), whereby the state protects weak industries in a competitive global economy and maintains control over strategic sectors such as energy. When it comes to political and social values, Russia has profiled itself as the defender of 'genuine' European values against a (Western) Europe that has betrayed its own traditional family and religious values. It goes without saying that this is a very conservative interpretation of what European values stand for, which in some elite circles has taken the form of a 'paleo-conservative ideology' (Morozov 2018, 36). It is a deliberate positioning against the idea of a decadent Europe.

What we can conclude from this is that there is definitely important repositioning going on when it comes to the norms and basic rules of international economic and political interaction. While the Chinese model may inspire leaders in other states as a blueprint for development, it remains doubtful whether considerable power is derived from this. For this to be the case, the model and associated norms should weigh heavily on international institutions and global practices. Moreover, although this model contests some principles of neoliberalism and applies different accents, it does not object to the core idea of free trade, which is in itself essential for China's export-oriented economy. Nor can we say that China and Russia are in a strong position to define the identities of others or to overhaul existing hierarchies; creating categories and hierarchies of 'acceptability' remains largely the prerogative of the West. However, the emphasis on alternative models (divorced from political liberalism) and on sovereignty have created a potential platform for contestation.

Rising to hegemony?

All of the above confirms that power relations are changing – and rapidly. Yet a new, alternative hegemonic structure is not necessarily in the making. As outlined above, the latter would require a coherent fit between material capabilities, institutions and ideas in such a way that they are mutually reinforcing.

The next question that needs to be answered, concerns the attitude of both powers towards the current hegemonic order and the strategies they pursue vis-à-vis this order. In this respect an interesting paradox can be noted between China as 'cautious riser' within this hegemonic order versus Russia as 'desperate challenger' of the hegemonic order (Krickovic 2017). As Krickovic notes, these positions go against the assumptions of Power Transition Theory, that expects rising powers to be the most likely challengers of an international order (Krickovic 2017, 299). He explains this as follows. In line with some of the findings above, Russia is a relatively declining power that hopes to reverse its decline by changing the international order. China, on the other hand, is a steeply rising power that has grown within the current international order and is freeriding on it (Krickovic 2017, 309–16). As will be outlined below, it has benefited from the neoliberal economic features of the established order and has little interest in overhauling it.

Russia's strategy

In terms of strategy, Russia has gone through an interesting evolution. During the 1990s, its strategy was mainly one of social mobility, whereby it strove to gain status by imitating the Western model, hoping this would lead to its integration into the leading community of (Western) states (Larson & Shevchenko 2014). This approach was replaced by strategies in which Russia aimed to gain status through competition and by challenging the dominant position of the West. Repeatedly and loudly, it voiced its opposition against the West that sought to impose its 'unilateral Diktat'. As Putin (2014) stated, 'Essentially, the unipolar world is simply a means of justifying dictatorship over people and countries.' In foreign policy rhetoric, Russia has profiled itself as an alternative to the West and has done so with an assertiveness that is hardly substantiated by its real power. In other words, Russia is loudly voicing its opposition to Western domination but is doing so from a position of relative weakness.

Moscow is drawing on a 'full spectrum approach' (Monaghan 2017, 3). It displays and pushes the limits of its power on many different fronts at the same time:

in its rhetoric; through military action in Syria; through surprise actions 'by denial', such as the green men in Crimea (Allison, 2014); by showcasing its new weapons; by promoting conservative values; and through Internet trolls, election meddling and other means. Again, subjectivity is crucial: a country's power is as great as it is perceived to be. It can be argued that Russia has been quite successful in being perceived as far more powerful than its real power base suggests; in other words, Russia has been punching above its weight. Whether this is temporary or has the capacity to last remains to be seen. Most likely, Moscow's approach is more tactical manoeuvring than a strategic master plan (Monaghan, 2017). In contrast to short-term gains, Russia has clearly also lost long-term opportunities. Its role in Ukraine, for example, has undoubtedly burnt many bridges and opportunities for influence in this country for years to come.

China's strategy and implications for a change of order

Beijing's strategy may be to work towards a potentially counter-hegemonic struc-ture, following a cautious and long-term strategy, but – in contrast to Russia – acting from a position of strength. On one hand, China is building up its cap-abilities economically as well as militarily. It has framed the development of tech-nology and infrastructure as key priorities. It is establishing alternative global institutions and steadily extending its networks. On the other hand, it is doing so within a rhetoric of non-exclusionary cooperation, win–win situations, and responsibility within a 'community of shared destiny'.[4] Based on the model of Cox, Figure 3.1 compares the US hegemonic order in the economic sphere with the alternative structure China is developing.

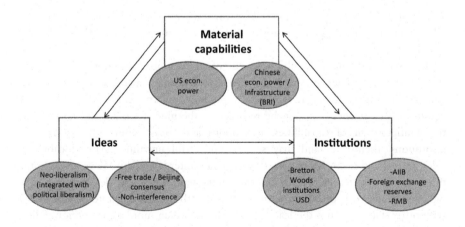

(based on Cox 1981)

FIGURE 3.1 US hegemony in the economic sphere and Chinese counter-hegemonic structure.

While this figure suggests a strong potential for China to lay the basis for a rivalling hegemonic structure, two factors may prove to form a considerable obstacle to create the neat 'configuration of forces' required for a stable hegemonic structure. The first one is an ideational factor, labelled as the 'distribution of identity' (Allan, Sucetic, Hopf 2018). The second is a material factor of particular importance to create a neat configuration of forces in Cox's scheme of hegemony, namely alliance formation.

Allan et al. formulate a Constructivist theory of hegemonic stability, contending that 'the distribution of identity among the great powers constrains and shapes the dynamics of hegemonic stability and transition. When the reigning hegemonic ideology is supported by the distribution of identity, then the hegemonic order is likely to remain stable even if the leading state is declining' (Allan, Sucetic, Hopf 2018, 840).[5] Building on the Gramscian notion of mass common sense,[6] the distribution of identity should be understood within the concept of 'thick hegemony', in which the rule based order is based on the beliefs of both masses and elites (and not only of the latter, as in the case of 'thin hegemony'). (Allan, Sucetic, Hopf 2018, 843). The authors claim that 'a counterhegemonic coalition is likely to be successful only if it can draw ideological strength from the distribution of identity itself. Otherwise, other states will not find the alternative order appealing or desirable and the challenger will be unable to build support for it' (Allan, Sucetic, Hopf 2018, 840). The authors claim that in many great powers there is quite widespread belief in the hegemonic discourse of democracy and neoliberalism, even in cases where there is no strong support for Western hegemony (for example Japan). China's national identity discourse – such as Xi's concept of the 'Chinese dream' or 'rejuvenation' – is regarded as too 'insular' to attract followers or change the hegemonic ideology from within (Allan, Sucetic, Hopf 2018, 841). As a result, the distribution of identity presents a 'system-level barrier to a Chinese hegemonic succession' (Allan, Sucetic, Hopf 2018, 841).[7] Other authors have also stressed that China has not developed a model that others emulate and nor has Russia (Krickovic 2017, 308).

A second factor that may inhibit the rise of a new global hegemonic order is the role of alliances. They may be regarded as a material capability in itself and a vehicle for enhancing a state's power by pooling military capabilities of different countries. But alliances can also be regarded as the glue, fostering and reinforcing the configuration of capabilities, institutions and ideas. They form 'secondary institutions' themselves and may serve as powerful instruments for distributing rules, norms and ideas. Moreover, they generate interdependent views on security, threats and key interests. While China has invested a lot in the development of a widespread network of infrastructure and trade (BRI), creating interdependencies with other states, it is not the leader of an alliance. Even more so, its foreign policy discourse is based on the principle of non-alliance. Nor can China and Russia be seen as forming a solid counter-hegemonic coalition. Clearly, they have common concerns about American dominance, but this is predominantly a negative basis for cooperation: it is the anti-Western attitude that determines their common attitude rather than a positive choice to form a coalition. Lo has argued that current relations between Moscow and Beijing are based on a fragile balance, whereby China recognises Russia's military primacy and Russia recognises China's economic primacy (Lo 2016). With China's military power growing, this balance increasingly comes under pressure.

The survival of a hegemonic structure without a hegemon?

Of key importance in Figure 3.1 is the idea of (economic) neoliberalism as an organising idea of the international economic order, which is shared both by the current hegemon, the United States and by China. This brings up the crucial question whether the changing concentration of power (the relative decline of the US and the rise of China) will erode the international economic order or not. According to Hegemonic Stability Theory (for example Keohane 1980), the international economic order is related to the distribution of power in the international system and reflects the preferences of the hegemon. In case the latter is liberal economic (the US), the theory expects trade structures will be open. However, when this hegemon is in decline, the trade structures will be weakened and less open (Lang 2008).

Ruggie has argued against this, contending that hegemonic orders may survive even in the case of decline of the hegemon (Ruggie 1982). According to Ruggie the internationalised political authority that sustains an international economic order does not only depend on the distribution of power, but is based on a fusion of power and legitimate social purpose.[8] If the legitimate social purpose is constant, a change of hegemon does not need to imply a change of international economic order: 'as long as purpose is held constant, there is no reason to suppose that the normative framework of regimes must change as well' (Ruggie 1982, 384). In other words, international regimes have a 'relative autonomy', because they are based on principles reflecting a shared social purpose and rely on an 'intersubjective framework of meaning' (Ruggie 1982, 385 and 380). In a situation where there is no clear hegemon, but there is congruence of social purpose among leading economic countries, Ruggie expects 'norm governed change', rather than 'norm transforming change' (Ruggie 1982, 384). This means that the normative framework (the neoliberal principles and norms of free trade) will remain unchanged, but the instruments (rules and procedures related to free trade) will change.[9]

Translated to the rise of China, this means that as long as China and other leading economies (the US, the EU, Japan, India in the future) continue to agree on the liberal norms and principles of the current international economic order, the latter may very well survive the decline of American hegemony. Given that China needs free trade to sustain high growth levels in its export-oriented economy, there is little reason to assume a fundamental change in China's attitude. Where we may expect change is in the instruments of the order, for example new institutional frameworks producing their own procedures and rules reflecting the 'Beijing consensus' and China's position.

Buzan and Lawson (2014, 2015) make a similar argument claiming that power is getting more dispersed, but there is a largely shared ideological adherence of great powers to capitalism. This convergence stands in sharp contrast with great power competition in the 1930s when ideological differences ran deep, also about the preferred type of political economy (Buzan and Lawson 2014, 86). They define the emerging world order as 'decentred globalism', in contrast to earlier Western-centred globalism (Buzan and Lawson 2014, 72). The core question becomes 'how to manage relations between diverse modes of capitalist governance' (p. 72). Buzan and Lawson present two possible scenarios: a more conflictual scenario of 'inter-capitalist competition' or a more cooperative 'concert of capitalist powers', in which great powers manage capitalist interaction (p. 86). They expect a setting of 'soft geo-economics' to be most likely, whereby capitalist powers both compete and cooperate (p. 89).

An analysis like this assumes a clear separation of ideas of economic liberalism and political liberalism, whereby the latter is seen as primarily a domestic issue rather than a building stone of hegemonic order. The (perceived) link between economic actors and states may potentially be of essence: are companies seen as operating on their own behalf or seen as closely intertwined with the states from which they operate? In this respect the trend to securitisation of trade issues by the Trump administration may indicate that a spill-over of economic competition into geopolitical competition is definitely possible, but of course it is too early for conclusions. Also the role of transnational actors is of key importance: which role do they play in determining the normative framework of the international economic order and how do they relate to states?

One or multiple international orders?

John Ikenberry opens his article 'The end of liberal international order?' with this sentence: 'For seven decades the world has been dominated by a western liberal order' (Ikenberry 2018, 7). Acharya, in contrast, refers to the idea of a US-led liberal hegemonic order covering most of the world since the Second World War as a myth. During the Cold War, this order did not include the Eastern bloc and the non-aligned countries. Therefore it was a 'limited international order' based on a 'US-UK-West Europe-Australasian configuration', rather than 'an inclusive global order' (Acharya 2017, 271).[10]

The bigger question to be answered is thus whether it makes sense to think in terms of one *global* hegemonic order. Acharya expects an evolution towards a 'multiplex world order', in which elements of the liberal order survive, but are 'subsumed in a complex of multiple, crosscutting international orders' (Acharya 2017, 272). From an English School perspective, Flockhart makes a somewhat similar point.[11] What emerges is a 'multi-order system', an international system consisting of 'several "orders" with multiple overlapping and diverging characteristics nested within an overall international system in which a complex network of "inter-order" relationships will determine the character of the coming "multi-order world"' (Flockhart 2016, 5). These orders should not be thought in geographic, regional terms, but will more likely be determined by a shared identity. The central dynamics in a multi-order world are likely to be 'within and between different orders, rather than between multiple sovereign states' (Flockhart 2016, 23). This implies that the liberal order will not have global reach and the world will be characterised by 'new forms of relationships between composite and diverse actors across complex lines of division and convergence' (Flockhart 2016, 3).

If the new international order is a complex patchwork of orders and dividing lines, rather than a homogeneous global order, this sheds new light on the role of rising powers. Many of their policies can be understood as attempts to establish or lead one of multiple orders. Russia, for example, has made a clear turn towards geographically determined Eurasian cooperation, but struggles to find a common identity for this order (see for example Katzenstein and Weygandt 2017; Lewis 2018). In the case of China, the emphasis is less on regional cooperation, but on more extended international networks (BRI and targeted investments). These can create strong interdependencies and leverage for China, but it is far from sure whether they have the potential to create a strong shared identity.

Conclusion

Power and hegemony are intrinsically linked, but have usually been theorised separately. This chapter has looked at two influential models, sharing a pluralist, integrative approach to hegemony and power. The Robert Cox model understands hegemony as a historical structure based on a relatively stable configuration of forces – material capabilities, ideas and institutions – which form a perfect fit and reinforce each other. In Barnett and Duvall's taxonomy, power operates continuously in different dimensions, producing diverse and changing effects. Power is the complex, evolving dynamic which ultimately determines the possibility of 'static' hegemonic and counter-hegemonic historical structures, but does not form a sufficient condition for such a hegemonic structure.

The current US-led hegemonic structure is traditionally based on the enlacement of American economic and military capabilities, neoliberal ideas and institutions such as the dollar and the Bretton Woods institutions. Today, this hegemonic order is challenged. This chapter compared China and Russia, two main challengers of Western hegemony, along different dimensions of power and along their capacity to form alternative hegemonic structures. China is operating from a position of relative and increasing strength but follows a rather cautious and gradual strategy, coined in a rhetoric of non-exclusionary cooperation. Russia, on the other hand, scores low on many power indicators but voices its protest against Western dominance loudly. By using a wide variety of power instruments, it seeks short-term status gains, often de facto punching above its weight. When it comes to hegemonic structures, only China seems to effectively establish new structures, built on its economic success, an adapted Beijing version of the idea of free trade and alternative institutional networks (such as the Asian Infrastructure Investment Bank or the Belt and Road Initiative). At this point in time, this does not indicate that China is about to displace US-led hegemony, but only that it has *potential* to put a substitute on the table.

Eventually, before we even consider the possible shift to a new international order, some bigger questions need to be answered. First, as hegemonic orders are rather stable, they may well survive without a hegemon. In particular the fact that China broadly shares the (neo-)liberal ideas behind the international economic order and trade regime, could imply that we will evolve to a world of 'inter-capitalist competition' or 'a concert of capitalist powers' (Buzan and Lawson), rather than a replacement of the current hegemonic historical structure. Moreover, the question needs to be raised whether the world will continue to be dominated by one global hegemonic order or rather develop into multiple hegemonic orders, in which the interests and preferences of great powers converge and collide along complex lines. China is likely to be well prepared for such a complex multi-order world.

Notes

1 This chapter draws on earlier work (Casier 2018a, 2018b, 2018c).
2 According to Owen Worth, hegemony has mainly been understood as 'a leading state and a form of ideology' (Worth 2015, 1).
3 Some authors have suggested that hegemony is also threatened from within, with a US administration under Trump that does not seem to uphold beliefs in the key ideas at the heart of its own model, such as free trade (see also Kupchan 2018, Ikenberry 2018).
4 Based on the content analysis of 108 Chinese academic articles, Zeng finds that there is a considerable diversity in Chinese views on how to defend core interests. The emphasis overall is on diplomacy, but also on military capability. The latter, however, does not equal the actual willingness to use military force in current circumstances (Zeng 2017).
5 From a very different theoretical perspective, Ikenberry argues that 'the more general organizing idea and impulses of liberal internationalism run deep in world politics' and are more than 'a creature of American hegemony' (Ikenberry, 2018, 8 and 9).
6 Gramsci refers to the common sense of the masses as 'the conceptualisation of the world that is uncritically absorbed' (Gramsci, quoted in Allan, Vucetic and Hopf, 2018, 846).
7 However, it should be noted that the meaning and significance of the 'Chinese model' for developing countries, as an alternative to the 'American model', is a matter of debate (see for example He 2018).
8 Social purpose refers to the role of the state in relation to the market and leads Ruggie to speak of 'embedded liberalism' as social purpose of the post-World War II international economic order.
9 A change of instruments can, for example, be witnessed in the 'shift from multilateralism to polycentrism' in global governance, seeing the rise of new 'informal, private, multi-stakeholder' institutional frameworks (Scholte 2018).
10 Acharya also reproaches the discipline of – predominantly Western – IR to be based on 'false universalisms' (Acharya 2011).
11 For Flockhart the concept of international order coincides with the English School concept of international society: 'an ideal-typical international society can be thought of as a cluster of sovereign states (usually) converging around a leading state, where the society will be defined by power and identity and by its primary and secondary institutions' (Flockhart 2016, 15).

References

Acharya, A. (2011) 'Amitav Acharya on the Relevance of Regions, ASEAN, and Western IR's False Universalism', Theory Talk 42, 10 August 2011. Available at: www.theory-talks.org/2011/08/theory-talk-42.html (accessed 20 March 2019).

Acharya, A. (2017) 'After Liberal Hegemony: The Advent of a Multiplex World Order', *Ethics and International Affairs*, 31(3): 271–285.

Allan, B., Vucetic, S. and Hopf, T. (2018) 'The Distribution of Identity and the Future of International Order: China's Hegemonic Prospects', *International Organization*, 72(4): 839–869.

Allison, R. (2014). 'Russian "Deniable" Intervention in Ukraine: How and Why Russia Broke the Rules', *International Affairs*, 90(6): 1255–1297.

Barnett M. and Duvall, R. (2005) 'Power in International Politics', *International Organization*, 59(Winter): 39–75.

Buzan, B. and Lawson, G. (2014) 'Capitalism and Emergent World Order', *International Affairs*, 90(1): 71–91.

Buzan, B. and Lawson, G. (2015) *The Global Transformation: History, Modernity and the Making of International Relations*. Cambridge: Cambridge University Press.

Casier, T. (2018a) 'Hegemony and Contestation: Why Changing Power Relations Do Not Mean a Change of International Order (yet)', in A. Malashenko, V. Popov and P. Schulze (eds), *Making Multilateralism Work: Dialogue for Peace, Security and Development*, Rhodes Annual Volume16, Berlin: DOC, 65–77.

Casier, T. (2018b) 'The Different Faces of Power in European Union – Russia Relations', *Cooperation and Conflict*, 53(1): 101–117.

Casier, T. (2018c) 'Unravelling Power and Hegemony: Towards a Differentiated Approach', DOC expert comment, 28 August 2018. Available at: https://doc-research.org/2018/08/unravelling-power-hegemony-towards-differentiated-approach/ (accessed 20 March 2019).

Cox, R.W. (1981) 'Social Forces, States and World Orders: Beyond International Relations Theory', *Millennium*, 10(2): 126–155.

DeBardeleben, J. (2018) 'Alternative Paradigms for EU-Russian Neighbourhood Relations', in T. Casier and J. DeBardeleben (eds), *EU-Russia Relations in Crisis: Understanding Diverging Perceptions*, London: Routledge, 115–136.

Flockhart, T. (2016) 'The Coming Multi-order World', *Contemporary Security Policy*, 37(1): 3–30.

Haugaard, M. (2006) 'Power and Hegemony in Social Theory', in M. Haugaard and H. Lentner (eds), *Hegemony and Power: Consensus and Coercion in Contemporary Politics*, Lanham, MD: Lexington Books, 45–66.

He, Y. (2018) 'Will China and US Enter a New "Cold War"?' *China Daily*, 9 July 2018. Available at: http://global.chinadaily.com.cn/a/201807/09/WS5b42a4f8a3103349141e16d7.html (accessed 20 March 2019).

Ikenberry, G.J. (2018) 'The End of Liberal International Order?', *International Affairs*, 94(1): 7–23.

International Monetary Fund (2018). 'World Economic Outlook Database'. Available at: www.imf.org/external/pubs/ft/weo/2018/01/weodata/index.aspx (accessed 20 March 2019).

Katzenstein, P.J. and Weygandt, N. (2017) 'Mapping Eurasia in an Open World: How the Insularity of Russia's Geopolitical and Civilizational Approaches Limits Its Foreign Policies', *Perspectives on Politics*, 15(2): 428–442.

Keohane, R.0. (1980) 'The Theory of Hegemonic Stability and Changes in International Economic Regimes, 1967–1977', in O. Holsti*et al.* (eds), *Change in the International System*, Boulder, CO: Westview Press.

Kile, S. and Kristensen, H. (2017). 'Trends in World Nuclear Forces, 2017', SIPRI Fact Sheet. Available at: www.sipri.org/sites/default/files/2017-2006/fs_1707_wnf.pdf (accessed 20 March 2019).

Kowert, P. (1998) 'Agent versus Structure in the Construction of National Identity', in V. Kubalkova, N. Onuf and P. Kowert (eds), *International Relations in a Constructed World*, New York: M.E. Sharpe, 101–122.

Krickovic, A. (2017) 'The Symbiotic China-Russia Partnership: Cautious Riser and Desperate Challenger', *The Chinese Journal of International Politics*, 10(3): 299–329.

Kupchan, C. (2018) 'The Clash of Exceptionalisms: A New Fight Over an Old Idea', *Foreign Affairs*, March/April. Available at: www.foreignaffairs.com/articles/united-states/2018-02-13/clash-exceptionalisms (accessed 20 March 2019).

Lang, A. (2008) 'Reconstructing Embedded Liberalism: John Gerard Ruggie and Constructivist Approaches to the Study of the International Trade Regime', in J.G. Ruggie (ed.), *Embedding Global Markets: An Enduring Challenge*, London: Routledge, 13–46.

Larson, D. and Shevchenko, A. (2014). 'Russia Says No: Power, Status and Emotions in Foreign Policy', *Communist and Post-Communist Studies*, 47(3–4): 269–279.

Lewis, D.G. (2018) 'Geopolitical Imaginaries in Russian Foreign Policy: The Evolution of "Greater Eurasia"', *Europe-Asia Studies*, 70(10): 1612–1637.

Lo, B. (2016) 'The Illusion of Convergence – Russia, China and the BRICS', *Russie.Nei. Visions*, 92(March). Available at: www.ifri.org/sites/default/files/atoms/files/ifri_rnv_92_bobo_lo_brics-eng_march_2016_0.pdf (accessed 20 March 2019).

Mahbubani, K. (2013) *The Great Convergence: Asia, the West, and the Logic of One World*. New York: Public Affairs.

Monaghan, A. (2017). *Power in Modern Russia: Strategy and Mobilisation*. Manchester: Manchester University Press.

Morozov, V. (2018). 'Identity and Hegemony in EU–Russia Relations: Making Sense of the Asymmetrical Entanglement', in T. Casier and J. DeBardeleben (eds), *EU–Russia Relations in Crisis: Understanding Diverging Perceptions*, London: Routledge, 30–49.

Puchala, D. (2005) 'World Hegemony and the United Nations', *International Studies Review*, 7: 571–584.

Putin, V. (2014) '[Speech at the] Meeting of the Valdai International Discussion Club', 24 October 2014. Available at: http://en.kremlin.ru/events/president/news/46860 (accessed 20 March 2019).

Ramo, J.C. (2004). *The Beijing Consensus: Notes on the New Physics of Chinese Power*. London: Foreign Policy Centre.

Ruggie, J.G. (1982) 'International Regimes, Transactions and Change: Embedded Liberalism in the Postwar Economic Order', *International Organization*, 36(2): 379–415.

Sakwa, R. (2010). *The Crisis of Russian Democracy*. Cambridge: Cambridge University Press.

Scholte, J.A. (2018) 'Global Governance 2030', in Germany and the World 2030. Available at: https://deutschland-und-die-welt-2030.de/en/article/global-governance-2030/ (accessed 20 March 2019).

Stockholm International Peace Research Institute (2018). 'SIPRI Military Expenditure Database'. Available at: www.sipri.org/databases/milex (accessed 20 March 2019).

Worth, O. (2015) *Rethinking Hegemony*. Basingstoke: Palgrave.

Xi, J. (2017, 18 October). *Secure a Decisive Victory in Building a Moderately Prosperous Society in All Respects and Strive for the Great Success of Socialism with Chinese Characteristics for a New Era*. Delivered at the 19 National Congress of the Communist Party of China. Available at: www.xinhuanet.com/english/download/Xi_Jinping's_report_at_19th_CPC_National_Congress.pdf (accessed 20 March 2019).

Zeng, J. (2017) 'Is China Committed to Peaceful Rise? Debating How to Secure Core Interests in China', *International Politics*, 54(5): 618–636.

4

GLOBALISATION AND THE DECLINE OF UNIVERSALISM

New realities for hegemony

Ivan Safranchuk

Acknowledgements

Research assistance from Bilguun Shinebayar, graduate student at Moscow State University, the faculty of political science, helped a lot in my work on this chapter. Advice from James Clement van Pelt from the Yale Divinity School, master of clarity, improved the final draft, and his line editing of this chapter helped me avoid any obvious embarrassments.

Introduction

The present chapter is built on two assumptions about hegemony – meaning one state's ability to sustainably impose and enforce arrangements on others, i.e. legitimated rule by dominant power. First, hegemony rests on both material and non-material components – which is to say power and consent. Second, the implementation of hegemony is dependent not only on who implements it and how, but even more on the circumstances within which it is to occur. In accordance with these two assumptions, a broader context is useful to understand hegemony. This context is provided by the distinction between material globalisation and ideational universalism, where the former refers to the world's interdependent physical infrastructure and the latter refers to the sharing of norms, ideals and values. Two combinations of material globalisation and ideational universalism are defined for the post-Cold War period: first, the convergence of material globalisation and ideational universalism, both on the rise; and second, the decline of ideational universalism and the resulting divergence of these material and non-material components. Although these combinations may have multiple applications, this chapter is focused on them as structural realities for hegemony in international relations.

DOI: 10.4324/9781003037231-4

Globalisation and universalism: On the rise and converging

The Age of Discovery and the colonisation of vast areas by European empires resulted in global interconnectedness by the beginning of the twentieth century. Two world wars and the dislocations of decolonisation did not halt that trend, which evolved into worldwide interdependence, and then globalisation. This long historic trend was correlated with a vast increase in Western material power and its geographical expansion. That material power was made possible through the advent of European Modernity (D'Souza 2002, 64, 66; Diamond 1998; Lewis 2002, 150).

Western expansion and then globalisation was not only material. Colonisation, despite its terrible cost to the colonised, contributed to social interconnectedness (D'Souza 2002, 40–1, 60). Communication infrastructure (including newspapers, publishing houses,and later radio), which colonisers had initially established for themselves, eventually attracted locals, and over time more and more of them. This infrastructure combined the activities and interests of both colonisers and colonised and both colonies and metropoles into a common web.

During the course of World War II, substantial ideational unity was achieved within this common web. On the one hand, wartime censorship curbed debates on issues about which there was widespread disagreement; on the other, wartime sacrifices brought colonisers and colonised together in a shared dedication to defeating fascism. The enemy was viewed within the essential moral dichotomy 'good vs. evil' so that the unity was value-based. This dramatically increased self-consciousness in colonies. With the end of WWII, censorship eased but the increased self-consciousness among the colonised could not be reversed. Consequently, debates in colonies, and in metropoles about colonies, became more intense: colonised peoples acquired more rights to debate with colonisers on equal terms, and the latter could not resist this.

Decolonisation, taking the form of national self-determination, was a strong contravention of ideational universalism. At the same time, the Cold War advanced universalism though two competing systems clashed over its particular expression. This resolved into a stand-off between two alternative universalities reaching for the same roots in European philosophical egalitarianism. Competing sides tended to extend their camps to achieve a geopolitical advantage, as well as to prove the success of their models. The two Cold War contenders provided economic and technical assistance on the condition that the beneficiaries lean toward the competing version of universal values represented by the donor state. The two superpowers had implicit belief in what was conceptualised in the second half of the twentieth century by modernisation theory, which provided that material progress is incompatible with traditional values and instead is linked to social progress (Lipset 1960, 45–76). Ultimately, to secure the victory of their universality system, each of the two competing camps sought to materially globalise and ideationally universalise the rest of the world.

The end of the Cold War, which brought the removal of political and security restrictions, had the effect of strengthening the combination of material globalisation and ideational universalisation even more. But this far-reaching com-bination did not go to validate the analytical model of either of the leading theories of international relations – institutional liberalism and structural realism. Contrary to what structural realism had theorised, the distribution of capabilities – military most of all – became so asymmetrical that it demotivated state actors from com-peting against the United States. States other than those with no chance of recon-ciling with the US, whom the US consigned to the 'axis of evil', sought to accommodate to US superiority rather than to balance it, let alone challenge it. On the other hand, contrary to the theory of institutional liberalism, the effects of interdependence that were supposed to rule out hegemony were far outweighed by the overwhelming superiority of the hard power of the US.

Even more important was the revival of ideational universalism and the accep-tance of idealism from which neoliberalism had substantially departed. The con-temporary understanding of universality emerged after the shift from metaphysics to the humanities, occurring in the spirit of the Enlightenment and leading to the dramatic progress occurring with the rise of empirical methods. With that shift, the previous understanding of what constitutes universal as the first principles of things was not needed anymore to explain the workings of nature. Instead, the philoso-phy of idealism asserted the possibility of the rational cognition of truths, absolute and universal. Fukuyama referred to Hegel, an icon of idealism, and even more to Alexandre Kojève when he declared that the conclusion of the Cold War brought with it the 'end of history' (Fukuyama 1989). In the great battle between the two universals, the capitalist thesis withstood the Marxist communist antithesis, com-pleting the Hegelian dialectic and crowning liberal universality the victor. This idealism did coincide with reality in the eyes of many. Popular culture proclaimed 'We Are the World', reflecting how much that world, suddenly freed from gen-erations-long fear and prejudice, came to take for granted the unity of material globalisation and ideational universalism, now fully fused in the notion of globali-sation, which overtook the minds of many in elites and among the masses.

However, idealistic universalism has a theoretical trap. Fukuyama claimed 'the end of history' and, at the same time, described the world as being divided into 'states at the end of history' and 'states still in history', in which the latter continued their unresolved grievances while the former could also be attacked (Fukuyama 1989, 17). However, Hegel anticipated that at 'the end of history' all elements of the world would become manifestations of the Absolute Spirit. Kojève too envi-sioned 'the end of history' as being universal, meaning non-expandable, and homogeneous, meaning non-transformable (Kojève 1969, 90, 95). The theoretical puzzle of idealistic universalism is how the two 'ends' are to meet – 'the end of history' as the completion of the dialectic in a process of political evolution and 'the end of history' as the total manifestation of the Absolute, the state of culmi-nation? Idealistic universalism implies that somehow this is to happen naturally.

But those who needed to act practically around the time the Cold War ended did not observe the victorious liberal principles be fully realised all over the world naturally and automatically. They saw the need for a benign force for this initial phase of the global-universal world, with that role being assigned to the United States. Besides, in the 1980s, progress in the direction of the liberal 'after hegemony' world had turned out to be exceedingly challenging (Wood 1987, 10–17). Given the aforementioned conditions, when hegemonic stability (with a strong liberal gene) once again became materially possible, there was little opposition to it from proponents of institutional liberalism.

All this contributed to the acceptance of American super-hegemony by the majority in the international community – even anticipation. That was not the acceptance of a hegemon in the traditional understanding of hegemony as a power able to establish and endorse arrangements in line with its interests, also providing absolute, even if unequal, gains for others, which legitimises one's hegemony. It was instead the acceptance of a super-hegemon in an idealistic interpretation: the leader whose intention is to forge and implement the practical design of the new world order based on victorious liberal universality, and whose legitimacy to execute hegemony arises from the premise of this mission. Figuratively, it was the acceptance of a version of the god Zeus who would behave like the titan Prometheus: an absolute power serving the universal interests of all.

Many scholars have paid attention to how the missionary interpretation of American exceptionalism developed (Huntington 2004; Sardar and Davies 2003; McDougall 1997). This culminated in the nineteenth-century doctrine of Manifest Destiny emerging in the context of the inevitability and justifiability of the territorial expansion of the US throughout the North American continent. This doctrine and others conceived of America as divinely favoured, with a mission both universal and global. The universal mission is to 'smite unto death the tyranny of kings, hierarchs, and oligarchs, and carry the glad tidings of peace and good will where myriads now endure an existence scarcely more enviable than the beasts of the field'. The global mission originates in the 'right of our manifest destiny to spread over this whole continent'; figuratively, 'Its floor shall be a hemisphere – its roof the firmament of the star-studded heavens, and its congregation an Union of many Republics' [sic] (Pratt 1927, 797). When that notion was developed the US was far from being materially capable to fulfil the task. Later, after engaging with the world at the beginning of the twentieth century, America took for a 'central drama' that 'it would have to implement its ideals in a world less blessed than its own' (Kissinger 1994, 54–5). The emerging global-universal world made the mission more implementable.

Besides this deeply rooted idea consistent with the role of super-hegemony, there was also a political force in the latter third of the twentieth century favouring the US to take the role: American 'reassertionism'. Claiming that 'confidence in ourselves (is) the crucial psychological element in any foreign policy' (Feinberg 1983, 15–16), 'reassertionism' treated the perceived setback of Vietnam and the setback in Iran during the Carter presidency as a self-fulfilling prophecy. Not surprisingly, the active stance of 'reassertionism' was taken up by the Reagan Administration (Sewell, Feinberg, Kallab 1985, 3–30), and it did not imply a new setback after capitalism's victory in the Cold War.

The problem was that no school of political thought promised success to super-hegemony: both classical and neo-realism foresaw relative decline of the US (Kennedy 1988, 418–535) and did not allow for the possibility of super-hegemony, while neoliberalism regarded any hegemony as being less possible and instead looked forward 'after hegemony', a world free of hegemony in general (Keohane 1984). But suddenly the neoliberal camp reinterpreted the nature of power, in particular, America's power, proclaiming that leadership was possible and advisable on the basis of soft (non-coercive) power (Nye 1990). America, with its strong union of values and interests, soft and hard power, was given a chance to lead.

Undeniably, after the end of the Cold War, progress was made in constructing the liberal world order via the development of international institutions based on liberal principles. Structural realism was critical to that development because this theory viewed it unsustainable and driven by disillusion. Institutional liberalism nonetheless favoured this development even though the construction of institutions was progressing not in a world without hegemony, as the theory had envisioned, but instead under the auspices of the American super-hegemony.

Globalisation with declining universalism

The processes of material globalisation persisted in the twenty-first century. Though it did not progress much further after the 2008–2009 world economic crisis, it was not dramatically reversed either. The same could not be said about the worldwide adherence to the principle of ideationally universal values.

Regional conflicts of the 1990s and the worsening problem of failed states were regarded at that time as remnants of the past, persisting only because some historic processes were still incomplete. The 9/11 terrorist attacks were also initially interpreted as being rooted in recent history, and especially in the Cold War end game. The 2002 National Security Strategy (NSS) of the US claimed that the 'great struggle of the twentieth century between liberty and totalitarianism ended with the decisive victory of the forces of freedom – and a single sustainable model for national success: freedom, democracy, and free enterprise'. In this context, terrorism was considered a threat from remnant forces of unfreedom. The 2006 NSS also linked terrorism to unfreedom and tyranny, combining the war on terror and the promotion of freedom as two inseparable priorities, but ceased to understand terrorism as a remnant of the past. Instead, the war on terror was presented as a prolonged struggle against a new totalitarian ideology (equating to fascism and communism in the recent past). Islamist terrorists were reinterpreted into 'evildoers', and the war against them into a Just War. Moreover, some saw it taking inter-civilisational shape (Mann 2003, 164). Voices against this inter-civilisational veneer of counter-terrorism and rare voices against it as a war against 'evildoers' (Brzezinski 2004, 28–2; Harvey 2003, 96) did not stop the US-led 'war on terror' from turning into the Just War (with some elements of inter-civilisational interpretation). This undermined the perception of an emerging ideationally universal world.

The new Just War theory was not the only development that contravened the anticipation of universalism. Modernisation theory asserted that developing societies should abandon their traditional values if they are to make progress toward economic prosperity. But what authors of that theory took for universal social law looked more like a deal in developing countries: they were to make some administrative reforms and social modernisation and in return they would get some foreign technical assistance and capital for economic development (provided by foreigners, majorly the two competing universalities). Developing countries did not see themselves as mere objects of social law, but rather conscious subjects making a rational choice in response to a given dilemma. Not surprisingly, with their acquired material capability they sought to defend their cultural and ideational uniqueness instead of melting in the thaw of universalism. In the natural course of development, successful followers of the West began to be critical of many of its ways, as Lee Kuan Yew demonstrated in his famous conversation with Fareed Zakaria for *Foreign Affairs* (Zakaria 1994).

The world economic crisis of 2008–2009 contributed to the reverse of universalism with a negative power even greater than the previous growth. That crisis had a tremendous and enduring impact on the worldview of developing countries; for them, it was not just another cyclic economic setback. Previously material success had often been viewed as a result of social and political modernisation (and for those practising a catch-up model of development, a reward). In the aftermath of the crisis, the calculus changed. Now the developing world saw the West even more as the cornucopia of Modernity, shopping it for technology, capital and other material inputs, but not for norms, models of economic development, sociopolitical order or cultural practices.

In the domain of global governance, opportunities to harmonise rule-setting were also missed. At the turn of the millennium, there were many rational and persuasively delivered calls for reforming global policymaking. Importantly, the strongest of them originated within the core of the global economic system, i.e. with the Western financial corporations. In 2001 Goldman Sachs stressed the increasing global economic impact of Brazil, Russia, India and China (BRIC) and further endorsed that thesis in 2003 by forecasting that BRIC together with the US and Japan would be the six largest world economies by 2040–2050. Those same voices from the West called for institutional reforms to reduce the international influence of Western nations (Stiglitz 2002, 130). The G7 countries hesitated to move in that direction. This finally happened in the aftermath of the 2008–2009 crisis, when the G20 became the new platform of global policymaking. By that time the momentum for a universal economic agenda had already been lost. Instead, the members of the G20 with the largest economies quickly consolidated into two factions: the G7 and BRICS (Denisov, Kazantsev, Lukyanov and Safranchuk 2019, 491–92, 496). The result: the G20 turned into a global but ideologically split – global but non-universal – body.

Socially, conventional wisdom at the beginning of the millennium suggested that the Internet and later social media – those truly global technical platforms, which have substantially contributed to material globalisation – should become powerful instruments of universalisation, unequivocally spreading the only post-Cold War ideational universality from the West to the rest of the world. Some expected that individuals could not be successful in the globalised world without a sort of socialisation: 'to self-include and self-identify in the context of the global information and communication flows is to self-exclude and dis-identify from the national flows' (Lash 2002, 5). In practice, however, the world did not harmonise with that brand of globalisation (Nye 2003, 95–9). On the contrary, it got onto the track of solidifying various identities (Castells 2010). In such circumstances, democracy could be found conflicting with liberalism (Zakaria 2003). Indeed, global technical platforms unleashed local initiatives and peoples' energies, which are hard to confine within universal ideations. Smaller and weaker actors got more voice and expanded opportunities, for the most part using this not to join the ideational universality but to enforce local and regional voices that can be inconsistent with liberal universalism.

This situation can be analogised to George Orwell's statement about the link between weapons and democracy: expensive and difficult to make weapons are 'inherently tyrannical' because they are not available to masses, thus ages when such weapons dominate are ages of despotism; on the contrary, cheap and simple weapons are 'inherently democratic', when they dominate 'people have a chance' to struggle for democracy (Orwell 1945). In the same way, the Internet and particularly social media became new 'democratic weapons'. People with something to say, in unprecedented numbers, gained access to the means of production of content and its dissemination; this inevitably has contributed to pluralism and is empowering those people who are unready or unwilling to accept ideational universality.

From all these different perspectives, the universality that was victorious by the end of the Cold War was undermined and even reversed. It is not that this universality was challenged with a new antithesis. Rather, a substantial part of the world consciously chose to resist being taken into the thesis, and this voluntary self-exclusion was too deep and widespread in scope not to undermine universalisation.

Worst of all, American culture failed to produce a working and comfortable combination of Zeus-like and Prometheus-like models of leadership and hegemony. The alternative view resolved into the conviction that if globalisation is a social process, then it needs to be properly managed to sustain 'good globalization' and prevent 'bad globalization' (Sachs 2005; De Soto 2000; Stiglitz 2002; Stiglitz 2003). To accomplish that degree of management implies less rigid control of the world powers, America first and foremost, together with increasing regulation of international norms and institutions (Bhagwati 2004; Drucker 1999; Soros 2004) – the very thing institutional liberalism had originally argued for. What this means, in essence, is that America is to be prepared to accept a future of decline: 'over the longer term, we can expect globalization itself to spread technological and economic capabilities and thus reduce the extent of American dominance' (Nye 2003, 95).

In line with the neoliberal approach, the recommended solution is for the US to become more reconciled to multilateralism, shifting its hegemonic powers from itself to international institutions, norms and values (Stiglitz 2002; Brzezinski 2004). In other words, America was urged to cease striving to use its massive economic and military might to be the Olympian god of globalisation and universalisation. Instead, the US was expected to abandon its self-assigned role as the world's universalising force and to accept its becoming no more than another object for universalisation on the same basis as all other states. Such a decisive shift, from universalising to being universalised, is viewed by many in America's leadership circles as a radical demotion and a fundamental denial of the exceptionalism on which the national identity has been founded for more than a century. American resistance to this alleged demotion, as the systems of globalisation gather steam, critically contributes to the divergence of universalism and globalisation in opposite directions.

Arguably, this reality – the materially globalising world order marching forward while ideational universalism is set on a declining course – is unique in the history of humankind. Prior to the modern era, the old world could be described as lacking global economic and political systems yet bound by strong universal ideas and values, mostly derived from deeply held religious beliefs. The emergence of the modern era has featured a prolonged trend of ever stronger globalisation together with a rise in secular universalism characterised by an ever-extending commitment to egalitarianism. By the end of the twentieth century, the world reached the threshold of globalised economic and political order in combination with strong universal values.

As the new millennium progresses, the globalising trends continue while inclinations toward universalism are quite noticeably in decline. Perhaps an analogy can be made between contemporary history and parallel developments at the turn of the nineteen century. During that transition, the world was growing materially interconnected, however far from the present pace of globalisation, and emerging national identities confronted old imperial identities and (although to a lesser extent) universal religious values. At the same time, universal ideas rooted in European Enlightenment philosophy such as egalitarianism ploughed into history on their way to becoming guidelines for new national identities, world politics and international order.

Finally, after two world wars and the subsequent consolidation of the world into two competing universalistic systems under the banners of Marxist communism and liberal capitalism, both globalisation and universalisation made further progress. Now, however, the reversal of universalism's progress looks to be a more lasting development, with some specific effects.

In this materially globalised world with declining ideational universalism, the phenomenon of interdependence acquires new features and seems to be working in a different way. Just as before, great states are sensitive to destabilisation. But beyond this, there are new mechanisms contributing to the tectonic power shift. The direct coercion of states by militarily supreme powers has become too costly, whether the goal is victory via offence or denying victory in defences – in particular in nuclear define. The projection of power against militarily weaker enemies in asymmetric conflicts has a controversial record of outcomes, for example from Vietnam to Afghanistan, and ultimately it is also found to be too costly. The greater the cost, the greater must be the appeal to universal values if that cost is to seem justifiable – especially when costs are measured in human casualties. Although Clausewitz advised sovereigns to stick to political objectives in war, in reality neither democratic nor authoritarian societies are inclined to sacrifice sufficient casualties to achieve merely material, practical fruits of victory. Universalistic claims are indispensable for mobilising masses for the extreme self-sacrifice warfare demands, shifting from the ancient battle cries to defend king and country to universal ideations like making the world safe for democracy. The ideational decline reduces the military power of major states because they lack justification required to unleash it in full force.

From the perspective of a certain level of interdependence, the materially globalised world integrates itself into a single system. Then it becomes subject to the second law of thermodynamics having to do with the idea of entropy as adapted to information theory (Hart and Gregor 2005). Entropy in this context is a quantification of randomness, uncertainty and disorganisation that must be released into the environment in order to maintain the stability of the system from which it originates; otherwise, the system will destabilise and collapse. This leads to the controversial question: what can be treated as the environment into which the single system of human beings and their social interactions can expel its entropy? The most obvious response is the natural environment that suffers the consequences of human activity. However, not all sorts of entropy produced by human systems can be discharged into nature. Even worse, nature itself produces entropy, an example of which is climate change, which at first is a by-product of human activity that then becomes a cycle negatively affecting human civilisation as a whole. The materially globalised world can be seen as a closed system since it is not located within an environment into which it can discharge its entropy. According to information theory, the causal closure of a system maximises entropy.

In addition, entropy increases not only with the closure of a system but also with its complexity. In the Flat World (Friedman 2007) there are myriad connections on different levels between different actors. This becomes a network de facto with minimal structural holes, which minimises the benefits of information and control that formerly empowered the major players, as network theory reasons (Burt 1992, 8–49). Consequently, in an increasingly globalised world, human interactions occur on various levels among individuals, non-state entities, states and international entities. The interactions of these actors are conditioned by varying attitudes toward one another (friends, enemies, etc.) on multiple issues (political, security-related, economic, material, ideational, etc.). Such interactions cause subjects, objects and circumstances to increase in quantity and to diversify in quality. This increases the number of possible microstates that can be randomly formed by elements of the system; the larger the number of microstates, the greater the overall complexity of the system. From this perspective, the globalised world becomes an increasingly complex closed system, within which entropy is maximised.

This description suggests that it is in the interest of the global system that entropy in the form of disorganisation and chaos should be minimised. The crucial question is: how can that be accomplished? Several ways are possible. Force and coercion can reduce entropy if successfully employed: due to the physical liquidation of elements, complexity decreases. But the use of coercion may not bring a clear resolution, either because the use of force is unsuccessful, or because the balance of power results in constraints from deterrence relationships, or else because a state may be reluctant to use force even though it may possess military primacy. Any and all of these are current realities and contribute to the complexity of the system and thus to the generation of entropy.

To co-opt with strong ideas is another way to reduce entropy. The triumph of universalism, as viewed by idealism as the 'end of history' with total ideational reconciliation, theoretically should stop the production of entropy from human activity, especially from social interactions. Progressing toward its terminal state but not yet completed, universalisation may have opposite effects – increasing or decreasing entropy – depending on the circumstances that prevail.

Universalistic alternatives can clash with one another as they did during the Cold War and thereby generate entropy; at the same time the competing systems universalised other actors and by doing so decreased the complexity of the system, which in turn decreased entropy. If one set of ideas wins the struggle to achieve universality, as in the outcome of the Cold War, but is not yet commonly accepted, then the victor needs to achieve general acceptance and then global pre-eminence. In that case, the means by which it is promoted on a global scale may generate more or less entropy, depending on what methods are applied. As a general rule, coercing uncommitted actors is likely to maximise entropy far more effectively than attempting to co-opt them. However, when universalism in general declines it becomes less likely that co-opting will work, which overall adds to the maximisation of entropy even more than when it is progressing in its acceptance but is not yet completed.

Cooperation is another technique through which the generation of entropy can be limited. In contrast to successful coercion or co-opting meant to decrease complexity, cooperation causes a system to be more able to manage complexity. However, the sources underpinning cooperation may vary, which determines the patterns of cooperation. Cooperation may be rooted in a belief in universalistic ideas. In that case, the strength of the universalistic idea determines the extent of cooperation. Alternatively, cooperation may originate from an absence of universalistic ideas. Thus cooperation can benefit from either the presence of strong shared universalistic ideas, but also from the absence of those ideas.

The central structural element of the current world is the mismatch between material globalisation and ideational universalism – the former continuing its ascendance while the latter declines. This mismatch leads to an erosion of the balance between entropy and an organising force – as seen by would-be hegemons' loss of power not only due to the effects of interdependence from material globalisation but even more because of the decline of ideational universalism. That makes states less capable of managing the global growth of entropy as it is generated in a closed complex system of the materially globalised world.

As ideational universalism falls into decline at the same time material globalisation continues, it can be observed that the latter has started working against the former with no less power than that with which it had once contributed to it. When globalisation and universalism converged into an integrated force, globalisation had empowered the melting pot of universalism. The rational decision for interconnected and interdependent entities was to choose universalism as the ideational ground on which their engines of material growth could prosper – whether those entities were societies or individuals, economies or cultures. But as the universalistic momentum leaks away, various elements get mixed by the power of material globalisation in various ways, yet they cannot be combined to form something new and common.

Conclusion

The end of the Cold War made a return to world hegemony possible but only in a very specific form: liberal super-hegemony. That was inconsistent with the expectations of institutional liberalism and structural realism alike: with the former's 'after hegemony' thinking and the latter's balance of power among competing hegemonies. The US liberal super-hegemony that emerged rested on the seeming culmination of the centuries-long trend of converging material globalisation and ideational universalisation. However, soon material globalisation and ideational universalism diverged, and as a consequence the foundation for super-hegemony is fading.

In today's materially globalised world, with the characteristics of a closed complex system, the production of entropy is unabated. But the major actors and especially the would-be hegemons now lack the means to effect its reduction. Universalistic aspirations are too weak now to sustain the use of co-optation or coercion with full force. At the same time, universalistic aspirations are still too strong for some powerful states to allow their genuine cooperation with other actors. Material globalisation and ideational universalism are mismatched in a kind of limbo, which defines the structural realities of the current world system.

This can be interpreted to support argument of institutional liberalism and structural realism alike. On the one hand, the decline of universalism enforces the argument of structural realism that harmonious liberal international design is a grand delusion (Mearsheimer 2018). On the other hand, the production of entropy in the materially globalised world rationalises a 'liberalism of fear': since unchecked power is too dangerous, institutional liberalism offers 'a source of hope for improvement coupled with institutional checks against retrogression' (Keohane 2012, 136).

In fact, the aforementioned ambivalent structural realities are terra incognita for power politics. There is no map, no bible to guide powerful actors toward their objectives in the materially globalised world whose foundation of universal ideas continues to erode.

Would-be hegemons tend to undertake spontaneous rather than thoughtful attempts to adjust their ventures to fit within these structural constraints. So far it is an open question as to what the great powers will finally do. Will they reshape the realities of the world by re-introducing strong and compelling universal ideas, in which case institutional liberalism would have more power to explain and guide; or by de-globalising the world so that it leans more toward economic and political nationalism, in which case structural realism would better explain and guide? Or might they learn to cope in the emerging global non-universal world with all its entropy and diversity?

References

Bhagwati, J. (2004) *In Defense of Globalization*. New York: Oxford University Press.

Brzezinski, Z. (2004) *The Choice: Global Domination or Global Leadership*. New York: Basic Books.

Burt, R.S. (1992) *Structural Holes: The Social Structure of Competition*. Cambridge, MA: Harvard University Press.

Castells, M. (2010) *The Power of Identity*. Malden, MA: Wiley-Blackwell.

Denisov, I., Kazantsev, A., Lukyanov, F. and Safranchuk, I. (2019) 'Shifting Strategic Focus of BRICS and Great Power Competition', *Strategic Analysis*, 43(6): 487–498.

De Soto, H. (2000) *The Mystery of Capital: Why Capitalism Triumphs in the West and Fails Everywhere Else*. New York: Basic Books.

Diamond, J. (1998) *Guns, Germs and Steel: A Short History of Everybody for the Last 13,000 Years*. London: Vintage.

Drucker, P.F. (1999) *Management Challenges for the 21st Century*. New York: HarperBusiness.

D'Souza, D. (2002) *What's So Great about America*. Washington, DC: Regnery Publishing.

Feinberg, R.E. (1983) *The Intemperate Zone: The Third World Challenge to U.S. Foreign Policy*. New York: W. W. Norton.

Friedman, T.L. (2007) *The World is Flat: A Brief History of the Twenty-First Century*. New York: Farrar, Straus and Giroux.

Fukuyama, F. (1989) 'The End of History?', *The National Interest*, 16(Summer): 1–18.

Hart, D.N. and Gregor, S.D. (2005) *Information Systems Foundations: Constructing and Criticising*. Canberra: ANU Press.

Harvey, R. (2003) *Global Disorder*. London: Constable.

Huntington, S.P. (2004) *Who are We? The Challenges to America's Identity*. New York: Simon & Schuster.

Kennedy, P. (1988) *The Rise and Fall of the Great Powers*. London: Unwin Hyman.

Keohane, R.O. (1984) *After Hegemony: Cooperation and Discord in the World Political Economy*. Princeton, NJ: Princeton University Press.

Keohane, R.O. (2012) 'Twenty Years of Institutional Liberalism', *International Relations*, 26(2): 125–138.

Kissinger, H. (1994) *Diplomacy*. New York: Simon & Schuster.

Kojève, A. (1969) *Introduction to the Reading of Hegel: Lectures on the Phenomenology of Spirit*. New York: Basic Books.

Lash, S. (2002) *Critique of the Information*. London: Sage.

Lewis, B. (2002) *What Went Wrong? Western Impact and Middle-Eastern Response*. New York: Oxford University Press.

Lipset, S.M. (1960) *Political Man: The Social Bases of Politics*. Garden City, NY: Doubleday.

Mann, M. (2003) *Incoherent Empire*. London: Verso.

McDougall, W. (1997) *Promised Land, Crusader State: The American Encounter with the World since 1776*. Boston, MA: Houghton Mifflin.

Mearsheimer, J.J. (2018) *Great Delusion: Liberal Dreams and International Realities*. New Haven, CT: Yale University Press.

Nye, J. (1990) *Bound to Lead: The Changing Nature of American Power*. New York: Basic Books.

Nye, J. (2003) *The Paradox of American Power: Why the World's Only Superpower Can't Go It Alone*. New York: Oxford University Press.

Orwell, G. (1945) 'You and the Atomic Bomb'. *Tribune*, 19 October. Available at: http://orwell.ru/library/articles/ABomb/english/e_abomb

Pratt, J.W. (1927) 'The Origin of "Manifest Destiny"', *The American Historical Review*, 32(4): 795–798.

Sachs, J. (2005) *The End of Poverty: Economic Possibilities for Our Time*. London: Allen Lane.

Sardar, Z. and Davies, M.W. (2003) *Why Do People Hate America?*Cambridge: Icon.

Sewell, J.W., Feinberg, R.E. and Kallab, V. (1985) *U.S. Foreign Policy and the Third World: Agenda 1985–86*. New Brunswick, NJ: Transaction Books.

Soros, G. (2004) *The Bubble of American Supremacy*. New York: Public Affairs.

Stiglitz, J.E. (2002) *Globalization and Its Discontents*. New York: W. W. Norton.

Stiglitz, J.E. (2003) *The Roaring Nineties. A New History of the World's Most Prosperous Decade*. New York: W. W. Norton.

Wood, B. (1987) 'Middle Powers in the International System: A Preliminary Assessment of Potential', WIDER Working Papers, Helsinki. Available at: www.wider.unu.edu/publication/middle-powers-international-system

Zakaria, F. (1994) 'A Conversation with Lee Kuan Yew', *Foreign Affairs*, March/April. Available at: www.foreignaffairs.com/articles/asia/1994-03-01/conversation-lee-kuan-yew-0

Zakaria, F. (2003) *The Future of Freedom: Illiberal Democracy at Home and Abroad*. New York: W. W. Norton.

5

RETHINKING HEGEMONY AS COMPLEXITY

Jan Aart Scholte

Introduction

As elaborated in the introduction to this volume, hegemony in world politics can be theorised in diverse ways. The preceding four chapters have developed several of those perspectives (i.e. world-systems, realist and neo-Gramscian approaches), updating them in the light of current world politics. Now this chapter asks whether contemporary circumstances warrant a more fundamental rethink of hegemony, not only drawing upon past theories, but also going beyond them to an alternative conception, here dubbed 'complex hegemony'.

Most established theories of (world) hegemony locate legitimated rule by dominant power in one principal force. Thus liberalism and realism situate hegemony in a leading state. Neo-Gramscian analysis roots hegemony in capitalism. Postcolonialism grounds hegemony in Western imperialism. Poststructuralism attributes hegemony to a disciplining knowledge structure. In all of these cases, hegemony appears to emanate in linear fashion from a single primary source.

Certainly these reductionist diagnoses of hegemony offer attractions of relative simplicity and parsimony; however, one may also ask whether they unduly oversimplify the dynamics of world politics. Already we have seen that world-system theory explains hegemony in terms of an interplay between capitalist development and interstate relations, whereby each of these two forces reciprocally shapes the other, and neither is reducible to the other. Similarly, the principle of intersectionality, discussed in the introduction to this volume, suggests that hegemony involves a combination of social stratifications (class, gender, race, etc.) rather than one primary structural hierarchy. World-systems and intersectional accounts find it unsustainable – theoretically and empirically – to pare hegemony down to a one-dimensional core. As such, they point in the direction of complexity.

DOI: 10.4324/9781003037231-5

This chapter foregrounds still more the principle of complexity: i.e. the notion that hegemony operates in complicated and substantially unpredictable ways through a co-constitution of multiple forces. The first section below sets out complexity as a general metatheoretical premise. The second section then relates the complexity principle more particularly to hegemony in contemporary world politics. The third section develops a more concrete account of complex hegemony in the context of today's global Internet governance. The conclusion suggests directions for future research of complex hegemony in world politics.

Turning to complexity

Rethinking hegemony in terms of complexity fits with a broader trend in contemporary scholarship. Since the late twentieth century, many quarters of natural and social sciences have undergone 'a paradigm shift' (Bogg and Geyer 2007, 1) with 'the complexity turn' (Urry 2005). Within this wider development, notions of complexity have also spread to theories of world politics (Rosenau 2003; Harrison 2006; Kavalski 2007, 2013; Kissane 2011). At least one other scholar has already brought a complexity perspective to the study of hegemony, albeit not world hegemony more specifically (Williams 2019). To this extent, the present chapter's exploration of complex hegemony in world politics treads an unbeaten path.

As invoked here, 'complexity' involves not a precise explanatory theory, but a general metatheoretical orientation. Nor does the present discussion engage with certain more technical concepts of complex systems science concerning 'emergence', 'feedback loops', 'punctuated equilibria', 'adaptation', and so on (Holland 1995; Arthur et al. 1997; Gould 2007). Rather, complexity is invoked here as a more generic way to understand the character of reality and build knowledge about that reality. In particular, a complexity approach reacts against the reductionism and linearity that have dominated modern science. Instead, complexity conceives of reality – including the realities of hegemony in world politics – in terms of systems with multiple co-constituting forces.

At its most elementary, complexity means not simple. Complexity rejects the premium that modern – frequently dubbed 'Newtonian' – science places on parsimony, i.e. on the quest to identify one or a few discrete causes to explain a phenomenon. This epistemology promises to discover precisely measurable impact for each key variable and, with that knowledge, to acquire the capacity to predict outcomes and to control a situation through the manipulation of the driver variables. For example, a parsimonious theory of world politics might pare causality down to the utilitarian calculations of states, or to the effective operation of institutions, or to the class dialectic of globalising capitalism, or to patriarchal gender subordination, or to some other discrete primary force. In all such cases, scholarship expects to explain and predict – and policy practice expects to control – world politics in terms of singular factors.

In contrast, a complexity orientation says that reality is qualitatively more complicated. This approach rejects parsimonious explanation – and associated prediction and control – as an untenable oversimplification. From a complexity perspective, world politics (as any other reality) is complicated because it involves multiple non-reducible forces. Here 'multiple' means more than a few, and 'non-reducible' means that none of these forces is wholly an outcome of another. In the words of complexity thinker John Urry, 'global ordering is so immensely complicated that it cannot be "known" through a simple concept or set of processes' (2003, 15). In a similar vein, James Rosenau has understood world politics in terms of 'turbulence', 'cascades' and 'fragmegration' (1990; 2003).

Hence, for a complexity analysis of world politics, the question is not whether states or non-state actors prevail, but how these various entities co-exist and inter-relate. Likewise, the question for complexity thinking is not the primacy of either ideational forces (e.g. associated with culture and psychology) or material forces (e. g. associated with ecology and economy), but their interconnections and reciprocal effects on each other (Scholte 1993). Causality lies not in either structure (i.e. social ordering patterns) or actor (i.e. behavioural unit), but in their co-constitution (Giddens 1984; Wendt 1999). A complexity approach assumes not a single determining world-order framework (be it the states system, liberal norms, capitalism, gender hierarchy, anthropocentrism, or other), but multiple interwoven and mutually shaping structures. Similarly, complexity reasoning presumes not one dynamic of history (be it a balance of power mechanism, progressive modernisation, a Polanyian double movement, a Kondratiev cycle, or whatever), but concurrent multidirectional trajectories, none of which consistently overrides the others.

In refusing reductionism, complexity rejects the ontological practice of breaking down a condition (such as world politics) into separate parts and then distributing discrete causal forces among these elements. Colin Wight speaks in this vein of 'potentially hundreds of interacting feedback loops … making it very difficult, if not impossible, to untangle the contribution of individual causal mechanisms, or combinations of them, in explaining specific outcomes' (2015, 63). Instead, complexity considers a situation as a whole and locates causation in the interconnections which form that whole.

For example, reductionism might divide world politics into separate countries and give each country its discrete force in shaping developments. In contrast, a complexity approach would treat world politics as a distinct whole whose own systemic properties – i.e. forces that interlink the countries – also constitute major drivers of events. On similar lines, a reductionist orientation might separate issue-areas in world affairs (culture, ecology, economy, military, etc.) and their respective regulatory arrangements (the environmental regime, the human rights regime, the peacebuilding regime, the trade regime, etc.). In contrast, a complexity perspective would focus on the interrelations and mutual effects of these policy fields. Another reductionist ontology might isolate and measure distinct structural forces of, say, multipolarity, capitalism, anthropocentrism, heterosexism, etc. In contrast, the holism of complexity would suppose intersecting and co-constituting world-order patterns. Reductionist thinking might imagine a single and even teleological course of history, whereas complexity thinking with its eye on multiple interrelated forces would regard the future to be substantially indeterminate and largely uncontrollable.

As preceding references to 'interconnection', 'interlinkage', 'interrelation' and 'intersection' indicate, complexity analysis rejects modern Newtonian notions of linear causation. Instead, says William Connolly, think of 'a world composed of heterogeneous, partially open, interacting force-fields' (2011, 215). Reductionist science formulates explanation in terms of unidirectional flows from cause to effect, whereby certain elements (often designated as 'independent variables') are the driver whereas others ('dependent variables') are the driven. The underlying presumption suggests that cause and effect can be ontologically separated. In contrast, complexity science speaks in terms of mutual determination, reciprocal effects and co-constitution. Causation thereby lies not only or even primarily in the parts, but in the systemic relations that interweave the elements. In this vein, for example, several historical sociologists have analysed world politics in terms of four inter-related sources of power (economic, ideological, military and political) (Giddens 1985; Mann 1986, ch. 1). Similarly, intersectional accounts of global inequality have situated its causation in interplays of age, class, gender, race and other social stratifications (Walby 2009; Collins and Bilge 2016). From another angle, political ecologists have embedded world politics in a planetary web of life (Cudworth and Hobden 2011). Certain liberal institutionalists have understood global governance in terms of 'regime complexes' that interlink multiple regulatory bodies (Alter and Meunier 2009; Orsini et al. 2013, 2019).

As the preceding discussion has intimated, complexity entails not a specific theory, but a metatheoretical orientation. There is no paradigmatic 'complexity theory' that offers a specific explanatory formula to rival other approaches to world politics such as liberalism, realism, Marxism, feminism and so on. Rather, corner-stones of complexity thinking such as complication, holism, co-constitution, and indeterminacy can be elaborated in diverse ways, including through world-systems theory, intersectional analysis, political ecology and more. Hence, the rest of this chapter presents not a definitive 'complexity theory' of hegemony, but offers just one possible complexity perspective on legitimated rule by dominant power in contemporary world politics.

Of course, critics of complexity thinking can object that this metatheoretical orientation makes knowledge – and the scientific methods to obtain knowledge – overly messy. Reductionism and linear causation have the attraction of generating neater and more manageable explanations – and explanations that answer modern demands for predictability and control of nature and society. Moreover, we have long experience of – and huge literature based on – reductionist methods, many of them by now highly sophisticated. Undeniably, modern strivings after parsimo-nious explanations have borne many advances of knowledge and practice. Hence, wholesale dismissal of Newtonian approaches would not be advisable.

Yet it is also clear that modern science based on parsimony, reductionism, line-arity and promises of prediction and control has important limits, including for the study of world politics and the more specific topic of hegemony. The focus on certain variables to the exclusion of others conceals as well as reveals: e.g., state-centrism hides societal actors, political economy hides ecology, class-centrism hides gender, and so on. Moreover, for all of the decades of efforts, reductionism in empirical research of world politics has arguably under-delivered in providing reliable and significant explanations of real-world conditions. As for predictability, reductionist social science has generally supplied poor forecasts of wars, reconfigurations of states, economic crises, technological developments, cultural trends, ecological changes, etc. Which Kremlinologists foresaw the end of the Cold War? Which reductionist economists anticipated the financial crisis of 2008? What linear theory predicted the Internet or can now confidently foretell the future of digitisation and artificial intelligence? What Newtonian model can with any precision anticipate the social consequences of global warming?

One answer to these criticisms is to say that the problem lies not with Newtonian principles, but with their as yet insufficient development: the project of modern science just needs more time and effort. Critics of reductionism, too, can acknowledge that the cup is half-full as well as half-empty and not throw the baby out with the bathwater. Our understanding of world politics has become much greater with modern science than without it; so one might continue to develop reductionist knowledge while also acknowledging (more than in the past) its limitations.

Those limitations provide strong arguments for pursuing a complexity alternative. The principle of multiple co-constituting forces with substantially indeterminate outcomes makes intuitive sense from concrete experience. Complexity orientations have already yielded some important insights into world politics through the aforementioned research. However, the overall promise of complexity thinking is thus far underdeveloped. In particular, the approach has little entered the study of hegemony in world politics, apart from previously noted partial steps in respect of world-systems theory and intersectionality. The moment can be ripe to push these explorations further.

Complex hegemony in world politics

As already underlined, complexity is a broad metatheoretical principle that can be developed in many different ways, including with respect to world politics. For example, complexity ideas go in diverse directions when liberal institutionalists speak of regime complexes, Marxists elaborate world-system theory, and feminists turn to the intersectionality concept. One might also expect complexity theories to vary over time, since the forces that shape world politics do not remain constant. For instance, non-state actors and anthropogenic ecological changes figure more in the complexity mix today than in the past. In addition, particular versions of complexity theory could vary depending on the object of study: for example, whether the research focuses on cultural heritage or on international migration.

Hence, the account of complex hegemony that is developed in this chapter reflects a theoretical proclivity (i.e. my perspective of critical global political sociology), its moment in time (i.e. the early twenty-first century), and the focus of my current empirical research (i.e. global Internet governance). So I do not claim here to offer *the* complexity theory of world hegemony, but rather give an illustration of how complexity thinking can be elaborated in a particular context. Another author, working at another time, and on another issue-area, might come to a quite different kind of complexity analysis.

My methodology in formulating the following conception of complex hegemony has been one of abduction (Friedrichs and Kratochwil 2009). That is, I have pursued neither deduction (i.e. imposing a pre-set theory on concrete circumstances) nor induction (deriving an explanation solely from a particular empirical context, without any theoretical presuppositions). As a third approach, abduction involves taking an array of existing theoretical propositions to a given context of empirical research and considering which of those notions – perhaps several, or even new ones – seem helpful to understand that situation.

In the present case, the relevant array of theories are those related to world-scale hegemony (as surveyed in the introduction to this volume), and the empirical context is the regulation of global Internet infrastructure. So on the table are a full range of possible drivers of hegemony and counter-hegemony in world politics, including:

- a leading state or group of states (as per liberal and realist theories)
- regime complexes (as per institutionalist theories)
- elite networks and social movements (as per theories of transnationalism)
- capitalism (as per Marxist theories)
- dominant norms and discourses (as per constructivist theories)
- Western-modern imperialism (as per postcolonial theories)
- anthropocentrism (as per political ecology theories)
- social stratifications (as per feminist, queer and other theories of hierarchy).

Moreover, a complexity perspective allows – even expects – that a combination of forces taken from several theories could elucidate the workings of hegemony in world politics. Thus, hegemony would not need to lie only in a leading state, or only in capitalism, or only in dominant discourses, and so on. Each of these propositions (and more) could be identifying an important dimension of hegemony, without capturing its entirety. As the case of Internet governance will illustrate below, the problem arises when reductionist theories, in their quest for parsimony, insist to limit hegemony in world politics to one aspect, to the exclusion of other forces that together could comprise (complex) hegemony.

Invoking the complexity principle, an alternative approach could consider whether a combination of forces that various reductionist theories highlight individually might generate hegemony together, through reciprocal relationships. Thus, one can examine a given concrete circumstance (such as global Internet governance) and ask whether empirical evidence from that setting corroborates the presence of the type of hegemonic force that different theories of world politics postulate. So, for example, does hegemony in that context involve a leading state or group of states that sponsors the rules, with the confidence and trust of other parties who are subject to those rules? Does the hegemonic situation in question have a regime complex, with legitimated (i.e. generally endorsed) dominance by a network of regulators that spans multiple interrelated institutions? Does the circumstance involve approved supremacy of capitalism and a transnational bourgeoisie? Of ruling discourses concerning, say, 'security', 'development', or 'human rights'? Of the principles and values of Western modernity? Of anthropocentrism and hyperextractivism vis-à-vis the web of life on earth? Of social hierarchies by age, class, gender, race, etc.? Moreover, might empirical evidence from the context under investigation suggest the presence of additional hegemonic forces that existing reductionist theories have not discerned?

To be sure, a complexity approach is interested not only in identifying various force fields that figure in a given situation, but also in teasing out how they interconnect as a systemic whole. Hence, a complexity analysis would explore how the various dimensions of hegemony in world politics reinforce and/or contradict each other. In the case of global Internet governance, for instance, how far might forces around a leading state, a regime complex, capitalism, reigning discourses, Western dominance, anthropocentrism and social stratifications buttress each other? Alternatively, and perhaps concurrently, how far might regulation of the global Internet evince tensions between these and potentially further dimensions of hegemony? Again, a complexity approach focuses on the relationships between and co-constitution of the elements rather than on the elements as discrete forces.

Finally, a complexity analysis could assess the overall strength or fragility of the multifaceted hegemony in question. If one considers the general balance of reinforcing and contradictory tendencies among the various forces comprising a given complex hegemony, does this legitimated dominance in world politics seem ensconced and stable, or instead unsettled and liable to change? To the extent that change is in prospect, does it entail shifts within the existing system structures: e.g. from one leading state to another, or from one capitalist faction to another, etc.? Alternatively, could the change be more transformative of the system structures themselves: e.g. with an end of hegemony through leading states, or with a transcendence of capitalism, or with a shift to new modes of gender relations, etc.?

Complex hegemony in contemporary global Internet governance

We now relate the more abstract questions raised above to the concrete circumstances of governing today's global Internet. The growth of a transplanetary digital communications network is one of the most striking developments in world politics of recent decades. The World Wide Web went public in 1991, and less than three decades later, as of 2019, the Internet had 4.5 billion regular users, amounting to 58% of humanity (Internet World Stats 2019; Statista 2019a).

This uncanny growth depended not only on technological innovations, commercial drivers and user interests, but crucially also on enabling global governance arrangements. To connect 4.5 billion people across the planet in one network requires substantial global standards and coordination: e.g. concerning cables, exchange points, accessible devices, addresses, data transmission, as well as some trans-border regulation of content and data. Thousands of such globally applied measures underpin today's Internet (Brown 2013; Nye 2014; Kurbalija 2016). Moreover, the adoption of one rule rather than another for the Internet has significant implications. It can deeply affect culture (e.g. the fate of languages), ecology (e.g. production of energy to operate the network), economy (e.g. who gains and loses from digital capitalism), geography (e.g. the growth and features of virtual spaces), politics (e.g. the nature and results of election campaigns) and psychology (e.g. modes of human consciousness and behaviour).

How has it been possible to produce and implement this mass of global Internet regulation, with all of its far-reaching consequences, and in such a relatively short time? Clearly a lot of governing capacity has been required. Yet no centralised world state has been available, let alone a world government legitimated with global democracy. Nor has the early twenty-first century presented a situation like 1945 or 1991, when the United States Government (USG) had sufficient concentrations of resources and power to exert hegemonic leadership. So where, if at all, has hegemony lain in global Internet governance?

The next paragraphs consider a number of candidate forces in turn, taken from various existing theories of hegemony in world politics. Empirically I draw upon five years of participant observation and interviews with nearly 700 participants in Internet governance, especially regarding the so-called Internet Assigned Numbers Authority (IANA) functions. These rules cover critical resources such as Internet Protocol (IP) addresses, the domain name system (DNS), and protocol parameters (i.e. technical standards for transmission of data across the Internet). Abduction between a menu of theories on the one hand and the Internet governance context on the other leads me to the particular notion of complex hegemony elaborated below.

Certainly the USG has played a leading regulatory role vis-à-vis the Internet, particularly in earlier phases of its development (Abbate 1999). The Advanced Research Projects Agency Network (ARPANET), created in 1969 within the US Department of Defense, laid core technical foundations for the Internet. The USG also sponsored the creation in 1986 of the Internet Engineering Task Force (IETF), to this day the main source of protocol parameters. Twelve years later, the USG established – under formal oversight of the Department of Commerce – the Internet Corporation for Assigned Names and Numbers (ICANN) to govern the domain name system and to manage the IANA functions. So far in our account, then, evidence points toward world hegemony through a single dominant state.

Yet criticism of USG leadership in Internet governance mounted as globalisation of the network accelerated in the new millennium. In particular, the World Summit on the Information Society, with global conferences in 2003 and 2005, saw major attacks on the situation where one state (through its unilateral oversight of ICANN and IANA) controlled an increasingly vital global resource. The George W. Bush Administration dismissed these critiques, but opposition mounted still further at the World Conference on International Telecommunications in 2012 and following the 2013 Snowden revelations of global Internet surveillance by the US National Security Agency. The Obama Administration in several steps loosened the USG hold, culminating in the termination of Washington's 'stewardship' of ICANN and the IANA functions in 2016. Today the USG is formally just one state amongst 177 other members in ICANN's Government Advisory Committee.

That said, on other evidence the retreat of USG hegemony in global Internet governance is not complete. As of 2020, ICANN headquarters and the IANA office (now called PTI, Public Technical Identifiers) remain in Los Angeles under State of California law. Management of the root zone, the pinnacle of the DNS, still lies with Verisign, a US corporation with head offices in the suburbs of Washington, DC. In addition, administration of 9 of the 12 root servers remains based in the USA. The quarterly Root Key Signing Key Ceremony (the core of security provisions for the DNS) alternates between El Segundo, California and Culpeper, Virginia. The IETF Secretariat is located in Fremont, California, while the IETF policy arm, the Internet Society, also has its main office near Washington.

None of these US-centred circumstances of global Internet regulation has attracted substantial criticism since the IANA stewardship transition. On the contrary, Internet governance insiders (including from seemingly unlikely quarters such as China, Iran and Russia) sooner voice positive support of these continuing US roles, inter alia citing technical soundness of the arrangements, the integrity of US courts, and USG support of human rights (author interviews 2016–2018). Thus some notable elements of legitimated dominance by US government and society in global Internet governance persist.

However, hegemony in Internet governance is by no means reducible to the USG. For example, realists and world-system theorists who anticipate a rise of *Pax Sinica* in the twenty-first century can find certain evidence to support their case (Arrighi 2005; Kueh 2013). China now has by far the largest number of regular online users by country, some 850 million people as of 2019 (Internet World Stats 2019). Five of the world's 20 largest Internet companies by market capitalisation are currently headquartered in China (Statista 2019b), and China-based firms have in recent years become more active at the IETF. Since 2014 the Chinese Government has hosted an annual World Internet Conference at Wuzhen as a Sino-centric site of deliberations about Internet governance. The Chinese Government has also convened an annual International Conference on ICT and Post-2015 Education at Quigdao. In 2016 China for the first time took a Vice Chair position in the Government Advisory Committee at ICANN. The Chinese Government and Communist Party have also articulated an alternative legitimating discourse for global Internet governance with ideas such as 'Internet sovereignty', 'harmonious society' and 'civilized citizenry' (Svensson 2017).

Still, more affirmative Chinese state involvement in global Internet governance by no means equates to hegemony. For one thing, Chinese Government and business hardly have an overriding material resource position in the global Internet. In addition, China-based actors have thus far played but a modest role in constructing rules for global digital communications, and the Chinese Government's rival legitimating discourse has attracted little international following. Some Internet governance insiders believe that 'China has a very long game' (author interviews), but the foreseeable future shows no shift of hegemonic pivot in global Internet governance to Beijing.

Indeed, no state looks to have – or acquire – a hegemonic position on its own in contemporary global digital politics. Alongside the USA and China, the European Union (EU) has taken various significant initiatives concerning the global Internet, such as the General Data Protection Regulation (GDPR), implemented from 2018. Moreover, several EU member states including France and Germany have gained international attention for their distinctive visions for Internet governance. The Brazilian Government has also taken a lead in developing general principles for Internet governance, inter alia with its multistakeholder Internet Steering Committee (CGI.br), established in 1995, and its Civil Rights Framework for the Internet (*Marco civil da Internet*), passed in 2014 (Knight 2014; Fraundorfer 2018, ch 6). In terms of collectives of leading states, Internet matters have figured regularly in declarations and initiatives of the Group of Seven (G7) and the Group of Twenty (G20) (G20 Information Centre 2020).

So, to the extent that the state feeds into world hegemony vis-à-vis today's Internet, it is a diffuse state hegemony. Certainly it is not a hegemony without states. However, resource dominance, sponsorship of rules and legitimation activities do not come from a single state. Several states take leading roles. Nor do those leading states always follow a common line on Internet policy. For example, the President of France, Emmanuel Macron, has distinguished three contending paths in current global Internet governance: a 'Californian model' of 'self-management', a 'Chinese model' of 'government control', and a 'European model' of 'regulation' (Macron 2018).

That said, hegemonic actors in today's global Internet governance also extend beyond states. True, relevant multilateral institutions such as the International Telecommunications Union (ITU) and the World Intellectual Property Organization (WIPO) rest on state membership. However, governments have little formal or practical role in a range of other important global standard-setting and coordination bodies for the Internet, including the IETF, the Institute of Electrical and Electronics Engineers (IEEE), the Regional Internet Registries (RIRs), Unicode, the World Wide Web Consortium (W3C), and regional associations of Internet exchange points (IXPs). Meanwhile, states play a secondary and mainly advisory role at ICANN, the European Telecommunications Standards Institute (ETSI), and the deliberative Internet Governance Forum (IGF).

Instead of multilateralism, these many institutions approach Internet regulation in a so-called 'multistakeholder' fashion, where rules emanate from collaborations among leaders from various affected sectors of society (Hallström and Bolström 2010; Raymond and DeNardis 2015). In the Internet sphere, these stakeholders generally include academe, business, civil society, government, technical experts, and users/general public. Multistakeholder institutions such as ICANN, IETF, IGF and the RIRs involve representatives of these different sectors together in deliberation and policy-making processes. Indeed, the past three decades of global Internet governance have seen more growth in multistakeholder arrangements than multilateral bodies (Mueller 2010; Antonova 2011; Flyverbom 2011; Mathew 2014).

All components of what Internet governance parlance calls 'the multistakeholder community' are elites. That is, whatever sector they come from, the stakeholder representatives in global Internet governance hold positions of influence in orga-nisations that strive to be politically influential. Moreover, they are a *transnational* elite that heralds from many countries. Indeed, 'the multistakeholder community' is generally more united by its common preoccupation with Internet governance than it is divided by national differences. It resonates of what other research has termed 'transnational social fields', 'epistemic communities', and a 'transnational capitalist class' (Haas 1992; Sklair 2001; Levitt and Schiller 2004). In the present context we might speak of a 'global elite network' in Internet governance.

This global elite network fits into complex hegemony for global Internet govern-ance. In line with hegemony, this conglomerate of rule-makers comes from organisa-tions that collectively hold a preponderance of resources in the Internet sphere. 'The multistakeholder community' also in hegemonic fashion envelops itself in legitimating discourses: for example, concerning 'free and open Internet', 'bottom-up policy-making', 'transparency and accountability', and 'global public interest'.

To be sure, this hegemonic elite in global Internet governance is far from monolithic. Academics, activists, bureaucrats, engineers and entrepreneurs approach Internet governance with diverse and sometimes contradictory mindsets. Divisions can also split the different sectors individually, as companies compete with each other for market share, civil society organisations promote opposing political visions, states pursue clashing goals, and academics espouse contending theories. Yet an underlying structural glue also bonds the global elite network across these internal differences. Several decades of institutionalised trans-sectoral collaboration in Internet governance has created a whole that is more than the sum of its parts. A supraterritorial nomadic tribe of sorts, 'the multistakeholder community' wanders together through world conference centres, airport lounges and online mailing lists. As a distinctive 'community of practice' (Wenger 1998), this global elite has its own unifying language, codes, rituals and friendships. In the words of two partici-pants, 'we learn to work together' and 'relationships built in the dialogue are quite durable' (author interviews). With this solidarity and experience, transnationalism has proved far more effective than state-centrism in generating rules that enable a planet-spanning Internet.

Yet the global elite network cannot claim full hegemony in Internet govern-ance, without supplementary involvement and backing from major states. The Brazilian and US governments were major sponsors of multistakeholder regulation for the Internet, and these arrangements would collapse if leading states in this issue-area opposed this model. Moreover, transnational trans-sectoral governance of the Internet has some fragile legitimacy. True, participants in multistakeholder Internet governance generally give these processes reasonably high confidence and trust. However, outside these insider circles – among broader elites and the general public – legitimacy for multistakeholder institutions is more limited. Most people are not even aware that these governance processes for the Internet exist, while informed outsiders often hold concerns about low democratic accountability and special-interest capture in multistakeholder arrangements (Gleckman 2018; Jongen and Scholte forthcoming; Scholte et al. 2019). As one fervent promoter has observed, 'the legitimacy point is perhaps the most critical component as we think about extending the multistakeholder process' (Strickling 2016).

Thus, hegemony in contemporary global Internet governance involves not only a shift from the USG to multiple major states, but also an extension beyond the states system to a transnational elite network with predominantly non-state components. Neither of these two dimensions – leading states and the global elite – succeeds on its own to generate world hegemony in the Internet arena. The major states have lacked adequate coordination, technical competence and institutional innovation to provide the necessary governance foundations for an exponentially growing global Internet. Meanwhile the multistakeholder elite network has lacked enough legitimacy in wider society to hold hegemony on its own.

Indeed, one may ask whether even the combination of major states and transsectoral elites generates sufficient legitimated rule by dominant power to qualify as hegemony in contemporary global Internet governance. Given the limitations just noted, it may be necessary to look beyond actors to discover the fuller dynamics of hegemony. After all, various theories suggest that power in world politics derives not only from actors (i.e. the features and motivations of behavioural units), but also from structures (i.e. the ordering patterns that frame social relations). As noted early on in this chapter, the complexity principle as applied to world politics encourages one to find hegemony in a co-constitution of actors and structures. Moreover, social structures could bring order to the 'chaos' of having many scattered hegemonic actors in today's Internet regulation (Raymond and Smith 2014).

Regarding specific structural forces that figure in global Internet governance, field observations suggest an important structural hegemony of 'technicism'. In other words, regulation of the Internet has generally both reflected and reinforced a mode of knowledge and practice that emphasises instrumental problem-solving through engineering fixes. Internet regulation has rested on a pretty well undisputed premise that the technology is inherently good, and the overriding priority has been to bring ever more connectivity and functionality to ever more people. Even when the Internet has raised social, political and ecological concerns, people have usually expected technical solutions, through the development of alternative devices and protocols. Reflective of structural power, the more technical bodies in global Internet governance – such as the IETF and the RIRs – attract the highest average levels of legitimacy beliefs, significantly more than nation-states or the intergovernmental International Telecommunication Union (ITU) (Jongen and Scholte forthcoming).

Under a hegemony of technicism, Internet governance has consistently accorded major and largely unquestioned authority to hardware and software 'techies'. In comparison, government officials and civil society activists have often struggled to obtain influence. Engineers by far outnumber any other vocational group in the 'Internet Hall of Fame'. Some technical pioneers are even draped in quasi-religious language as 'technology evangelists' (Kawasaki 1990).

Technicism also shapes the language of legitimation in global Internet governance. Litanies such as 'security, stability and resiliency' rank among the most pervasive narratives around the Internet: to invoke this vocabulary is to call uncontested power to one's side. Most Internet governance institutions insistently characterise themselves as 'technical' bodies, well aware that this descriptor can insulate them from political contestation.

That said, technicism lacks full structural hegemony by itself in global Internet governance. Certainly technical fixes satisfy engineering circles, and other constituencies gain confidence and trust when the Internet functions technically. However, more than technology per se has driven the exponential growth of the Internet, and many rules of Internet governance go beyond technical rationales. While technically oriented military and academic concerns underpinned the early Internet, commercial and consumer interests became major stimulants for globalisation of the digital communications network from the 1990s onwards.

Commercialisation draws attention to the hegemony of capitalism in contemporary global Internet governance. Indeed, most Internet engineers today work for corporate business rather than governments, universities and social movements. The Internet lies at the heart of contemporary surplus accumulation (Schiller 1999; Castells 2009). The global digital network is a vital enabling infrastructure for capitalism in general and furthermore has become a major focus of accumulation in its own right. Internet hardware, software, data and content all offer lucrative profit-making opportunities. Internet companies now rank among the largest firms on the leading stock exchanges.

Not surprisingly, then, capitalism has been a dominant power in the past quarter-century of Internet governance. The rules exist largely to facilitate surplus accumulation through digital channels. Indeed, business corporations participate centrally in the main global Internet governance processes: domain name entrepreneurs and intellectual property firms at ICANN; Internet service providers at the RIRs; e-commerce concerns, social media giants and search engine companies at the IETF; etc. For-profit companies are also the main financial sponsors of these regimes, paying the main membership dues and splashing their logos across the meeting halls. In this context, the director of a leading institution in the field has mused that 'sometimes I think Internet governance is a commercial association', while a leader at the IETF has affirmed that 'the money factor is a big thing' (author interviews). Tellingly, most US-based Internet corporations actively supported the IANA transition, suggesting that at this juncture capitalist hegemony outweighed USG hegemony.

For the most part, in conformity with hegemony, the dominant power of capital in global Internet governance attracts considerable legitimacy. Most participants in the regulatory processes view the leading forces of the profit motive and the business sector as unproblematic or positively appropriate (Jongen and Scholte unpublished). Although leading states and the global elite in Internet governance almost never call 'surplus accumulation' by name, they inhabit a neoliberal imaginary that embraces 'the market' (code for capitalism) as an unquestioned good.

That said, critiques of capitalism also circulate around Internet governance and suggest that this structural hegemony is not sufficiently strong to stand on its own. For example, iconic Internet pioneers such as Vint Cerf and Tim Berners-Lee have spoken against big money in the DNS. Likewise, many in the RIRs have 'frowned upon' the commercialisation of Internet Protocol addresses as 'unethical' (author interviews). Some reformists in hegemonic states and global elite circles have raised 'public interest' concerns about possible corporate capture of global Internet governance. Meanwhile some social movement groups have articulated foundational critiques of the capitalist Internet (cf. Just Net Coalition 2014). These cracks in the neoliberal consensus suggest that capitalist rule in Internet governance is not fully secure and needs supplementary buttressing from other facets of complex hegemony.

Such reinforcement comes not only from major states, global elites and technicism, as identified earlier, but also from mental structures in the shape of disciplining discourses. We consider these linguistic and narrative dimensions of complex hegemony since: (a) conceptually, critical theories underline the legitimating consequences of ideology (Froomkin 2003); and (b) empirically, field observations reveal pervasive legitimating discourses in global Internet governance. The 'disciplining' quality of these discourses lies in their power to normalise certain frames of consciousness as 'common sense' and to marginalise alternative ways of being and knowing. In particular, hegemonic discourses silence – usually subtly but sometimes overtly – consciousness that could subvert the governing power of major states, global elites, technicism and capitalism in the Internet.

Hegemonic discourses take multiple forms in contemporary global Internet regulation. Different scripts tap into different modern touchstones of legitimacy, especially around the triumvirate of technocracy, democracy and fairness (Scholte and Tallberg 2018). Regarding the first, technocratic discourse affirms that a given governance arrangement provides efficiency, expertise and problem-solving effectiveness. In contemporary global Internet governance, technocratic legitimation often occurs with language concerning 'security, stability and resiliency', 'market forces', and 'customer satisfaction'. Second, democratic discourse asserts that a given political situation offers all affected people due involvement and control. In today's global Internet governance, common discursive touchstones for democratic legitimation include 'multistakeholder participation', 'free and open Internet', 'transparency', 'accountability', 'global public interest' and 'bottom-up policymaking'. Third, fairness discourse claims that a governance framework fulfils criteria such as impartial treatment, dignity for all and distributive justice. Common markers of fairness legitimation in contemporary global Internet regulation include 'diversity' and 'human rights'.

To emphasise again, these various discourses serve a disciplining function for hegemony. Thus people who invoke the legitimating scripts just mentioned are more likely to gain entry to and influence in the conversation of Internet governance. In contrast, actors who neglect these key linguistic signals tend to struggle to get a hearing until they shift their language to fall into line with prevailing discursive frameworks. Meanwhile counter-hegemonic voices (such as the aforementioned Just Net Coalition) that openly challenge the dominant discourses usually face marginalisation, if not open ridicule from the mainstream. After all, how can one not believe in 'security', 'freedom', 'transparency', and the like?

The broad range of legitimating scripts ensures that linguistic tools of power are available for pretty well every audience and every situation in global Internet governance. Thus, people and circumstances that want technocratic narratives can turn to 'security, stability and resiliency', etc. Contexts that want democratic assurances can appeal to 'multistakeholder participation', etc. Moments that want a fairness story can call upon the language of 'diversity', etc. Often scenarios in global Internet governance want a combination of technocratic, democratic and fairness scripts in order to realise hegemonic power. Hence, no single disciplining discourse suffices on its own to provide overall hegemony in the Internet sphere: multiple narratives in combination are required.

Indeed, certain legitimating scripts can become sources of vulnerability rather than power when actual conditions in Internet governance appear to contradict them. For example, charges of weak accountability have spurred several major reforms of ICANN. Other critics have despaired at inefficiencies and infighting of (facetiously termed) 'multisnakeholder' participation. Hierarchies of regions, genders, languages, races, etc. have exposed all quarters of global Internet governance to critiques regarding inadequate diversity, unequal access and unfair distribution of benefits. Many participants in Internet governance look warily upon the introduction of human rights discourse, seeing it as potentially disruptive of commercial and technical operations.

With such notable weak points, disciplining discourses cannot provide full structural hegemony in global Internet governance, without additional (and mostly complementary) forces from technicism and capitalism. As complexity thinking would suggest, ideational and material dimensions of hegemony are mutually dependent. Thus, as with the co-constitution of major states and the global elite network in actor aspects of hegemony, none of the structural facets of complex hegemony – technicism, capitalism or disciplining discourses – suffices on its own or sits causally prior to the others.

Finally, to unite the whole that makes complex hegemony in contemporary global Internet governance, the various actors and structures are co-determining in a process of interrelation that Anthony Giddens (1984) has evocatively called 'structuration'. From this perspective, the core of complex hegemony lies in a five-faceted interconnection of technicism, leading states, capitalism, global elite networks and disciplining discourses. The hegemonic actors have not led so much through their own resources and initiatives, but through their general alignment with certain powerful patterns of world order. Conversely, the hegemonic structures have not guided global Internet governance so much through their own forces, but through their general alignment with the motivations and decisions of powerful actors. In structuration dynamics, neither actors or structures are causally prior and only exist in combination.

Nor is the overall complex of hegemony depicted here necessarily stable. Certainly this chapter has noted many points of mutual reinforcement between the various facets of complex hegemony in relation to global Internet governance. However, the discussion has also identified points of inconsistency and weakness, including certain contrasting priorities among actors and contestation around certain disciplining discourses. These tensions indicate that the system of complex hegemony does not necessarily revert to equilibrium. On the contrary, the past three decades of global Internet governance show considerable fluidity and change in complex hegemony. To cite just two shifts, USG hegemony has given way to multi-state hegemony, and human rights scripts that were out of bounds in early years have recently moved toward the mainstream. One should expect such systemic dynamism to bring further (and perhaps quite unexpected) changes to the contours of complex hegemony in future global Internet governance.

Conclusion

Hegemony is a key aspect of contemporary world politics, including global governance in particular. Today's more global world requires substantial planet-spanning rules. Otherwise a global Internet, global finance, global disease control, global peacebuilding, and so on are not possible. Global governance, like any governance, requires substantial power for its creation and maintenance. That power can benefit enormously from legitimacy, inasmuch as legitimacy allows the governors to avoid burdens of coercion, manipulation and stealth vis-à-vis the governed. Hence, world-scale hegemony – legitimated rule by dominant power that has a planetary reach – can be a boon for global governance. Under conditions of world hegemony, regulation of global matters faces a minimum of resistance and needs little or no compulsion.

This chapter has advanced a proposition that, contrary to traditional reductionist theories, contemporary world hegemony does not reside in a discrete site. Thus, the 'dominant power' that exerts 'legitimated rule' today does not take form as one particular actor (e.g. a leading state) or one particular structure (e.g. capitalism). Instead, world hegemony in the twenty-first century involves a complex of interweaving forces. This 'complex hegemony' is more challenging to tease out analytically and empirically, but this more diffuse and nebulous character does not make the hegemonic power any less strong.

The second half of the chapter has engaged with global Internet governance to identify specific contours of complex hegemony in that context. The analysis started by examining the USG, given that much established theory has conceived of hegemony in terms of a single leading state, as well as that historical evidence shows much USG initiative, especially in the early development of the Internet. Yet our examination revealed significant limits to USG hegemony; so the discussion turned to other major states and concluded that legitimated rule by dominant power in today's Internet is spread across multiple leading governments. However, we also noted that much of the actual governing of the Internet occurs through non-governmental actors, many of them with substantial power and resources apart from states. We therefore expanded our concept of complex hegemony to encompass an interplay of leading states and the global elite network of a 'multi-stakeholder community'.

At this point we posited that geographically and sectorally scattered hegemonic state and non-state actors would need some kind of structural power to bring relative coherence to the overall complex. The hegemonic role of techno-scientific problem-solving knowledge – or 'technicism' – is evident from the earliest days of Internet governance. Later, structural forces of capitalism complemented technicism to generate regulatory frameworks that enabled the rapid global expansion of the Internet. Meanwhile hegemonic disciplining discourses have played a key role to pre-empt contestation of the emergent global Internet regime. Just as neither leading states nor the global elite network could exert hegemony without the other, so technicism, capitalism and disciplining discourses have been mutually dependent.

In sum, then, complex hegemony in today's global Internet governance has comprised: (a) an interconnection of states and a global elite network in respect of actors; (b) an interrelation of technicism, capitalism and disciplining discourses in respect of structures; and (c) a co-constitution of these actors and structures through processes of 'complex structuration'. Each facet by itself is insufficient to generate world hegemony in current Internet governance. However, through their combination – where each quality is generally reinforcing (though also sometimes contradicting) the others – the whole entails more than the parts.

Admittedly, this chapter has only offered an exploratory sketch of complex hegemony in contemporary world politics. The concept wants further elaboration, including more specification than this chapter has offered concerning the dynamics that interweave the various dimensions of the complex. Moreover, additional empirical analysis beyond global Internet governance is called for, in order to see how complex hegemony might operate similarly or differently across various issue-areas. Methodologically, we need to see whether and how the mathematics of complexity science might be adapted to quantitative analysis of complex hegemony and/or how to develop suitable qualitative research techniques. This chapter has also not brought normative theory to bear on complex hegemony: what moral implications arise, for example, in terms of democracy, justice and responsibility?

However, such next steps regarding theory and evidence are for later. This chapter's more limited objective, in the context of the present volume on 'reimagining power in global politics', has been to suggest that contemporary world politics and global governance require a wholesale rethink of hegemony. Old forms of legitimated rule by dominant power may have passed, but a complexity perspective opens up alternative conceptions of hegemony that shed new light on where world politics is today and might go in the future.

References

Abbate, J. (1999) *Inventing the Internet*. Cambridge, MA: MIT Press.

Alter, K. and Meunier, S. (2009) 'The Politics of International Regime Complexity', *Perspectives on Politics*, 7(1): 13–24.

Antonova, S. (2011) '"Capacity-Building" in Global Internet Governance: The Long-Term Outcomes of "Multistakeholderism"', *Regulation & Governance*, 5(4): 425–445.

Arrighi, G. (2005) 'Hegemony Unravelling', *New Left Review*, 32 and 33.

Arthur, W.B., Durlauf, S.N. and Lane, D.A. (eds) (1997) *The Economy as an Evolving Complex System II*. Boulder, CO: Westview.

Bogg, J. and Geyer, R. (eds) (2007) *Complexity, Science & Society*. Oxford: Radcliffe.

Brown, I. (ed.) (2013) *Research Handbook on Governance of the Internet*. Cheltenham: Edward Elgar Publishing.

Castells, M. (2009) *The Rise of the Network Society*, 2nd edn. Oxford: Wiley-Blackwell.

Collins, P.H. and Bilge, S. (2016) *Intersectionality*. Cambridge: Polity Press.

Connolly, W. (2011) 'Complexity and Relevance', *European Political Science*, 10(2): 210–219.

Cudworth, E. and Hobden, S. (2011) *Posthuman International Relations: Complexity, Ecologism and Global Politics*. London: Zed Books.

Flyverbom, M. (2011) *The Power of Networks: Organizing the Global Politics of the Internet*. Cheltenham: Edward Elgar Publishing.

Fraundorfer, M. (2018) *Rethinking Global Democracy in Brazil*. London: Rowman & Littlefield.

Friedrichs, J. and Kratochwil, F. (2009) 'On Acting and Knowing: How Pragmatism Can Advance International Relations Research and Methodology', *International Organization*, 63(4): 701–731.

Froomkin, M.A. (2003) 'Habermas@discourse.net: Toward a Critical Theory of Cyberspace', *Harvard Law Review*, 116(3): 749–773.

G20 Information Centre (2020) Search for 'Internet'. Available at: https://find.utoronto.ca/search/?site=default_collection&client=default_frontend&output=xml_no_dtd&prox ystylesheet=default_frontend&as_dt=i&as_sitesearch=www.g8.utoronto.ca&q=internet (accessed 20 January 2020).

Giddens, A. (1984) *The Constitution of Society: Outline of the Theory of Structuration*. Berkeley, CA: University of California Press.

Giddens, A. (1985) *The Nation-State and Violence*. Cambridge: Polity Press.

Gleckman, H. (2018) *Multistakeholder Governance and Democracy*. Abingdon: Routledge.

Gould, S.J. (2007) *Punctuated Equilibrium*. Cambridge, MA: Belknap Press.

Haas, P.M. (1992) 'Introduction: Epistemic Communities and International Policy Coordination', *International Organization*, 46(1): 1–35.

Hallström K.T. and Boström, M. (2010) *Transnational Multi-Stakeholder Standardization: Organizing Fragile Non-State Authority*. Cheltenham: Edward Elgar Publishing.

Harrison, N.E. (ed.) (2006) *Complexity in World Politics: Concepts and Methods of a New Paradigm*. Albany, NY: State University of New York Press.

Holland, J.H. (1995) *Hidden Order: How Adaptation Builds Complexity*. New York: Helix Books.

Internet World Stats (2019) 'World Internet Usage and Population Statistics: 2019 Mid-Year Estimates'. Available at: www.Internetworldstats.com/stats.htm

Jongen, H. and Scholte, J.A. (forthcoming) 'Legitimacy in Multistakeholder Global Governance at ICANN', *Global Governance.*

Jongen, H. and Scholte, J.A. (unpublished) *Survey of 550 Participants in Internet Governance.*

Just Net Coalition (2014) 'The Delhi Declaration for a Just and Equitable Internet'. Available at: https://justnetcoalition.org/delhi-declaration

Kavalski, E. (2007) 'The Fifth Debate and the Emergence of Complex International Relations Theory', *Cambridge Review of International Affairs*, 20(3): 435–454.

Kavalski, E. (ed.) (2015) *World Politics at the Edge of Chaos: Reflections on Complexity and Global Life.* Albany, NY: State University of New York Press.

Kawasaki, G. (1990) *The Macintosh Way.* New York: Harper Collins.

Kissane, D. (2011) *Beyond Anarchy: The Complex and Chaotic Dynamics of International Politics.* Stuttgart: Ibidem.

Knight, P. (2014) *The Internet in Brazil: Origins, Strategy, Development, and Governance.* Bloomington, IN: AuthorHouse.

Kueh, Y.Y. (2013) *Pax Sinica: Geopolitics and Economics of China's Ascendance.* Hong Kong: Kong University Press.

Kurbalija, J. (2016) *An Introduction to Internet Governance*, 7th edn. Geneva/Belgrade: Diplo.

Levitt, P. and Schiller, N.G. (2004) 'Conceptualizing Simultaneity: A Transnational Social Field Perspective on Society', *International Migration Review*, 38(3): 1002–1039.

Macron, E. (2018) 'IGF 2018 Speech by French President Emmanuel Macron'. Available at: www.intgovforum.org/multilingual/content/igf-2018-speech-by-french-president-emmanuel-macron

Mann, M. (1986) *The Sources of Social Power*, Vol. 1: *A History of Power from the Beginning to A.D. 1760.* Cambridge: Cambridge University Press.

Mathew, A.J. (2014) 'Where in the World Is the Internet? Locating Political Power in Internet Infrastructure'. PhD dissertation, University of California, Berkeley.

Mueller, M. (2010) *Networks and States: The Global Politics of Internet Governance.* Cambridge, MA: MIT Press.

Nye, J.S. (2014) *The Regime Complex for Managing Global Cyber Activities.* Waterloo/London: Centre for International Governance Innovation/Royal Institute for International Affairs.

Orsini, A., Morin, J.-F. and Young, O. (2013) 'Regime Complexes: A Buzz, a Boom, or a Boost for Global Governance?', *Global Governance*, 19(1): 27–39.

Orsini, A.*et al.* (2019) 'Forum: Complex Systems and International Governance', *International Studies Review.* Available at: https://doi.org/10.1093/isr/viz005

Raymond, M. and DeNardis, L. (2015) 'Multistakeholderism: Anatomy of an Inchoate Global Institution', *International Theory*, 7(3): 572–616.

Raymond, M. and Smith, G. (eds) (2014) *Organized Chaos: Reimagining the Internet.* Waterloo: Centre for International Governance Innovation.

Rosenau, J.N. (1990) *Turbulence in World Politics: A Theory of Change and Continuity.* Princeton, NJ: Princeton University Press.

Rosenau, J.N. (2003) *Distant Proximities: Dynamics beyond Globalization.* Princeton, NJ: Princeton University Press.

Schiller, D. (1999) *Digital Capitalism: Networking the Global Market System.* Cambridge, MA: MIT Press.

Scholte, J. A. (1993) *International Relations of Social Change.* Buckingham: Open University Press.

Scholte, J.A. and Tallberg, J. (2018) 'Theorizing Institutional Sources of Legitimacy in Global Governance', in J. Tallberg, K. Bäckstrand and J.A. Scholte (eds), *Legitimacy in Global Governance; Sources, Processes and Consequences*, Oxford: Oxford University Press, 56–74.

Scholte, J.A., Tallberg, J. and Verhaegen, S. (2019) 'Elite Attitudes towards Global Governance'. Available at: www.statsvet.su.se/leggov/leggov-elite-survey/leggov-elite-survey-1.447763

Sklair, L. (2001) *The Transnational Capitalist Class*. Oxford: Blackwell.

Statista (2019a) 'Global Digital Population as of October 2019'. Available at: www.statista.com/statistics/617136/digital-population-worldwide/

Statista (2019b) 'Market Capitalization of the Biggest Internet Companies Worldwide as of June 2019'. Available at: www.statista.com/statistics/277483/market-value-of-the-largest-Internet-companies-worldwide/

Strickling, L.E. (2016) Statement of the United States Assistant Secretary of Commerce at the Internet Governance Forum, Guadalajara, 5 December. Available at: www.ntia.doc.gov/speechtestimony/2016/remarks-assistant-secretary-strickling-Internet-governance-forum-12052016

Svensson, M. (2017) 'Internet Visions and IT Entrepreneurs in China'. Paper for the Digital Culture and Society Conference, Fudan University. Available at: https://lup.lub.lu.se/search/publication/169a876d-4ed4-4441-b0d9-3364b543f8bd

Urry, J. (2003) *Global Complexity*. Cambridge: Polity Press.

Urry, J. (2005) 'The Complexity Turn', *Theory, Culture & Society*, 22(5): 1–14.

Walby, S. (2009) *Globalization and Inequalities: Complexity and Contested Modernities*. London: Sage.

Wendt, A. (1999) *Social Theory of International Politics*. Cambridge: Cambridge University Press.

Wenger, E. (1998) *Communities of Practice: Learning, Meaning, and Identity*. Cambridge: Cambridge University Press.

Wight, C. (2015) 'Theorising International Relations: Emergence, Organised Complexity and Integrative Pluralism', in E. Kavalski (ed.), *World Politics at the Edge of Chaos: Reflections on Complexity and Global Life*, Albany, NY: State University of New York Press, 53–78.

Williams, A. (2019) *Political Hegemony and Social Complexity: Mechanisms of Power after Gramsci*. London: Palgrave Macmillan.

PART 2

Practices of hegemony

6

HYBRID WAR AND HEGEMONIC POWER

Elinor Sloan

One of the salient features of the contemporary global landscape is that major state actors are seeking novel ways through which to maintain, achieve or re-establish hegemony at the regional or global level. 'Hegemony', here, refers to a state exercising preponderant influence over another actor or actors, usually one or more states. The central ingredient for hegemony is 'power', a concept that can be understood both in terms of tangible and intangible inputs (population, GDP, size of military, soft power, etc.), and in terms of outcomes – the ability to get others to do something they otherwise would not do, or to achieve a circumstance to their liking that other actors would not choose.[1] In between inputs and outcomes there is necessarily a translation aspect, a strategy that bridges means with ends. Today, one of these 'intervening strategies' is hybrid war.

In pursing hybrid war, states are achieving a degree of power and influence over other actors beyond that which would be predicted or possible if the state were to confine itself to traditional tangible and intangible inputs. Hybrid war therefore does not fit into the realist conception of hegemony, which centres on controlling or dominating others through the exercise of overwhelming preponderant material power (Schmidt, Chapter 2 this volume). But neither does hybrid war accord with existing liberal theorist conceptions of hegemony. Writing in this volume, Schmidt notes that for liberals such as John Ikenberry, Charles Kupchan and, we might add, Joseph Nye, brute power is not enough to understand hegemony. Rather, we also must look at processes, mechanisms, socialisation and leadership. But theirs is a sunny picture, neatly captured by Nye's famous idea of 'soft power' – controlling or influencing others by 'getting others to want what you want' (Nye 1990, 31). Hybrid war, by contrast, is not a particularly sunny picture; it can be insidious, sneaky, smart and calculated, and might best be characterised as the dark side of soft power.

This chapter examines how states are using tools and techniques of hybrid warfare to increase their power, exercise influence over other actors and achieve

DOI: 10.4324/9781003037231-6

self-interested outcomes. Although both state and non-state actors pursue hybrid war, and indeed the term was first applied to non-state actors (see below), this chapter contributes to the more recent and less extensive literature on state actors and hybrid war. The first section outlines the parameters of what is meant by hybrid war, highlights key characteristics of this form of warfare, and raises some possible reasons *why* states are pursuing hybrid war today. Working from this basis, section two specifies some indicators to look for when determining if and to what degree a state is following a hybrid war approach and examines the actions of several states in terms of these indicators. While Russia is the country that is most often associated with hybrid war approaches, it is by no means the only state actor to see its benefits and adopt its methods.

Section I: Setting the stage

What is hybrid war?

At the most basic level, the 'hybrid' in hybrid warfare refers to the coordinated use of conventional and irregular tools of warfare within the same battlespace. Conventional weapons include all military instruments that are not weapons of mass destruction (WMD), i.e. not nuclear, biological or chemical. Irregular tools of warfare have traditionally included terrorism, criminal activity, insurgency and guerrilla war (the tactics of 'hit and run'). More recent 'novel' irregular approaches include cyber war or digital attack against adversary computer systems, the use of special operations forces, and the use of unmarked soldiers and proxies.

Some scholars and policy makers include wider, non-military tools as part of hybrid war. From this perspective, a hybrid threat is an adversary that simultaneously employs a combination of conventional and irregular methods along with political, military, economic, social and information means.[2] Examples might include intense diplomatic pressure, large military exercises along borders, controlling access to key economic assets like oil and gas resources, exploiting nationalist identities and cultural differences, and waging a media campaign of false information on the Internet.[3] For some, the return of political warfare – the employment of military, intelligence, diplomatic, financial and other means, short of conventional war, to achieve national objectives – is the defining feature of the contemporary security environment (Jones 2018).

New ways of waging information operations are a core component of what is conceived today as hybrid war. Information operations are measures designed to influence or corrupt adversary information. Types of information operations include cyber war, psychological operations (PSYOPS), electronic warfare, and even the kinetic strike of command and control sites. PSYOPS, an age-old component of war, are meant to induce emotions in enemy thinking that are amenable to one's own side. Such operations can range from the non-technical dropping of leaflets on adversary populations to today's Internet-based spread of 'fake news' through social media. The degree to which adversaries are waging media campaigns of false information via the Internet is such that cyber-related activity is increasingly the centrepiece of hybrid war discussions.[4] Thus when it comes to hegemony, or a state exercising preponderant influence over another actor or actors, the concept of hybrid war points us to the idea of a state using a full range of tactical, operational and/or strategic approaches to achieve its goals. For those who would wage hybrid war the digitally connected world creates new opportunities, especially, at the operational level.

Hybrid war then and now

The types of actors involved in hybrid war have changed over the past few decades. As originally conceived in the 1990s and early 2000s, hybrid war described an activity carried out by non-state actors. Scholars characterised the Chechen struggle against Russia as hybrid, for example, because the Chechens employed, alongside their predominant guerrilla tactics, modern military communications technology and large coordinated military operations that are normally associated with state-based warfare.[5] Similarly, during and after the 2006 Israeli war against Lebanon scholars described Hezbollah as waging hybrid war because it combined terrorist activity and cyber war with the use of high-tech military capabilities like anti-satellite weapons to stymie Israeli objectives (Hoffman 2006, 37; 2007).

It was not until after the Russian annexation of Crimea in 2014 that hybrid war became associated with state behaviour. Casting around for a descriptor of Russian action in Crimea and Ukraine, NATO argued that the Russian method was one of hybrid war.[6] Since then scholars and policy makers have focused on hybrid war as a state-led activity that incorporates non-state actors and other components.

With the change in primary actor has come a change in objectives. Both state-led and non-state-led hybrid wars target the adversary's military forces and civilian population. Their goals, however, will differ. Non-state actors wage a hybrid war for things like secession, or to forestall a state actor from intervening. A state actor, by contrast, will have in its mind objectives that are larger in geographic scale or strategic in nature. Whether waged by a non-state or state actor, hybrid war targets state actors. This can be contrasted with counterinsurgency and civil war where state and non-state actors, respectively, target non-state actors.

Today, observers and experts often characterise hybrid war as existing in the 'grey zone' between peace and war because states seek to carry out their objectives without crossing the threshold to open conventional war. Since the traditional trigger to conventional war is clear-cut military aggression, states waging hybrid war pursue activities that are amenable to non-detection, non-attribution, plausible denial of responsibility, or a 'masquerade of non-involvement' (Bachmann and Gunneriusson 2015, 202). Hybrid war is about as far away from a formal declaration of war, the overt statement of an impending or existing use of military force, as a conflict can get. It may involve very limited actual combat, defined as 'violent struggle' (Cooper and Shearer 2017, 307), or even no combat at all. The idea is to create enough ambiguity in the mind of the state's adversary to forestall any conventional military response. Those who wage hybrid war pursue a 'long game' of seeking, below the radar of open conventional war, cumulative tactical successes that ultimately add up to a situation where the state has exercised preponderant influence over one or more states and thereby achieved hegemony.

The importance of non-attribution for keeping tensions below the use of force threshold points us to the central role cyber war can play in a hybrid war. Depending on the skill of the perpetrator, it can be very difficult to determine who or what entity launches a cyber attack. Cyber attack is thus particularly amenable to non-attribution. For some, the challenges associated with the identification of perpetrators in cyber space mean that 'cyberspace will be the crux of future hybrid war' (Saalman 2016–2017, 145). Although at one time it was thought the cyber domain could level the playing field between state actors and non-state actors like terrorists, in fact it is states that have proven to be the most formidable cyber warriors because of the substantial resources that they can devote to capability development.

Why hybrid war?

In adopting a hybrid war approach, major powers are calculating that their interests are best served by pursuing their objectives without triggering a major conflict or waging conventional war. Why are states going to pains to pursue their objectives indirectly, patiently, through sustained measures just short of war, when in another age they might have simply gone to war?

A fundamental reason great powers seek to achieve their goals through hostile measures short of overt war is the existence of nuclear weapons and the risk that a conventional war between the great powers will escalate. This situation, of course, is not new, so nuclear weapons alone do not explain the contemporary currency of hybrid war. But nuclear weapons remain 'the ultimate disincentive for great powers to wage [conventional] war against each other'[7] and thus a critical backdrop to other factors.

The rise of hybrid war as a state-led strategy might also be a response to over-whelming conventional US power. Dramatic advances in America's conventional military capabilities, particularly in the areas of command, control, communications, intelligence, surveillance, reconnaissance and precision strike, were first revealed during the 1991 Gulf War and subsequently reinforced in other wars of the 1990s and 2000s. In the intervening years America's conventional strength has only grown; since 2010 the United States has been pursuing a concept called Conventional Prompt Global Strike, with the goal of being able to strike anywhere in the world with conventionally armed long-range precision weapons within one hour.

The message US opponents have taken, today and from the early days of the post-Cold War period, is to avoid America's overwhelming conventional strengths and seek alternative paths. 'Asymmetric' warfare was the term that originally appeared in the late 1990s and early 2000s by US thinkers)[8] to describe adversaries who sought to target America's weaknesses and vulnerabilities, rather than engage in a direct confrontation. By waging hybrid war, America's opponents avoid exposing themselves to severe conventional force retribution, whether by the United States or a wider US-led coalition of countries.

Third, waging hybrid war allows powers to seek goals in circumstances where existing laws of war and global norms would not permit a use of force. Scholars note that in traditional just war doctrine the *jus ad bellum* (or 'war decision') included the right to wage an offensive war to protect vital interests that had been unjustly threatened or injured (O'Brien 1981, 22). For centuries after the rise of the inter-state system in the 1600s, states accepted 'reprisals' as an international norm. However, the UN Charter framework removed this option. Under the UN Charter, all members must refrain in their use of force against the territorial integrity or political independence of any other state. Apart from collective security measures authorised by the UN Security Council, the only permitted use of force is self-defence when a threat is apparent or imminent.

Over the past several decades, global norms against war, conquest and territorial violations have continued to strengthen (Lanoszka 2016, 180). While they have not stopped conflict, they have forced great power leaders to attempt to justify their actions in normative terms. Waging war without waging war enables states to make their way around this framework. Hybrid war, and particularly its cyber component, allows states to bypass international legal norms regarding the use of force and territorial sovereignty (Bachmann and Gunneriusson 2015, 205), in pursuit of territorial gain or what in another era might have been called reprisals.

Finally, the rise of contemporary hybrid war cannot be divorced from changes in the structure of the international system. During the Cold War, under a bipolar structure of power, the United States and the Soviet Union pursued a hybrid approach particular to the time: nuclear stand-off combined with proxy wars. In the unipolar era of the 1990s America's overwhelming power precluded contenders. Since then, competitors' relative increases in power, as defined in tangible terms of economic capacity and military strength (including nuclear), are allowing them to push back against the US-led order. The nascent return to a multipolar world, now taking place for the first time in a nuclear era, is incentivising great powers to seek hybrid warfare approaches as means as pursuing hegemony, i.e. their power of influence, over others.

Section II: Assessing the contenders

With this short discussion of hybrid war's parameters and characteristics in mind, it is possible to identify some themes we can look for when determining if a state is following a hybrid war approach. For ease of reference the first three sets of criteria can be referred to as activities at the tactical, operational and strategic levels, respectively.

- At the tactical level, is the state engaged in the coordinated use of conventional tools of warfare (traditional military instruments) and irregular tools of warfare (terrorism, criminal activity, insurgency, guerrilla war, cyber war/

digital attack, special operations forces, and/or unmarked soldiers and proxies) within the same battlespace?

- At the operational level, is the state employing conventional and irregular tools of warfare in combination with political (e.g. diplomatic pressure), military (e.g. large military exercises), economic (e.g. controlling access to key economic assets like oil and gas resources), social (e.g. exploiting nationalist identities and cultural differences), and/or information (e.g. waging a media campaign of false information on the Internet) means?
- At the strategic level, is the state pursuing a series of activities that lie below the threshold to conventional war, the cumulative success of which will add up to a changed strategic situation (i.e. 'grey zone' tactics)? Is the state engaged in political warfare, using all means short of war (political, military, economic, social and informational) to achieve its objectives?
- Is a state's involvement in activities in any of these levels amenable to, or pursued in the context of, a plausible denial of responsibility or a 'masquerade of non-involvement'?

The West

An ironic aspect of the contemporary hybrid war dialogue is that while the West sees state-waged hybrid war as the Russian approach to conflict (see below), in fact Russia attributes it to Western actions and behaviours over the past several years and even decades. In 2013 Russian General Valery Gerasimov wrote an article in which he stated the 'role of non-military means of achieving political and strategic goals has grown, and, in many cases, they have exceeded the power of force of weapons in their effectiveness'. Those means included the use of special operations forces and propaganda to create an operating front within enemy territory.[9] The article itself was little known until Russia invaded and annexed Crimea, and supported separatists in the Donbass, prompting the West to interpret Gerasimov's words as presaging what was to come. But in his article Gerasimov, who continues to hold his post as Chief of the General Staff of the Russian Armed Forces, was describing his view of *Western* behaviour, i.e. a new US way of war, not Russian doctrine. The notion of a 'Gerasimov doctrine' on Russian hybrid war has become so misattributed that the original purveyor has sought to correct the record (Galeotti 2018).

For Russia, it is the West that carries out hybrid war. Gerasimov's article reflected how the Kremlin interpreted the Arab Spring uprisings of 2010–11, and the colour revolutions in Russia's neighbourhood against Moscow-friendly regimes (Ukraine 2004, Georgia 2012 and, ultimately, Ukraine 2014). Moscow's perspective is that these events were the result of planned Western interventions using hybrid warfare (Allen and Moore 2018, 60). 'The Russians honestly – however wrongly – believe that these were not genuine protests against brutal and corrupt governments, but regime changes orchestrated in Washington, or rather, Langley' (Galeotti 2018). At an international security conference in Moscow in 2014 Russia blamed the West for instigating colour revolutions, fomenting protests and destabilising countries through political warfare (Kofman and Rojansky 2015). Thus, in essence, each side believes the 2014 revolution in Ukraine represents the others' successful hybrid operation Charap 2015–2016, 57).

If one were to characterise the West as using hybrid war, it would be primarily at the strategic level, i.e. political, military, economic, social and/or informational measures that do not involve actual combat. Russia views many US policies, especially long-standing democracy promotion programmes, as a form of political warfare targeting Moscow's interests (Chivvis 2017b, 320). It believes the colour revolutions were sparked by the West's use of technology and information to manipulate a population's protest potential (Thomas 2016, 558). Chinese authors, too, also draw a link between the West and the various colour revolutions, arguing that America engaged in proxy warfare using non-governmental organisations and online propaganda (Saalman 2016–2017, 139). Some Russian commentators go so far as to argue Russia has been under sustained information attack from the West for decades, with perestroika from the 1980s and multilateral organisations like the IMF and World Bank all considered instruments of irregular war designed to destabilise Russia.[10]

Economically, the European Union's move towards a (political and economic) Association Agreement with Ukraine and a related Deep and Comprehensive Free Trade Area agreement played an important and well-known contextual role in the 2014 Ukrainian revolution. Russia had wanted Ukraine to join not the EU but a Russia-led customs union. The Ukrainian government's decision in the autumn of 2013 to back away from signing the EU agreement helped catalyse massive anti-government street protests, which ultimately became violent and led to the overthrow of the government.

In the politico-military realm, since 2014 NATO and its member states have launched an expanding series of complex military exercises in close proximity to Russia's western border and in the adjacent seas and airspace (Clem 2018). NATO's biggest military exercise since the Cold War, Trident Juncture, took place in fall 2018 in and around Norway, a country so geographically close to Russia that it shares a 200-kilometre border. By contrast, a previous large NATO exercise took place off the coast of Spain, thousands of kilometres from Russian territory. Trident Juncture involved more than 50,000 sea, land and air forces drawn from almost all 29 NATO allies. Still closer to Russian 'home', in the autumn of 2018 NATO also launched, for the first time, a large-scale multinational air exercise in Ukraine, a country which is not part of NATO and over which Russia seeks to have influence and secure a strategic buffer. In Russian eyes, NATO's incorporation of non-NATO countries into exercises, and promoting interoperability between NATO and non-NATO forces (such as those of Georgia and Ukraine), might be seen as a Western version of grey zone tactics, i.e. a cumulative series of activities short of war that add up to a changed strategic situation.

If one includes special operations forces in the list of irregular warfare tools, as the schema noted above does, then the West has arguably engaged in hybrid war at the tactical level on several occasions since the turn of the century. 'One of the striking developments in the conduct of war [in the 2000s]', I have pointed out elsewhere, 'was the degree to which SOF and conventional forces were integrated at the tactical level' (Sloan 2017, 31) America used SOF during World War Two and the Cold War, but these forces really 'came of age' in the period after 9/11, playing important roles, in conjunction with conventional forces, in Afghanistan, Iraq, Libya and Syria.[11] In Afghanistan in the autumn of 2001, for example, US Special Forces worked with indigenous Afghan forces to overthrow the ruling Taliban. Observers have criticised recent US administrations for relying so much on special operations forces to achieve foreign policy objections, but they also acknowledge the value of SOF to the US as a means of applying American military power in the growing number of circumstances where competitors operate below a threshold that would trigger a direct response (Lohaus 2018).

Cyber war and digital attack are also elements of 'tactical' hybrid war that one might see in Western behaviour. It is widely believed, for example, that the Stuxnet computer worm used to attack Iranian nuclear facilities a decade ago was developed by the United States and Israel. Computer network attack, although not without its shortcomings (Sloan 2017, 153–4), is an attractive as a tool of warfare because it can be used to achieve military and political objectives through means that do not involve bloodshed.

Russia

The evidence suggests that Russia is pursuing hybrid war at the tactical, operational and strategic levels. In Crimea in February 2014 Russia engaged in the coordinated use of irregular and, to minimum degree possible, conventional tools of warfare within the same battlespace to achieve political objectives. Russia inserted unmarked militia groups to occupy official governmental buildings in the capital, Simferopol (Lanoszka 2016, 175), occupy other key objectives like the Simferopol Airport (Schnaufer 2017, 26), block military and police facilities, and set up barricades and checkpoints all over Crimea (Veljovski, Taneski and Dojchinovski 2017, 296). Russia also employed a computer network attack in the Crimean theatre, isolating the Ukrainian security services in a massive electronic knockdown (Allen and Moore 2018, 64). These actions paved the way for Russia to use regular forces stationed at the Sevastopol naval base, home of Russia's Black Sea Fleet, to seize control of the peninsula. Russia also engaged in a 'masquerade of non-involvement' as it repeatedly denied it had any role in events. The militias themselves indicated they had 'self mobilized' (Woo Pyung-Kyun 2015, 390); the armed men wearing Russian style uniforms with no markings would not reveal their state of origin but told reporters they were simply volunteers (Schnaufer 2017, 26).

At the operational level, Russia coordinated conventional and irregular tactics with a wide range of political, military, economic, cultural and informational means. In the lead up to the actual annexation Russia fomented local pro-Russian demonstrations and then oversaw a disputed referendum a month later in an effort to lend an air of legitimacy to the action (Lanoszka 2016, 175). This was preceded by a long-standing information operation campaign along cultural and ethnic lines in which Russia sought to influence the Russian diaspora in Crimea, convincing them that Ukraine was not a real country and had no independent culture separate from Russia. As a result, 'instead of waking up in a different country, Crimeans woke up in a country they had been conditioned to believe was theirs all along' (Allen and Moore 2018, 64).

Roughly concurrent with the Crimea operation, in the Donbass region of eastern Ukraine, Russia deployed special operations forces in support of separatists in Ukraine (Johnson 2018, 142), and provided the separatists with sophisticated armaments and equipment (Veljovski et al. 2017, 296), all the while denying it was directly involved in armed hostilities between Kiev and the separatists (Lanoszka 2016, 175). Evidence suggested the Russian-backed separatists attempted to organise along conventional lines, rather than strictly as insurgents (Savage 2018, 81). At this tactical level, Russia also engaged in cyber war or computer network attack. Press reports indicate Russia's move into Ukraine was accompanied by distributed denial-of-service attacks against computers in Kiev and Poland, as well as the European Parliament and European Commission (Wirtz 2017, 108). As the conflict progressed and the separatists proved ineffectual, Russian battalion tactical groups intervened directly in combat against the Ukrainian army, thereby combining irregular war with the conventional use of force. Fighting involved armoured, artillery and infantry forces, along with the use of drones for surveillance and target acquisition (Giegerich 2016, 85). But Russia was careful not to use its air force in the conflict, so as to not give up its ability to deny direct involvement in the conflict (Bachmann and Gunneriusson 2015, 206).

At the 'operational' level of hybrid war in the Donbass, before hostilities broke out Russia provoked historical sentiments, vowed to protect the Russian-speaking population, and encouraged separatist sentiments and pro-Russian groups through its intelligence services (Savage 2018, 81). It deployed military forces on the border with Ukraine in a show of force (Veljovski et al. 2017, 302), while Russian-backed separatists carried out phased operations in coordination with negotiations at the diplomatic level, often escalating activity before and after ceasefire talks with Ukraine (Snegovaya 2015, 13). Russia also attempted to blackmail Ukraine over gas supplies; in 2015 Gazprom halted its gas supplies to Ukraine while continuing to export to the European Union. During this period NATO described Russia's actions 'a combination of military action, covert action and, in particular, an aggressive program of disinformation'.[12]

In Eastern Ukraine Russia was able to maintain its actions below the threshold to *major* conventional war, but not to conventional war itself, notes one analyst, despite the massing of Russian forces across the border, and the provision of logistics and special operations support, cyber operations and airspace dominance, without the ultimate deployment of Russian military force the rebels would have been defeated by the Ukrainian army (Charap 2015–2016, 55). 'In the event, the regular Russian military intervened in a very old-fashioned, non-hybrid way, using artillery barrages' (ibid.). Russia's direct military intervention was necessary, at least in part, because unlike in Crimea the Russian-speaking Ukrainian population did not respond strongly enough to the cultural narrative to sustain an entirely indigenous uprising (Kofman and Rojansky 2015).

In the period since 2014 and 2015 Russia has continued hybrid war activities at the strategic level. It engages in information operations to shape the political narrative in many countries through such outlets as *Sputnik News* and *Russia Today*; uses targeted television programming; and employs fake news farms to spread misinformation through the Internet Chivvis 2017a, 3). Russian trolls, i.e. individuals who spread false information online, report on events that never happened with the hope that legitimate news media in the West will pick it up and report on it without fact-checking (Schnaufer 2017, 27).

Just as Russian information operations along cultural lines began in Ukraine several years, even decades, before Russia's intervention, so too is Russia increasing its political and social pressure in the Baltic (Wither 2016, 83). Russia provides funds to pro-Russian groups and to some political parties (Chivvis 2017a, 7), notably the Harmony party in Latvia which is openly aligned with Russian President Vladimir Putin's United Russia Party (Chivvis 2017b, 318). Scholars also document renewed Russian political warfare efforts in the Balkans, building on its historical ties to the region (ibid.). It is thought, for example, that Russia is seeking to establish a 'humanitarian operations centre' in Serbia, a traditional ally of Russia, as a base from which to conduct covert operations across the Balkans (Chivvis 2017a, 6).

The strategic use of military exercises and activities in the context of political warfare has emerged as a prominent feature of Russian behaviour. Russian forces operate on an almost continual basis near NATO territory, whether it be aircraft, ships or submarines. To intimidate and shape public opinion in Europe it has undertaken unannounced 'snap' exercises along NATO's borders (Chivvis 2017b, 317), and conducted large military exercises on Russian territory in areas close to NATO, such as Zapad in 2017 in the Baltic Sea region, Western Russia and Belarus. Russia has also deployed an extensive air defence system around its Western perimeter, extending over eastern NATO territory, leading the United States and its allies to characterise this as an 'anti-access, area-denial "bubble"' (Clem 2018). In all cases, Russia is careful to pursue these military activities below the threshold to war, i.e. in a manner that does not trigger NATO's use of conventional force (Lanoszka 2016, 190).

Russia's hybrid war approach to warfare is not unique to the contemporary era. During the 2008 war in Georgia, for example, Russia combined conventional forces with special operations forces and South Ossetian and Abkhazian militias (Wither 2016, 75). These tactics mirrored those used by the Soviet Union in the initial stages of the invasion of Afghanistan in 1979, which began with 700 special forces troops wearing Afghan uniforms (Popescu 2015). Similarly, Russian's information operations and political warfare efforts against Europe are nothing new and were pursued in the Soviet era. As an example, the Soviet Union established a web of foreign-language news outlets and sympathetic thinks tanks in Western countries, a practice Russia continues today (Snegovaya 2015, 14). What *is* new is the tools and opportunities to engage in elements of political warfare. With the advent of the Internet, cable news and above all social media the volume and ambition of Russia's information campaigns are much greater (Chivvis 2017a, 8).

China

China is also characterised as being engaged in hybrid war efforts, especially within the strategic arena of 'grey zone' tactics that incrementally seek a changed strategic situation via cumulative efforts below the threshold to war (sometimes referred to as 'salami' tactics). The best-known element is China's progressive building of islands in the South China Sea. Since 2015 China has been pouring sand and concrete onto various reefs – seven disputed features in the Spratly Islands all told – to create artificial islands and building upon them sophisticated military facilities. These islands create a changed strategic situation by virtue of the potential for China to control access to the Strait of Malacca, a critical ocean fairway between East Asia and Africa/the Middle East. China has installed anti-ship cruise missiles and surface-to-air missile systems on three of its fortified outposts in the South China Sea (Macias 2018). It has also deployed anti-jamming equipment in the region, but it has not yet deployed military forces (ibid.).

China's political warfare has been evident in several other areas. The country rejected an international tribunal's ruling on Beijing's South China Sea claims; deployed an oil rig into waters claimed by Vietnam; has engaged in economic coercion, such as limiting rare earth exports to Japan and fruit imports from the Philippines; and unexpectedly established, in 2013, an air defence authorisation zone in the East China Sea which covers contested islands with Japan. China carries out extensive cyber espionage efforts against Western governments and companies, targeting especially its industry and research centres (such as universities) for technological information that can assist the country economically. It is also conducting a sophisticated propaganda campaign aimed at an international audience. Whereas at one time the government's efforts to shape opinion centred overwhelmingly on its domestic audience, today and for the past several years it has sought to shape its image abroad. This has involved, among other things, inserting supplements in respected international publications, establishing Chinese TV satellite offices around the world and hiring local journalists, and paying for foreign journalists to go to China to complete free graduate programmes in communications (Lim and Bergin 2018). As some observers note, 'In information warfare – as in so much else – Deng Xiaoping's famous maxim of "hide your strength and bide your time" is over' (ibid.).

Yet it is not just at the strategic level in terms of political warfare that we can see Chinese hybrid war activity. At the tactical level China mixes conventional naval platforms with coast guard assets and a fleet of civilian shipping vessels to enforce claims both in the South and East China Sea. For example, China contests ownership of the Senkaku/Diaoyu Islands in the East China Sea, also claimed by Japan, with a combination of Peoples Liberation Army Navy (PLAN) ships, coast guard ships and fishing vessels (Burke et al. 2018, 9).

Over the past several years a growing number of Chinese fishing vessels and small trawlers, now in the thousands, have appeared to act in concert with, or in place of, the PLAN to achieve Chinese maritime and ultimately political objectives. Sometimes referred to as 'little blue men' (in reference to the 'little green men' of the Crimean theatre) (Saalman 2016–2017, 143), this 'maritime militia' is controlled by, or at least acts in coordination with, the Chinese military. In maritime areas of dispute a small or large number of fishing vessels will suddenly come together to disrupt, block or harass the ships of other countries (Cavas 2016a). On one occasion, Chinese fishing vessels blocked a US Navy surveillance ship and tried to grab away its towed listening gear (Cavas 2016b). In its 2018 report to Congress on Chinese military capabilities the Pentagon referenced the force directly, even assigning it an acronym – the People's Armed Forces Maritime Militia or PAFMM. It argues the PAFMM assists and trains with the coast guard and navy and has been involved in several coercive activities since 2009 to achieve China's political goals by means short of war (Department of Defense 2018, 72).

Like Russia, China counters that it is the United States that is engaged in hybrid war. Chinese scholars point to America's soft power as one means by which the United States has undertaken a long-standing war of economic penetration and political subversion of China. This includes, among other things, the spread of democratic principles through non-governmental organisations, online propaganda and exchange students.[13] They also speak of America as instigating proxy warfare against China by neighbouring countries with which it has historical disputes (ibid.). 'Much as in the case of Moscow's dealings with Ukraine, Beijing has repeatedly pointed to Washington's enabling of China's neighbors. Chinese analysts categorise Beijing's actions in the East China Sea, South China Sea and elsewhere as "reactive" or "forced" behavior driven by American actions' (Saalman 2016–2017, 147).

Iran

Finally, Iran is also a country that noticeably pursues its political objectives in the space short of conventional war. To gain increased influence in the Middle East, a central goal of the government, it supports local groups in Syria to bolster the regime of President Bashar al-Assad, and proxy groups like Houthis in Yemen and Hezbollah in Lebanon (Dalton 2017, 313). The latter group is especially important to Iran because Hezbollah acts as a 'strategic asset that extends Iranian influence to the Mediterranean' (Feltman 2019). Like China, Iran's hybrid war activity at the tactical level has a notable maritime dimension. Iran has two navies, the conventional Islamic Republic of Iran Navy and the Islamic Republican Guard Corps Navy, which is a paramilitary force. The latter operates in the Persian Gulf and Strait of Hormuz and uses small vessels to swarm US naval ships, carry out naval ambushes and conduct hit and run operations. Operating close to home, the force takes advantage of the element of surprise as well as its greater manoeuvrability as compared to the large US ships (Dalton 2017, 313).

Iran also makes extensive use of computer network attack. Its cyber war/digital attack capabilities, though still inferior to those of Russia, China and the United States, are growing in sophistication and impact. It is thought that Iran is behind an 'unprecedented' number of cyber attacks in recent years against governments and communications infrastructure across the Middle East, Europe and North America (Tweed 2019). Its information warfare measures extend from the tactical to strategic levels, from video footage of detained US sailors to give an inflated image of Iranian power (Dalton 2017, 313), to a systematic disinformation campaign abroad that promotes anti-Saudi, anti-Israeli and pro-Palestinian themes in line with Iranian foreign policy (Tabatabai 2018). Scholars note that for Iran, information warfare is nothing new. It was practised extensively in the 1970s as a means of toppling the Shah and bringing into power Ayatollah Khomeini, albeit without the facilitating force of today's online technology (ibid.).

Conclusion

Key state actors today are using hybrid war to increase their power and influence over other actors and thereby seek their self-interested objectives. Operating at just below the threshold to open warfare, hybrid war enables states to pursue their interests without risking nuclear escalation and/or conventional annihilation, and to do so in a manner that plausibly maintains their behaviour within global norms on the use of force. While Russia is operating across all three levels of hybrid war, it is not the only power to do so. Since the turn of the century the West has on occasion engaged in activities that are associated with tactical hybrid war, and at the strategic level it is charged in some quarters with having pursued political warfare for decades. China operates primarily at the strategic level of grey zone behaviour, with some tactical hybrid war components, while Iran's behaviour lies primarily in the tactical realm while capitalising on the strategic potential of cyber attack and digital information warfare.

There is no obvious place for hybrid war in existing theoretical understandings of hegemony. Realists equate hegemony with preponderant military power, but Russia, China and Iran are using hybrid war to dominate others specifically *because* they do not have preponderant military power in their region. Idealists start from the view that material power alone is not sufficient for hegemony, but their assertion of what is necessary focuses on objectively positive things like consensus-building, leadership and the provision of public goods. The tools and techniques of hybrid war do not fit well with this 'glass half full' perspective. There is room for future theoretical work on where to place hybrid war within the international relations literature on hegemony.

Hybrid war is not new and even these limited cases include examples that go back decades. Nonetheless, states across the spectrum are stepping up their pursuit of hybrid war. The particular tools available to them today are especially amenable to this form of warfare; the alternative is to risk nuclear escalation and/or conventional annihilation; hybrid war allows states to operate outside the bounds of global norms on the use of force; and the decline in America's relative power vis à vis other states has opened up opportunities for countries to act on their discontent with the US-led world order. Unanswered in all of this is how state actors can use hybrid war to influence non-state actors, an important area of future research.

Most importantly in the context of this chapter's overall theme, hybrid war is proving to be particularly amenable to hegemony, to the ability of a state actor to exercise preponderant influence over other state actors. The West really has expanded NATO to Russian borders; Russia really has incorporated Crimea and parts of Ukraine into Russian territory; China really has dramatically increased its control over the South China Sea with progressive island building. In this era of growing great power tension hybrid war is likely remain a central feature of the global security environment. The next challenge will centre on how major powers respond to one another.

Notes

1 The literature on defining power is vast. See, for example, Hans Morgenthau (1973, 9 and 28), Robert Dahl (1057, 202–3), Robert Keohane and Joseph Nye (2001, 10), Kenneth Waltz (1979, 191–2) and John Mearsheimer (2001, 57).
2 See, for example, Russell Glenn (2009).
3 Others argue that this sort of grand strategic approach, where tactical aspects of hybrid war are only part of a larger subversive and indirect weakening of the enemy, is better labelled 'non-linear warfare'. See Tad Schnaufer (2017, 22).
4 See for example Sorin Ducaru (2016).
5 W.J. Nemeth (2002) as discussed in Andras Racz (2015, 28).
6 'Hybrid War – Hybrid Response?' *NATO Review* video posted 3 July 2014 at https://www.nato.int/docu/review/2014/Russia-Ukraine-Nato-crisis/Russia-Ukraine-crisis-war/EN/index.htm (accessed 11 May 2018).
7 'The Odds on a Conflict between the Great Powers', *Economist*, 27 January 2018, special report, p. 6.
8 See, for example, Winn Schwartau (2000). For an overview of the discussion of asymmetrical war at the turn of the century, see Elinor C. Sloan (2002), chapter 7.
9 As quoted in Michael Charap (2015–2016, 53).
10 As paraphrased in James Wither (2016, 80).
11 Stephen J. Cimbala (2005, 28), as quoted in Sloan (2017, 32).
12 As quoted in Wither (2016, 76).
13 Chinese scholars as referenced in Saalman (2016–2017, 141).

References

Allen, T.S. and Moore, A.J. (2018) 'Victory without Casualties: Russia's Information Operations', *Parameters*, 48(1): 59–71.
Bachmann, S.D. and Gunneriusson, H. (2015) 'Russia's Hybrid Warfare in the East: The Integral Nature of the Information Sphere', *Georgetown Journal of International Affairs*, 16. Available at: www.researchgate.net/publication/277953401_RUSSIA%27S_HYBRID_WARFARE_IN_THE_EAST_USING_THE_INFORMATION_SPHERE_AS_INTEGRAL_TO_HYBRID_WARFARE

Burke, E.J.*et al.* (2018) *China's Military Activities in the East China Sea*. Santa Monica, CA: RAND Corporation.

Cavas, C. (2016a) 'Time to Call Out China's Maritime Militia?' *Defense News*, 18 September. Available at: https://www.defensenews.com/2016/09/19/chinas-maritime-militia-time-to-call-them-out/ (accessed 29 September 2016).

Cavas, C. (2016b) 'China's Maritime Militia a Growing Concern', *Defense News*, 21 November. Available at: https://www.defensenews.com/naval/2016/11/22/chinas-maritime-militia-a-growing-concern/(accessed 27 November 2016).

Charap, M. (2015–2016) 'The Ghost of Hybrid War', *Survival* 57(6): 51–58.

Chivvis, C.S (2017a) 'Understanding Russian "Hybrid Warfare"', in *Testimony before the United States House of Representatives Committee on Armed Services*. Santa Monica, CA: RAND Corporation.

Chivvis, C.S. (2017b) 'Hybrid War: Russian Contemporary Political Warfare', *Bulletin of the Atomic Scientists*, 73(5): 316–321.

Cimbala, S.J. (2005) 'Transformation in Concept and Policy', *Joint Force Quarterly*. Available at: https://ndupress.ndu.edu/portals/68/Documents/jfq/jfq-38.pdf

Clem, R. (2018) 'Military Exercises as Geopolitical Messaging in the NATO–Russia Dynamic', *Texas National Security Review*, 2(1). Available at: https://tnsr.org/2018/11/military-exercises-as-geopolitical-messaging-in-the-nato-russia-dynamic-reassurance-deterrence-and-instability/

Cooper, Z. and Shearer, A. (2017) 'Thinking Clearly about China's Layered Indo-Pacific Strategy', *Bulletin of the Atomic Scientists*, 73(8): 305–311.

Dahl, R. (1957). 'The Concept of Power', *Behavioral Science*, 2(3): 201–225.

Dalton, M.G. (2017) 'How Iran's Hybrid-War Tactics Help and Hurt It', *Bulletin of the Atomic Scientists*, 73(5): 312–315.

Department of Defense (2018) *Annual Report to Congress: Military and Security Developments Involving the People's Republic of China*. Washington, DC: Office of the Secretary of Defense.

Ducaru, S. (2016) 'The Cyber Dimension of Modern Hybrid Warfare and its Relevance for NATO', *Europolity*, 10(1): 7–23.

Feltman, J. (2019) 'Hezbollah: Revolutionary Iran's Most Successful Export', Brookings Institution. Available at: www.brookings.edu (accessed 19 April 2019).

Galeotti, M. (2018) 'I'm Sorry for Creating the "Gerasimov Doctrine"', *Foreign Policy*, 5. Available at: https://foreignpolicy.com/2018/03/05/im-sorry-for-creating-the-gerasimov-doctrine/

Giegerich, B. (2016) 'Hybrid Warfare and the Changing Character of Conflict', *Connections: The Quarterly Journal*, 15(2): 65–72.

Glenn, R. (2009) 'Thoughts on Hybrid Conflict', *Small Wars Journal*. Available at: http://smallwarsjournal.com/blog/journal/docs-temp/188-glenn.pdf (accessed 10 May 2018).

Hoffman, F. (2006) 'Hizbollah and Hybrid Wars: U.S. Should Take Hard Lesson from Lebanon', *Defense News*, 14 August. Available at: https://advance-lexis-com.proxy.library.carleton.ca/api/document?collection=news&id=urn:contentItem:4KPN-8850-TWX0-Y324-00000-00&context=1516831

Hoffman, F. (2007) *Conflict in the 21st Century: The Rise of Hybrid Wars*. Arlington, VA: Potomac Institute for Policy Studies.

Johnson, R. (2018) 'Hybrid War and Its Countermeasures: A Critique of the Literature', *Small Wars & Insurgencies*, 29(1): 141–163.

Jones, S.G. (2018) 'The Return of Political Warfare', Center for International & Strategic Studies. Available at: www.csis.org/analysis/return-political-warfare (accessed 18 May 2018).

Keohane, R.O. and Nye, J.S. (2001) *Power and Interdependence*, 3rd edn. New York: Longman.

Kofman, M. and Rojansky, M. (2015) 'A Closer Look at Russia's "Hybrid War"', *Wilson Center Kennan Cable*, no. 7. Available at: www.files.ethz.ch/isn/190090/5-KENNAN% 20CABLE-ROJANSKY%20KOFMAN.pdf

Lanoszka, A. (2016) 'Russian Hybrid Warfare and Extended Deterrence in Eastern Europe', *International Affairs*, 92(1): 175–195.

Lim, L. and Bergin, J. (2018) 'Inside China's Audacious Global Propaganda Campaign', *The Guardian*, 7 December 2018. Available at: https://advance-lexis-com.proxy.library. carleton.ca/api/document?collection=news&id=urn:contentItem:4KPN-8850-TWX0-Y324- 00000-00&context=1516831 (accessed 12 April 2019).

Lohaus, P. (2018) 'A New Blueprint for Competing Below the Threshold: The Joint Concept for Integrated Campaigning', War on the Rocks. Available at: https://warontherocks. com/2018/05/a-new-blueprint-for-competing-below-the-threshold-the-joint-concept-for- integrated-campaigning/

Macias, A. (2018) 'China Quietly Installed Missile Systems on Strategic Spratly Islands in Hotly Contested South China Sea', *CNBC*, 2 May 2018. Available at: https://www. cnbc.com/2018/05/02/china-added-missile-systems-on-spratly-islands-in-south-china-sea. html (accessed 12 April 2019).

Mearsheimer, J. (2001) *The Tragedy of Great Power Politics*. New York: W. W. Norton.

Morgenthau, H.J. (1973) *Power among Nations*, 5th edn. New York: Alfred A. Knoff.

Nemeth, W.J. (2002) 'Future War and Chechnya: A Case for Hybrid Warfare', Thesis, Naval Postgraduate School, Monterey, California.

Nye, J.S.Jr. (1990) *Bound to Lead: The Changing Nature of American Power*. New York: Basic Books.

O'Brien, W. (1981) *The Conduct of Just and Limited War*. New York: Praeger Publishers.

Popescu, N. (2015) 'Hybrid Tactics: Neither New nor Only Russian', *European Union Institute for Security Studies*, January: 1–2. Available at: https://www.iss.europa.eu/sites/ default/files/EUISSFiles/Alert_4_hybrid_warfare.pdf

Pyung-Kyun, W. (2015) 'Russian Hybrid War in the Ukraine Crisis', *Korean Journal of Defense Analysis*, 27(3): 383–400.

Racz, A. (2015) *Russia's Hybrid War: Breaking the Enemy's Ability to Resist*. Helsinki: The Finnish Institute of International Affairs.

Saalman, L. (2016–2017) 'Little Grey Men: China and the Ukraine Crisis', *Survival* 58(6).

Savage, P. (2018) 'The Conventionality of Russia's Unconventional Warfare', *Parameters* 48 (2): 135–156.

Schnaufer, T.A. (2017) 'Redefining Hybrid Warfare: Russia's Non-Linear War against the West', *Journal of Strategic Security* 10(1).

Schwartau, W. (2000) 'Asymmetrical Adversaries', *Orbis*, 44(2): 197–205.

Sloan, E.C. (2002) *The Revolution in Military Affairs*. Montreal: McGill-Queen's University Press.

Sloan, E.C. (2017) *Modern Military Strategy*, 2nd edn. London: Routledge.

Snegovaya, M. (2015) *Putin's Information War in Ukraine*. Washington, DC: Institute for the Study of War.

Tabatabai, A.M. (2018) 'A Brief History of Iranian Fake News', *Foreign Affairs*. https:// www.foreignaffairs.com/articles/middle-east/2018-08-24/brief-history-iranian-fake-news (accessed 2 April 2019).

Thomas, T. (2016) 'The Evolution of Russian Military Thought: Integrating Hybrid, New-Generation, and New-Type Thinking', *Journal of Slavic Military Studies*, 29(4): 554–575.

Tweed, D. (2019) 'Iranians May Be Behind Unprecedented Cyber Hacks, FireEye Says', *Bloomberg News*, 10 January 2019. Available at: https://www.foreignaffairs.com/articles/ middle-east/2018-08-24/brief-history-iranian-fake-news (accessed 18 April 2019).

Veljovski, G., Taneski, N. and Dojchinovski, M. (2017) 'The Danger of "Hybrid Warfare" from a Sophisticated Adversary: The Russian "Hybridity" in the Ukrainian Conflict', *Defense and Security Analysis*, 33(4): 292–307.

Waltz, K. (1979) *Theory of International Relations*. Boston, MA: McGraw Hill.

Wirtz, J.J. (2017) 'Life in the "Gray Zone": Observations for Contemporary Strategists', *Defense & Security Analysis*, 33(2): 106–114.

Wither, J.K. (2016) 'Making Sense of Hybrid War', *Connections: The Quarterly Journal*, 15(2): 73–87.

7

GLOBAL HEGEMONY FROM A *LONGUE DURÉE* PERSPECTIVE

The dollar and the world economy

Randall Germain

Introduction: The dollar and global hegemony

The US dollar has been the world's 'global currency' since the end of World War II.[1] There are many reasons offered for this role: the size of the US economy relative to other major economies; the centrality of US financial and stock markets in the global financial system; the role of US multinational firms in international transactions; the global reach of the US alliance system; the paramount political position of the US in international relations; and the central role of the dollar in foreign exchange markets. Over the past decade, however, many have questioned the viability of the US dollar to continue acting as the world's global currency (Helleiner and Kirshner 2008; Cohen 2019). Is it a reliable store of value? Do persistent and large American budgetary and current account deficits spell out a future in which the supply of dollars will outstrip demand? With the rise of emerging market economies and especially China's determined effort to internationalise the renminbi (RMB), not to mention the establishment of the euro as a fully fledged reserve currency, many feel justified in questioning how much longer the dollar will maintain its historic role.

In this chapter I consider how much longer we can expect the dollar to continue in its role as the world's most important currency through an engagement with the work of the French historian Fernand Braudel. The hallmark of Braudel's work is what might be termed his world-economy framework, in which he assesses the structural characteristics of a world economy in terms of its coherence as a singular totality, albeit one that can be divided in several different ways. I shall divide the world-economy in two ways: between overlapping social spaces and interrelated social times. By outlining the world-economy in this way, I advance a conceptual framework that suggests a somewhat different way to apprehend the production and sanctioning of global currencies. It is a framework organised

DOI: 10.4324/9781003037231-7

around a set of dialectical relationships that anticipates how the US dollar will continue to act as the world's global currency into the immediate and medium-term future, due to the particular way in which American-style capitalism has become infused with key structural features of the world-economy.

I proceed by first outlining Braudel's conceptual framework, drawing special attention to the way in which he conceives a world-economy as organised through overlapping social spaces and interrelated social times, which are in turn refracted through the juxtaposition of competing *ensembles* of political, economic, cultural and social hierarchies. I then ask how such a framework might consider the fit between global hegemony and a global currency. Two historical cases are used to illustrate the operation of a global currency within a hegemonic world-economy: sterling during the era of the pre-1914 international gold standard, and the dollar during the contemporary period. Considering these two cases reveals in a different way the enduring features of the dollar's status as the world's global currency.

A Braudelian framework for thinking about global hegemony: Overlapping social spaces and interrelated social times

Carving up social space: Capitalism, market economy, material life

The term hegemony (much less global hegemony) is not part of Braudel's lexicon, yet I want to suggest that he provides us with a valuable framework through which to consider the coherence and durability of global hegemony, framed around four sets of dialectical relations. His starting point is that history is connected and its parts are comprehensible in terms of the whole. He defines this whole in political economy terms as a 'world-economy', an 'economically autonomous section of the planet able to provide for most of its own needs, a section to which its internal links and exchanges give a certain organic unity' (Braudel 1984, 22). Relating part to whole in this way provides the first key dialectical relationship through which we can consider global hegemony as a multi-dimensional phenomenon. It allows us to place problems such as the provision of a global currency into a broad context, rather than to define it singularly as either a 'political' or an 'economic' phenomenon.

Once established, the coherence of a world-economy may be mapped in several ways: through boundaries that mark one world-economy off from others; through its central axis of power, which for Braudel runs through cities; and through its hierarchical zones, extending from core to periphery (Braudel 1984, 25–44). Within the context of his historical materialist method, this coherence is in part a function of the application of political power and the ongoing effects of a fusion between state prerogatives and market activities. But Braudel also directs our attention to the linkages between what he describes as a world-economy's 'core' building blocks, which he identifies as the social arenas of capitalism, market economy and material life. These are the separate yet interrelated terrains of social space that provide the 'envelope' within which we can situate the history of discrete parts. The 'whole' of the world-economy is constituted by these terrains, whose parts are in turn moved by quite different rhythms, dynamics, agents and forms of contestation. These intricate interrelations mark out the second dialectical feature of Braudel's approach.

Here, we enter into one of the most controversial aspects of a Braudelian framework, due to his insistence (i) that capitalism does not (indeed cannot) subsume every aspect of social life under its purview, (ii) that it is as old as the hills, and (iii) that social space is not homogeneous in its organisation and experience. These claims allow him to consider not only that the historicity of capitalism extends as far back as recorded time but also that capitalism needs to be distinguished from markets and the market economy. Contrary to common usage, Braudel asks us to accept that capitalists and their preferred arena of activity – capitalism – differ substantially from all other producers, traders and consumers in their many and overlapping interactions. Most importantly, for him capitalism is the terrain in which competition is minimal, monopoly and oligopoly are the norm, transparency is rare, information is necessarily asymmetric in its generation and availability, and power is explicitly recognised and exercised in economic and commercial activities. It is as far from the transparent, competitive market economy as one can imagine; indeed, on occasion he refers to capitalism as the 'counter-market'. As I will suggest below, it is the natural 'home' of global hegemonic practices.

Braudel sketches the architecture of the world-economy in terms of a pyramid, with the smallest, top-most section reserved for the terrain of capitalists. Even if we agree with Braudel that the world-economy might be portrayed as a pyramid, this is a counter-intuitive inversion of the standard depiction. For most of us, the economic imagination we deploy sees the terrain of capitalism as the largest section of the pyramid – its biggest, most powerful portion – precisely because this captures the enormous sway that capitalism exerts over the economy. In fact, for most of us capitalism and the economy are inseparable; capitalism *is* the economy. Contemporary arguments about global capitalism tell us that today it is busy drawing more and more extensive lands and peoples into its maw. To argue that capitalism is not this super-dominant system is to go against the grain of nearly all modern political economy analyses.

Yet, this is exactly what Braudel asks us to do. For him, if the idea of *capital* is to be treated in an historically accurate manner, it should be most centrally connected to money, to the form of wealth which is directed to reproducing itself through accumulation and for the purposes of accumulation (Braudel 1982, 232–43). Capital is moneyed wealth, built up over time rather than consumed. This is why until very recently capital has almost always been a property of families: the connection between family and capital has enabled capitalism to become an organised terrain of activity (Braudel 1977, 66–75). Most importantly, of course, it has been merchant families who have engaged in accumulation; hence their association with capitalism as he defines it.[2]

For Braudel, the defining characteristic of capitalists has always been their capacity to choose where to deploy their capital, and thus to shift the means of accumulation according to the profitability of particular types of activities. Long-distance trade and money-lending, for example, have long been chosen preserves of capitalists. It was only in the seventeenth and eighteenth centuries that production became profitable enough to warrant their attention. Today it is speculative activities along many fronts – finance, property, technology – that mostly capture their attention. We can think of venture capitalists as practising the purest form of capitalism. The point Braudel brings home is that capitalists have never desired to control the entire economy; rather they insert themselves into the commanding heights of economic and commercial activity where the easiest and juiciest profit margins lie. As for the rest of the economy, the 'market economy', capitalists are often happy to leave that to others.

This market economy encompasses the middle section of our economic pyramid, changing in size over time. Transparency is its defining feature. The economic and commercial activities which mark out the market economy are well-understood, easily calculable because of the wide availability of information, open to competition and capable of sustaining many participants. Over the years and centuries the market economy has organised and entertained the kinds of routine exchange that have in turn sustained villages, cities and even nations. These range from the provision of basic necessities to local services to the stable economies associated with trade in non-luxury items produced through comparative specialisation: olives for wine; cloth for timber; and in our time, metals and commodities for manufactured products.

The crucial point about the market economy is that it is entirely about the production, exchange and consumption of everyday items, where the possibility of realising super-profits does not exist outside rare and unusual circumstances. The economic and commercial activities that constitute the market economy are obviously profit-oriented, but these profits are not themselves directed for the most part towards accumulation. Of course, some people will begin in the market economy and move into the arena of capitalism – that is to say, they will become *capitalists* – but this is not a widespread occurrence and most importantly it is not one which upsets the essential stability of the market economy. At the same time, the market economy is vulnerable to incursions from capitalists, such as when new technologies provide new economies of scale that recalibrate profit margins in established sectors, or when special circumstances transform stable commodities into highly profitable opportunities (as for example during a drought or famine). But this is not a common development. As Braudel reminds us, there are simply too few profitable opportunities (in an accumulation sense) for capitalists to bother with the market economy on a grand scale. It is not the preferred site of global hegemonic practices, most simply because it is not worth the expenditure of effort.

Distinguishing between capitalism and the market economy allows Braudel to negotiate two problems that plague much contemporary analysis. The first is the tendency to assume the homogeneity of social space, wherein we are compelled to designate an entire social space such as an economy in only one manner (i.e. capitalist, socialist, feudal, etc.). While this may offer a tempting form of analytical parsimony, Braudel is convinced that this is factually inaccurate, especially if one examines the kinds of dynamics and imperatives which move actual historical agents.[3] Distinguishing between the structural characteristics of capitalism and the market economy is helpful in this respect, for it helps us to locate the preferred terrain of hegemony, which as Braudel suggests is the arena of capitalism.

The second problem is the tendency to assume a monochromatic reading of causality. Braudel's framework introduces multiple and competing causal factors that push and pull historical agents in different directions depending upon the terrain of activity in which they are involved. The terrain of capitalism responds to markedly different dynamics than those at work in the market economy, and we need to be aware of these distinctions if we are to accurately evaluate future trends and possibilities. Here the utility of Braudel's insistence that capitalism is a specialised terrain of activity is useful, precisely because it alerts us to the different kinds of push-and-pull factors that animate human agency. This allows us to conceive of a world-economy that is structured and organised around a multiplicity of historical imperatives, rather like the unfolding of social life itself.

The last part of the world economy pyramid Braudel identifies is the terrain of *material life*, that vast pool of activities dominated by routine, repetition and unreflective behaviour. It is the domain of what is often portrayed as the 'natural order of things', what some have called 'the political economy of the everyday', and which Antonio Gramsci famously called 'common sense'. For the eras which most occupy Braudel – the Mediterranean world during the reign of Philip II of Spain, and the European world economy from the fifteenth to eighteenth centuries – the domain of material life constituted the single largest arena of social activity, simply because most people were involved in webs of exchange that extended no further than a few miles, and which were directed primarily towards reproducing family and village life on a subsistence basis. The money economy – the hallmark of the market economy and vitally necessary for capitalism – was not widely entrenched, and many forms of economic exchange were wrapped up in non-economic or uneconomic demands. The parallel here with Karl Polanyi's (1944/1957) understanding of an 'embedded economy' is clear.

Braudel conceives of material life as comprised of 'those aspects of life that control us without our even being aware of them; habit or, better yet, routine – those thousands of acts that flower and reach fruition without anyone's having made a decision ...' (Braudel 1977, 6–7). He offers the historical choice of grain for foodstuff as a prime example: wheat in Europe, maize in the Americas, and rice throughout Asia. Each crop demanded different techniques and imposed particular consequences upon the social organisation of its respective economy (Braudel 1977, 11–12). At the same time, even though each foodstuff was initially confined to the domain of material life, over time it became subject to routine long-distance trade – a sign of inclusion in the market economy – and even, in unusual circumstances, capitalism itself, as when it became a plaything of capitalists during famines or unusual trading circumstances (Braudel 1982, 457). Historically, human organisation has been mostly *imprisoned*, as Braudel would have it, within the lived experience of material life; it is one of the hallmarks of modernity that increasing swathes of our lives have become part of the market economy, where new ideas, inclusive participation and fluidity and mobility can be so impactful. Another way of emphasising this point is to note that for most people, most of the time, they have almost no real lived experience of global hegemony, because so much of their everyday lives take place outside the social arena of capitalism.

Braudel's world-economy framework is thus pitched as a triptych, a three-dimensional model that sets the basic structural parameters within which human agency takes form. Yet, this structural framework also works through another set of macro-constraints, which he identifies as a 'set of sets', or as the ensemble of polity, economy, society, and culture (Braudel 1984, 45–70). On this front the dialectical nature of Braudel's framework becomes explicit, for if the economy is capable of invading other terrains, so too is it open to incursions from other forms of activity. He presents this as a possible set of equations:

1   politics + economics + culture = society
2   economics + culture + society = politics
3   culture + society + politics = economics
4   society + politics + economics = culture

In fact, we may identify this as the third dialectical feature of Braudel's frame-work, namely the holistic and interactive web of his history, which demands that we employ not only a global historical perspective but also a holistic one that sets different forms of activity into tension and contestation with one another.

The particular conflict that Braudel emphasises is the way in which the terrain of capitalism sets upon and utilises for its own purposes the various social hierarchies it encounters. This idea is crucial, because for Braudel capitalists are able to seize control of, or insert themselves into, the commanding heights of the economy precisely by taking advantage of pre-existing social hierarchies. This is how capit-alism grows and expands; not so much by devouring its own as through a search to exploit the differences which these hierarchies present to those with capital, infor-mation, power and resources. Once the niche yields its treasure, however, the capitalist moves on. This refusal to specialise is in fact the key to their ability to survive: capitalists simply pick up and move on when loopholes are closed to them and the hierarchies they feed on are ameliorated.

Braudel's framework, by conceptualising a world-economy in terms of three terrains which are overlapped by the hierarchies associated with politics, econom-ics, society and culture, enables us to consider the question of global hegemony in terms of how deeply it penetrates into a world-economy, and the particular way in which its key practices extend, reinforce or undercut existing hierarchies. A global currency epitomises one such practice, as a global currency extends the arc of economic exchange, reinforces the fusion of political and economic power, and can fasten onto existing hierarchies by channelling resources towards those agents who are entangled in the accumulation of capital. As we shall see, the US dollar today has a more extensive role than the pound sterling did in the pre-1914 gold standard period; we might say that the dollar's role extends beyond the usual terrain of an internationally used currency, which is more typically associated only with the terrain of capitalism. For this reason the US dollar today is a critical support element to the practice of American global hegemony.

To sum up this section, Braudel's framework suggests that we draw our attention to three key features of the world-economy: the constant movement between individual agency and global context, or part and whole; the conflicts and tensions between actors situated in different terrains of activity (capitalism, market economy and material life); and the conflicts inherent to different social hierarchies as they are exploited by capitalists, who in Braudel's universe are the flag-bearer's of hegemony. But these dialectical features are not simply organised spatially. Crucially for Braudel, they are also informed by the differential movement of social time.

Carving up social time: The event, the conjuncture, the longue durée

I suggest that one of Braudel's key insights concerns how the prism of time affects our understanding of events. He is here reacting to the idea that history is primarily about great men' or singular events. This vision of history is marked out by the short time span, or what Braudel identifies as *histoire événementielle*, the time of the event. It focuses upon what some see as the surface appearance of history, disconnected from deeper structures which might enable its narrative to be given meaning. While Braudel recognises the lure of this method of thinking about time, he is not a fan: it is history 'in the raw', focusing on the time span that is 'the most capricious and the most delusive of all' (Braudel 1980, 28–9). Ultimately, such a view of social time fails to provide history with any depth.

To gain access to historical depth involves conceiving of a longer time span that can be measured over decades. What Braudel terms the *conjuncture* is a time span that can chart movements from 10 to about 50 years (which is the timespan of the Kondratiev wave, a price series named after the early twentieth century Russian economist who initially formulated it). This medium-term time span is valuable precisely because it sets the time of the event into a more appropriate context, to enable connections to be made between collective action and structural context. One example of the conjuncture is the business cycle, that staple of supply and demand which demonstrates how different elements of economic activity (production, exchange and consumption) are balanced out over a set period of time.

As this example indicates, the conjuncture is a time span whose greatest utility can be found within the context of the market economy. Here, with supply and demand a function of competition, transparency and routine transactions, prices move in relatively regular cycles which can be plotted and mapped in order to explore their appropriate causal factors. Thus we have commodity booms and busts, trends which can be identified and linked to industrialisation, inflation, technological developments and population changes. By plotting such cycles the market economy becomes visible and almost – within certain parameters – predictable.

But it is not the conjuncture which is Braudel's main concern in his writing, despite its importance. The timespan which commands his primary attention is the *longue durée*, a timespan that stretches over many decades and can even extend over centuries. The *longue durée* is as much a *mentalité* or mental framework as it is a timespan; that is, it is a mode of experience through which history is encountered. One expression of the *longue durée* is the secular price level, which moves in slow and undulating cycles over centuries, but yet which can be severed at certain crucial points. This is for Braudel the key aspect of social time, and the principal reason why we need to recognise its different 'moments': time, while continuous, can also be broken or ruptured, and in order to recognise these points we need to be able to contrast the fast paced time of the event to the slower-paced movement of the conjuncture, and contrast both to the 'common sense' glacial stream of the *longue durée* (Braudel 1980, 26).

The *longue durée* is most commonly applicable to the terrain of material life, where the long-term span of time is composed of routine practices and hereditary actions that change only slowly. This is where our most basic habits are formed and our most durable predispositions are shaped. Such predispositions may sometimes be equated with 'human nature', but really these are simply the settled preferences which become our 'common sense'. Examples drawn from the early modern period might include the power with which seasonal changes ruled agricultural communities, dictating many aspects of behaviour, or the capacity which religious belief possessed to reinforce particular status hierarchies. Contemporary examples might include in western industrialised countries the stubborn persistence of the idea of individual responsibility, which infuses values across widely disparate income groups, or the equally stubborn and paradoxical valorisation of nationalist impulses, which seem in so many ways to be counter-intuitive to the thrust of globalisation. Braudel's point here is that even in today's world, there are long-held ideas and material practices which remain almost impervious to the onslaught of commercial pressures.

This points to the fourth dialectical relationship that a Braudelian framework highlights: the tensions produced by different experiences of time. Just as we need to relate parts to the whole, we need also to be mindful of how the short and medium-term relate to the *longue durée*. As he put it in an important article first written over 60 years ago:

> nothing is more important, nothing comes closer to the crux of social reality than this living, intimate, infinitely repeated opposition between the instant of time and that time which flows only slowly. Whether it is a question of past or of the present, a clear awareness of this plurality of social time is indispensable to the communal methodologies of the human sciences. (Braudel 1980, 26)

These tensions should not be conceived as disembodied, abstract experiences of time, but rather as lived experiences in which the rhythms and cycles of practices organised across different terrains of social space interact and shape our understandings of what is possible for human agents to achieve within their given circumstances. It is an awareness that time and space are historical categories which push and pull at our values and objectives, and through this exert an impact on the consequences of our actions. It is above all a call to recognise that the social sciences are on the same plane as the historical sciences, and that we may approach issues commonly associated with the social sciences through what might be termed, following Robert Cox (1981, 131), an historical mode of thought.

We have now arrived at the point where we can outline a Braudelian framework for understanding global hegemony, and establish how this might provide insights into the question of the future of the US dollar as a global currency. Such a framework begins by establishing the global context of such a currency, which is nothing more than a description of the extent of global hegemony, and then juxtaposes the social terrains through which the global currency is active, to determine how deeply entrenched it is in relation to the extent of its hegemonic context. Next it sets up the hierarchies that are central to how and where the currency operates, and then finally considers the long-term *mentalité* that underpins and/or undermines its form, which can then be juxtaposed to short- and medium-term time-frames. It is this last element that sets the entire framework in motion. I now consider this framework with reference to the examples of sterling and the dollar as global currencies.

A 'world-economy' view of global currencies: Sterling versus the dollar

Parts and wholes

Braudel's first dialectical relationship concerns parts and wholes, which is the relative depth and strength of a world-economy's structural coherence. A global currency is an important part of this coherence; thus our first question must be to gauge in some manner the coherence of the contemporary world-economy in comparison with its pre-1914 antecedent. The nineteenth-century world-economy was marked out by the predominant political and economic position of Great Britain and the City of London, the spread of the values and ethos of liberal capitalism, the consolidation of the bourgeoisie as a class across many nations, the rise and then decline of free trade in relation to the renaissance of what some termed the 'new imperialism', and the incorporation of new geographic areas into the orbit of capitalist development together with the rapid industrialisation of many non-European countries (e.g. Japan, Canada, Australia, Germany and the US).

Within this context, sterling played a very important role. It was first and foremost the currency used by the London markets, together with all of Great Britain's colonies and dependencies when they raised funds in the City. The use of sterling as the principal currency for international credit meant that the international financial system in effect functioned on a sterling standard rather than the nominal gold standard that is often used to describe it (Germain 1997). In Braudel's terms,

we may say that sterling received a good part of its capacity to act as a global currency from the strength and breadth of the terrain of capitalism.

Beyond the domain of capitalism, however, throughout the market economy
and material life, sterling was much less prominent, even in Britain's colonies. Few
British colonies used sterling for everyday transactions, although of course sterling
did function throughout these economies as high-powered money, backing up
colonial currencies as foreign reserves. And there were some countries, such as
Argentina, Russia and the US, which maintained large sterling balances in London,
thus further supporting the reserve role of sterling. Nevertheless, the reach of sterling into other social arenas was not striking, which indicates that while the domain
of capitalism certainly supported the use of sterling as a global currency, its reach
did not travel too deeply into the remaining fabric of the extant world-economy.

This position can be contrasted to the contemporary period, when the use of the
dollar both in the terrain of capitalism and beyond is much more widespread. With
the growth in the number of countries drawn into the web of the world-economy – especially since 1989 – the actual reach of the dollar as a global currency has
expanded. In particular, the use of the dollar by China and many other countries as
their key foreign currency reserve dwarfs any similar use made of sterling during
the nineteenth century. At the same time, due to the growing dollarisation of
many economies, the dollar has extended its role into the market economy.
Examples can be found throughout Central and Latin America of de facto and *de
jure* dollarisation, but similar developments can also be found in other parts of the
world. Here what is important to note is that the dollar is playing a larger role
throughout the world-economy than sterling did in its heyday. This may be one
indication that, despite many recent challenges to American hegemony, the
coherence of the contemporary world-economy remains robust.

Indeed, if we consider the extent of American power today versus that of Britain
in the pre-1914 era, we cannot help but be impressed by the ideational and
material supremacy of the United States. Ideationally, despite the spread of dis-
satisfaction with and opposition to American government policies, the resilience, or
better, the reservoir of belief in a version of America's founding ideals continues to
run deep. To the extent that these ideals remain in character a pragmatic (rather
than fundamentalist) version of liberalism, they will continue to resonate with the
hopes and aspirations of many across the industrialised and even the developing
world as witnessed by the continued numbers of people who are intent on fleeing
or moving to America, or who simply desire to trade with American companies
(cf. Hardt and Negri 2000). In this sense the *Pax Americana* has much more social
depth than the *Pax Britannica* ever possessed: today's world-economy is more
thoroughly Americanised than the nineteenth-century version was Anglicised.

Social arenas

Another way in which we might think of this coherence or fit is by asking how
deeply the terrain of capitalism extends into and is able to influence the terrains of the

market economy and material life. For Braudel, the nineteenth century represented a new structural turn in the evolution of capitalism, as capitalists discovered and entered the field of production and in the process cemented a new relationship to both the state and the market economy. But, even as capitalists entered new fields, they left alone large sections of existing economies, which continued to operate outside full-blown market relations. In India and China, for example, large parts of their economies and societies remained firmly tethered to the arena of material life, largely organised around village life and subsistence economic exchange. Even as the coastal fringes of Africa were being exploited and drawn into the terrain of capitalism through the slave trade, much of its inland social organisation followed older norms and customs (Wolf 1982). That is to say, what marked out the expansion of the world-economy during this period was the extension of capitalism to new parts of the world through investment into infrastructure and state-building, which required massive capital sums. But capitalist encroachment on the market economy and material life was neither extensive nor transformative. Large domains of social activity remained subject to pre-existing rhythms and dynamics.

The post-1945 era, in contrast, saw the geographic range of capitalism shrink with the consolidation of the Cold War, which divided the world into an American trading area and a relatively autarchic Soviet zone. Additionally, China withdrew from the world-economy and India turned towards self-reliance after independence. Denied its previous geographic range, capitalism turned inward and began instead to encroach upon both the market economy and material life. These arenas became the necessary sites of capitalist accumulation, which deepened the reach of capitalism within national economies. The 1950s and 1960s especially saw this incursion most vividly, as large swathes of the American national economy were brought into the orbit of capitalist operations as Braudel would comprehend them. This incursion was associated most clearly with the rise of large corporations and the growth of conglomerates, which attempted to gain control over entire production and distribution systems.

This deepening of capitalism gained a new fillip in the late twentieth century with the opening up of China, the moderate liberalising of India and the collapse of the Soviet Union. When coupled with developments associated with the resurgence of a renewed liberalism – often identified as neoliberalism and associated with the Washington Consensus – capitalism once again recaptured its historic globality and sought windfall profits in the transition economies of central and eastern Europe and newly opened 'emerging markets', especially in Asia. At the same time, the market economy also expanded on the back of the ethos of commercialising activities which had heretofore resided outside the cash nexus. The result is that today the world-economy has been reconstituted with an enhanced arena of capitalism, a bolstered market economy and a diminished arena of material life. In other words, the natural terrain of global hegemony – the arena of capitalism – has expanded considerably.

What this means today for the role of the US dollar as the global currency is that the enabling conditions of the world-economy are more robust in the contemporary period than they were during the era of sterling. The arenas of capitalism and the market economy are stronger and more deeply entrenched compared with the arena of material life, providing increased scope for the dollar to circulate as the world's global currency. It is in this sense that the dollar is more strongly embedded in the contemporary structure of the world-economy than was sterling under the *Pax Britannica*. As a global hegemonic practice, the US dollar today occupies a strengthened position as compared to its nineteenth-century counterpart.

Hierarchies

Hierarchies and inequalities are a central organising feature of the world-economy, and even though capitalism did not create them it is well positioned to exploit them for its own uses. The main hierarchy which capitalism utilises today is the international hierarchy of political power, and here we may suggest that the role of the US dollar is stronger now than was sterling previously, precisely because the ambit and reach of American state power outweighs and outdistances its nine-teenth-century British counterpart. It does so in two ways, one internal to the organisation of the American state and one external to it in terms of the interna-tional balance of power.

Internally, the American state benefits from an extremely durable state-society complex, which provides it with access to resources that are more wide-ranging than its competitors. Because it is a democracy, its capacity to tax its citizens and honour its debt obligations has enabled the American state to support global mili-tary and political operations on a scale that vastly surpasses anything the British state could support during the nineteenth century, or the Soviet state during the Cold War. From our perspective, what is important to note here is that the United States has been at war almost continuously over the past 80 years, without harming the role or value of the dollar. This is truly an astonishing feat that reflects the tight fit between the operation of global hegemony and the global status of the dollar.

This internal ability to generate resources is complemented by an external component, which is the capacity of the US to attract funds from abroad. Since the mid-1980s, when the US became a net international debtor (first on its current account, and then subsequently on its capital account), this capacity took the form of what Susan Strange (1987) called a 'super-exorbitant' privilege, which is nothing else than the ability to exploit the international political hierarchy. This hierarchy of course is clearly buttressed by the international balance of military power, whose apex the US has held since 1945. It is also reinforced by the global institutionali-sation of American power through a network of political, military and economic institutions standing guard over the evolution of a multilateral world-economy. Together, the fusion of these internal and external elements constitutes a formid-able structure of American power.

This international political hierarchy, as several chapters in this volume suggest, is now in certain respects under stress. With the re-emergence of China and to a more limited extent Russia as political and economic powers, the rise of India and even Brazil, it appears that this external element of American power is eroding. Direct challenges to America's military supremacy may not yet exist; but the ability of the US to prosecute two wars at the same time has become stretched, while the ability of the US to draw on the international institutional fabric of the post-1945 world order appears constrained. UN backing for the war on Iraq was not granted, and the divisions that emerged within NATO over the Afghanistan mission further indicate that the US must sometimes push harder to maintain its dominant hold over the international political hierarchy. And throughout most of its term, the Trump administration has oddly attacked the existing international balance of power as tilted against its own interests.

Nevertheless, this erosion is not unequivocal. The US has not had problems financing its current account and budgetary deficits at a very reasonable cost. Its consumer-driven economy is still a magnet for the exports of developing (and developed) economies. Its corporations remain among the biggest, best capitalised, most innovative and highly profitable on the planet (Starrs 2013). And when it comes to devising the rules for the global economy, America's interests are rarely ignored or trammelled upon, even when the US government seems to call existing rules into question. In short, the US is and will undoubtedly remain for some time the richest and most militarily powerful country in the world, and this position will continue to generate resources for it to use and exploit.

Time

The temporal aspect of Braudel's world-economy framework draws our attention to two elements. The first is a common sense element: global currencies and their role change only slowly, thus providing their issuers with many opportunities to stem the tide (Cohen 2019). The second element is more complex: the use of global currencies depends crucially upon a particular *mentalité*, which is itself constituted by several ideational and cultural features. A *longue durée* view of the question of global currencies embraces a range of factors above and beyond a narrowly 'economic' rationale for their use. Global currencies are part of a world-economy that is itself composed of a 'set of sets' that extends beyond the strictly economic.

As Cohen (2019) points out, global currencies are historical creations, and have come and gone throughout history. They can take a long time to depart the scene: indeed, sterling still retains its position as a (minor) international reserve currency to this day, which is part of the role played by all global currencies. Even if the dollar is in decline, this will take quite some time to run its course. However, if we turn to consider the ideational supports for a potential rival to act as a global currency, we need to ask if such currencies can match the enduring global appeal of the American economy's *mentalité*? In terms of countries or regions that can potentially exert this kind of pull – as witnessed by a desire to trade with or migrate to it – only one appears to offer such a rival *mentalité*: the

EU and the euro. This is partly because it is a magnet for refugees and economic migrants (unlike the much more limited appeal here of China, Japan, India, Brazil and Russia), and partly because it shares with the US a version of liberalism that seems to resonate beyond its borders. Although this appeal is not quite as strong or global as that of America's, it at least resonates with a similar set of values. The lack of alternatives on this front suggests that throughout the contemporary world-economy, it is the US that will continue to hold fast to the world's economic imagination, and thus it will continue to provide the core *mentalité* for the dollar to uphold the global currency role.[4]

The dollar's longue durée

I have advanced a conceptual framework that explores the enabling conditions required to provide and sanction a global currency. The crucial point stressed throughout is to consider the question of global currencies in the light of the overall structural organisation of the world-economy, which is the material underpinning of global hegemony. Until the basic structure of a world-economy is altered, the provision of its global currency is unlikely to change. From this perspective, the most important question to pose is whether the world-economy itself is being transformed?

There are two main components involved in answering this question. First, are the basic structural arrangements of the world-economy under threat? The answer provided above is: not really. The different arenas of activity (capitalism, market economy and material life) are indeed changing, as they have throughout history, but they are not yet changing at a pace that is genuinely transformative. Indeed, an important change has already occurred, namely the squeezing of the terrain of material life by the market economy, but this has not resulted in a diminution of the role of the US dollar as the world's single most important currency. Quite the contrary in fact: it has widened the scope for the use of the dollar. The main reason is that the arena of capitalism has inserted itself more forcefully into the arenas of the market economy and material life, and the dollar has followed in this slipstream. The US dollar has legs, and they are grounded in the strong material support afforded to the dollar by the continuing hegemonic structure of the world-economy.

Reinforcing this material condition is the ideational support provided to the dollar by the prevailing *mentalité* that inclines commercial and other agents to consider the dollar as part of a broader political economy framework associated with liberalism, open economies and international transactions. From a *longue durée* perspective, this *mentalité* affords the dollar as much support as does the unparalleled liquidity for its assets and the complete openness of the US capital account. Global hegemony is a deep, multilayered structure that Braudel's world-economy framework is well positioned to capture. Until this structure fractures, the dollar will continue to remain the world's most important – indeed indispensable – global currency.

Notes

1 I am using the term 'global currency' here in a way that encompasses but also goes beyond the more common term 'international reserve currency'. It is akin to what Susan Strange (1971) and Benjamin Cohen (1998) identify as a Top Currency. A top currency (a global currency in my terminology) is more than a reserve currency (used by governments for their foreign reserves); it is the dominant currency used for international economic transactions and credit flows around the world. Recent assessments which demonstrate the continued dominance of the US dollar include Thimann (2008) and Cohen and Benney (2014).

2 Interestingly, many contemporary efforts to 'map' class formation and circuits of capital at the global level note the continuing significance of families as repositories of serious wealth (Carroll 2010).

3 J.K. Gibson-Graham (1996) offer a further reason to join Braudel in resisting a homogeneous conception of social space: it restricts our imagination for considering alternatives, in this case to capitalist social relations.

4 Harold James (2011) makes this same point in his consideration of whether China might provide an alternative set of core values around which a potential challenge to American global hegemony might cohere.

References

Braudel, F. (1973/1967) *Capitalism and Material Life: 1400–1800*, trans. M. Kochan. London: George Weidenfeld and Nicolson.

Braudel, F. (1977) *Afterthoughts on Material Civilization and Capitalism*, trans. P.M. Ranum. Baltimore, MD: Johns Hopkins University Press.

Braudel, F. (1980/1958) 'History and the Social Sciences: The *Longue Durée*', in *On History*, trans. S. Matthews, Chicago: University of Chicago Press.

Braudel, F. (1982/1979) *Civilization and Capitalism, 15th–18th Century*, Vol. 2: *The Wheels of Commerce*, trans. S. Reynolds. New York: Harper & Row.

Braudel, F. (1984/1979) *Civilization and Capitalism, 15th–18th Century*, Vol. 3: *The Perspective of the World*, trans. S. Reynolds. London: William Collins.

Carroll, W. (2010) *The Making of a Transnational Capitalist Class: Corporate Power in the 21st Century*. London: Zed Books.

Cohen, B. (1998) *The Geography of Money*. Princeton, NJ: Princeton University Press.

Cohen, B. (2019) *Currency Statecraft: Monetary Rivalry and Geopolitical Ambition*. Chicago: University of Chicago Press.

Cohen, B. and Benney, T. (2014) 'What Does the International Currency System Really Look Like?', *Review of International Political Economy*, 21(5): 1017–1041.

Cox, R. (1981) 'Social Forces, States and World Order: Beyond International Relations Theory', *Millennium*, 10(2): 126–155.

Germain, R. (1997) *The International Organization of Credit*. Cambridge: Cambridge University Press.

Gibson-Graham, J.K. (1996) *The End of Capitalism (As We Knew It)*. Minneapolis: University of Minnesota Press.

Hardt, M. and Negri, A. (2000) *Empire*. Boston, MA: Harvard University Press.

Helleiner, E. and Kirshner, J. (eds) (2008) *The Future of the Dollar*. Ithaca, NY: Cornell University Press.

James, H. (2011) 'International Order after the Financial Crisis', *International Affairs*, 87(3): 525–537.

Polanyi, K. (1944/1957) *The Great Transformation*. Boston, MA: Beacon Press.

Starrs, S. (2013) 'American Economic Power Hasn't Declined – It Globalized! Summoning the Data and Taking Globalization Seriously!', *International Studies Quarterly*, 57(4): 817–830.

Strange, S. (1971) *Sterling and British Policy: A Study of a Currency in Decline*. London: Oxford University Press, for the Royal Institute of International Affairs.

Strange, S. (1987) 'The Persistent Myth of Lost Hegemony', *International Organization*, 41(4): 551–574.

Thimann, C. (2008) 'Global Roles of Currencies', *International Finance*, 11(3): 211–245.

Wolf, E. (1982) *Europe and the People without History*. Berkeley: University of California Press.

8

THE ROLE OF IDEAS

Western liberalism and Russian left conservatism in search of international hegemony

Elena Chebankova

Ideational factors in sustaining hegemony

Hegel claimed the Absolute (the eternal spirit) elevates some states to a position of 'world historical hero', grants those states a moment of geopolitical glory, and then that same spirit forces them to fade from the historical scene (Pinkard 2002). Indeed, many areas of the world have experienced periods of geopolitical triumph by building impressive empires and ruling vast landmasses before eventually losing such positions to new claimants. Eschewing the Hegelian explanation of the eternal *spirit*, which factors have been decisive in the rise and fall of such empires? From a rationalist perspective, it could be argued that, while economic and military factors play an important role in constructing world hegemonies, ideational components exert a significant, if not decisive influence. In most cases, world leaders had economic and military resources to maintain their hegemony, but were undermined by ideational limitations. These included the corrosion of spiritual consolidation within society, the dissolution of a base consensus on core values, internal corruption, the breakdown of consensus among the domestic elite, and changes in the political and ideational environment in the wider world.

A closer look at military and economic factors points to their dependence on ideational aspects. The military dimension of hegemony, for example, necessitates a state of exception in which war becomes a possibility and during which the sacrifice of life may sensibly be demanded. Such a *political* (in Schmittian terms) state of affairs calls for the elite's ideological commitments to advance their hegemonic plans and to request their citizens' readiness to die in defence of the community. Equally, it demands an adequate level of public commitment and trust to volunteer one's life for the benefit of the community. Economic hegemony can hardly be seen as fully fledged hegemony as in general terms it contains an anti-political force. The unimpeded pursuit of economic freedoms creates a world of mere

DOI: 10.4324/9781003037231-8

entertainment, illusory comfort and hedonism; it devalues the meaning of human life and threatens to reduce humanity to the Hobbesian 'ideal of civilisation' – one in which humanity becomes a partnership between 'production and consumption' (Meier 2006, 34). In its logical conclusion, personal freedoms move to an increasingly borderless, self-indulgent, transitory and commitment-free plane. Such a society becomes open to manipulation and unable to resist the tyranny of external and domestic claimants. It is powerless to assert world hegemony as a result.

From this perspective, hegemony is achieved mainly via the ability of a particular civilisation to invoke a positive response to its core values in the rest of the world, to become a metaphysical inspiration, an example to follow, and a rival to envy. In Fichtean terms, it is the ability to produce and advance a specific *Kultur* (culture, ideology, and metaphysical environment) that will exert a claim on discursive hegemony, establish a specific 'regime of truth' (Foucault), and produce knowledge that appeals to the compelling desire of humans to resolve existential issues such as 'the nature of ... happiness and reality' (Berlin 2002, 32–3). A reliance on ideational factors as sites of domination, resistance and change represents, according to Lévi-Strauss, a universal condition of humankind that sustains all human societies, be it the modern Western community or beyond (Giddens 1979, 21; Harkin 2009, 45–6). Claims over the authorship of hegemonic ideas grants countries, civilisations and cultures the ability to take hold of intellectual, cultural, and economic leadership (Ikenberry and Kupchan 1990, 285–6; Keohane 1984).

Discursive ideas were agents of the rise and fall of civilisational hegemony well before the Age of Communication and the Industrial Revolution. A brief look at history sustains this. Dissemination of Christianity, Islam, and Confucianism had a decisive impact on the evolution of different world civilisations (Fukuyama 2015, 534–5). European crusades to Jerusalem and the Eastern Roman Empire led to the emergence of Thomism, scholasticism and the adoption of the Justinian legal code which ultimately fuelled the developments of the Renaissance, Reform of the Church and Industrial Revolution – ideas that subsequently secured Western accession to world hegemony (Frankopan 2013; Herrin 2007; Meyendorff 1989). Advances in the communication technologies of the twenty-first century significantly facilitated the interchange of knowledge and made the entire political process ever more dependent on the discursive mapping of historical and spatial redistributions.

The contemporary West and the crisis of hegemony

Western Europe began to secure its discursive and civilisational hegemony from the fifteenth century onward. Admittedly, the West still enjoys a leading position in the economic and military spheres. At the same time, a range of ideological and political dilemmas are currently chasing the Western world from its hegemonic heights. While the Western intellectual tradition encompasses different lines of thought, the liberal trend lent its tenets to the foundations of the contemporary moral, political and institutional timber of the West. At the same time, the twentieth century unfolded under the banner of anti-liberalism, or liberal revisionism. Liberalism was seriously challenged by fascism and communism, as well as various non-totalitarian centre right and centre left collectivist doctrines, intellectually upheld by Joseph Schumpeter and Karl Polanyi. These competitors, however, left the political scene one by one during the course of the twentieth century. Fascism collapsed at the end of World War Two. The political and institutional waning of socialism, communism and other forms of collectivism occurred between the 1970s and 1990s. Ideological disaffection with Soviet socialism within the USSR and the rest of the Warsaw Pact countries made a significant contribution to the fall of the Berlin Wall in 1989, as well as the collapse of communist states in Eastern Europe and the fall of the Soviet Union in 1991.

Around the same time, neoliberalism emerged as the triumphant public doctrine to inform policy in Western society and soon conquered global hegemonic discourse. Liberalism was viewed not as just another ideology but as an endogenous part of behaviour informing human conduct. The ideas of liberalism have been proclaimed as leading to the most effective economic growth and social development. The application of any other ideological doctrine was regarded as 'fanciful, utopian and fraught with highly damaging unintended consequences' (Gamble 1996, 5–10). The Western realm, as the politico-institutional heartland of the liberal doctrine, has become a natural leader and political mentor to other states wishing to join the 'correct' way of social development. At the same time, the demise of existing ideological alternatives has been fraught with various forms of ideological tyranny that, in the long run, began to dampen the liberal victory – and with it the Western grip on global ideational hegemony.

What is responsible for this possible tyranny? David Runciman (2006, 25–6) foresaw the emergence of oppression from within the realm of the modern nation-state; a force that will attempt to harness increasingly aloof and non-committed liberal citizens to its political and ideational logic. However, one could argue that the idea of the modern nation-state has been significantly redefined since the end of World War Two and that the nation-state itself has been in danger of rising ideological oppression and control. The watershed event was the adoption of the Universal Declaration on Human Rights by the United Nations in 1948. Here, it was admitted that there are universal matters more important than the sovereignty of a particular state. This signified a shift from the Hobbesian idea of the state as an imaginary being that represents historical territory, its people, its leaders, and its particular institutions to a supra-national mechanism dependent on international bureaucracy and the overarching ideology of human rights. The latter began to manipulate the modern nation-state to act in its interest and to advance its political and economic agenda.

In this light, Foucault (1991, 90–1) draws a theoretical distinction between the state and government. The *reason of the state* is primarily concerned with the exercise of sovereignty, while the reason of a government is responsible for managing the well-being of its citizens, setting the rules for the growth of its population, and other practical matters. In the contemporary context the state and the government enter into a form of existential conflict in which sovereignty becomes at odds with the interests of global business and international organisations. The rapid growth of such organisations together with the global reach of multinational corporations led to the expansion of instruments by which such actors could influence, manipulate and even coerce the state via the instrument of government. By the end of the 1990s the practical application of new liberalism had begun to stagger and the consequences of that process have become evident. New forms of soft tyranny exercised in thought control, political manipulation, the production of ideational simulacra, and political hypocrisy have surfaced. This model has threatened Western hegemony and inflicted damage on its global moral authority. The West experienced this process on four separate planes involving the economic, ideological and social spheres.

First, economic crises and radical redistribution of wealth towards the rich revived debates on the nature of contemporary capitalist society. Liberalism can only exist within the bounds of the market economy generating significant economic inequality. Liberals welcome this inequality as an instrument of innovation and growth although they argue that this political structure must guarantee equal access to the economic system. The equality of such access became highly problematic because, in the apt observation by Francis Fukuyama (2015, 464–6), political and economic elites sought to convert their wealth into unequal political influence. Since the launch of neoliberal reforms, excessive monopolisation of power coupled with extreme socio-economic inequality became the main challengers to the stability of the Western political system. It drained the attractiveness of the Western way of life and undermined its socio-political myth as to the overall richness, prosperity and wealth of the so-called 'golden billion'.

From this perspective, classical liberalism is still viewed in Voltaire's original sense as an appreciation of personal autonomy understood as the absence of external arbitrary interference implemented with impunity. At the same time, it is also regarded as an ideology that originated with the birth of modernity, obtained some universal purchasing power during the course of its life and had ceased to be the unique property of the West by the end of the twentieth century. *Contemporary* liberalism (or neoliberalism), on the other hand, has been increasingly seen as a distinct Washington Consensus product. Hence, it is often narrated in rather crude terms as an institutional and value system that serves the interests of global financial and industrial capital. It is also seen as a system that submerges multiple aspects of human life to the economic needs of the market. Among those are the foundational principles of modern social existence such as a broad education, social solidarity, commitments to local and national community, social justice and cultural preservation. From this angle, liberalism is experiencing difficulties with its discursive hegemony in both Western and non-Western realms. The Trump presidential victory, as well as the successful performance of the maverick Democratic candidate Bernie Sanders, was not accidental. The same could be said of radical European parties on both the right and left ends of the political spectrum. These developments demonstrate a serious disaffection among ordinary people with their political leaders as well as the extant political system.

Second, contemporary Western discourse shifted from its original liberal, and in many ways idealistic, ambition of promoting a value neutral state that ensures the survival of differing ideas of the good life. This was seen in the political and media marginalisation of non-liberal and traditionalist lifestyles pursued by the political liberals. From this point of view, the neoliberal state began to exercise thought control via the politics of political correctness, identity and toleration resulting in self-censorship among those who shared traditionalist principles. This in turn raised doubts about the extent to which an individual could exercise a choice between meaningful alternative lifestyles. Carl Schmitt's observation that within liberal society an individual is left alone to be 'his own priest … his own poet, his own philosopher, his own king, and his own master-builder in the cathedral of his personality' (cited in McCormick 1997, 20) seems dated now. Demands placed on a person to search for 'individual self-expression' and 'identity' developed into a mass phenomenon that has pushed liberal society to the brink of becoming a mass-based society.

Third, the traditional morality of modernity, which had been the crux of the moral attraction of the West since the Enlightenment, began to give way to new forms of postmodern morality. In the wake of this process, the nature of liberal morality has made a transition from the *Morality of Right* (Recht or *Droit*) into the *Morality of Emancipation* (Lukes 1985).[1] While the classical liberal state claims to pursue the morality of right, its postmodern version has concerned itself with the morality of emancipation. This was seen in the furthering of the rhetoric of *lifestyle* or *self-actualisation* and brought various political, economic and social minorities to the centre of public discourse (Giddens 1998, 156).

It is also important that while the morality of emancipation is *originally* Marxist, its contemporary postmodern left liberal legacy exhibits some crucial differences. The object of emancipation is different in both cases. The new process of emancipation is mainly concerned with 'subaltern minorities' instead of the Marxian masses of exploited classes. Contemporary liberal discourse has focused mainly on emancipating an individual *from* various forms of oppressive collective identities. Dispensing with these redundant identities served the needs of a rapidly growing global capitalism. Among these 'oppressive' identities have been nationality, culture, ethnicity, gender, family, food preference, age group, and several others. And while the new liberal morality of emancipation cast aside the notion of class struggle, it nevertheless adopted the very Marxist idea of shaking the bondage of history and changing our traditional understanding of human nature to fit new economic and socio-political realities. Modern assumptions about human physical capabilities, attitudes to work, home, locality and family life have been significantly recast.

Consequently, ideological rigidity and a single-minded obsession with the defence of 'cultural diversity' and minority rights tends to reduce Western liberalism to its most radical agenda. This moral environment opens the floodgates to irrationalism and fanaticism and also induces the desire for a stronger state to enforce newly obtained freedoms, as per Erich Fromm's suggestions. It also silences far more important issues confronting the Western world, which as Christopher

Lasch (1995, 91) observes, include 'the crisis of competence, the lack of genuine beliefs in institutions, the spread of apathy; the fear of speaking one's mind due to the universal enforcement of politically correct language and thought' (see also Glazer 1987).

Fourth, the crisis of leadership forms part of this larger picture and seriously impacts the hegemony of the West. The contemporary climate pushes out inspiring intellectuals and outstanding leaders on the fringes of the political process. Figures like Henry Kissinger and the late Zbigniev Brzezinski began to represent rapidly vanishing exceptions among the contemporary cohort of Western politicians. Instead, careerists and mediocre conformists climbed up the political ladder. This contrasts with the period of high modernity during which intellectuals secured a tight grip over the political process and consolidated Western intellectual hegemony. François Guizot, John Stuart Mill, William Gladstone, Benjamin Disraeli and Woodrow Wilson were all outstanding intellectuals and produced academic and literary works of the highest quality (Mezhuyev 2018). In the contemporary world, however, intellectuals of that calibre are removed from public echelons of political power. Systematic research into this problem shows that the government is the last place where intellectuals wishing to effect socio-political, economic and ideational change choose as the field of their professional activity (Light 2008, 126; Volker 1989 and Volker 2003; Fukuyama 2015, 460). Fukuyama (2015, 461) argues that the American bureaucracy has moved away from the Weberian ideal of an energetic, motivated, talented, well-educated and mission-driven cohort. The system no longer employs people who are motivated by the ideals of service or any other idealistic considerations.

These developments have serious repercussions on the validity of the ideational doctrine that informed much of Western foreign and domestic policy as well as its discursive hegemony in the global arena. Clearly, the Western world is undergoing what Gramsci branded a 'conjuncture' moment, in which elites are trying to cling to their carefully constructed political order, though the public is deeply sceptical about its nature. At the same time, countries dominated by non-liberal collectivist and traditionalist public doctrines began to present a challenge to Western-style technocratic government and demonstrated impressive economic growth. A number of alternative developmental patterns have emerged and the erstwhile argument as to the variety of world civilisations has resurfaced. Indeed, as civilisational paradigms become more subjective, the Western liberal 'regime of truth' seems to have exhausted its professed universality. A large number of non-Western countries and regions such as Japan, Turkey, Latin America have begun to drift away from the Western geopolitical orbit, while Iran, Russia and China have once again begun to emerge as serious contenders to international hegemony.[2]

Russia's claims to alternative hegemony

At this point I would like to focus on the nature of those alternative claims to Western liberal hegemony. Let me select Russia as a potential contender for the holder of global (or regional) hegemonic discourse. It is important to note at the outset that Russia's political scene is divided into two separate streams: pro-Western liberal and traditionalist. The first group does not seek to challenge Western hegemony and is eager to follow cultural, ideological and economic suit of the Euro-Atlantic community. The traditionalist group, however, actively constructs counter-hegemonic discourse. It seeks to challenge Western intellectual hegemony and confront it at the level of politics and civil society, both domestic and international. Many thinkers falling into the second group roam broadly over various metaphysical theories of the West and seek to develop an alternative to the existing international political order. Their critique outspokenly focuses on the problematic aspects of contemporary Western development outlined above and proposes alternative cultural solutions which we will treat in detail below. A large number of such thinkers form public opinion via electronic media, discussion clubs, educational institutions, and a number of governmental agencies and social movements. Sergey Glaziev and Andrey Belousov were former consultants to the president on economic matters. Sergey Kurginyan actively participates in political processes and helps in forming Russia's discursive agenda. Evgeny Spitsyn, Mikhail Delyagin and Mikhail Khazin all exert influence on the media and educational institutions. There is a large number of such thinkers in the realm of cinematic art and literature. Their median ideological inclination is to combine the ideas of social justice and human development with the Christian moral imperatives that created Western European civilisation. It is hoped that such discourse could attract the rest of the world spiritually and make Russia a beacon of hope defending humanity and traditional cultures.

This proposal combines both left and conservative ideas. The ideas of social justice, equality, economic redistribution, reification of men and liberation from capitalist imperialism represented the left side of its story, while the traditional lenience towards Abrahamic morality and Mosaic law and the insistence on cultural distinctiveness stood for the conservative side of the spectrum. Soviet thinkers enshrined this complex idea in the Moral Code of the Builder of Communism with its general assumptions about the nature of human conduct. Contemporary Russian thinkers follow this left conservative stance by openly declaring their desire to adhere to traditionalist morality – and also some core principles of European modernity – while at the same time advancing the socialist idea of emancipating human beings from the chains of economic oppression. Let us examine the 'left' and 'conservative' elements of Russia's contemporary philosophical critique.

The idea of emancipation of humans represents its foremost left-leaning ingredient. Returning to our earlier distinction between the Morality of *Recht* (Droit) and Morality of Emancipation, these distinct moral dynamics buttress the right and left ethical paradigms respectively. Left-leaning ideas are founded in the cardinal trajectories of emancipation, while right-leaning perceptions pursue the procedural commitments to rights that remain indifferent to inequality. The idea of emancipation goes hand in hand with the idealistic treatment of humans and feeds into the left-leaning spectrum of the contemporary Russian idea. Indeed, Maxim Gorky's famous phrase 'mankind that sounds proud' became their existential motto. However, a closer look at the nature and the object of emancipation returns a more nuanced picture and divorces Russia's left *conservatism* from the left (or social in the US terminology) *liberalism* emanating mainly from the West. Both these left-leaning ideas share the same methodological source. Namely, the constructivist rationalism which praises human reason and sets forth belief in the power of knowledge, human will and the possibility of reconstructing human society and its institutions to eradicate social evils such as poverty, violence, and ignorance (Gamble 1996, 32–3).

Such rationalism is focused on creating a 'new' type of 'emancipated' individual. At the same time, the left conservative endeavour mainly relies on past human experiences and accounts for physical realities, human contingencies and appeals to idealistic creative tasks. The left liberal variant, on the other hand, focuses on the material, sensual and bodily aspects of the changes around intersectional issues of lifestyle, ethnicity, race and gender liberation. Gamble (1996, 33) argues that constructivist rationalism at large originated in the nineteenth-century British liberalism that laid the foundation for socialism in the twentieth century. Gamble's theorisations, however, must be refined. We should instead claim that two types of 'socialism' have emerged from this nineteenth-century doctrine: liberal-leaning 'socialism' and conservative-leaning 'socialism'.

The left conservative variant of emancipation also concerns itself with the task of liberating humans from the chains of global capitalism that, in conjunction with technical progress, aims to subvert humanity to its practical needs. Western liberalism, it is argued, has learned how to develop in the realm of technical progress, but has not learned how to develop a human being alongside such progress. Instead, contemporary Western ideologues seek to harness human anthropology to the needs of the market, economic and technical progress, which will inevitably result in a diminishing population and extreme inequality – economic as well as physical. Rapidly globalising markets require highly effective and highly mobile labour that can quickly relocate to different parts of the world to follow the movement of capital. Globalising capitalism also seeks to reduce the world population to match the rapid mechanisation of the production process. Advancing various forms of lifestyle emancipation politics becomes fundamental to such tasks. Russia's left argue that this kind of political dynamic considers profit and capital as the highest value and expresses contempt towards humanity. This approach turns human beings into an instrument of enrichment, a tool for gaining power and votes, or a mere servant of capital and property. At the same time, humans are being fooled by the market-enabling simulacra of emancipation of the left liberal nature, which detract from the practical dangers facing humanity. In other words, humanity is being taken away from people using the very slogans of humanism (Kurginyan 2018).

Russian left conservatism appeals to the desire to liberate humans from the dictum of globalising markets. This endeavour comes across as a claim to counter-hegemony for it has an air of hope for masses of ordinary people around the world.

Education comes across as the main instrument of this plan. The Soviet educational system was praised for producing world-leading scientists in the fields of natural sciences. It also ensured that ordinary Soviet people had an impressive breadth of knowledge. From this point of view, higher-quality education – away from the market-driven European 'Bologna' system – is considered a primary aspect of human emancipation. Left conservatism aspires to promote the exercise of 'higher pleasures', understood in J.S. Mill's view as metaphysical aspirations for intellectual, scientific, artistic and professional achievements. Indeed, J.S. Mill's initial assessment of man as a progressive being was responded to in subsequent left conservative theories on human intellectual growth and self-mastery, as well as corresponding socialist policies towards the development of human talent.

Let us discuss purely conservative aspects now. Conservatism is normally pre-occupied with community and tradition; it is also a standpoint (rather than a value-package) political ideology that strives to preserve some existing state of affairs (Huntington). From this perspective, Russian ideologues insist on some inviolable moral principles (usually derived from Abrahamic religions) that individuals must follow. These thinkers single out faith and family as two important conservative ideals that in their mind form the cornerstone of European civilisation. Family, as the most effective disseminator of conservative values, was considered a particularly important institution that could defend the state and ensure public obedience during the nineteenth and first half of the twentieth century. In early modernity, family was often likened to the state and was deployed in defence of the institution of monarchy, as seen in Robert Filmer's work (Pateman 1988, 77–115).

Faith was another conservative value that reinforced public order. As Hayek rightly notes, only those religions that promoted *family* and *property* were able to survive into the modern European era (Gamble 1996, 30). The situation began to change by the middle of the twentieth century. The introduction of the institution of unlimited credit and unlimited consumption during the 1960s and 1970s ensured those values were no longer needed to defend public order. Hence, they were to be reconstructed to accommodate new social realities (Khazin 2018). The conservatism of Russia's left-wing thinkers is also evident through their tireless defence of the core principles of modernity. These include the nation-state, will to reason and the social-democratic economic welfare package that was adopted in modern European states during the twentieth century, but is now gradually being dismantled by the neoliberals.

Finally, the merger between the left and conservative ideals is seen in the striving for universal solidarity and peace among humans albeit based on the principles of mutual recognition of cultures, traditions, and civilisational differences. On the one hand, it is the recognition of equality and solidarity; on the other, it admits the importance of culture, community and tradition. Russian left conservatism follows the writings of Nikolay Danilevsky and Nikolay Strakhov, Arnold Toynbee, Oswald Spengler, Ferdinand Braudel and Samuel Huntington with its claims that the world is composed of different civilisations whose institutions, customs and habits have been formed throughout generations. Hence, existing social arrangements within those civilisations reflect the experience of multiple individuals whose cumulative wisdom is higher than that of any particular individual proposing to radically reform one or another society to suit the experience of more economically developed communities. Russia's left conservatives believe the notion of civilisational difference translated into the multipolar world order doctrine would give Russia a chance to become a new moral authority in the international arena. This facet of left conservative thinking has been internalised by Russia's Foreign Policy Concept in 2016 (The Foreign Policy Concept of the Russian Federation 2016). As opposed to the Western realm that demands countries to follow their ideological doctrines in order to forge positive economic and political relations, Russia offers to keep economics, politics and culture strictly separate and allows countries freedom to choose their cultural and ideational path. This feature represents a potential point of attraction for the rest of the world, which could give Russian foregin policy a fair chance in challenging the extant Western hegemony.

Links to Western modernity

Russia's left conservative thinking is lodged in the overarching Western civilisational matrix of modernity, yet draws on its subordinate counter-discursive dimensions. Let us examine this matrix. Figure 8.1 illustrates redistribution of the most significant ideologies, although we must bear in mind that such water-tight examples do not exist in real-life politics. The left–right axis runs horizontally. It depicts the aforementioned difference between ideas of emancipation coupled with social justice and discourse on rights coupled with procedural commitment to legal equality. The vertical axis distinguishes between liberal and conservative realms.

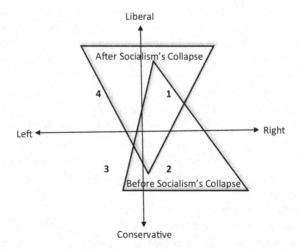

FIGURE 8.1 Distribution of Ideological Variants in the Western Ideational Matrix.

Let us assume here that liberalism seeks to remove external constraints on individual conduct and ensure that society is engaged in granting an ever-expanding range of rights to its participant members. Conservatism emphasises duties to community, shared tradition, solidarity and mutual obligation. The triangles symbolise the relative significance of the existing ideological quadrants during the twentieth and twenty-first centuries before and after the collapse of communism.

How was this modernist matrix formed? Western Europe passed through an important moment of metaphysical bifurcation during the Renaissance period. The dominant moral identity of Western modernity, as well as the prevailing conventions and dominant ideology of the era, were conceived during that time. The fateful choice was between two competing metaphysical bases: republican humanism (roughly located in Quadrant 3) and juridical liberalism (located in Quadrant 1) (Tully 1988, 17). The latter secured the position of a dominant ideology, while the former has become a subordinate counter-ideology. Among many nuances that separate these two systems, the idea of freedom buttressing the subsequent development of polity seems the most important. Juridical liberalism sought to grant the maximum number of individuals equal access to the maximum number of rights. Such a path to freedom is linked to the contemporary idea of negative liberty, which states that an individual needs to be left alone without external interference to pursue his/her happiness to the best possible outcome. This approach suited the nascent bourgeoisie of the early industrial age (Skinner 2002), yet it is also responsible for the nihilistic crisis of today, which we discussed above. The focus on liberal rights, liberties, free market and a compact state is evident, and this dominant discourse of modernity falls into the liberal right category located in Quadrant 1.

The humanist alternative sees freedom in satisfying a psychological need of humans to be part of a social structure and to exhibit virtues such as courage, responsibility, nobility and prudence. This approach assumed that certain duties needed to be performed at the expense of purely individual and private ends if freedom were to be assured to all community members. This ideology also aims to achieve greater equality among individuals. Initially, it sought to break the links between noble heritage and virtue with the ideas of Thomas More being the prime example. Here, we are able to trace both left and conservative inclinations of this thought and can place such discourse in Quadrant 3. Quadrants 2 and 4 are complementary to the first two. Left liberal Quadrant 4 emerged as the postmodernist offspring of Quadrant 1 and shares most of its globalist, rights-focused agenda. It emphasises social justice understood mainly in the intersectional cultural identity terms. Quadrant 2 also focuses on solidarities, duties and traditions, yet it is concerned with the procedural idea of merit more than with the striving for justice and emancipation.

Until the collapse of communism at the end of the twentieth century, Quadrants 1, 2 and 3 were at the apex of Western political discourse. Right liberal and right conservative options, however, occupied the political mainstream in the West, with left conservatism acting as a subordinate challenger. At the same time, with all its successes and shortcomings, Quadrant 3 has been adopted by nearly one-third of the planet and was clear in the political rhetoric of the USSR, states within the Soviet sphere of influence, political practice of Scandinavian socialism, the ideational rhetoric of Eurocommunism as well as Latin American Salvador Allende and others. The situation changed with the demise of the Soviet Union. Right liberal ideology (Quadrant 1) consolidated its dominant position in the guise of the globalist neoliberalism of Thatcher, Reagan and similar types. The main axis of the political mainstream switched to a dialogue between Quadrants 1 and 4, thereby supressing the prior importance of Quadrant 2. Contemporary Quadrant 2 represents the nation-state focused alternative to globalist liberalism and is currently reflected in contemporary right-wing and nationalist parties in Europe and the Make America Great Again movement in the United States. It was the collusion between Quadrants 1 and 4 that propelled the backlash of this Right-Conservatism in its most radical version. Curiously, contemporary left conservatism stands as an alternative to left and right liberalism and forms a situational alliance with right-conservatism.[3]

The final aspect of this discussion, however, pertains to the ability of the world to remain within the existing ideological quadrants of modernity. Pitirim Sorokin in his *Social and Cultural Dynamics* distinguished three types of human societies: ideational (spiritual, rigorous, and doctrine-oriented); idealistic (encompassing scholastic revision of doctrine to match material realities); and sensate (in which bodily and material functions have been liberated from the constraints of a spiritual soul). These types follow each other in strict sequence. It means that when our current sensate, materialist world loses its discursive hegemony, it must be followed by some rigorous ideational doctrine. The nature of this doctrine is unclear. It might grow organically out of the totalitarian inclinations of left liberal Quadrant 4 or appear in an entirely new ideational guise. One fundamentally different route could lie in the adoption of an entirely new and previously unexplored matrix. Russia's proposed option to meaningfully explore Quadrant 3 represents a mere perpetuation of Western modernist idealism and it is far from clear whether this possibility is still on the table.

Conclusion

This discussion has shown that ideational factors play a crucial role in creating world hegemonies. It has also been argued that recent decades revealed the crisis of liberalism as the core ideology buttressing the West's victory over the world's hegemonic discourse. Economic factors raised a range of existential ideological dilemmas, while customisation of the formerly inviolable values and assumptions on human conduct around the needs of the global market and political goals of international elites fuelled further scepticism. In this environment, alternative centres of power began to emerge. Ideologically, large segments of Russian discourse proposed a left conservative doctrine that claims to mitigate the dilemmas of contemporary liberalism and assert new claims to discursive hegemony. At the same time, the extent to which the Russian ideational doctrines could become a new hegemonic alternative is questionable. As we have seen, Russia's left conservative theorising resembles a number of modern Western doctrines. From that perspective, Russia is mainly proposing a return to the Western ideational positions that were relevant during the mid-twentieth century. The nature of the subsequent trajectory of this return remains open, as does the practical success of such hegemonic claims.

Notes

1 To clarify, the former is concerned with ensuring the rights of men as members of civil society and with granting everyone equal economic and civil liberties (Marx and Engels 1848, 162). Morality of Right originates from the ideals of the 1789 French Revolution and the Civil Code developed by Napoleon. The Civil Code, or the Code Napoleon, guaranteed property rights, called for legal equality, and invoked the principles of social mobility (Fukuyama 2015, 15–8). This morality laid the foundation for the modern bureaucratic machine in Europe and represented a feature of a broad European socio-political consensus. Significantly, this type of morality has a distinct liberal foundation. Morality of emancipation, on the other hand, takes its source from Marx and refers to the liberation of large masses of population from the chains of injustice, inequality and servitude. It is aimed at the creation of free people liberated from the bondage of history, culminated in the idea of exploitation. It also refers to the ideal of social unity and individual self-realisation.
2 There is an argument that both Japan and Turkey actively search to balance their involvement in the Western orbit by more active cooperation with Russia, Iran, China and other South-East Asian nations in the spheres of energy and trade. Equally, both countries have some serious left-wing opposition. Japanese left-wing opposition, in particular, represents the third largest party in the country and argues in favour of greater cooperation with Russia and lesser involvement with the United States.
3 With this in mind, it comes as no surprise that Trump finds an affinity with Putin in that they could be viewed as situational ideological allies in their existential struggles with liberals.

References

Berlin, I. (2006) *Political Ideas in the Romantic Age*. Oxford: Oxford University Press.

Foucault, M. (1991) 'Governmentality', in G. Burchell, C. Gordon and P. Miller (eds), *The Foucault Effect: Studies in Governmentality*, Hemel Hempstead: Harverster Whatsheaf, 87–227.

Frankopan, P. (2013) *The First Crusade: The Call from the East*. London: Vintage Books.

Fukuyama, F. (2015) *Political Order and Political Decay*. London: Profile Books.

Gamble, A. (1996) *Hayek. The Iron Cage of Liberty*. Cambridge: Polity Press.

Giddens, A. (1979) *Central Problems in Social Theory: Action, Structure and Contradiction in Social Analysis*. Berkley: University of California Press.

Giddens, A. (1998) *The Consequences of Modernity*. Cambridge: Polity Press.

Glazer, N. (1987) *Affirmative Discrimination: Ethnic Inequality and Public Policy*. Cambridge, MA: Harvard University Press.

Harkin, M. (2009) 'Lévi-Strauss and History', in B. Wiseman (ed.), *The Cambridge Companion to Lévi-Strauss*, Cambridge: Cambridge University Press, 39–59.

Herrin, J. (2007) *Byzantium: The Surprising Life of a Medieval Empire*. London: Penguin Books.

Hindess, B. (1996) *Discourses of Power: From Hobbes to Foucault.* Oxford: Blackwell Publishers.

Ikenberry, G.J. and Kupchan, C.A. (1990) 'Socialisation and Hegemonic Power', *International Organisation,* 44(3): 283–315.

Keohane, R. (1984) *After Hegemony: Co-operation and Discord in the World Political Economy.* Princeton, NJ: Princeton University Press.

Khazin, M. (2018) 'V Mire Proizoshel Radikalnyi Slom Ideinoi Bazovoi Modeli', *Radonezh,* 2 January. Available at: http://radonezh.ru/recommend/mikhail-khazin-v-mire-proi zosh-l-radikalny-slom-ideynoy-bazovoy-modeli-177885.html (accessed 16 December 2019).

Kurginyan, S. (2018) 'Bolshoe Interview', in Vecher s Vladimirom Soloveyovym, 16 April. Available at: www.youtube.com/watch?v=ZYz0e340l8w (accessed 16 December 2019).

Lasch, C. (1995) *The Revolt of the Elites and the Betrayal of Democracy.* London: W. W. Norton and Company.

Light, P. (2008) *A Government III Executed: The Decline of the Federal Service and How to Reverse It.* Cambridge, MA: Harvard University Press.

Lukes, S. (1985) *Marxism and Morality.* Oxford: Oxford University Press.

Marx, K. and Engels, F. (1848) *Collected Works,* Vol. 6: *Manifesto of the Communist Party.* London: Lawrence and Wishart.

McCormick, J. (1997) *Carl Schmitt's Critique of Liberalism: Against Politics as Technology.* Cambridge: Cambridge University Press.

Meier, H. (1995) *Carl Schmitt and Leo Strauss: The Hidden Dialogue.* Chicago: The University of Chicago Press.

Meyendorff, J. (1989) *Byzantium and the Rise of Russia.* New York: St Vladimir's Seminary Press.

Mezhuyev, B. (2018) 'Idiotizatsiya Mirovoi Politiki Razbudit Zverinuyu Nenavist Intellektualov', ForPost. Novosti Sevastopolya, 31 May. Available at: https://sevastopol.su/point-of-view/idiotizaciya-mirovoy-politiki-razbudit-zverinuyu-nenavist-intellektualov (accessed 14 May 2020).

Pateman, C. (1988) *The Sexual Contract.* Cambridge: Polity Press.

Pinkard, T. (2002) *German Philosophy 1760–1860: The Legacy of Idealism.* Cambridge: Cambridge University Press.

Runciman, D. (2006) *The Politics of Good Intentions: History, Fear and Hypocrisy in the New World Order.* Princeton, NJ: Princeton University Press.

Skinner, Q. (2002) *Vision of Politics,* Vol. 1: *Regarding Method.* Cambridge: Cambridge University Press.

Sorokin, P. (1937–1985) *Social and Cultural Dynamics,* 4 vols. New York: American Book Co.

The Foreign Policy Concept of the Russian Federation (2016). Mid.ru (Ministry of Foreign Affairs), 1 December. Available at: www.mid.ru/en/foreign_policy/official_documents/-/asset_publisher/CptICkB6BZ29/content/id/2542248

Tully, J. (1988) *Meaning and Context: Quentin Skinner and His Critics.* Princeton, NJ: Princeton University Press.

Volker, P. (1989) *Rebuilding the Public Service.* Washington, DC: National Commission on the Public Service.

Volker, P. (2003) *Revitalising the Federal Government for the 21st Century.* Washington, DC: National Commission on the Public Service.

9

TWILIGHT OF HEGEMONY

The T20 and the defensive re-imagining of global order

Leslie A. Pal

There is widespread agreement that the prevailing, hegemonic world order is fragile and fractured (Acharya 2014). It was an order 'organized around American hegemonic authority, open markets, cooperative security, multilateral institutions, social bargains, and democratic community' (Ikenberry 2011: 193). The crisis can be seen as being of economic and political institutions, including American leadership, dominance and support (Bremmer 2018; Diamond, Plattner, and Walker, 2016; World Economic Forum 2018), or of liberal-democracy and cosmopolitan values (Deneen 2018; Eatwell and Goodwin 2018; Mounk 2018). This pessimism is now a matter of routine punditry, and long foretold, at least with respect to American dominance of that order (Keohane 1984). In a 12 July 2018 column in the *Washington Post*, Robert Kagan, a Senior Fellow at the Brookings Institution and no friend of the current American administration, wrote: 'The democratic alliance that has been the bedrock of the American-led liberal world order is unraveling. At some point, and probably sooner than we expect, the global peace that that alliance and that order undergirded will unravel, too. Despite our human desire to hope for the best, things will not be okay. The world crisis is upon us' (Kagan 2018).

This chapter takes the crisis of global hegemony as given, and focuses on how that hegemonic order is responding, primarily through how it is re-imagining itself. Defenders and re-imaginers are everywhere of course, within the media and academe, and even within governments that appear to be chaffing at the order (e.g. elements of the Trump administration). As we explain below, we take one network as our empirical example (the T20 network of global think tanks, and engagement group of the G20), and examine its evolution and contributions to global debates and reformulations. Its version of re-imagining of the current order consists of both a strong defence of core norms and their extension to broader inclusiveness and equity.

DOI: 10.4324/9781003037231-9

Hegemony: Defence and Re-imagining as 'neural networks'

Hegemonies in crisis do not go gentle into that good night. Definitions and debates over hegemony are rehearsed in other chapters in this book, but it has both material and non-material sources (Clark 2011). In this chapter we emphasise the non-material, or ideological dimension of hegemony, of how hegemonic orders legitimise themselves. This legitimacy is a key ingredient in defending and ratio-nalising the order (Gilpin 1987: 73) Hegemonies rely on a web of discursive rationales and norms, in this case in support of a 'liberal world order' with its normative, institutional and material foundations. When hegemony is at its zenith, these discursive rationales, even when they are routinely contested, appear as affir-mations of the system's obvious and unassailable logic. When hegemony is fragile and challenged, the discursive rationales have to be reconstituted, adjusted, revised and renovated in order to defend, not simply affirm. Some important recent work in international relations theory has focused on contestation of norms (Deitelhoff and Zimmermann 2013; Krook and True 2010; Lantis and Wunderlich 2018), but less so on overarching or hegemonic regimes. The question we address in this chapter is the nature of these defensive strategies in re-imagining the hegemonic world order.

How to locate discourses designed to defend, renovate and, if necessary, re-imagine the hegemonic order? The conventional research strategy would be to round up the usual suspects of global governance – the UN, the World Bank, World Economic Forum, the OECD, the IMF, etc. – and parse the speeches of their leaders and proponents. But the order, as a hegemonic one, was embedded in a complex network of international organisations and institutional processes, most of which reflected US and Western (broadly defined as the major developed economies) interests, but which were broader than the interests of a single hege-mon or even some peak organisations. A good example is the global trade regime – progressively freer trade at first was broadly supported by the US because it served its interests, but once embedded in the world system could be used to the advan-tage of other emerging economies as well, China being the textbook example. Now that the US faces some serious competitors in that system, it is pushing to change it (attacking the WTO, pulling out of TPP), and the system (the institu-tions that make it up, and those who support it both within and outside the US) is fighting back defensively.

The irony is that the old global hegemonic order, while initially American-led, became bigger than the US, and now must defend itself against a crisis partially initiated by American (Trumpian) assertiveness. But how does a 'global hegemonic order' respond to crisis, especially if the government of its leading member is part of that crisis? This chapter argues that we can conceive of the global order as containing a 'neural network' consisting of governments, international organisa-tions, think tanks, NGOs, universities, political parties and media who loosely but consistently 'think' and 'imagine' that order, and indeed constitute it through their publications and debates, their statements and re-statements of the order itself.

There is no central coordination to this messaging, but there is an emergent consistency that comes through the self-referential nature of the defensive networks, and their entanglements and overlaps and mutually reinforcing interactions (as we show below). A truly hegemonic world order, even a fragile one, will be supported by a deep and extensive 'neural network' of experts and analysts in traditional media (e.g. *The New York Times*), academe, think tanks and foundations, supplemented by platoons of like-minded NGOs. We use this metaphor of a neural network deliberately, in that it captures the distributed nature of ideas and how they flow and are shaped in support of a regime, with endless iterations, inconsistencies, debates and resolutions, producing not a single coherent ideological system of beliefs, but a synaptic flaring of ideas and concepts that create a conceptual justificatory space.

We think the notion of a 'neural network' is a useful rendering of how these discursive spaces function, but at the same time makes it difficult to isolate any uniquely influential quadrants or pathways – a neural network is complex, distributed and layered. An input like a Trump tweet or a Brexit vote will have the network firing and processing responses in cyclical, cascading and kaleidoscopic waves, usually first through media and Internet, and then subsequently among research centres, institutes, and other 'expert' opinion. But we can hypothesize that a global 'neural network', like the human brain, has concentrated locations that perform higher-order thinking functions, particularly the 'sense of self'.

A plausible example for this sort of network within the global neural network is the Think20 (T20), an 'engagement group' of the G20. The G20 has emerged 'in practice as well as proclamation, the centre of global economic governance for a globalized world' (Kirton 2013: 373).[1] We are not arguing that the T20 is somehow dominating global discourses, or superior to other more prominent venues like the World Economic Forum or the World Bank or the IMF. Rather, our argument is fourfold. First, because of its status as an engagement group to the G20, it has a proximity to a (if not the) key transnational organisation engaged in managing the global order. Second, its members and its connections (to the World Bank, the IMF, the OECD, etc.) give it a salience as a widely distributed network, designed to generate, debate, refine and project ideas to steer the world. Third, while it presents itself as a research network (which it certainly is), it also is a political one, dedicated to what it considers the self-evident principles of multilateralism and modern liberal-democratic capitalism. Fourth, while the T20 collectively defends and supports the hegemonic global order, it also works hard to critique and re-imagine it.

The next section provides background on the development of the T20 since its formalisation in 2012. It is followed by a discussion of the most recent global meetings of the network in May 2018 and March 2019 in Berlin within the context of the 'Global Solutions Summit', intriguingly subtitled 'The World Policy Forum'. Through a combination of document analysis and ethnographic observations, the chapter shows how the T20 and its positioning within a complementary network of supporting institutions are working to re-imagine the global order.

The T20: Origins and development

The G20 was established in 1999, in the wake of the Asian financial crisis of 1997, initially as a meeting of finance ministers and central bank governors of the '19 most systematically significant countries and the European Union' (Kirton 2013: 3). The 2008 financial crisis was the G20s watershed moment, a global shock to the hegemonic order of global capitalism that required a high-level global response. The 14–15 November 2008 G20 Summit in Washington was therefore the first with heads of government attending. The next was in London in 1–2 April 2009, and an 'Anglo-alliance' of representatives of leading think tanks (Brookings Institution, Peterson Institute, CIGI (Centre for International Governance Innovation)) were invited there to advise on the global stimulus package.

This injection of high-powered, international, think tank advice in 2009 was formalised three years later under the Mexican G20 presidency. The first T20 meeting had representatives from 17 well-established think tanks and academic institutions from 14 different G20 countries (Table 9.1).

In the first few G20 summits after its formation in 2012, the T20 remained on the sidelines. Germany assumed the presidency of the G20 for 2017, and delegated two German think tanks to coordinate the T20: the German Development Institute (Deutsches Institut für Entwicklungspolitik) (DIE), and the Kiel Institute for

TABLE 9.1 T20 attendees, Mexico City, Mexico, 27–28 February 2012

Organisation	Country
Centre for International Governance Innovation (CIGI)	Canada
Centre for Strategic and International Studies	Indonesia
China Institutes of Contemporary International Relations (CICIR)	China
Council on Foreign Relations	United States
Economic Policy Research Foundation of Turkey	Turkey
Foundation for International Relations and Foreign Dialogue	Spain
German Development Institute	Germany
Getulio Vargas Foundation	Brazil
Heinrich Boell Foundation	Germany
Japan Institute of International Affairs	Japan
Korea Development Institute	South Korea
Lowy Institute for International Policy	Australia
Mexican Council on Foreign Relations	Mexico
Nanyang Technological University	Singapore
Russian International Affairs Council (RIAC)	Russia
Stanford University	United States
Stanley Foundation	United States

the World Economy (Kiel Institut für Weltwirtschaft) (IfW). They knew, in broad terms, what the German Chancellery's priorities were, and so structured the T20 Task Forces in part around them. They also consulted the T20 members on what they thought the topics should be. The first T20 conference ('Cohesion in Diversity') was held on 1–2 December 2016. The conference brought together the T20 think tanks, but also experts and government officials, and so was more multistakeholder from the start than previous T20 exercises.

The T20 Task Force approach was introduced by the Germans in 2017, but then adopted (with modifications) by Argentina (2018) and Japan (2019). Table 9.2 shows the Task Forces for each T20 exercise. Japan as the G20 president in 2019 wanted to focus on ageing, given the country's demographics, and so this became a T20 focus as well (combined with immigration, not 'migration'). Gender equity and food security had been task force themes under Germany and Argentina, but disappeared under Japan. The change in tone was palpable: social justice and equity dropped off the formal agenda; economic and financing issues took their place. These shifts in agendas reflect the balance of the national priorities of the country that has assumed the presidency, and the sense of what the major collective global issues are that require attention. Given that the global economy was only gradually and fitfully recovering throughout this period, a sense of 'global crisis' remained the backdrop for discussions, soon to be supplemented by political shocks like Brexit and rising populist movements, parties and leaders. Combined, these appeared as grave challenges to the economic, political and normative foundations of the global order.

The German T20 Summit was held as part of the first Global Solutions Summit on 29–30 May 2017, and had over 1,000 attendees. The German chairs decided to organise a multistakeholder event, with presentations by the Task Forces balanced with feedback and discussion. The Summit was the culmination of the work of 12 Task Forces assembling 170 think tanks from around the world, yielding 75 policy briefs and over 300 authors. In principle, this all fed into the summary of recommendations submitted by the T20 chairs to the G20, entitled *20 Solution Proposals to the G20 from the T20 Engagement Group* (T20 Engagement Group, 2017).

These recommendations were framed within a 'new global vision' consisting of three elements: (1) learning to stabilise and manage the global commons (climate systems, interconnected financial systems, but also universal access to education, health and housing), (2) investments in social innovations leading to collaborative collection action, and (3) globalisation and global governance that is people-centred, focused on delivering global well-being, human flourishing and empowerment. Many of the more detailed elaborations of the recommendations were tilted in the social justice direction, emphasising fairness, equity, redistribution or service and support to lower-income groups and countries. Given the importance of this narrative 're-framing', we cite the relevant passage from the report at length. It clearly positions the G20s core priorities in terms of social discontent with globalisation, and the manifestations of that discontent in

TABLE 9.2 T20 Task Forces

Germany (2017)	Argentina (2018)	Japan (2019)
1. Future of Work	1. Future of Work and Education for the Digital Age	1. Future of Work and Education for the Digital Age
2. Climate Action and Infrastructure for Development	2. Climate Action and Infrastructure for Development	2. Climate Change and Environment
3. 2030 Agenda for Sustainable Development	3. 2030 Agenda for Sustainable Development	3. 2030 Agenda for Sustainable Development
4. Social Cohesion, Global Governance and the Future of Politics	4. Social Cohesion, Global Governance and the Future of Politics	4. Social Cohesion, Global Governance and the Future of Politics
5. Migration	5. Migration	5. Aging Population and its Economic Impact + Immigration
6. International Financial Architecture for Stability and Development	6. International Financial Architecture for Stability and Development	6. International Financial Architecture for Stability and Development/Crypto-assets and Fintech
7. Trade, Investment and Tax Cooperation	7. Trade, Investment and Tax Cooperation	7. Trade, Investment and Globalisation
8. Food Security and Sustainable Agriculture	8. Food Security and Sustainable Agriculture	8. Cooperation with Africa
9. Circular Economy	9. Cooperation with Africa	9. SME Policy faced with Development of Financial Technology
10. Cooperation with Africa	10. Gender Economic Equity	10. Economic Effects of Infrastructure Investment and its Financing
11. Gender Economic Equity		
12. Digital Infrastructure and Security		

populism and electoral backlash – all fundamental challenges to hegemony, though that term is never used:

> The fundamental mission of the G20 should be to promote the creation of a global framework of institutions, policies and norms that meet human needs. In particular, the G20 should support a world order in which evolving human needs – beginning with the most basic and urgent ones – are satisfied adequately through the workings of the world economy. In times when the success of well-managed economies is closely tied to societal success, it is appropriate for the G20 to focus on global economic management. When economic and social progress diverge, the G20 agenda needs to extend beyond purely economic concerns. (T20 Engagement Group, 2017, 4)

Argentina assumed the presidency of the G20 for 2018. The Argentinian T20 exercise produced more than 80 policy briefs, and also culminated in 20 key recommendations (T20 Argentina 2018). Those recommendations were prefaced with a 'Vision' focused on (1) cooperation to overcome the challenges to multilateralism, and (2) representativeness, diversity and flexibility. There were similar tropes and even similar formulations to the German global vision cited above, though a somewhat stronger emphasis on the balance between multilateralism and national distinctiveness.

This short history of the T20 to 2018 shows a network in rapid formation, with evolving and often quite plastic structures. The formalisation of the network continued in 2017–2019. After the successful T20 Summit in Berlin in 2017, the Kiel Institute decided to provide some institutional backbone to the T20 by continuing with annual event – the Global Solutions Summit (GSS) or World Policy Forum – that will be independent of the T20 but have many of the same players and provide what it calls a 'new, permanent supportive, advisory structure to the G20 and G7'. The GSS held in Berlin in May 2017 was almost entirely a T20 event. The second (28–29 May 2018) and third (18–19 March 2019), broadened out to be a wider forum (the World Policy Forum), and were sponsored by the Council for Global Problem Solving (CGP). The CGP was established in 2015, and was designed to run an annual GSS and to support the T20 process, but is distinct from it. It is a members-only group of 28 of the world's top think tanks, some academic institutions and government organisations.[2]

The CGP and the GSS are both embedded in the Global Solutions Initiative (GSI).[3] It builds on four 'interlocking innovations': (1) global research contribution: a global network of research institutions centred around the CGP, (2) implementation-oriented contribution: a solutions focus, bridging research and decision makers, (3) organisational continuity, and (4) narrative contribution: developing a joint understanding across stakeholders motivating solutions. The work of the GSI is to be channelled through Task Forces and Policy Briefs, which will be presented on the G20 Insights Platform (www.g20-insights.org/).

The GSI is an early experiment, and the T20 has challenges of coherence and impact, but their joint evolution in just a few years has been remarkable. The aspiration (*sotto voce*) clearly has been to create a sort of 'brains trust' (what we termed a neural network) for the G20, and perhaps more ambitiously, a generator and repository of ideas in defence of the achievements of the liberal hegemonic global order (again, the term hegemonic is not used). Its hope is to be truly global – its members are deliberately drawn from around the world, though anchored in the core of the CGP. It is not sector specific, and deliberately tries to weave together recommendations on economic policy with social and political advice as well. The effort has been framed within the development of a 'global vision' and a 'narrative' of the decoupling of social cohesion from economic prosperity. An opportunity to observe the network in action came with the Global Solutions Summit/T20 meetings in May 2018 and again in March 2019, in Berlin.[4]

Global solutions summits ('The World Policy Forum'), May 2018 and March 2019

The GSS is the Global Solutions Summit, with the subtitle of 'The World Policy Forum'. The March 2019 GSS also was a platform for T20 Task Force meetings, and presentation of some of the early research results, but less prominently than in 2018. The 2018 GSS had about 1,000 attendees with over 40 sessions; the 2019 version had almost 1,600 attendees and over 50 sessions. We offer some observations on organisational format and objectives, and on content and themes. The salient point however, in terms of the theme of this chapter, is that the GSS aspires to its name – 'global solutions'. It is a site for a particular network of organisations and actors to convene, discuss and propose solutions. As we show below, despite some differences of views and emphases, the attendees are fervent supporters of at least the core of the global order (i.e. multilateralism – not US dominance; cooperation; most international institutions; broadly liberal values; progressive capitalism; social and economic equity). They are appalled and perplexed by populism, which they instinctively equate with xenophobia, racism and authoritarianism. They are equally appalled and even infuriated by President Trump and all that he represents. They believe in globalism, and are searching for renovations and re-imaginings that will make its current manifestation work.

Organisational format and objectives

A good part of the two GSS was devoted to presenting the first results of T20 Task Force work and even some recommendations, though this was stronger in the 2018 event than in 2019. But if the GSS is in large part a T20 exercise, it could have been organised very differently, on a smaller and more focused scale. Why the wider ambition? Why a 'Summit'? The answer is that the Summits serve the larger purposes of legitimation, validation and amplification, of what we have termed re-imagining.

Both meetings of experts took place under the shadow of political factors. Panellists often noted that continued inequality and systemic shocks had generated political backlash against 'global elites'. But this of course was a meeting of those same elites. The GSS, as a larger forum than the T20, even if it was still a forum of elites, gave some sense of representational legitimacy. A large summit of this sort can also serve as an idea aggregator, and give more force and legitimacy to the T20 when it meets with the G20 sherpas. Policy advice on global economic steering, when the global economy is under political threat from populists, has to balance technical validity with political legitimacy. For expert venues like the GSS, the closest it can come to political legitimacy is the demonstration of strength in numbers, of representation, and some consensus on key issues. In 2019, much was made of Young Global Changers (YGC) – a programme that provided full scholarships to attend the GSS for 90 candidates selected from a pool of 3,500 applicants from 15 countries. This provided another type of legitimacy – cross-generational, multi-racial (several of the YGCs, who were usually invited to ask the first question after panel presentations, noted the lack of regional, racial, and gender diversity in the GSS and the need for 'more people who look like me' – a flagellation warmly received by the audience).

The wider ambition also served the objective of network building. This was explicit in the design of the CGP and in the promotion of the conferences as well, but we can add several less obvious dimensions to this. First, the network of T20 think tanks and research institutions is strengthened and extended through this exercise, but so is the strategic advantage and influence of the key players, as represented in the CGP. Second, beyond the core, the Summit can attract a periphery of networked actors who are outside the think tank world, but engaged in global issues and themselves linked to other institutions. One stated Summit ambition is to create and reinforce a 'global network of problem solvers'. Third, the Summit does serve as an echo chamber, as well as an amplifier. While at the policy level, there were Task Forces meetings, and specific recommendations in fields as different as the future of work and of climate change, there was also a common discourse among the participants. As an example (more below), there was an unquestioned support for multilateralism and (mostly) free trade, and a universal repugnance for populism and nationalism.[5] There was also a mutually reinforcing catechism of social concern for the poor and the excluded. Linking to the previous point on legitimation, this echo chamber effect helps amplify the Summit message – there is consensus on the virtues of multilateralism, the evils of nationalism, the decoupling of social and economic progress and the need for 'recoupling' (this was the explicit theme of the 2019 Summit). This consensus is the frame within which specific recommendations are then channelled to the G20 leaders. It also constitutes the results of an extended exercise in debating the global order, articulating both its value and its liabilities, and proposing ways to re-imagine it in policy terms. This became quite literal when participants were enjoined to come up with a new 'narrative' on globalism, to combat the competing (anti-globalist) populist narratives.

Content and themes

The substantive content of the 2018 Summit consisted primarily of the Task Force reports ('Key Policy Recommendations: Presented at the Global Solutions Summit 2018') and the T20 Concept Note ('T20 Argentina Concept Note: Proposals for a Productive, Inclusive and Sustainable World'). In 2018, the Task Force sessions took up over half the Summit, and consisted of presentations on policy briefs to date, and some tentative recommendations. These were reflected in the Concept Note, with preliminary proposals. It is impossible to summarise the lengthy list of detailed recommendations, but we can note their dual character. On the one hand, many of them were entirely conventional and uncontroversial. In the Concept Note, for example, under Recommendation #1 on 'Policies and commitments to promote equal opportunities for quality education', G20 leaders were urged to 'implement a set of comprehensive policies addressing curriculum, such as the implementation of teacher training and administering educational resources to develop labor and democratic skills'. On the other hand, there were signals and tonalities that were less 'conventional' and obvious, and registered in a key that spoke to anxieties about disruptions to the global order and to globalisation's own disruptions. Table 9.3 lists some of these.

We identify these as 'conventional' in the sense that they emanate from a conventional globalist, cosmopolitan and broadly social democratic world view. We would not characterise these as 'neoliberal' as the more left-wing critics of the G20 would – there is too much genuine concern about inequality and climate change. At the same time, there is a firm commitment to freer trade and deeper global economic integration, under the watchful eye of the G20 and other global institutions. More state action and spending are required in areas like infrastructure and climate change mitigation. Taxes on fossil fuels should be increased; green energy encouraged. Adjustments and policy interventions will be painful, but democratically achieved. If a label is needed for this world view, it might be 'technocratic inclusive liberal globalism'. This is the re-imagining of what a cooperative global order could look like.

The theme in 2019 was 'Recoupling Social and Economic Progress: Towards a Global Paradigm Change'. Dennis Snower, President of the GSI, once again gave the opening keynote, excoriating conventional economics and its emphasis on materialism and self-interest, urging 'recoupling' and 'paradigm change'. In the roundtable following his remarks, he was jokingly labelled a 'revolutionary', to somewhat uncomfortable laughter in the audience. Gabrielle Ramos, representing the OECD, made equally critical remarks about contemporary capitalism as not being sufficiently inclusive or people-centred (citing the OECD's work on 'New Approaches to Economic Challenges' (NEAC)). Data on inequality and fraying social cohesion were presented, and there were a number of explicitly labelled 'paradigm change' sessions (e.g. The Future of the Corporation; Toward New Economic and Moral Foundations for Capitalism; Globalisation and Vulnerability; Radical Uncertainty; Rethinking Society for the 21st Century).

TABLE 9.3 T20 Argentina proposals

No.	Proposal header	Unconventional/New/Anxieties
1	Policies and commitments to promote equal opportunities for quality education	• Develop 'democratic skills' – a counter to populism • Non-formal learning
2	The future of work will not be the same everywhere	• Technological change may generate 'significant job losses and greater inequality' • Policy solutions have to be tailored for different conditions in emerging and developing economies (e.g. inequality of Internet access)
3	The role of cities to mitigate climate change: a new urban paradigm and urban infrastructure	• Infrastructure focused on cities; low-carbon, climate-resilient cities
4	Addressing food security concerns through special arrangements between large net importer and exporter countries	• Create a special group of countries who are leading net exporters and importers of food
5	A commitment to a rule-based international trade system with mechanisms to compensate losers from trade	• Trade frictions increased noticeably in 2018 • Adjustment costs are large, and there is insufficient compensation for those who lose from trade • 'Call a stop' to unilateral trade restrictions • Enhance mobility of displaced workers (possibly globally and across borders)
6	A strong commitment to achieve gender economic equity	• Address unpaid care • Invest in care infrastructure • Maternity and paternity leave regimes to reach all families
7	Resource mobilisation through a fair international tax regime: End harmful tax competition and provide a level playing field for taxation and investment	• New phase of tax competition leading to a 'ruinous race to the bottom' • Introduce a minimum corporate tax rate • Agree on a consolidated corporate tax base (CCTB) and treat multinationals as single entities
8	Scaling up development finance for our common future	• Mobilise private capital for infrastructure development • Projects aligned to climate change mitigation strategies • More resources and better coordination among multilateral development banks (MDBs)
9	Moving forward on the 2030 Agenda	• Implementation of SDGs modest • Build stronger monitoring and reporting mechanisms

(continued)

TABLE 9.3 (*continued*)

No.	Proposal header	Unconventional/New/Anxieties
10	Developing green fiscal reform plans for just energy transitions	• Green fiscal reforms 'cannot be introduced directly' and 'a gradual and step-wise approach raises the political feasibility' • Adverse distributional impacts of higher energy prices
11	Global sustainable development will only be achieved if African economies are part of the consensus	• Trade structures are still 'disadvantageous' to African countries
12	Strengthening the global financial safety net	• Conduct a quota review of the Global Financial Safety Net, 'for this will favour the legitimacy, credibility and effectiveness of the IMF'
13	The crypto-assets experience: giving technology a chance without milking users nor investors	• The G20 should 'design a cross border framework to put Crypto-Assets (CA) on a regulatory level playing field with other financial instruments'

Source: T20 Argentina Concept Note: Proposals for a Productive, Inclusive and Sustainable World.

This world view suffused the Summit proceedings, providing a subterranean and consensual foundation that could then support any incidental disagreements over details. Some other core, if unspoken, ingredients of this world view were:

- Strong emphasis on a global commons, on global public policy challenges that affect all or most countries (climate change, global trading system, digital technologies and the global financial system).
- Importance of rules-based and institutionalised multilateralism, with its corollary of extreme antipathy to 'nationalism', which was equated with unilateralism and populism.
- Angst, but also some incomprehension, about rising populism (the 2018 Summit took place as a populist coalition government was being formed in Italy; the 2019 as Brexit was approaching on 29 March), which is connected to disturbing trends in the decline of democracy, the impact of social media, and rising authoritarianism.
- 'Recoupling' of social and economic prosperity. The 2018 theme had been 'decoupling'; the 2019 theme, logically enough, was 'recoupling', though spiced with the injunction for paradigm change.

An interesting theme of the 2018 Summit – in the light of our metaphor of a 'default network' – was an argument made by Dennis Snower in the opening keynote for a new 'narrative'. Recoupling would require, in part, a renewed popular social engagement and identification with multilateralism. To the extent that electorates and populations identify with localities, with nations, with their ethnic groups or religions, they are susceptible to nationalist and populist appeals. Counter-appeals have to be mobilised on the same terrain, a terrain that is not entirely or purely technical. In this sense, a global meeting of technocrats seemed to agree that technocratic solutions would not be enough – that hearts and minds need to be changed, and that technocratic solutions need to be framed in ways that resonate with popular feelings. This was carried over in the 2019 Summit, though in the form of a call for 'paradigm change'. While multilateralism was still defended, there were several panels where the individualism of conventional economics was attacked in favour of resuscitating communities, families, culture and values.

Colin Bradford (senior fellow Brookings Institution and one of the participants in the 2008 'Anglo-alliance' of think tanks mentioned above, and a highly respected figure in the T20 and G20 processes) summed up the consensus: '… systemic transformation is an imperative rather than one of several pathways to sustainability. Incrementalism, technical fixes, policy tweaks and marginal changes have run out of relevance' (Bradford 2019: 288).

Conclusion

The global order has not been overturned, even with the pandemic, but it is fragile, assaulted from all sides (even from within, with some leaders and electorates openly attacking its foundations), and perhaps in twilight until its sun can rise again. In the meantime, it has to be defended and re-imagined, and not just on the platforms of practice such as the GSS, but in academe as well (Mearsheimer 2018). But how does a hegemonic global order do this, when its leader, the United States in the person of Mr Trump, turns on that order? The key point is of course that the order – the leading members of that global order – consist of vast and distributed networks of complicit leaders across multiple sectors. If one member defaults, others can be expected to step up. For every Trumpian tweet, there will be waves of rebuttals from political leaders, leading organs of conventional wisdom, media stars, pundits, NGOs, CEOs and others. But these are all reflexive, like an amoeba recoiling instinctively from negative stimuli. A sophisticated defence of the hegemonic order requires deeper and more deliberate strategies and articulations.

Our approach in this chapter has been to focus on a newly emerged 'neural network' of think tanks in the T20, CGP and GSI nexus. It has the advantage of being directly connected to the leading instrument of global hegemonic leadership, the G20, and of being self-consciously designed to marshal deep and informed research to deal with global problems. The network was certainly constructed by design. Its leading members (now the members of the CGP) felt strongly that the 2008 global economic crisis needed a coordinated, and policy informed, response. They successfully mobilised and leveraged advice in the 2008–2010 period. As the G20 evolved and became more institutionalised, so did the think tanks, eventually congealing in the T20 in 2012. By the 2019 Global Solutions Summit, that small membership has exploded into a global network of almost 200 think tanks, institutes and universities, not to mention associated NGOs, and business observers.

The process of multiple meetings, slaloming through Task Force tracks and summits, culminating in the final T20 meeting before the leaders' summit and producing a short list of recommendations, creates the mirage of some single, coherent voice. That in fact is not the real point, and several T20 and GSS participants remarked on the incoherence and fragmentation of the exercise if that exercise is seen as one intended to influence the G20 agenda. From our perspective, the T20 nexus of processes is better conceived as a global neural network of discursive contributions to a broader defence and re-imagining of the hegemonic order, a defence and re-imagining that will only, initially, find muted echoes in G20 communiqués. The network is struggling to produce a fresh narrative of globalisation with a human face, of a recoupling of social and economic progress, of inclusion, and of measured response to the impending disruptions of digitalisation, AI and climate change. That narrative is too radical in tone to be whole-heartedly embraced by the G20 leaders, though the specific policy recommendations that it nourishes (e.g. on financial reforms; digital workplaces; climate change) might be. Of course, 'radical' is a relative term here. Both Summits had nanoseconds of ironic if uncomfortable appreciation that the attendees themselves are beneficiaries of the systems they claim need fundamental change. And the change and paradigm shift being demanded was actually more often that of grafting than of overthrow.

One can debate the conceptual nuances of hegemony and the hegemonic order, but there is ample evidence of angst over 'system challenges', whether of the norms and institutions of liberalism (Deneen 2018; Frum 2018; Goodhart 2017; Harari 2018; Mounk 2018; Sunstein, 2018; Zielonka 2018) or the international political and economic system (Eurasia Group 2019; World Economic Forum 2018). This chapter has explored how supporters of the system respond, systemically; that is, through networks of ideas and debates. The T20 and the Global Solutions Summits are prime examples of new 'neural networks' engaged in the defensive re-imagining of the global hegemonic system in ways that will keep it intact (in terms of norms that we discussed above), but adaptive. Many of the adaptations and re-imaginings remain consistent with the core principles of the order, but some stretch its precepts (especially economic) to respond to challenges. The impact on G20 leaders may ultimately be slight, and *realpolitik* may dominate, but the legitimation and self-understanding of the order hinges on it.

Notes

1 There are other candidates, such as the annual World Economic Forum in Davos or other 'thought leader' networks (Garston and Sörbom, 2018; Giridharadas, 2018). Indeed, a fuller discussion of this global default network would connect the various 'global policy summits' that have emerged in recent years as venues for the good and great to discuss world issues and, in effect, to discursively rationalise and reimagine the global hegemonic order.

2 Members as of April 2019: ADB Institute; Bertelsmaan Stiftung; Blavatnik School of Government; Brookings Institution; Brugel; Centre for Economic and Financial Research (CEFIR); Centre for International Governance Innovation (CIGI); Center for Strategic and International Studies (CSIS); Centro de Implementación de Políticas Públicas para la

Equidad y el Crecimiento (CIPPEC); Consejo Argentino para las Relaciones Internacionales (CARI); G20 Research Group; Fundação Getulio Vargas (FGV); Gateway House (Indian Council on Global Relations); Hertie School of Governance; Institute for New Economic Thinking (Oxford Martin School); Kiel Institute for the World Economy (IFW); Institut français des relations interantionales (IFRI); International Institute for Applied Systems Analysis (IIASA); International Panel on Social Progress (IPSP); Italian Institute for International Political Studies (ISPI); The New Economic School (NES); Observer Research Foundation (ORF); OECD; Oxford Martin School; Renmin University of China; South African Institute of International Affairs (SAIIA); Stiftung Mercator.

3   The following draws on 'Global Solutions Initiative: Description of Concept' (December 23, 2017), courtesy of the Counsel on Global Problem-Solving.
4   The author attended both as an observer.
5   In the 2019 panel on the Future of Politics, Julia Pomares (Executive Director, CIPPEC) noted that 'we can't label everything we don't like as populism'.

References

Acharya, A. (2014) *The End of American World Order*. Cambridge: Polity Press.
Bradford, C. (2019) 'Changing dynamics: From Conflict to Transformation', *Global Solutions Journal*, 4(March): 287–292.
Bremmer, I. (2018) *Us vs. Them: The Failure of Globalism*. New York: Penguin.
Clark, I. (2011) *Hegemony in International Society*. Oxford: Oxford University Press.
Deitelhoff, N. and Zimmermann, L. (2013) *Things We Lost in the Fire: How Different Types of Contestation Affect the Validity of International Norms*. PRIF Working Papers, 18. Frankfurt am Main: Hessische Stiftung Friedens-und Konfliktforschung. Available at: https://nbn-resolving.org/urn:nbn:de:0168-ssoar-455201
Deneen, P.J. (2018) *Why Liberalism Failed*. New Haven, CT: Yale University Press.
Diamond, L., Plattner, M.F. and Walker, C. (eds) (2016) *Authoritarianism Goes Global: The Challenges to Democracy*. Baltimore, MA: Johns Hopkins University Press.
Eatwell, R. and Goodwin, R. (2018) *National Populism: The Revolt against Liberal Democracy*. New York: Pelican.
Eurasia Group (2019) 'Top Risks 2019'. Available at: www.eurasiagroup.net/files/upload/Top_Risks_2019_Report.pdf
Frum, D. (2018) *Trumpocracy: The Corruption of the American Republic*. New York: Harper.
Garston, C. and Sörbom, A. (2018) *Discreet Power: How the World Economic Forum Shapes Market Agendas*. Stanford, CA: Stanford University Press.
Gilpin, R. (1987) *The Political Economy of International Relations*. Princeton, NJ: Princeton University Press.
Giridharadas, A. (2018) *Winners Take All: The Elite Charade of Changing the World*. New York: Knopf.
Goodhart, D. (2017) *The Road to Somewhere: The Populist Revolt and the Future of Politics*. London: Oxford University Press.
Harari, Y.N. (2018) *21 Lessons for the 21st Century*. New York: Spiegel & Grau.
Ikenberry, G. (2011) *Liberal Leviathan: The Origins, Crisis and Transformation of the American World Order*. Princeton, NJ: Princeton University Press.
Kagan, R. (2018, 12 July). 'Things will not be OK', *The Washington Post*. Available at: www.washingtonpost.com/opinions/everything-will-not-be-okay/2018/07/12/c5900550-85e9-11e8-9e80-403a221946a7_story.html?utm_term=.10af28706dd1
Keohane, R.O. (1984) *After Hegemony: Cooperation and Discord in the World Political Economy*. Princeton, NJ: Princeton University Press.

Kirton, J.J. (2013) *G20 Governance for a Globalized World*. Burlington, VT: Ashgate.

Krook, M.L. and True, J. (2010) 'Rethinking the Life Cycles of International Norms: The United Nations and the Global Promotion of Gender Equality', *European Journal of International Relations*, 18(1), 103–127. doi:10.1177/1354066110380963

Lantis, J.S. and Wunderlich, C. (2018) 'Resiliency Dynamics of Norm Clusters: Norm Contestation and International Cooperation', *Review of International Studies*, 44(3), 570–593. doi:10.1017/S0260210517000626

Mearsheimer, J.J. (2018) *The Great Delusion: Liberal Dreams and International Realities*. New Haven, CT: Yale University Press.

Mounk, Y. (2018) *The People vs. Democracy: Why Our Freedom Is in Danger and How to Save It*. Cambridge, MA: Harvard University Press.

Sunstein, C.R. (ed.) (2018) *Can It Happen Here?: Authoritarianism in America*. New York: Harper Collins.

T20 Argentina 2018 (2018) Communiqué. T20 Summit 2018, Buenos Aires, Argentina: Consejo Argentino para las Relaciones Internacionales (CARI) and Centro de Implementación de Políticas Públicas para la Equidad y el Crecimiento (CIPPEC). Available at: https://t20argentina.org/wp-content/uploads/2018/09/Communiqu%C3%A9-T20-Argentina.pdf

T20 Engagement Group (2017) '20 Solution Proposals for the G20 from the T20 Engagement Group'. Available at: www.ifw-kiel.de/publications/policy-papers/20-solution-proposals-for-the-g20/

World Economic Forum (2018) *The Global Risks Report 2018*, 13th edn. Geneva: World Economic Forum. Available at: http://www.3.weforum.org/docs/WEF_GRR18_Report.pdf

Zielonka, J. (2018) *Counter-Revolution: Liberal Europe in Retreat*. Oxford: Oxford University Press.

10

SHIFTING HEGEMONIES IN GLOBAL MIGRATION POLITICS AND THE RISE OF THE INTERNATIONAL ORGANIZATION FOR MIGRATION (IOM)

Martin Geiger

International migration is a highly state and sovereignty-relevant policy field. Over the last three decades it has nevertheless witnessed a growing involvement of private and non-governmental actors, and first and foremost intergovernmental organisations (IGOs). Focusing on the International Organization for Migration (IOM), a leading IGO in migration, section I highlights the need to advance existing assumptions concerning migration politics and the role of states, IGOs and other actors. Section II discusses how the ideational concept of 'migration management' came to serve the IOM in taking a global lead in migration politics. 'Migration management', which started as an umbrella term and discourse, has materialised into a tool-based approach, marketed and implemented by the IOM. As a result, the IOM has become an indispensable organisation which, as this chapter argues, is able to act as a supplementary hegemon. The IOM has not replaced states yet, neither does it contest the existing international order, but the IOM is already powerful enough to exercise decisive influence in migration politics. Section III concludes by discussing future scenarios for the IOM as well as global migration politics, giving the example of the IOM and its fostering of new alliances, including with China, in a shifting global order, not exclusive to migration politics.

(I) Re-conceptualising migration politics and who is involved

Migration is a powerful social, economic and political process which deeply transforms societies, nation-states and the international order. Following the end of the Cold War, and in the context of increasing globalisation, the question has become unavoidable of who else is gaining influence, other than states and their governments, and which additional actors are increasingly required to assist states in the management of migration (e.g. Ghosh 1993; Geiger 2013, GCIM 2005; Loescher 2001; UN 2016/2018a/2018b). The existing international order concerning

DOI: 10.4324/9781003037231-10

migration is based on a hegemonic position of the most economically, politically and militarily capable states, and simultaneously the most important immigration countries – first and foremost the United States and other G7 and Western countries. However, the influence of the Global South and traditional non-Western states is growing (e.g. Boucher 2008; Schierup et al. 2018; Rother 2018) – also non-governmental and private entities, and first and foremost IGOs have become important (e.g. Betts 2011; Geiger and Pécoud 2014; Loescher 2001).

The project of a common migration, asylum and border policy in the European Union (EU) is a prime example of new mechanisms that actively involve IGOs in the design and implementation of migration-related measures and full-fledged policy programmes (e.g. Georgi 2007; Lavenex 2007; Geiger 2011). Since the mid-1980s, a multitude of consultative forums have emerged around the world (e.g. Hansen 2005; Thouez and Channac 2006; Oelgemoller 2017). These forums bring state as well as non-state and inter-state actors together in order to address negative aspects of migration more effectively (e.g. irregular migration, trafficking), and at the same time make migration 'work for development' and for the benefit of sending and receiving societies as well as migrants (e.g. GCIM 2005; UNDP 2009). Many of these forums are held under the auspices of the UN, UNHCR (United High Commissioner for Refugees) and ILO (International Labour Organization); however the IOM is by far the most important organiser and player in these forums.

There has also been an increasing trend of outsourcing policy interventions aimed at addressing specific types, flows and aspects related to migration, including e.g. anti-trafficking or measures to enhance border security. The IOM has established itself as the most important provider of such programmes, and states around the world have become strongly dependent on this particular organisation (see section II). In turn, this has enabled the IOM to move into a position of decisive influence and what could be called a 'supplementary' hegemonic position.

The aforementioned aspects challenge long-held assumptions about states and their role and prerogative over migration. The prevailing way the world has responded to migration has already changed from a system that was based mostly on unilateral state responses to arrangements that increasingly involve partnering with not only other states but also with non-state, private, and aforementioned specialised IGOs (Betts 2011; Boucher 2008; Geiger 2013; Geiger and Pécoud 2010). The debate surrounding IGOs, in particular, remains dominated by a state-centric perspective. While some still question whether IGOs really 'matter' (e.g. Mearsheimer 1994), and the long-standing reduction of IGOs to 'arenas' for states to confer with one other; or as dependent 'instruments' or 'agents' of states (Karns and Mingst 2010; Davies and Woodward 2014), newer discussions stress the agency and genuine 'actorness' of IGOs (e.g. Avant et al. 2010; Lyne et al. 2006). Recent studies on the role of IGOs in migration are echoing these discussions by pointing out the growing agency, capabilities, self-interests and actorness certain IGOs have acquired (i.e. the IOM), despite the remaining focus on state sovereignty in migration politics (e.g. Georgi 2007/2019; Geiger and Koch 2018). As put forward in the following it is possible to take the newer strand of studies of migration politics and the role of IGOs (Geiger and Koch 2018) and link it with recent inquiries into shifting hegemonies and the rise of non-state and intergovernmental actors (e.g. Sørensen 2016; Witt 2019).

(II) 'Migration management': A new discourse and its translation into practices. The IOM's rise in global migration politics

2.1 The IOM as a more pragmatic, not norm-centred and flexible organisation

Today's IOM had several predecessors, the first being the PICMME, the Provisional Intergovernmental Committee for the Movements of Migrants from Europe, which was created in 1951 as an instrument for the US and its allies to intervene in the case of specific migration-related situations (Georgi 2010/2019; Perruchoud 1989). The PICMME was purposely set up outside the UN to shield off any Communist influence. Even following the end of the Cold War, the IOM remained outside the UN system, and it was only in 2016 that the IOM finally became an organisation within the UN (section III). Since 1951, the PICMME and all subsequent predecessors,[1] including the IOM, acted as an alternative and competitor to the ILO and UNHCR (Georgi 2010/2019). In contrast to the ILO and UNHCR which always formed an official part of the UN system, the IOM remains unique to this day. It is not bound to a specific normative framework (Georgi 2019; Guild et al. 2020), while, for example, the UNHCR is committed to safeguarding and monitoring state compliance with the Geneva Refugee Convention.

Traditionally led by a US citizen, the IOM was the 'go-to' organisation of the US, EU and other states in the Global North for decades. Operating for most of its existence outside the UN system, provided the IOM with an unparalleled degree of flexibility and range of possibilities to act as an assumingly more pragmatic, technical and effective IGO. To this day, this gives the IOM a key advantage over the ILO and UNHCR. It is also a key factor enabling the rise of the IOM in global migration politics. The IOM has emerged as a particular type of a 'supplementary hegemon' which itself is not interested in norm design and propagation. Instead, it aims to maintain its major resource – its unparalleled degree of freedom which allows the IOM, contrary to other organisations (i.e. ILO and UNHCR) to operate in many more situations which are highly sensitive and more 'problematic' for competitor organisations to become involved in.

Examples of the IOM's involvement in politically sensitive situations include the provision of assistance to Hungarians and other populations to resettle to non-communist countries during the Cold War (e.g. IOM 2019b), and the evacuation of migrant workers stranded in conflict areas (e.g. Kelly and Wadud 2012). Assistance provided by the IOM also often includes the disarmament and professional re-training (e.g. as firefighters) of militias (e.g. the UÇK in Kosovo: Di Lellio

2005). The IOM has been in strong demand and has become one of the biggest intergovernmental organisations in the world. Today, the IOM has 173 member and 8 observer states, close to 13,000 staff, and is able to work with an annual budget of almost $1.6 billion (IOM 2019a).

2.2 'Migration management', the IOM's ideational concept for shaping migration politics

The IOM's character and self-understanding as a more pragmatic, solution-oriented and explicitly not rights and norm-centred organisation has its foundation in a particular ideational concept from which the IOM operates, and which is important to the understanding of why states around the world not only continue to fund the IOM but since the 1990s are also increasingly outsourcing specific activities to this particular IGO.

Key to the IOM's rise in global migration politics is a term which, thanks to massive lobbying and the IOM's strong publishing activities (1,794 publications, and approximately 2.2 million downloaded IOM publications, as of 31 December 2018: IOM 2019c), has formed a new global discourse, concept and leitmotif – 'migration management'. The IOM copied the term of 'migration management' and parts of its concept from Bimal Ghosh, a UN migration expert, who in the early 1990s proposed to the Commission on Global Governance (1995) the establishment of a 'New International Regime for Orderly Movements of People' (NIROMP) (Ghosh 1993/2000; Geiger and Pécoud 2010). Ghosh opted for the term 'management' instead of 'governance'. The latter term had drawn resistance from governments that were reluctant to share their sovereignty, which the term 'governance' would have implied (Ghosh 2012). While the NIROMP was never realised, the IOM continued to use and further develop his concept of 'migration management'.

Central to the IOM 'migration management' is the overall aim to depoliticise and de-problematise and, simultaneously, strongly positivise the debate on migration (Georgi 2010; Kalm 2010; Geiger 2016). 'Migration management' aims to realise three policy goals, originally stipulated back in the 1990s by Ghosh: (1) A 'balanced approach' combined with (2) 'regulated openness' – meaning: strict control and prevention of unwanted and illegal migratory flows combined with a stronger liberalisation of flows that are deemed beneficial; and (3) the goal to aim for a 'triple win' – to develop and implement programmes and measures which are likely to facilitate such migration flows (e.g. temporary and circulatory migration, high-skilled migration) and to result in positive market outcomes (benefits) not only for receiving states, but also for countries of origins and their emigrants (Ghosh 1993/2000).

The fact that the IOM is holding a majority of the migration policy forums worldwide and is exclusively using the concept of 'management' in all its other lobbying, publications as well as in its field operations have been successful to the extent that 'migration management' pervades all major discussions on migration today. Instead of 'governance' and 'politics', 'management' has become the 'language' and 'mantra' predominantly or exclusively used today in most globally relevant policy documents (e.g. GCIM 2005; UN 2018; UNDP 2009; for critique and detailed analysis see Boucher 2008; Geiger and Pécoud 2010; Pécoud 2015).

It is the policy talk of 'managing' migration 'more effectively', 'to make migration work better for development' and 'in the interest of migrants and countries of origins', etcetera, which many officials are using and 'speaking' today. In this understanding, the IOM has successfully created and propagated a certain language and concept which has found wide acceptance, and which fits the discussion and description of what hegemony is and what a hegemonic actor is able to achieve, as proposed in this book. The IOM's ideational concept has become embedded in the mindsets of all relevant stakeholders – they, in turn, have simultaneously become assured of the IOM's expertise, its ability to 'lead the world', and also of it being the 'rightful' and appropriate organisation to which they can delegate particular measures.

2.3 Material practices of hegemony. The translation of the IOM's concept into concrete measures

Aside from the whole range of social media tools (Twitter, Facebook, Instagram, YouTube), its general (www.iom.int) and close to hundred regional and country offices websites, the IOM publishes hundreds of reports and brochures each year. Among these, two annual reports stand out: (1) the 'World Migration Report' (e.g. IOM 2018) and (2) the IOM's 'Migration Initiatives' (e.g. IOM 2015). Both are of primary importance for the IOM when translating the 'migration management' discourse into actual practices. The 'World Migration Reports' include statistics and information that the IOM collects through its project activities and more than 400 country and project offices worldwide. The IOM's 'Migration Initiatives' (e.g. IOM 2015) goes a step further by first synthesising the most pressing migration-related challenges in specific states and regions, and then making the (business) case for measures and programmes the IOM deems necessary and is able to offer. Here, the IOM translates its 'management' concept into concrete policy practices. These practices (programmes and specific measures) are pre-designed 'in-house' by the IOM and each come in the annual 'Migration Initiatives' report with a price tag. Donor states and other entities can choose to opt and 'buy-in', commission, fund and receive specific assistance and support measures from the IOM. The IOM's policy programmes and measures are highly 'standardised' and resemble 'package solutions' that can theoretically be purchased by everyone who is interested and has the necessary funding, and can be implemented in different places, ignorant to a large extent of concrete 'on the ground' situations and contextualities (e.g. Bartels 2018; Geiger 2011).

The IOM's catalogue for specific countries and regions includes a wide range of tailored logistics and other operative support, such as measures to increase border security, verify documents, conduct health and background checks, and pre-departure orientation programmes e.g. for migrants leaving for Canada (e.g. Dupeyron 2016; Geiger 2018). The IOM is also known for its 'assisted return' programmes that with the help of financial and in-kind support incentivise rejected asylum-seekers and irregular migrants to 'voluntarily' return to their home countries. The IOM has been openly accused of misinforming or even coercing migrants and for promoting generally contentious practices (Koch 2014; Webber 2011).

For some countries the IOM has become indispensable in implementing major parts of their own national policies. Funded by the EU and with the help of additional US co-funding, the IOM has designed holistic 'migration strategies' for several of the major sending and transit countries of unwanted and irregular migration flows (e.g. Ukraine, Albania). One of the earliest IOM projects was the 'National Strategy on Migration' for Albania (Government of Albania/IOM 2005) which was promoted by the IOM as well as its main donor, the European Commission, as a strategy to not only manage Albanian migration but also to bring Albania 'closer to membership in the European Union' (Government of Albania/IOM 2005: 1). The IOM acted as an EU instrument to further the EU's hegemonic interests. At the same, it used the opportunity to further its own interests and advance its position as an indispensable actor in regional migration, and to a certain degree in EU accession politics.

It is this 'market place' in particular that the IOM has successfully created, and the unique tool-based approach to 'migration management' which over the last three decades has turned the IOM into an almost indispensable IGO in global, regional and even national migration politics. States have become strongly dependent on the IOM, which makes a case for calling the IOM a new supplementary hegemon in migration politics. However, it is important to note that the IOM's concept of 'migration management' in and of itself does not intend to create and invoke genuine (good, better, i.e. norm-based) governance, neither does it intend to replace states nor contest state government and sovereignty. This is at least not the official orientation of the IOM and its concept, though in the actual implementation of IOM migration management, this could often be open for debate. Certain activities, including drafting, selling and to a large extent implementing the migration policy of an entire country, certainly have not only a tendency but also actual power to compliment and even replace traditional aspects of sovereignty and state power. The IOM's catalogue of 'tools' of migration management offers to relieve states of some of the burdens and tasks of designing and implementing policy measures. At the same time, the IOM undoubtedly strives to take a global lead in proposing and selling to the world community at large, including its traditional hegemons, new approaches to migration and its organisational capabilities to implement them.

(III) Shifting hegemonies and global migration management in the future

While the international order concerning international migration is still characterised by a persistent prerogative of states in the field of migration politics, and there is a strong element of hegemony exercised by the US, its G7 and other Global North partners, there are fundamental changes underway. A major development is the increasing influence of non-governmental, private, and first and foremost intergovernmental organisations in the once strongly state-exclusive domain of migration. Partnerships and mechanisms have emerged that, like in the case of the EU, increasingly involve actors from 'beyond' the state. In particular the IOM has become an indispensable organisation for states and other entities. The IOM's unparalleled degree of freedom, its ability to largely shape and determine the global discourse on migration, and the fact that its 'tools' of migration management have found many clients across the world, validate the argument which considers the IOM to be a supplementary hegemony in global migration politics.

The existing global migration policy system is rapidly changing, with the influence of major Global South and main sending countries of emigrants which has steadily grown since the end of the Cold War. There is also growing pressure from 'below', including from migrant activist and other non-state and civil society groups for stronger and more equal participation in all relevant discussions on migration (e.g. Rother 2018; Piper and Grugel 2015). The rising number of migrants and refugees worldwide is another clear challenge to traditional modes of state control over migration and the existing international order. These developments, which result in and are often called 'crises', provide the IOM with an opportunity to advance its own power and influence, which leads to the question of the IOM's future role, power and share of 'sovereignty' and hegemony.

2016 can be identified as a fundamentally important year in the IOM's history, as well as in global (migration) politics. The IOM celebrated its 65th anniversary, and the People's Republic of China, which had been merely an observer state for several years, made the decision to join the IOM as its 165th member state. William Swing, the IOM's Director General at the time, welcomed China as a new member state, furthering the IOM's global significance and making it a truly global organisation (IOM 2016b). At the same time, it was likely no coincidence that China's accession to the IOM in June 2016 happened only weeks before the IOM Council decided to give up the IOM's 65th year of formal independence from the UN in July 2016, calling for the IOM to join the UN as a 'related organization' (IOM 2016a). A few months later, in September 2016, the UN General Assembly adopted the 'New York Declaration for Refugees and Migrants' (UN 2016) which resulted in the adoption of two new frameworks on migration in the end of 2018 – the UN Global Compact for Safe, Orderly and Regular Migration (UN 2018a) and the UN Global Compact on Refugees (UN 2018b).

It was highly meaningful for China, the IOM, global migration politics and the world community in general, that these developments all happened in the same year. In 2016 it was also decided by the UN that the IOM, and not the ILO (the longest existing UN organisation specialising in migration, founded in 1919) would take the lead on the Global Compact for Migration, while the UNHCR's leadership position on refugees was reconfirmed by making it the leader for the Compact on Refugees. The IOM not only joined the UN, it also immediately became the lead organisation for the Global Compact on Migration. China's accession brought the IOM a potential ally with its own growing global influence, and a member state which is the one of the world's most important migrant-sending countries (IOM 2018: 17), and receives the second-largest amount annually in remittances from its fourth-largest diaspora in the world (World Bank 2018, 5). China has the fourth-largest diaspora in the world, and is also becoming increasingly important as a transit and destination country for migrants.

Moreover, the IOM's ambitions are likely to be linked with the current ambitions of China to create a global 'neighborhood' for itself. Official Chinese statements linked the new membership in the IOM to China's ongoing process of 'opening up', its 'rapid economic and social development' but, in particular, its 'Belt and Road Initiative' (BRI) (PRC 2016). This project, which is projected to span the whole world, will undoubtedly make China a new key player in any migration-related decisions in regional or global migration politics. It will also fundamentally challenge the existing order, undermining and shifting the existing US and Global North/Western hegemony in migration and other fields of global politics. China is expecting guidance and support from the IOM in many highly relevant sub-fields of national but also regional and global migration politics, such as border control, human trafficking, irregular migration, enhancement of visas and passports, return of migrants, but also the long-term integration of migrants, conflict resolution, disaster prevention and reduction (e.g. PRC 2016/2018).

Judging from a Western geopolitical perspective, China's move to join the IOM at this decisive point in history could be considered a clever 'counter-hegemonic' move. Considering the IOM's own accession to the UN and China's new membership in the IOM, the IOM's freedom to operate undoubtedly increases, making it more independent from the US and other Global North and Western states. Simultaneously, other Global South and major sending countries of migrants from Asia, Africa and Latin America are now able to explore strategic alliances with China, while they are less dependent on Global North and US support in particular.

Important for this discussion is also the particular status the IOM's member states have reserved for the IOM before the organisation joined the UN. The IOM only became a 'related organization' (Guild et al. 2020). This is a status in the UN which, in contrast to 'special organization' (ILO, UNHCR), reserves a significantly higher degree of independence from the UN (e.g. it is not obliged to report to other UN bodies, can follow its own founding documents and decisions of its own member states). It retains much of the IOM's key advantage over its competitor organisations; by joining as a related organisation only, the IOM is likely to further advance its position, despite and perhaps regardless of the fact that it is now officially a UN organisation.

The double accession of China to the IOM, and of the IOM to the UN in its importance can be even further emphasised by the fact that the US influence over the IOM, the UN and global politics in general, has been fundamentally changing and diminishing over the last two years. At the beginning of Donald Trump's presidency, the US withdrew its support from the two Global Compact processes (Wintour 2017); it also started to decrease its support for the UN and the IOM. These decisions had a direct consequence in 2018 when, as a first in the IOM's history, the US failed to get their candidate for the Director General of the IOM elected. Instead, Antonio Vitorino, the first-ever European to lead the IOM was confirmed (*The Straits Times* 2018). As in other fields of global politics, the particular disinterest of the current US administration in global partnerships is working in favour of countries of the Global South and, in particular, China. In stark contrast to the US and a small number of other countries that voted at the end of 2018 against or abstained to either one or both Global Compacts, China not only participated in several of the discussion processes on the two Compacts but even joined the vast majority of UN member states in formally adopting both the Global Compact on Migration and the Compact on Refugees (UN 2018a/b). Afterwards, China declared that it will integrate relevant parts of both Compacts into its own future migration-related policies (Xinhua News 2018). The influence of China at the global level, as well as in many BRI countries, is likely to grow and therefore it is quite probable that its collaboration with the IOM will become more importance. China could copy the EU's neighbourhood approach in funding specific measures in Central Asian and other BRI countries, and to delegate measures and their implementation to the IOM.

It will be important to empirically observe the IOM's new partnership with China, in particular, in the coming years in order to gain a truly global understanding of the IOM and the changing nature of global migration politics. The fundamental question remains who, in the future, will be 'governing' people on the move, and who will not only have an active say but also have actual power to determine the direction and definition of migratory flows (e.g. as 'irregular' or 'regular'). Who might in the future have the power to perhaps even command how states must respond to migration and refugee flows? There are at least three different scenarios:

1   Continuation of privatisation and outsourcing of policy interventions to the IOM and perhaps additional new inter-state, non-state and private entities. Challenges and risks: The question is to what extent will states accept the continued intervention of inter-state and non-state actors in the domain of migration? Furthermore, to what extent will activities of the IOM or other organisations take over sovereignty from states in the future? Many activities of the IOM have been criticised for being un-democratic, unsustainable and ineffective in governing and e.g. preventing irregular flows. The problem is that a continuation of outsourcing is not likely to result in more effective and sustainable migration-related solutions. It will also not help to tackle growing citizens' concerns, and the well-being of migrants and refugees. Considering growing migratory pressures, and unsolved fundamental problems (e.g. conflicts and under-developments), as well as growing new challenges (e.g. climate and demographic change), a continuation of 'business as usual' is problematic, but not unlikely given the current state of affairs. If there is a

continued trend of outsourcing and privatisation, perhaps followed up by additional countries (e.g. China, other Global South states, Russia), the likely result is that the IOM will further grow in relevance and continue expanding its hegemonic position.

2   Adopting at the regional level, e.g. Europe and EU, new mechanisms of migration management involving the IOM and other entities but forcing these organisations to actively engage more with sending and transit states and their governments (e.g. twinning programmes, trainings but also equal partnership). A key requirement would be to impose strict control and limits on what activities donor states are able to outsource, and the extent to which the IOM and other implementers are able to circumvent local entities including state governments, in their actions. Mandatory evaluations and joint assessments of programmes involving target state governments are warranted, in true and equal partnership among all actors involved. Given the growing pressure to respond more effectively to migration and refugee flows, this alternative would not be too difficult to achieve, and could potentially lead to a more effective and genuine partnership-based governance of migration, with the help of highly specialised organisations such as the IOM. Since the IOM already has a global advantage over other organisations, there is a potential to strengthen alternative organisations and share tasks among different service-providers, hereby limiting the monopoly and power of the IOM.

3   At the global level, further developing the IOM as a 'service provider' explicitly for all UN member states and funded by the UN, rather than individual donor states. A central UN funding mechanism for the IOM (and similar organisations) could be generated, with regular contributions from UN member states and other donors, involving clear oversight. This alternative, in combination with regional policy changes, would require a strong global consensus on the role of the UN as an entity tasked to help states with growing migration in the light of humanitarian crises and conflicts. This also means an acceptance that specialised organisations tasked by the UN, such as the IOM, require some level of sovereignty to act on behalf of the international community during key events. It is currently unlikely that donors would transfer sufficient funds to fully implement broader solutions, although this is envisioned in the UN Global Compacts. Also, at the global level, stronger monitoring and joint assessment of activities implemented by the IOM and other entities would be required. States would have to tolerate and support these activities, accept their findings and implement policy changes, which is currently unlikely to happen in the near future.

Note

1 In 1952, the PICCME became the 'Intergovernmental Committee for European Migration' (ICEM), in 1980 the 'Intergovernmental Committee for Migration' (ICM), and in 1989, the name changed again into today's 'International Organization for Migration' (IOM).

References

Avant, D.D.*et al.* (eds) (2010) *Who Governs the Globe?*Cambridge: Cambridge University Press.

Bartels, I. (2018) 'Practices and Power of Knowledge Dissemination', *Movements*, 4(1): 47–66.

Betts, A. (ed.) (2011) *Global Migration Governance*. Oxford: Oxford University Press.

Boucher, G. (2008) 'A Critique of Global Policy Discourses on Managing International Migration', *Third World Quarterly*, 29(7): 1461–1471.

Davies, M. and Woodward, R. (2014) *International Organizations: A Companion*. Cheltenham: Edward Elgar.

Di Lellio, A. (2005) 'A Civil Alternative: An Evaluation of the IOM KPC Program'. Available at: www.beyondintractability.org/casestudy/dilellio-civil

Dupeyron, B. (2016) 'Secluding North America's Labor Migrants: Notes on the International Organization for Migration's Compassionate Mercenary Business', in R. Zaiotti (ed.), *Externalizing Migration Management: Europe, North America and the Spread of 'Remote control' Practices*, Abingdon: Routledge, 238–258.

GCIM (Global Commission on International Migration) (2005) *Migration in an Interconnected World: New Directions for Action*. Geneva: GCIM.

Geiger, M. (2011) *Europäische Migrationspolitik und Raumproduktion. Internationale Regierungsorganisationen im Management von Migration in Albanien, Bosnien-Herzegowina und der Ukraine*. Baden-Baden: Nomos.

Geiger, M. (2013) 'The Transformation of Migration Politics: From Migration Control to Disciplining Mobility', in M. Geiger and A. Pécoud (eds.), *Disciplining the Transnational Mobility of People*, Basingstoke: Palgrave Macmillan, 15–40.

Geiger, M. (2016) 'Policy Outsourcing and Remote Management', in R. Zaiotti (ed.), *Externalizing Migration Management*, London: Routledge, 261–279.

Geiger, M. (2018) 'Ideal Partnership or Marriage of Convenience? Canada's Ambivalent Relationship with the International Organization for Migration', *Journal of Ethnic and Migration Studies* (JEMS), 44(10): 1639–1655.

Geiger, M. and Koch, M. (2018) 'World Organization in Migration Politics: The International Organization for Migration', *Journal of International Organizations Studies*, 9(1): 25–44.

Geiger, M. and Pécoud, A. (2010) 'The Politics of International Migration Management', in M. Geiger and A. Pécoud (eds), *The Politics of International Migration Management*, Basingstoke: Palgrave Macmillan, 1–20.

Geiger, M. and Pécoud, A. (2014) 'International Organisations and the Politics of Migration', *Journal of Ethnic and Migration Studies*, 40(6): 865–887.

Georgi, F. (2007) *Migrationsmanagement in Europa. Eine kritische Studie am Beispiel des International Centre for Migration Policy Development*. Saarbrücken: VDM.

Georgi, F. (2010) 'For the Benefit of Some: The International Organization for Migration and its Global Migration Management', in M. Geiger and A. Pécoud (eds), *The Politics of International Migration Management*, Basingstoke: Palgrave Macmillan, 45–72.

Georgi, F. (2019) *Managing Migration?: Eine kritische Geschichte der Internationalen Organisation für Migration (IOM)*. Berlin: Bertz und Fischer.

Ghosh, B. (1993) *Movements of People: The Search for a New International Regime*. Geneva: Commission on Global Governance.

Ghosh, B. (2000) '*Introduction*', in B. Ghosh (ed.) *Managing Migration: Time for a New International Regime?*, Oxford: Oxford University Press, 1–5.

Ghosh, B. (2012) 'A Snapshot of Reflections on Migration Management. Is Migration Management a Dirty Word?', *IMIS-Beiträge*, 40: 25–32.

Government of Albania/IOM (2005) *National Strategy on Migration and National Action Plan on Migration*. Tirana: Government of Albania/IOM.

Guild, E.*et al.* (2020), 'Unfinished Business: IOM and Migrants' Human Rights', in M. Geiger and A. Pécoud (eds), *The International Organization for Migration: The New 'UN Migration Agency' in Critical Perspective*, London: Palgrave Macmillan.

Hansen, R. (2005) 'Interstate Cooperation: Europe and Central Asia', in International Organization for Migration/Federal Office for Migration (Switzerland) (eds), *Interstate Cooperation and Migration*, Berne/Geneva: Federal Office for Migration, 9–33.

IOM (International Organization for Migration) (2015) *Migration Initiatives 2015*. Geneva: IOM.

IOM (2016a) 'IOM becomes a Related Organization to the UN'. Available at: www.iom.int/news/iom-becomes-related-organization-un

IOM (2016b) 'International Organization for Migration Welcomes China's Application for IOM Membership'. Available at: www.iom.int/news/international-organization-migration-welcomes-china-application-iom-membership

IOM (2018) *World Migration Report 2018*. Geneva: IOM.

IOM (2019a) 'About IOM'. Available at: www.iom.int/about-iom

IOM (2019b) 'IOM History. The 1950'. Available at: www.iom.int/1950s

IOM (2019c) 'IOM Snapshot'. Available at: www.iom.int/sites/default/files/about-iom/iom_snapshot_a4_en.pdf

Kalm, S. (2010) 'Liberalizing Movements? The Political Rationality of Global Migration Management', in M. Geiger and A. Pécoud, (eds), *The Politics of International Migration Management*, Basingstoke: Palgrave Macmillan, 21–44.

Karns, M. and Mingst, K. (2010) *International Organizations: The Politics and Processes of Global Governance*. Boulder, CO: Lynne Rienner Publishers.

Kelly, B. and Wadud, A.J. (2012) *Asian Labour Migrants and Humanitarian Crises*. Geneva: IOM.

Koch, A. (2014) 'The Politics and Discourse of Return: The Role of International Actors in the Governance of Return', *Journal of Ethnic and Migration Studies*, 40(6): 905–923.

Lavenex, S. (2007) 'The External Face of Europeanization: Third Countries and International Organizations', in T. Faist and A. Ette (eds), *The Europeanization of National Policies and Politics of Immigration*, Basingstoke: Palgrave Macmillan, 246–264.

Loescher, G. (2001) *The UNHCR and World Politics: A Perilous Path*. Oxford: Oxford University Press.

Lyne, M.M.*et al.* (2006) 'Who Delegates? Alternative Models of Principals in Development Aid', in D.G. Hawkins*et al.* (eds), *Delegation and Agency in International Organizations*, Cambridge: Cambridge University Press, 41–76.

Mearsheimer, J.J. (1994) 'The False Promise of International Institutions', *International Security*, 19(3): 5–49.

Oelgemoller, C. (2017) *The Evolution of Migration Management in the Global North*. London: Routledge.

Pécoud, A. (2015) *Global Governance and International Migration Narratives*. Basingstoke: Palgrave Macmillan.

Perruchoud, R. (1989) 'From the Intergovernmental Committee for European Migration to the International Organization for Migration', *International Journal of Refugee Law*, 1(4): 501–517.

Piper, N. and Grugel, J. (2015) 'Global Migration Governance, Social Movements and the Difficulties of Promoting Migrant Rights', in Carl-Ulrik Schierup*et al.* (eds), *Migration, Precarity and Global Governance*, Oxford: Oxford University Press, 261–279.

PRC (People's Republic of China) (2016) 'Statement by H.E. Ambassador Ma Zhaoxu'. Available at: https://governingbodies.iom.int/system/files/en/council/108/GD/China.pdf

PRC (2018) 'China's Supreme People's Court and Supreme People's Procuratorate Cooperates with IOM to Discuss How to Deal with Human Trafficking'. Available at: www.court.gov.cn/zixun-xiangqing-88362.html

Rother, S. (2018) 'The Global Forum on Migration and Development (GFMD) as a Venue of State Socialization', *Journal of Ethnic and Migration Studies*, 45(8): 1258–1274.

Schierup, C.-U.*et al.* (2018) 'Migration, Civil Society and Global Governance', *Globalizations*, 15(6): 733–745.

Sørensen, G. (2016) *Rethinking the New World Order*. Basingstoke: Palgrave Macmillan.

The Straits Times (2018) 'Portugal's Vitorino Elected Head of UN Migration Agency IOM'. Available at: www.straitstimes.com/world/europe/portugals-vitorino-elected-head-of-un-migration-agency-iom

Thouez, C. and Channac, F. (2006) 'Shaping International Migration Policy: The Role of Regional Consultative Processes', *West European Politics*, 29(2): 370–387.

UN (United Nations) (2016) *New York Declaration*. New York: UN. Available at: https://refugeesmigrants.un.org/declaration

UN (2018a) *The Global Compact on Migration*. New York: UN. Available at: https://refugeesmigrants.un.org/sites/default/files/180713_agreed_outcome_global_compact_for_migration.pdf

UN (2018b) *The Global Compact on Refugees*. New York: UN. Available at: www.unhcr.org/5b3295167

UNDP (United Nations Development Program) (2009) *Human Development Report 2009*. New York: UNDP.

Webber, F. (2011) 'How Voluntary are Voluntary Returns?', *Race Class*, 52(4): 98–107.

Wintour, P. (2017) 'Donald Trump Pulls US out of UN Global Compact on Migration'. Available at: www.theguardian.com/world/2017/dec/03/donald-trump-pulls-us-out-of-un-global-compact-on-migration

Witt, M.A. (2019) 'De-globalization: Theories, Predictions, and Opportunities for International Business Research', *Journal of International Business Studies*, 50(7): 1053–1077.

World Bank (2018) *Migration and Development Brief 29. Migration and Remittances: Recent Developments and Outlook*. Washington, DC: World Bank. Available at: https://www.knomad.org/sites/default/files/2018-04/Migration%20and%20Development%20Brief%2029.pdf

Xinhua News (2018) China's Ministry of Foreign Affairs briefly introduces relevant facts about the Global Compact on Migration [外交部发言人介绍《移民问题全球契约》相关情况]'. Available at: www.xinhuanet.com/world/2018-12/11/c_1210013487.htm

PART 3
Hegemony in action

11

THE US–CHINA TRADE WAR AND HEGEMONIC COMPETITION

Background, negotiations and consequences

Yong Wang

Introduction

The US–China trade conflict began at a special time. The year 2018 witnessed the celebration of the 40th anniversary of China's reform and open doors policy, as well as the 40th anniversary of the establishment of diplomatic relations between China and the United States. It is no coincidence that the launch of reforms, the opening up and the establishment of China–US diplomatic relations took place at the same time when Soviet expansion turned the United States and China into quasi-allies and brought China and the world into a new era. Since then, China has changed from a poor third world country into the world's second-largest economy. While China has greatly increased its weight in the global economy, it has also emerged as a regional and even a global power. President Trump was elected largely because many voters shared his goal of MAGA (Make America Great Again), and the Trump administration defined China as a major 'strategic competitor' and 'revisionist state' in the National Security Strategy Report released in December 2017 (NSS 2017). As a result of this new China strategy, the Trump administration launched a trade war against China.

This chapter aims to explore the following questions. What are the major goals of the US trade war against China? What does the trade conflict imply for the competition between the US and China for hegemony? How should one evaluate the domestic structural changes of both countries and their influence on the US–China trade war? How should one assess the US argument about its trade deficit and the perceived technological competition? Will the Phase One agreement, concluded between both parties, stop the spiralling of the strategic and hegemonic competition between the two major powers and can China and the US shake off the prospect of a new Cold War? These are the main questions this chapter will discuss. In order to answer these questions, three important elements are explored

DOI: 10.4324/9781003037231-11

in order to analyse the trade conflict between the US and China: (mis)perception, the domestic factor and economic competition.

Trade war and hegemonic competition

The rise of China is widely perceived as a vital challenge to the US hegemonic power in the international system. Since the global financial crisis of 2008, China's power and influence have been growing in an unprecedented pace and China now begins to challenge the US predominance in various fields: economic, technological as well as ideological. The hawkish elements in the US accuse globalists and moderates of misjudging China, arguing that integrating China into the global economy, since the nation's access to the WTO, failed to bring forth the political changes inside the country (Friedberg 2017). President Trump's hostile policy towards China represents some consensus among US power elites that the United States must act to slow down China's growth, otherwise it will be too late to do so. The China hawks agree that the most effective way to weaken China is to limit the country's access to the US market and to the advanced technology created by the US companies. They hold that some kind of 'economic decoupling' would definitely serve the goal of containing China's growth of power.

On 22 March 2018, the Office of the US Trade Representative (USTR) released a Section 301 report on China's trade practices (USTR 2018a). Based on that report, President Trump issued a presidential memorandum that called for countering China's 'economic aggression', and instructed his administration to impose extra import tariffs on US $ 50 billion in goods from China and to restrict Chinese investments in the US. The report mainly accused China of restricting the ownership rights of foreign enterprises and of demanding the establishment of joint ventures, thus forcing US companies to transfer technology to Chinese companies. Prior to the decision, the USTR published a report expressing regret that the US allowed China to join the WTO in 2001 (USTR 2018b).

As a matter of fact, the Trump administration has launched a trade war against several of the US's trading partners. Before the Section 301 action on China, on 8 March 2018, the US announced the results of an investigation under Section 232 (the 'national security' exemption) of the US Trade Expansion Act of 1962. The USTR declared that the US plans to impose a 25% tariff on imports of steel into the US and a 10% tariff on aluminium imports. US allies, including Canada, the European Union (EU), and Japan became targets of the Section 232 measures. Since 1 June 2018, the US and the EU have been engaged in an exchange of tariff measures, and the EU, China and other countries have opened a lawsuit against US measures on steel and aluminium. So far, only South Korea has agreed to accept 'voluntary' export restrictions to reduce trade in steel and aluminium products. At the same time, the Trump administration has prepared sanctions on cars made in Germany and other countries, and recently threatened to impose a tariff on imports from India.

Trump's trade policy reflects his 'America First' political philosophy and the deep belief that the unfair trade practices of other countries have been the main source of the US trade deficit, though most economists, including Trump's own Council of Economic Advisers, insist that the trade deficit is not a big problem and is caused by the US's low saving rate (Tankersley 2018; Chandran and Soong 2018).

Obviously, the Trump administration's trade actions remind observers of the US's 'aggressive' unilateralism in the 1980s, which also took place during a period of perceived declining international competitiveness. Trump and his advisers tend to believe that all countries that have a trade surplus with the US are engaged in 'unfair' trade. To correct this, they believe the US must leverage its domestic laws to impose or threaten sanctions on its trading partners. The Section 301 and Section 232 actions are derived from US domestic trade laws, and are unilateral by nature and in violation of the obligations of the US as a WTO member. These unilateral measures have severely impacted the multilateral trading system the US itself helped to establish after the Second World War. Additionally, the US is blocking the appointment of new judges for the WTO dispute settlement body, a move aimed at paralysing the mechanism in order to prevent it from ruling on unilateral US measures. As a result, the World Trade Organization is losing its authority for the resolution of trade disputes.

Some analysts believe in the good intentions behind and positive outcomes of the US unilateral actions. They assume that the US actions may play a big role in pushing forward deadlocked WTO reform (Lamy 2018). With a sanction stick in hand, the Trump administration is lowering tariff and non-tariff barriers (NTBs) by applying hard pressure in negotiations with major trading partners. Furthermore, the US has worked with the EU and Japan on a high standard WTO reform programme, which some analysts believe will revitalise the WTO (EU, Japan and US 2019).

US goals for the trade war against China

In economic theory, China and the United States are natural trading partners and have mutually beneficial relations. Their complementarity and mutually beneficial relations account for the rapid growth of bilateral trade. There are three main reasons why the US government launched a trade war against China.

First, the Trump administration hopes to reduce the US trade deficit with China substantially. Trump started to think in the 1980s that the trade deficit was not conducive to the development of the US. As part of its demands, the US initially asked for a reduction of US$ 100 billion a year in the US deficit, and later raised the target to US$ 200 billion. In order to reduce the US trade deficit, China agreed to purchase an additional $200 billion in US goods over the year of 2020 and 2021 as part of the 'phase one' trade deal, and the additional purchases will come on top of the 2017 US export numbers (Franck 2020). Trump's purposes are very clear: to bring jobs back to the United States and to consolidate his election position in 'swing states'.

Secondly, Trump hopes that China will open its market to the United States and improve the market access of American companies. Since 2008, US companies have complained that the Chinese market is becoming less and less open. They point out that in terms of government procurement, the Chinese government favours state-owned enterprises over foreign-invested companies. Particularly on the grounds of 'national security' and 'information security', China has strengthened market access restrictions on US companies in the information industry and related services. US companies and chambers of commerce have kept exerting pressure on the US government to take tough action on China.

Thirdly, the United States hopes to change China's current industrial policies to subsidise emerging industries, forcing China to abandon the 'Made in China 2025' plan and especially the 'unreasonable' practice of 'forced technology transfer' from foreign companies. The Section 301 report accused China of limiting foreign investors' ownership in joint ventures for acquiring transfer of technology or even 'theft' of technology. On the other hand, the US also points at China's overseas mergers and acquisitions of foreign companies subsidised by cheaper financing. Actually, as a developing country, China has applied a 'market-for-technology' policy over the decades of reform and opening up, and the outcomes of such a policy are controversial. In his speech on China on 25 October 2018, which was perceived as an announcement of a new Cold War with China by many people (Perlez 2018), US Vice President Pence expressed deep concern that China will take a leading position in some technologies within one or two years, highlighting the role of the Made in China 2025 plan (Pence 2018). Hence, the specific goals of the US trade war are clearly aimed at hampering the advancement of China's technology and innovation. On the other hand, some American analysts insist that China's industrial policies and especially its local incentive policies are likely to lead to overcapacity, export dumping, and as a result, the distortion of the global trade order (CCG 2018a). The shift of US positions on trade talks mirrored the increasingly tougher demands on China. Both sides basically reached an agreement in May 2018, focusing on China's commitments to procure more American products to balance bilateral trade within 6 years, to provide better protection of US intellectual property and to open its markets to US companies.

Obviously, China's large-scale increase in imports of agricultural products and liquefied natural gas (LNG) from the US will help President Trump keep his campaign promise of shrinking the US trade deficit with China, hence maintaining the political support of US farmers and the US energy sector. In the meantime, China has taken many unilateral steps to meet the demands of the US. In 2018, it announced a large-scale reduction of tariffs on automobiles, drugs, cosmetics, and other goods, and accelerated the opening up of its financial sector. Foreign financial institutions became entitled to own a majority of shares in securities companies by the end of June 2018, rather than having to wait three years. However, US security hawks and the US business community are more concerned about the impact of Beijing's 'Made in China 2025' plan on US predominance in the fields of security and technology. To a large extent, Trump's change of mind in June 2018 was driven by the joint endeavours of these two groups, though US businesses keep saying they do not think imposing tariffs is a good idea.

The case of ZTE demonstrates the extent of the dependence of Chinese industries on some key technologies provided by the United States. ZTE is one of the largest state-owned telecommunication companies of China, engaging in manufacturing mobile phones and network facilities, and its market extends to Africa, Asia as well as the US. The US government accused ZTE of violating sanctions against Iran and North Korea and imposed the ban prohibiting US companies from supplying ZTE with US-made components. In the end, the Chinese company accepted Washington's hefty penalty of US$ 1 billion and the inclusion of a US-appointed compliance team within the firm, in return for a US agreement to halt the ban, allowing the company to continue operations and avoid the loss of some 70,000 jobs (Schneider 2018). As part of the US strategy of trade war, senior US officials travelled the world to lobby allies not to procure 5G equipment produced by China's telecommunication company, Huawei. Given the fact that Huawei has obtained a clear advantage in 5G products, the US's European allies, such as Germany and the United Kingdom, find it hard to ban Huawei and distance themselves from the US position, holding they can manage the potential security risks with domestic regulations (Kakissis 2019).

China has made a lot of concessions to prevent the escalation of the trade conflict. In addition to the big procurement programme, China made promises to address other issues of US concern, such as intellectual property protection, market access, agriculture, exchange rates, and so on. On the 'Made in China 2025' plan, Vice Minister Wang Shouwen promised that it is mainly 'guidance' rather than a 'mandatory' plan (Chinese State Council Information Office 2018).

Obviously, if the US and China finally reach, to borrow Trump's term, an 'epic' deal, all the concessions will be enough to enable him to claim that he has won a trade war with China and that he is the strongest president safeguarding the national interest, which will greatly help him in his 2020 campaign for a second term. On the other hand, by arguing that the deal is in line with the direction of China's market-oriented reform and plays a stimulating role in the Chinese economy, comparable to the effect of China's WTO accession, China can also claim victory. More importantly, the deal can help to prevent US security hawks from 'decoupling' the two economies. But one should be aware of the fact that domestic politics of the two countries play a big role in deciding the results of the negotiations. When the talks collapsed on 10 May 2019 and the US imposed more and higher tariffs on the exports of China, Vice Premier Liu He blamed that US hardliners' pressure for more Chinese concessions and the imbalanced terms of the deal made the negotiations very difficult (Han and Gao 2019).

Putting the trade war in context

The trade war, combined with differences in ideologies, development models and political systems, may push China and the US into the dangers of a 'new Cold War', Which may be characterised by worldwide ideological competition and a power struggle akin to the rivalry between the US and the former Soviet Union in the period from the 1950s to the 1980s. When we explore the causes of current trade frictions, it is advisable to put trade issues in a broader context. Overall, the trade frictions have deep roots in the restructuring of domestic politics taking place in the world's two largest economies, as well as in the changes of mutual perceptions of one another.

When we examine the trends in economic policies of the US and China over the past 30 years, we surprisingly find that the policies of both countries have been moving in similar directions. In the first two decades, both the US and China embraced globalisation. While the US played the leadership role in globalisation, China participated, as the largest developing country, as an active follower, and later on became an important driving force. Both believe in the benefits of economic globalisation, and globalisation indeed has brought tremendous growth to both countries. The two countries' collective efforts in implementing free market and privatisation policies in the first 20 years led to a highly interdependent economic relationship, which was dubbed 'Chimerica' (Ferguson 2008). However, economic globalisation has also produced a serious negative consequence – widening disparities between the rich and the poor within each country – though it may be controversial to argue that globalisation has created the wealth gap. The wealth gap in the US has become the worst among developed economies, actually regressing the US to the situation of one hundred years ago, and China has fallen into one of the deepest wealth gaps among the largest developing countries. As gaps between the rich and poor cause much internal tension, it is hard to imagine that the continuation of widening disparities will be sustainable.

As part of their response to cope with the severe wealth gap, China and the US have made efforts respectively to readjust domestic policies, especially after the global financial crisis in 2008. However, due to differences in their political systems, different adjustment policies have been adopted. The election of Donald Trump manifested the rise of populism and protectionism, and 'America First' has become the primary goal of US foreign policy. The Trump administration has launched a broad trade war against each major trading partner. China's policy adjustments started earlier, beginning with the 'harmonious society' goal set during the Hu-Wen period. Since President Xi Jinping came to power in 2013, the Chinese government has adopted much more intensive policy readjustments, including those focusing on anti-corruption, poverty alleviation and rural rejuvenation, environmental protection and overall security (prevention of financial crises, cyber security, and so on). In order to push forward the tremendous reforms, President Xi Jinping has gradually restructured party and state institutions to recentralise power and strengthen the authority of the central government and leadership.

Trump's election and mode of governance have brought great changes to the US. First, the centres of gravity and power have shifted from the North-eastern part of the country (the Boston–New York–Washington corridor) and the West Coast, which had dominated the US for many years, to the new power centres formed by the 'Rust Belt states' of the Midwest and conservative agricultural states (Wang 2018c). As a smart businessman, Trump is clearly concerned with winning voter support in the 'swing states' of the Midwest, which figured prominently in his election victory. By launching a full-scale trade war, he has attained an approval rating surpassing that of former President Barack Obama in the same period of his presidency (Agiesta 2018).

Second, Trump and his supporters in the Midwest have pushed the US to adopt a 'reverse globalization' policy. In terms of economic and trade policies, Trump seems to be reversing the US policy of emphasising the growth of the online and high-tech sectors over the past 20 years, in favour of reviving the manufacturing sector to correct trade imbalances. In terms of foreign policy, Trump has changed the long-held view of US leadership of the liberal international order and put protectionist trade pressure on allies, demanding that they increase defence spending and purchase more US weapons – measures aimed at reducing the US fiscal burden. As a result, US allies have been increasingly sceptical of Trump's intentions and plans with regard to the so-called liberal international order. The leading countries of the EU, France and Germany, are strengthening their efforts to be independent and initiatives have been taken to enhance EU defence cooperation in order to reduce reliance on US military protection.

Third, more substantially, Trump's presidency has brought about a fierce clash of values, and the country's social and political consensus has been greatly weakened. Trump and his supporters have been accused of adhering to such ideas as white supremacy and other extreme conservative viewpoints that are incompatible with the liberalism advocated by pro-globalisation elites, leading to unprecedented divisions in US society. As some analysts argue, the US left wing and right wing have been divided on almost all domestic policies, but both call for the hardening of the China policy, arguably pushing US–China relations in a very dangerous direction.

Through changes over the past five or six years, China's leadership, with Xi as the core, has re-established its authority, restructured policy institutions and formulated a clearer medium- and long-term development strategy for the country, as proposed in a blueprint raised by Communist Party of China (CPC)'s 19th Party Congress. Although China's national development goals and strategies have maintained a strong continuity, the ways and means for achieving them have changed through major reforms of the party and state system. Central authority has been re-strengthened, and at the same time, supervision over the exercise of public power has been bolstered. The US–China trade conflict is better understood if it is put in the context of the 'revolutionary' structural changes in the US and China (Wang 2018b). Simply put, the changes that have taken place in both countries are revolutionary, and the domestic restructurings have produced spill-over effects that have aggravated the misunderstandings and tensions between China and US.

Reconfirming the truth about US–China trade

The US and China are two natural trading partners, and their economic and trade relations have brought enormous benefits to both sides (Wang 2018a). However, in the eyes of US security hawks and trade protectionists, the trade relationship with China is hurting American national interests (Navarro and Autry 2011). Such views have negatively distorted the US public's understanding of the nature of trade relations.

First of all, the US–China trade has been shaped in the broad context of economic globalisation. Because the trade is driven mainly by companies and follows market prices, one has sound reasons to argue that the bilateral trade relationship between China and US is generally free and fair, and the distribution of interests is overall even. Nobody wants to do business to lose money. While the American public does not understand the nature of China–US trade, US politicians intentionally or unintentionally conceal the truth for election purposes (Wang 2018a).

Secondly, the so-called huge US trade deficit with China does not accurately reflect the real distribution of the trade benefits. The rise of the global supply chain, driven by economic globalisation, largely accounts for the rapid development of China–US trade, but it also greatly exaggerates the gains earned by China. In the global supply chain, Chinese companies are generally in low-end sectors, although China has made progress in high-end sectors. China's exports to the US are largely generated by foreign companies invested in China, because these firms mainly treat China as a cheap place to assemble imported components and re-export them to other markets. The profits of Chinese factories and workers are far lower than those of Western investors and multinational companies. Apple's iPhone is a vivid example of this situation. Chinese factories and workers earn only 5% of the value added; Apple gains nearly 60%, and the rest goes to parts suppliers from Japan and Germany (MOFCOM 2017). This case reflects the reality of international trade in the era of economic globalisation: China's foreign trade may be large in volume, but the proportion of profits it collects is still small. This is further illustrated by another example: China's state-owned enterprises account for only 10% of the total exports of the country; most exports are created by foreign companies investing in China. Unfortunately, the American public and politicians do not understand this reality and complain about the high trade deficit with China. Some members of the elite in China do not understand the true nature of China–US bilateral trade either and are misled to be complacent about China's export surplus and competitiveness in so-called 'high-tech' products (Wang 2018a).

Thirdly, US politicians are not interested in disclosing the full picture of the trade flows, speaking only of trade in goods. In fact, the United States has a surplus of US$50 billion to $90 billion per year in terms of services, not to mention the $500 billion sales achieved by US-owned companies annually in the Chinese market, which includes a large amount of US-made spare parts and intellectual property (MOFCOM 2017). If all aspects of China–US economic and trade relations are added up, the two sides are generally balanced.

As most American economists argue, the trade deficit is not a problem caused by China's so-called 'unfair' trade policy, and is mainly a result of the US's too low savings rate (Tankersley 2018; Chandran and Soong 2018). Further, the claimed loss of 20 million jobs in manufacturing in the first decade of the twenty-first century is largely attributable to the progress of technology innovation.

Negotiations and consequences

Though the US–China relationship is defined by ideological and radical views on strategic rivalry over hegemony, economic interdependence and shared stakes set the ground for negotiation and possible compromise between the two countries. It is important to remember how economic interdependence puts checks on strategic competition.

Judging from the demand list (USTR 2018a) used by the US during the negotiations, its goals are to open up the Chinese market, curb the development of so-called state capitalism, slow down China's scientific and technological progress, and hence slow down China's rising momentum and challenges to the US position as a hegemon. In order to achieve these goals, the Trump administration has taken a set of comprehensive and combined actions, including the Section 301 high tariff sanctions, export controls and investment restrictions; restrictions on international student exchange; and high standard WTO reform proposals.

China's strategy for the talks aims to stabilise trade relations and the US–China relationship as a whole by promising big procurement orders and opening up Chinese markets to US-invested companies. By doing this, China has actually mobilised four major interest groups in the US, encouraging them to continue their support for reaching an earlier trade agreement. These interest groups represent agriculture, energy, Wall Street capital, and multinational corporations (MNCs) who have invested in China, along with chambers of commerce representing their interests. And the Chinese side also believes that the US state governments can provide a positive role in stabilising the US–China relationship, as most of the US state governments wish to conduct commercial cooperation with China as usual. The four groups plus local governments are believed to play a big role in balancing the influence of those deemed 'security hawks' or 'dragon slayers' in the federal government. The competition for influence on China policy is exemplified by the tensions between Wall Street and Peter Navarro, the China hawk in the White House. Just before the leaders of the two countries met in Argentina in December 2018, Peter Navarro accused former US Secretary of Treasury Henry Paulson and others to be 'self-hired' China lobbyists (CSIS 2018). While Paulson and Wall Street tycoons worked behind the scenes to bridge the gap between the two countries, they also sent a strong warning on the forthcoming 'economic iron curtain' to Chinese leaders (Paulson 2018; CCG 2019), hinting that the US trade and security hawks in power will dominate Washington's China policy if China does not make concessions on trade and investment issues. They also delivered these tough remarks to the domestic audience in the United States to prove that they too are defenders of US interests.

Because of differences in expectations and goals of the two sides, high uncertainties exist on the question whether China and the US can strike a deal or not, though the two sides signed the so-called Phase One agreement in January 2020. It is valuable to develop scenarios about the final results of the ongoing negotiations.

The first scenario is one in which the US and China reach a deal to end the tariff war. The US will benefit greatly from the huge amount of purchases from China, and US-invested companies will greatly improve their market access to China. These concessions will satisfy Trump's goal of re-election in 2020 – reportedly China is committed to large-scale purchases for six years. The long-term dream of opening up China's market will materialise if the deal is implemented well.

For China, the deal will help to deescalate, at least temporarily, the so-called strategic competition between the two countries and hence stabilise China's external environment. Since last year, the Chinese government has prepared to address US concerns on the trade imbalance and market barriers by informing the public that the concessions to the US will be in line with China's market-oriented reforms. Strengthening intellectual property protection and expanding market access will benefit China's economic growth. The media and officials argue that China's accession to the World Trade Organization in 2001 ushered in an explosion of tremendous growth and wealth. It is likely that such an agreement can boost the confidence of domestic investors and attract foreign capital into China, helping to overcome certain difficulties the Chinese economy faces now. Clearly, once the 'epic' deal (as called by Trump) is struck and truly implemented, the Chinese economy may experience another wave of relatively high growth. With such large stakes on the table, the possibility of reaching a big deal has greatly increased, though one cannot disregard the chance of a failed deal given the fluid mindset of Trump.

The second scenario is that the two countries do not strike a deal, especially the Phase Two agreement. One can list several reasons to argue for no deal. With the Section 301 tariff sanctions in hand, President Trump and trade hawks could seek a deal involving China's total surrender. Chinese leaders find such a deal politically unacceptable because it is too one-sided, too detailed and too technical, and it would force China to modify many of its domestic laws. The nature of such a deal is easily interpreted by Chinese people as violating the country's sovereignty.

The third scenario is that while an agreement is reached, both sides soon find themselves trapped in conflict over the interpretation of the agreement.

As part of its spill-over effects, the US–China deal will probably influence the economies of other regions. While China promises to import more food and energy products from the US, it may reduce its purchases from other regions, particularly Latin America, Australia, Canada and Saudi Arabia. As a result, the world may increasingly feel the power of 'Chinese procurement' and the 'Chinese market' and the influence of any big deal between the US and China. Decision makers from multiple countries will have to watch the impact of China's import readjustment on their economies and on the relations with China, which may become more complicated.

The China–US deal, if there will be one, will have an impact on WTO reform and the global governance system. As China promises to open up its market, based on the principle of national treatment, the gap between China and the US on WTO reform will narrow. With the implementation of the deal, China may find it easier to accept higher standards for market access in WTO reform discussions. The China–US trade deal could foster consultation and discussion on WTO reform.

Future trade: Stability or economic decoupling?

There is a saying in China that economic and trade relations play the role of 'stabilisers' and 'ballast stones' in Sino-US relations (Xinhua 2017). Given the current trade conflict and strategic rivalry, the question has emerged whether economic and trade relations will continue to play such a role.

The leaders of the US and China have played a leading role in all the negotiations on the trade deal. Though President Trump and President Xi pay attention to the differences of goals and interests, they tend to recognise the existence of common interests and hope to compromise on this basis.

As the case of putting Huawei on the US export control 'entity list' has shown, security hawks in the US government have taken advantage of the collapse of the 11th trade talks to push the policy of economic decoupling forward. While we should be vigilant about the decoupling prospect, one should note that the complex interdependence formed during the era of economic globalisation will probably work to constrain any substantial deterioration in China–US relations in the near future.

First, US–China trade has reached nearly US$700 billion (trade in goods and services combined), and the idea of 'decoupling' proposed by some trade and security hawks, can be very costly to both sides. In addition to trade, China–US monetary and financial relations are close, forming a relationship called the 'balance of financial terror' (a phrase coined by former US Secretary of the Treasury Lawrence Summers) (Summers 2004). China's continued purchase of US Treasury bonds has provided important support for the US economy and the status of the dollar. On the other hand, if China wants to have greater influence on the international financial and currency markets, it will also be unable to decouple from the dollar and the US market.

Second, after more than 40 years, the relations between the two countries have formed a dense network of close interpersonal relationships and various channels of dialogue. The relationships are linked to academic circles, financial circles and ordinary families. This is also an important constraint on the notion of a 'decoupling' between the two countries.

Third, the personal relationship between the leaders of China and the US is particularly important at present. So far, the interactions between Xi and Trump have been good, and a relatively smooth communication channel has been formed.

Fourth, China does not intend to replace the US's position in the international system. China's foreign policy is mainly based on international economic cooperation, and it supports existing international mechanisms and hopes to promote their reforms. While many people in the US tend to believe that China's development model and philosophy pose a challenge to the US, this argument does not make much sense because China does not advocate exporting ideology and emphasises respect for the right of each country to choose its own development path.

However, the so-called 'epic' deal cannot eliminate the strategic rivalry between the two countries. First, Trump and his team of advisers believe in his 'America First' policy and identify themselves with maintaining US hegemony. In the

Trump administration's first National Security Strategy Report released in December 2017, Russia and China are singled out as major social and economic threats. With the escalation of the trade conflict, China is believed to have actually replaced Russia as the biggest long-term threat to US national interests. Therefore, while the trade deal may imply a suspension of the economic competition, the US will continue to struggle with China's rise, using a whole-of-government and a whole-of-society approach (Pence 2018). The Trump administration recognises that it should improve the interagency and inter-branch coordination of policy making on China, and at the same time mobilise the social forces of different sectors to deal with the China challenges to its dominance in the world. US security hawks will continue to take advantage of the Taiwan issue, the South China Sea issue, and US dominance in the high-tech sector to build pressure on and slow down the pace of emerging China.

Secondly, US trade and security hawks, including Vice President Mike Pence, former National Security Adviser James Bolton, Director of Trade and Manufacturing Policy Peter Navarro, and former Trump adviser Steve Bannon, tended to believe that China is launching an economic war against the US and perceive the bilateral relationship as a strategic competition characterised by a 'zero-sum' game, neglecting the essence of mutual benefit between the two countries. The possible trade deal may frustrate their plans for a short time, but they will continue to work towards 'decoupling' the two economies.

Thirdly, following the 2018 mid-term elections, the Democrats and the Democrat-controlled House of Representatives will surely launch more actions against President Trump in order to win the support of voters ahead of the 2020 presidential election. It is quite possible that over the next two years, Democrats and Republicans, as well as Congress and the Trump administration, will compete with each other to get tough on China.

Rebuilding political trust as key to dealing with strategic rivalry

The hegemonic competition between the two countries is generated not only by the conflict of commercial interests but also by misperception. For a better relationship, the top priority should be rebuilding political trust and reducing misunderstanding, both of which are key to limiting the impact of strategic rivalry over the hegemonic position in world affairs.

The most important thing is to properly understand each other's policies. For Chinese leaders, it is important to understand that the adjustments made to domestic policies should not be too far away from internal and external expectations and it may be advisable not to go to extremes in the name of maintaining political security. They hold that the advocacy of the 'core values' of socialism does not contradict so-called 'universal' values.

On the other hand, American elites should learn more about China's changes over the past five years, particularly the changes represented by the CPC 19th Party Congress. As many studies show, the programme of the CPC 19th Party Congress has been one of the key factors driving US liberals and China experts to be more disappointed about the direction of China's transformation (Orville and Shirk 2019).

Clearly, China's policy adjustments in recent years can be perceived as necessary to solve the problems accumulated over past decades; the old development model is no longer sustainable – politically, economically or environmentally.

These policy adjustments introduced are not driven by a sense among elites of being a strong economy, but driven by their fears over the weakness of the Chinese economy, including declining labour competitiveness in labour-intensive exports and the middle income trap. That is to say, the core driver behind these adjustments is not a desire for China to compete with the US for global hegemony (for example, the Belt and Road Initiative), but rather fear of a 'governance deficit' and a shortage of 'international public goods', including institutions and resources to support international cooperation (Xi 2019).

Faced with the increasingly complex situation at home and abroad, the Chinese leadership has stressed the need to deal with three major 'traps'. The first is the 'middle-income trap'. China's comparative advantage in producing labour-intensive products is gradually disappearing. In order to maintain economic growth, China must rely on innovation, upgrading its industrial level and technology. The Made in China 2025 plan was conceived in this context, with the hope of using policy incentives to improve the competitiveness of the Chinese economy.

The second is the 'Tacitus trap', which refers to the challenge of losing government credibility. The Chinese government hopes to win back the hearts of the people and to consolidate its legitimacy by eliminating poverty by 2020.

The third is the 'Thucydides trap' (in some sense, the 'Kindleberger trap'). China has tried its best to avoid the 'Thucydides trap', in which an emerging power collides head-on with an established power (Allison 2017). At the same time, in the face of the increasingly inadequate supply of international public goods, China has made it ever clearer that it is willing to provide more international public goods to strengthen the global governance structure. In order to cope with the 'Kindleberger trap' (Nye 2017), which assumes that an emerging power is unwilling to provide international public goods, China has come up with initiatives such as the Belt and Road Initiative (BRI) and the Asian Infrastructure Investment Bank (AIIB). China is already the second-largest donor country in the United Nations and contributes the largest number of international peacekeepers employed abroad.

A good understanding of these three 'traps' could help US elites to understand China's domestic political and economic changes. Actually, these 'traps' that worry the Chinese leadership, can become a great opportunity for the two largest economies to work together for the sake of peace and the prosperity of mankind. China's peaceful rise and its lifting of hundreds of millions of its people out of poverty have been tremendous achievements, and both benefited from open markets and international cooperation. On one hand, the US has made huge contributions to China's development. On the other hand, while China has offered to give assistance to the US's infrastructure projects and other programmes (CCG 2017), it unfortunately has not yet received a positive response.

Finally, as the world's two largest economies, the US and China should keep in mind the lessons of history: the trade protectionist measures adopted by the US Congress during the Great Depression of the 1930s caused the global economy to be torn apart and ultimately led to the outbreak of World War II; the 'Cold War' resulted in several regional 'hot wars' in the Asia-Pacific region and led to head-to-head confrontation between China and the US for decades before the historic visit of US President Nixon. Both countries should work together to find ways to reconcile the differences of economic and political systems and to ensure that the competition between them, even a hegemonic struggle, remains manageable.

References

Agiesta, J. (2018) 'CNN Poll: 42% Approve of Trump, Highest in 11 Months', *CNN*. Available at: www.cnn.com/2018/03/26/politics/cnn-poll-trump-approval-rating-rises/index.html (15 April 2019).

Allison, G. (2017) *Destined for War: Can America and China Escape Thucydides's Trap?*. New York: Houghton Mifflin Harcourt.

CCG (2017) 'Sino-US Cooperation in the Field of Infrastructure and Project List [中美基础设施领域合作前景与项目清单]'. Beijing: Center for China and Globalization. Available at: www.ccg.org.cn/Research/view.aspx?Id=6289 (15 April 2019).

CCG (2018a) 'The China-US Trade Relations since the Mar-a-Lago Meeting'. Beijing: Center for China and Globalization. Available at: http://en.ccg.org.cn/the-china-us-trade-relations-since-the-mar-a-lago-meeting-a-year-in-review-and-whats-ahead/ (1 May 2018).

CCG (2018b) 'Sino-US Trade Relations and Challenges: Past, Present, Future and Policy Options [中美贸易关系和挑战:过去、现在、将来与政策选项]. Beijing: Center for China and Globalization. Available at: www.ccg.org.cn/Research/View.aspx?Id=9938 (accessed 15 April 2019).

CCG (2019) 'Lawrence Summers and Graham Allison Speak at CCG in Beijing'. Beijing: Center for China and Globalization. Available at: www.ccg.org.cn/uploads/2014-01-27/20190329en.html?from=groupmessage&isappinstalled=0 (accessed 15 April 2019).

Chandran, N. and Soong, M. (2018) 'US–China Trade Deficit Is Set to Keep on Rising, Yale's Stephen Roach Says', *CNBC*. Available at: www.cnbc.com/2018/03/25/US–China-trade-deficit-to-rise-stephen-roach-at-china-development-forum.html?&qsearchterm=US–China%20trade%20deficit%20is%20set%20to%20keep%20on%20rising,%20Yale's%20Stephen%20Roach%20says (accessed 15 April 2019).

Chinese State Council Information Office (2018) '"Made in China 2025" is Transparent and Open ["中国制造2025"是透明的开放的]'. Available at: www.scio.gov.cn/xwfbh/xwbfbh/wqfbh/37601/38181/zy38185/Document/1626850/1626850.htm (accessed 15 April 2019).

CSIS (2018) 'Economic Security as National Security: A Discussion with Dr. Peter Navarro'. Washington, DC: The Center for Strategic and International Studies (CSIS). Available at: www.csis.org/analysis/economic-security-national-security-discussion-dr-peter-navarro (accessed 15 April 2019).

EU, Japan and US (2019) 'Joint Statement of the Trilateral Meeting of the Trade Ministers of the European Union, Japan and the United States'. Available at: https://eeas.europa.eu/delegations/united-states-america/56329/joint-statement-trilateral-meeting-trade-ministers-european-union-japan-and-united-states_en (accessed 15 April 2019).

Feldstein, M. (2019) 'There Is No Sino-American Trade War'. Project Syndicate. Available at: www.project-syndicate.org/commentary/real-purpose-of-US–China-tariffs-not-trade-deficit-by-martin-feldstein-2019-01 (accessed 15 April 2019).

Ferguson, N. (2008) 'Team "Chimerica"', *The Washington Post*, 17 November, A19.

Franck, T. (2020) 'Here's What China agreed to Buy from the US in the Phase One Trade Deal', *CNBC* website, 16 January. Available at: www.cnbc.com/2020/01/15/heres-what-china-agreed-to-buy-from-the-us-in-the-phase-one-trade-deal.html (accessed 24 February 2020).

Friedberg, A.L. (2017) 'A New US Economic Strategy toward China?', *The Washington Quarterly*, 40(4): 97–114.

Han, J. and Gao, P. (2019) 'Liu He: Won't Give in on Major Principles, Oppose Levying Duty'[刘鹤:重大原则决不让步,坚决反对加征关税], *The Beijing News*. Available at: www.bjnews.com.cn/news/2019/05/11/577841.html (accessed 19 May 2019).

Kakissis, J. (2019) 'Despite U.S. Pressure, Germany Refuses to Exclude Huawei's 5G Technology', *NPR*. Available at: www.npr.org/2019/03/20/704818011/despite-u-s-p ressure-germany-refuses-to-exclude-huaweis-5g-technology (accessed 15 April 2019).

Lamy, P. (2018) 'WTO reform. Trump's Protectionism Might Just Save the WTO', *Washington Post*, Available at: www.washingtonpost.com/news/theworldpost/wp/2018/11/12/wto-2/?utm_term=.6043451f.2b60 (accessed 15 April 2019).

Ministry of Commerce, PRC (MOFCOM) (2017) 'Research Report on Sino-US Economic and Trade Relations [关于中美经贸关系的研究报告]'. Available at: http://images.mofcom.gov.cn/us/201705/20170526035246599.pdf (accessed 15 April 2019).

National Security Strategy (NSS) (2017) Available at: www.whitehouse.gov/wp-content/up loads/2017/12/NSS-Final-12-18-2017-0905.pdf (accessed 15 April 2019).

Navarro, P. and Autry, G. (2011) *Death by China: Confronting the Dragon-A Global Call to Action*. Upper Saddle River, NJ: Pearson Prentice Hall.

Nye, J. (2017) 'The Kindleberger Trap', Project Syndicate. Available at: www.project-syndicate.org/commentary/trump-china-kindleberger-trap-by-joseph-s–nye-2017-01 (accessed 15 April 2019).

Paulson, H. (2018) '*Remarks on the United States and China at a Crossroads*'. Delivered at the Bloomberg New Economy Forum, Singapore. Available at: www.paulsoninstitute.org/news/2018/11/06/statement-by-henry-m-paulson-jr-on-the-united-states-and-china-at-a-crossroads/ (accessed 15 April 2019).

Pence, M. (2018) '*Remarks by Vice President Pence on the Administration's Policy toward China*', Hudson Institute, Washington, DC. Available at: www.whitehouse.gov/briefings-statements/remarks-vice-president-pence-administrations-policy-toward-china/ (accessed 15 April 2019).

Perlez, J. (2018) 'Pence's China Speech Seen as Portent of "New Cold War"', *New York Times*. Available at: www.nytimes.com/2018/10/05/world/asia/pence-china-speech-cold-war.html (accessed 15 April 2019).

Schell, O. and Shirk, S. (2019) *Course Correction: Toward an Effective and Sustainable China Policy*. Asia Society Task Force Report.New York: Asia Society. Available at: https://asia society.org/center-US–China-relations/course-correction-toward-effective-and-sustainable-china-policy (accessed 15 April 2019).

Schneider, A. (2018) 'China's ZTE to Pay US$1 Billion Fine to Settle U.S. Trade Case', *NPR*. Available at: www.npr.org/2018/06/07/617849382/chinas-zte-to-pay-1-billion-fine-to-settle-u-s-trade-case (accessed 10 May 2018).

Summers, L. (2004) '*The United States and the Global Adjustment Process*'. Remarks delivered at the Third Annual Stavros S. Niarchos Lecture. Available at: https://piie.com/commentary/speeches-papers/united-states-and-global-adjustment-process (accessed 5 May 2018).

Tankersley, J. (2018) 'Trump Hates the Trade Deficit. Most Economists Don't', *New York Times*. Available at: www.nytimes.com/2018/03/05/us/politics/trade-deficit-tariffs-economists-trump.html (accessed 15 April 2019).

USTR (2018a) *Section 301 Report into China's Acts, Policies, and Practices Related to Technology Transfer, Intellectual Property, and Innovation*. Available at: https://ustr.gov/sites/default/files/Section%20301%20%20FINAL.PDF (accessed 1 May 2018).

USTR (2018b) *2018 Report to Congress on China's WTO Compliance*. Available at: https://ustr.gov/sites/default/files/2018-USTR-Report-to-Congress-on-China%27s-WTO-Compliance.pdf (accessed 15 April 2019).

Wang, Y. (2018a) 'The Chinese View: Ten Truths about U.S.-China Trade', *Los Angeles Times*. Available at: www.latimes.com/opinion/op-ed/la-oe-wang-china-tariffs-20180731-story.html (accessed 15 April 2019).

Wang, Y. (2018b) 'Trade Trap: China and the US Must Avoid a "New Cold War"', *Global Asia*, 13: 36–41.

Wang, Y. (2018c) 'Domestic Structural Changes and the Future Direction of Sino-US Relations [国内结构变革与中美关系的未来走向], *Contemporary International Relations* [现代国际关系], 6, 11–13.

Wang Y. (2019a), 'Interpreting US–China Trade War Background, Negotiations and Consequences', *Journal of China International Strategy Review*, 1(1), 111–125.

Wang, Y. (2019b) 'Zhongmei jijiang kaiqi xieyi shidai Beijing tongshi boyi huafu sida jituan [China and the United States are about to start the agreement era, and Beijing is playing for the four major groups of the US]', *Duowei News*. Available at: http://talk.dwnews.com/news/2019-04-10/60128286_all.html (accessed 15 April 2019).

Xi, J. (2019) 'Wei jianshe gengjia meihao de diqiu jiayuan gongxian zhihui he Liliang – zai zhongfa quanqiu zhili luntan bimushi shang de jianghua [Contribute wisdom and strength to building a better earth homeland: A speech at the closing ceremony of the China-France Global Governance Forum]'. Available at: www.xinhuanet.com/world/2019-03/26/c_1124286585.htm).

Xinhua (2017) 'Xi Jinping: jingmao hezuo shi zhongmei guanxi de wendingqi he yacangshi (Xi Jinping: Economic and trade cooperation is the stabilizer and ballast stone of Sino-US relations)', *Xinhua News Agency*. Available at: http://money.163.com/17/1110/07/D2S7QQ0M002581PP.html (accessed 15 April 2019).

12

COMPETITION IN CONVERGENCE

US–China hegemonic rivalry in global capitalism

Xin Zhang

The dramatic trade war between the United States and China since early 2018 for many represents the opening scene of hegemonic rivalry between an incumbent hegemon, the United States, and a major challenger, China, in the international system. According to mainstream views, such hegemonic rivalry is part of a natural progress we have started to witness since the beginning of the twenty-first century. From the very beginning, the confrontation, competition and contestation between the US and China has already been clearly framed, especially in the West, as rivalry between two systems of fundamental different natures in all major aspects, political, economic, ideological and cultural. Influential scholars in the Anglophone world were already very open about that back in 2008: 'Russia and China are not just great powers challenging the west. They also represent alternative versions of authoritarian capitalism ... the biggest potential ideological competitor to liberal democratic capitalism since the end of communism' (Ash 2008). US think tankers also echoed such an view by claiming, relative to radical Islamism, 'the ... more significant, challenge emanates from the rise of nondemocratic great powers: the West's old Cold War rivals China and Russia, now operating under authoritarian capitalist, rather than communist, regimes' (Gat 2007: 59). After a decade, US government's strategic reports reinforce such a view:

> [t]he central challenge to U.S. prosperity and security is the reemergence of long-term, strategic competition by what the National Security Strategy classifies as revisionist powers. It is increasingly clear that China and Russia want to shape a world consistent with their authoritarian model – gaining veto authority over other nations' economic, diplomatic, and security decisions. (Department of Defense, 2018, 2)

DOI: 10.4324/9781003037231-12

Accordingly, the 2018 trade war then is regarded as an avoidable showdown between democratic and authoritarian regimes, and between a liberal market economy and a state-led non-liberal economy.

However, we argue that in a dynamic sense, on multiple fronts the United States and China, and the two national political economies are actually converging at a pace and in a manner that very few have anticipated. The two countries have been converging towards re-juvenilisation of industrial capacities, under the same pressure of struggling between finance capital and industrial capital. Besides, their convergence has been subject to the same global trend that defines the basic features of the global capitalist system: financialisation. Therefore, the combined convergence between the two countries makes the bilateral relationship more resemble intraspecific competition over the same ecological niche, rather than the inter-specific competition across different ecological niches.[1]

'Twin surplus' vs. 'twin deficit' and rebalancing

From the fall of the Berlin Wall to the erection of the border wall between the United States and Mexico, intercepted by the 1998 and 2008 financial crises with two one-decade intermissions, global capitalism enters a new cycle. The financial crisis of 2008 in particular struck a big blow against the belief in the efficiency and legitimacy of capitalism, '[b]ecause of the unprecedented scale of the crisis but also because it emanated not from the periphery but from the very core of the system, especially the U.S.' (Deeg and O'Sullivan 2009, 754). The past three decades of post-Cold War globalisation under the American hegemonic leadership helps the liberal principles expand to almost the whole international society. Such expansion of liberal principles leads to universalisation the liberal principles both in terms of geographic coverage and coverage of issue arenas (Ikenberry 2009). However, since the 2008 financial crisis, we have also witnessed varieties of resistance against this order, ranging from various anti-globalisation movement, the 'Occupy' movement, to the rise of right-wing populist parties in a large part of the developed world. After the 2008 financial crisis, G20 was convened for the first time to seek a multiple-party solution to better coordinate macro-management of the global economy and avoid such crisis in the future. It is in this context that the US–China trade war broke out in 2018, which further indicates that the rebalance of world economy since 2008 turned out to fail.

We locate the hegemonic rivalry between US and China, represented by the recent trade disputes, in the context of long-term cyclic changes in the capitalist world system. In particular, we argue that the recent financialisation, as the running theme of this recent round of global capitalist expansion, influences both the incumbent hegemon (the United States) and the potential challenger (China). The ongoing trade war between the two countries is a key result of their converging from different starting positions in the world system during the era of financialisation, in particular, in a period of rebalancing for major economies as well as for the whole global economy.

The economic model of mainland China since the early 1980s has been built on large scale of exports of cheap labour-intensive goods to primarily the US market and markets in some of key US allies (e.g. Japan, South Korea). As a result, China has maintained a large-scale current balance surplus. Meanwhile, it also has kept a large surplus in its capital account and holds huge foreign currency reserves in the form of US treasury bonds. Such an unusual combination of 'twin surplus', while creating overall economic growth on the macro-level, essentially constitutes large scale of economic inefficiency and welfare transfer both domestically and internationally (Gao 2018; Hung 2008; Yu 2012). Domestically, an unusually high share of household income goes to Chinese businesses and to local governments, reflected in a very high level of domestic saving and subsidies for production paid for by ordinary households, resulting in a depressed exchange rate, lax environmental regulations and negative real interest rates that helps to transfer income from household savers to subsidise the borrowing of state-owned enterprises and local governments (Pettis 2019). Externally, such an accumulation regime in China channels large profits, particularly those created by Chinese low-end labour, from China to US while the holding of large amount of US treasury notes by Chinese government helps maintaining low consumer prices for US consumers and low inflation rates for the financial liquidity of the US financial market (Hung 2009). As some scholars put it, such a domestic accumulation regime in China is equivalent to 'resolving domestic issues with external solutions' (Gao 2018).

In contrast to the 'twin surplus' of Chinese economy, almost as a perfect mirror image, since the 1970s US economy has been characterised by 'twin deficits': large amounts of deficit in both its current and capital accounts. During the 1950s and 1960s the United States used to be a net exporter of manufactured products and capital to the rest of the world's war-stricken major economies. By the 1970s such a balance had started to shift and since then the US economy has functioned as the ultimate balancer of the global capitalist system by absorbing the excessive capital from around the world and providing accordingly the necessary demand for consumption for the global market. As a consequence, the US consumers enjoy generally low consumer prices and low interest rates and Americans rely on debt-finance more and more over time. The unique status of the dollar as the de facto global currency provides the United States with huge coinage to support such a trade imbalance, further ensuring lower costs of finance and lower consumer prices at home.

Since the 1980s, the rise of China as a new centre of global accumulation comes along with ever increasing dependence on export and debt-finance investment on the one hand, and on low domestic consumption on the other hand. As a result, over the past four decades the ever growing Chinese export-dependent economy and America's debt-financed and real-estate bubble-induced consumption spree have constituted two intertwined processes that account for nearly half of global economic growth (Hung 2008). Jointly, the mutually supporting structures of the American and Chinese national economies provide an important foundation for the global capitalist accumulation regime.

However, many economists have long regarded such a structure as 'global imbalances' and call for drastic correction for rebalancing this non-sustainable structure in the long run (Yu 2012). On the global level, over the past two decades, it has become increasingly difficult for the world to fix its massive trade imbalances; the very mechanisms that created them also make them harder to absorb (Pettis 2019). Roughly since the mid-1990s, push for such drastic correction from within both China and the US started to emerge. In the case for China, one started to witness serious signs of over-accumulation in the Chinese economy: decreasing return to capital investment along with increasing reliance on capital injection, overinvestment, under-consumption, and overcapacity in certain manufacturing and resource sectors, etc. (Zhang 2017). Consequently, demand for restructuring has been voiced through both official channels and the expert community. For example, Chinese top leaders have already openly criticised the China's once successful export-driven growth strategy as 'unstable, unbalanced, uncoordinated and ultimately unsustainable' as early as 2007 (Wen 2007). In the 'Made-in-China 2025', an ambitious plan to restart China's 'manufacturing renaissance', released by Chinese government in 2015, it is also clearly stated '[w]ith resource and environmental constraints growing, costs of labour and production inputs rising, and investment and export growth slowing, a resource and investment intensive development model that is driven by expansion cannot be sustained' (State Council 2015, 4). Chinese scholars have already been actively advocating for a dramatic shift in the basic structures of Chinese economy and the growth model: to shift from the current 'external-demand export driven model' to 'quasi-high-speed growth based on domestic demand' and 'consumption driven growth model based on the rise of real wages' (Gao 2018).

One recent policy initiative along this line is the China International Import Expo held in Shanghai in 2018. The Expo was specifically designated for 'imports' and one popular promotional slogan for the Expo was to set it as 'a platform for *Buy, Buy, Buy*' (Xinhua 2018). Such portrayal of the Expo indicates the Chinese central state's interest in at least experimenting with increasing imports with the intension of reversing the external balance structure of the Chinese economy. As the 2018 China International Import Expo in 2018 was regarded as a success, the Chinese central state decided to make the Import Expo an annual event.

Although policy makers and experts in China hold different views about specific policy choices, strong consensus seems to have emerged that to place growth on a sustainable path, China must continue to implement comprehensive policy measures to rebalance the economy, which not only engenders changes for China's domestic political economy but also holds direct implications for its engagement with the outside world, the US included.

On the US side, as the size of the US economy shrank relative to those of its trading partners, the cost of playing the global balancer rose accordingly. The US economy has also shown signs that it no longer is capable of continuing absorbing so much of the world's excess savings and no other national economy is large enough to play this role or no other country can accommodate the political costs associated with such a role. In addition, since the 1970s, the US economy has experienced significant de-industrialisation and during the same period financialisation of the US dramatically rose. Thus, reconsideration and efforts, similar to those held by Chinese political and economic elites, are also evident within the United States to restructure the domestic economy, which became particularly evident in the middle of the first decade into the twenty-first century. For example, although the US historically didn't have a tradition of industrial policy (Mann 1997), both Obama and Trump administrations actually respond to the de-industrialisation crisis and new industrial revolution in a very similar manner and both consistently advocated for re-industrialisation though 'promotion of industries', despite their partisan differences in many other policy fields. Since manufacturing revitalisation actually requires similar approaches for a matured post-industrial economy such as the US as for a catch-up industrialiser such as China, the two countries are thus also converging along the dimension of rebalancing through re-industrialisation, hence the enhanced competition for the same 'ecological niche' in international political economy.

Financialisation in the cyclic changes of global capitalism

Another background of the US–China trade disputes is the shifting nature of international system itself, on top of the common drives for rebalancing in both countries' domestic political economy. In this regard, the world-system analysis provides a helpful framework through which one can examine the international and domestic nexus that may help make sense of hegemonic rivalry in the era of financial capitalism. The world-system analysis looks at modern world-system as a set of nested and overlapping interaction networks linking all units of social analysis, so that the whole interactive system is more than the sum of the composing parts (e.g. all the nation states). Among various world-systemists, Giovanni Arrighi's account of systemic cycles of accumulation in the world system is of particular relevance for our analysis. Arrighi identifies two opposing logics of power through paraphrasing Marx's general formula of capitalist production M-C-M' into the 'capitalist logic' of power (M-T-M') and the 'territorial logic' of power (T-M-T') (Arrighi 1994). The former portrays territory (T) as a means for acquiring additional material wealth, while the latter takes money (M) as an intermediate link in a process aimed at the acquisition of additional territories. The choice between and different combination of these two logics drives a state's behaviour both internally and externally under different circumstances. Building on these concepts and insights, Arrighi analyses the 700-year history of the modern world system as a series of four century-long cycles of accumulation. He sees each of these cycles occurring through the alteration between a phase of 'material expansion', in which profits accrue through commodity production and trade, and a phase of 'financial expansion', in which profit making shifts from trade and commodity production to financial channels. The phase of material expansion coincides with the emergence of a new hegemonic power, the ascension of which in the capitalist world system rests on novel approaches of organising capital. Each of these cycles also begins in one territorial state actively engaging in territorial expansion, followed by a shift in the locus of capital accumulation to the financial sector, and ends with another new round of territorial expansion.

In this context, financialisation offers an account of present day capitalism where the scale and scope of current financial accumulation and innovation are primary drivers of change. In a nutshell, financialisation represents the transformation of the capital accumulation process of M-C-M' to M-M' by skipping the section of C, resulting in systemic 'profiting without producing' (Krippner 2005). Profits are channelled mainly through financial means rather than trade or production. Financialisation can manifest in various forms: the primary of shareholder value maximisation takes over as the defining principle of corporate governance; equity market takes over banking system as the main form of financial market; financial transactions represented by derivatives take primacy; financial knowledge promotes a specially privileged and unchallengeable expertise group; the role of financial literacy becomes a necessity for ordinary people, etc. (Krippner 2005; Montgomerie 2008). Beginning with the New Economy in the mid-1990s in parts of the western world, through to the global credit crunch in 2008, individuals, firms and domestic economies are increasingly mediated by new relations with financial markets, which is closely associated with the break out of the 2008 financial crisis in some of the core capitalist economies (Davis and Kim 2015).

The reality in the global system since the 1970s resonates well with the description of long cycles of expansion and contractions identified by Arrighi. The relative decline of the US hegemonic domination and the recent quick rise of China as a potential contender for global domination matches Arrighi's characterisation of the recent cycle of global accumulation. While both the United States and China have been subject to the same trend of financialisation, one can logically extrapolate from Arrighi's framework that the 2008 financial crisis heralds the transition to the ending stage of this long cycle under American hegemony (Arrighi 1994; Arrighi, Silver and Ahmad 1999). Arrighi also looks at China as the potential leading country to bring new dynamics to the global system thanks to its unique combination of imperial tradition, socialist legacy and reform era market practices (Arrighi 2007).

However, what is not completely accommodated by Arrigh's optimistic prediction about China is the more recent changes in Chinese capitalism: the increasing financialisation in both the Chinese economy and Chinese state's approach of economic management. The process roughly started 1993, the beginning of a new round of rapid liberal economic reform and high-speed growth after the 1989–1992 political backlash against further reform as the result of the 1989 Tiananmen political incident. It led directly to rapid increase of financial sectors' income in total national income and increasing inequality between the financial and non-financial sectors. Since 2005–6, Chinese capitalism has been undergoing a rapid shift from a material-expansion stage dominated by industrial capital to potentially a financial-expansion stage where financial capital may play the dominant role, thus approaching the peak of a major cycle in Arrighi's grand periodisation of world capitalism. The CCP's 18th Party Congress in 2012 essentially achieved two major goals in furthering financialisation. One is to further legalise land privatisation, especially in rural area, represented by the full circulation of rural land. As a result, the party line essentially breaks the independent, supportive role of land system to labour under the current constitutional framework. That may help to finally establish the full dependence of labour on capital in the long run.

Secondly, the 18th Party Congress helped to establish the dependence of small capital on big capital, making them the 'employed capitalists', ending the relative independent accumulation models for them. The origin of small capitals in China will thus increasingly become dependent on big capital, rather than relatively independent capital accumulation. Consequently, the Chinese political economy will place investment/financial capital in the leading position, helping consolidating a hierarchical system in finance capitalism. As part of the same process, heightened speed of capital circulation is also widely evident, particularly thanks to the abundant of finance capital. Overall, the relative ratio between industrial capital and finance capital is moving towards the latter's favour.

By most of the metrics, the speed of financialisation of the Chinese economy is now comparable to, or even faster than that of the United States economy. One important indicator in this regard, the ratio of financial sectors added value over GDP, has been picking up in China rapidly since 2005 and in 2018 reached 7.68%, about the same as that of the United States. During the years of 2015, 2016, and 2017, this measurement for China has been even higher than that of the United States.

Another illustrative metrics is the presence of so-called unicorn firms, which are privately held startup companies valued at over $1 billion. The global distribution of such firms clearly demonstrate US and China as the leading counties of origin, with a significant edge over other countries. Among others, a recent report by Deloitte and China Venture concludes that in 2017 China accounts for 38.9 per cent of the total number of unicorns globally, and the United States accounts for 42.1 per cent (Chen 2017). These unicorn firms from both countries are heavily concentrated in finance and Internet-related service sectors, which can be taken as major representatives of finance capital. In contrast, traditional major manufacturing economies such as Germany and Japan are distant followers in this global ranking of unicorn firms.

The same trend of financialisation has also changed the governance mentality of the Chinese state, which increasingly refashions itself as a shareholder and institutional investors, using all kinds of financial tools to manage state assets and public projects. Since the 1990s, as a 'shareholding state', the Chinese state has resorted to financial means to manage its ownership, assets and public investments, through multiple approaches involving the introduction of shareholder values in managing state assets, the expansion of state asset management bodies, and the provision of structured investment vehicles by these institutions to fund fixed asset investment (Wang 2015).

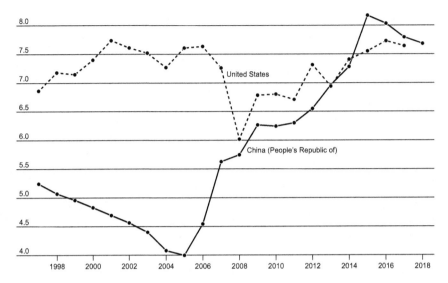

FIGURE 12.1 Ratio of financial sectors added value over GDP (US–China Comparison 1997–2018).

Source: OECD National Accounts Statistics https://data.oecd.org/natincome/value-added-by-activity.htm

Thus, China is rapidly building the infrastructural foundation for financial capitalism. Ironically, the seemingly stringent financial regulation by the Chinese state does not contain such a trend. Instead, it may protect and even speed up such a trend. Once such infrastructural structure is established, the protection role of financial regulation is then finished. Later, reversely, such infrastructural structure will push forward and protect the Chinese financial capitalism and its derived policies. Thus, one can draw the parallel between US and China in the sense that China now is undergoing the transition from Carnegie-style industrial capital to Morgan-style finance capital, similar to the United States during the early twentieth century.

Trade war and China–US hegemonic rivalry

The recent trade war results from the twin-transformation for both the US and China, the flip side of convergence of US–China as the result of enhanced financialisation and convergence in the rebalancing efforts on both sides. The first key event of the trade war took place in April 2017, when Chinese President Xi Jinping visited Mar-a-Lago estate in Florida to meet US President Donald Trump, where they agreed to set up a 100 Day Action Plan to resolve trade differences. On 22 March 2018, Office of the United States Trade Representative (USTR) formally issued the 'Findings of The Investigation Into China's Acts, Policies, and Practices Related To Technology Transfer, Intellectual Property, and Innovation under Section 301 of the Trade Act of 1974', along with request for levying additional 25% tariff over a series of Chinese imports. This represents the official opening of the bilateral trade war. The trade disputes lasted for about 22 months and the two governments reached a temporary deal in early 2020 (so-called 'phase one trade deal'). This temporary deal serves only as the prologue to a potentially long-drawn US–China competition on multiple fronts (Setser 2020).

Although the 'phase-one deal' seems to focus mostly on trade and tariff issues, '[w]hat is really going on is not about trade; it is about who will lead global innovation in the 21st century' (Garrett 2018). The core interest of the US in the backdrop of US–China trade disputes goes beyond balancing the international payments. Rather, it is about the revitalisation of manufacturing during the era of automation, artificial intelligence, and other key sectors in the so-called 'industrial revolution 4.0'. Re-industrialisation of US is characterised by efforts to meet the challenges from post-automation and post-intelligentisation, while the strong intention and ambitions to launch new round of industrialisation in China is more of pre-automation and intelligentisation. In this way, as both countries try to claim the leading role in this new round of industrial revolution, they are also converging from two different staring points.

On the China side, the most significant efforts in its re-industrialisation efforts is the 'Made in China (MIC) 2025', released by the Ministry of Industry and Information Technology of China in 2015 (State Council 2015). The document, even though released only as a policy proposal promoted at the ministerial level, has since become a bone of contention for the trade war between the United States and China. On the one hand, MIC 2025 seems to follow a long line of state-directed plans to channel government support and subsidies towards the development of industrial sectors and companies. On the other hand, the MIC 2025 goes beyond state-directed industrial development and takes on an even more ambitious tone to call for domestic enterprises to take a leading role in not just Chinese markets, but also global ones (Laskai 2018). The original document of MIC 2025 set ten key sectors as the focus of future development: electrical equipment, farming machines, new materials, energy saving and new energy vehicles, numerical control tools and robotics, information technology, aerospace equipment, railway equipment, ocean engineering equipment and high-end vessels, and medical devices (Hopewell 2018). All of these ten sectors clearly aim at new leading roles in the next round of major industrial and technological revolution. With similar intention behind the 2018 China Import Expo, MIC 2025 advocates for tapping into China's increasingly wealthy home consumer base as well as the value-added global sourcing segment to engineer a shift for China from being a low-end manufacturer to becoming a high-end producer of goods.

Consequently, although the US–China trade war seems to have centred on bargains over tariffs, the core of disputes is on the fate of (re)industrialisation in the era of industrialisation 4.0, evolving around issues such as intellectual property protection, forced technology transfer, cyber theft, reform of subsidies to state-owned-enterprises, and opening up of domestic financial markets, etc. (Zhang 2019). To the Trump administration, the MIC 2025 is a prime example of how

China's development model promotes unfair competition and disadvantages US businesses by subsidising Chinese companies and limiting market access to foreign ones. In March 2018, President Trump released a major investigation from the US Trade Representative's office highlighting MIC 2025's role in what it called China's 'unreasonable' trade practices. MIC 2025 critics in the US then gained evidence that the plan's ambitious targets motivate some of the questionable behaviours US officials have accused China of. Within weeks of Trump's first tariff announcement in June 2018, the Chinese government started to downplay MIC 2025 and has avoided mentioning the plan since then in official channels (Harada 2019). However, experts on both sides believe that the real ambition for industrial catch-up for China is not changed at all.

Behind the trade disputes, China is now struggling between an increasingly strong tendency towards financialisation on the one hand and, on the other hand, ambitious structural transformation of its key industrial sectors and uplifting its industrial capacity domestically and globally in the era of industrial revolution 4.0. Just like any other major late-comer in industrial competition, the rise of manufacturing in non-leading capitalist countries historically all required substantial trade protection and protection of domestic industries. The Chinese state has to rely on various means of subsidies and trade protection to achieve such strategic goals. Therefore, China is willing to make significant compromises in other fields in order to fulfil the MIC 2025 plans, despite the seeming back-down by giving up the MIC 2025 narratives in public. Thus, it is little wonder that the deep issues of the ongoing US–China trade negotiation are intellectual property, subsidies of SOEs and financial sectors. Disputes around bilateral trade issues between China and the US will linger on even if the two countries can reach some compromise in the short-run during this round of trade war

Even though the starting point of China as a national political economy seems dramatically different from that of the United States; the structural features of the two economies on multiple fronts are actually converging, in particular, due to the trend of financialisation and consequent drives for re-industrialisation on both sides. Thus, US–China hegemonic rivalry involves increasing competition for the same 'ecological niche' in the international system. In other words, the increasing confrontational relations come not from the fundamental difference in the two countries' economic, political and ideological systems, as have been argued by scholars and commentators in the West. Rather, it is the gradual but swift convergence between the two systems that drives the recent competitive mode. That is why the 2018 US trade war with China ultimately has little to do with President Trump's personal animosities or re-election strategy. It simply represents the most visible part of a much deeper global imbalance and the joint attempts from both sides of the trade war to rebalance their domestic political economy and gain a leading edge in future industrial revolution (Pettis 2019).

Such rivalry between the two countries may even push them to converge on the same institutional configuration. Without the competitive pressure of the Chinese telecommunications giants, such as Huawei, it'd be almost impossible for the almost taboo word 'nationalisation' to enter the US public policy debate. Even though in the end, the US government has not adopted the nationalisation of 5G proposed by the National Security Council. In a similar fashion, despite the deep suspicion towards industrial policy,[2] US mainstream economists are revitalising the debate on industrial policies and possibly lending some newly gained legitimacy to the idea of industrial policy. For example, two Massachusetts Institute of Technology economists, Jonathan Gruber and Simon Johnson, in their new book suggest more than one hundred places where the US could jump start the industrial policy, in a manner quite similar to the policy of 'special economic zones', widely used in China since the 1980s (Gruber and Johnson 2019).

Concluding Remarks

Much in the same way as Jan Tinbergen, the first recipient of the Nobel Prize for Economics, proposed in early 1960s that 'socialist economies' and 'free economies' at that time were already undergoing fundamental institutional changes, where market mechanisms were being increasingly introduced into the former and public sectors were playing a bigger role in the latter (Tinbergen 1961), we argue that the US and China are in a similar pattern now in the age of financial capitalism. Even though these two national political economies will not necessarily end up in the exactly same institutional configuration, evidence of convergence on multiple fronts since early 2000s are solid and clear. In the backdrop of intensifying financial capitalism, both the US and China are struggling to balance the relationship between financialisation and industrial production for the new industrial revolution as a key way to redefine its role in global capitalism. Such balancing acts for both countries require significant political will and manoeuvring, both domestically and internationally.

Although we take a critical political economy perspective similar to De Graaff and Van Apeldoorn (2018) and share their basic stance that 'making sense of US–China relations and their development with respect to world order requires a deeper understanding and analysis of respective domestic political economies, each of which is increasingly linked to a global capitalist economy' (115), we differ from their prediction of the future mostly scenarios of 'co-existence' between the two countries, where 'the United States and China would each maintain their own distinct political and economic system, both systems being – in different ways – part of and compatible with a capitalist and globally interlinked world economy' (115). Instead, we see the competition driven for the same 'ecological niche' is raising the stakes of the rivalry. We also deviate from the liberal view that integration of China into the US-led liberal order will ultimately transform China into an entity similar to the liberal political economy. The significant convergence between US and China, as we have observed, is not unilateral move from the China side alone. Rather, it is a joint movement of convergence from very different starting points for both countries, driven by the same larger social/political trend on the global level, financialisation and re-industrialisation in particular.

Although the bilateral trade disputes may have reached a temporary solution, US–China competition for the same 'ecological niche' in the international system is doomed to be more intense in the near future. How such competition in convergence will play out in the near future will not only determine the potential trajectory of US–China hegemonic rivalry but also shape the fate of global system in the era of financial capitalism.

Notes

1 For the use of 'ecological niche' in social sciences, please see Popielarz and Neal (2007).
2 John Sununu, former White House chief of staff once openly claimed, 'we don't do industrial policy' (Buigues and Sekkat, 2009, 170).

References

Arrighi, G. (1994) *The Long Twentieth Century: Money, Power, and the Origins of Our Times*. London: Verso.

Arrighi, G. (2007) *Adam Smith in Beijing: Lineages of the Twenty-First Century*. London: Verso.

Arrighi, G., Silver, B.J. and Ahmad, I. (eds) (1999) *Chaos and Governance in the Modern World System: Contradictions of Modernity*. Minneapolis: University of Minnesota Press.

Ash, T.G. (2008) 'We Friends of Liberal International Order Face a New Global Disorder', *The Guardian*, 11 September.

Buigues, P. and Sekkat, K. (2009) *Industrial Policy in Europe, Japan and the USA: Amounts, Mechanisms and Effectiveness*. New York: Palgrave Macmillan.

Chen, C. (2017) 'Who Has the Most Unicorns – China or the United States?', *South China Morning Post*, 7 September.

Davis, G.F. and Kim, S. (2015) 'Financialization of the Economy', *Annual Review of Sociology*, 41(1): 203–221.

Deeg, R. and O'Sullivan, M.A. (2009) 'The Political Economy of Global Finance Capital', *World Politics*, 61(4): 731–763.

De Graaff, N. and Van Apeldoorn, B. (2018) 'US–China Relations and the Liberal World Order: Contending Elites, Colliding Visions?' *International Affairs*, 94(1): 113–131.

Department of Defense (2018) 'Summary of the 2018 National Defense Strategy of the United States of America'. Available at: https://dod.defense.gov/Portals/1/Documents/pubs/2018-National-Defense-Strategy-Summary.pdf (accessed 14 May 2020).

Gao, B. (2018) 'Revitalization or Strengthening the Bones and Muscles: Kaleckian Macroeconomics and the Future Model of Economic Growth for China', *Beijing Cultural Review*, 6: 43–57.

Garrett, G. (2018) 'What is Really Going On Is Not about Trade; It Is about Who Will Lead Global Innovation in the 21st Century', 9 April. Available at: https://knowledge.wharton.upenn.edu/article/u-s-china-trade-war-really-future-innovation/

Gat, A. (2007) 'The Return of Authoritarian Great Powers', *Foreign Affairs*, 86(4): 59–69.

Gruber, J. and Johnson, S. (2019) *Jump-Starting America: How Breakthrough Science Can Revive Economic Growth and the American Dream*. New York: Public Affairs.

Harada, I. (2019) 'Beijing Drops "Made in China 2025" from Government Report', *Nikkei Asia Review*, 6 March. Available at: https://asia.nikkei.com/Politics/China-People-s-Congress/Beijing-drops-Made-in-China-2025-from-government-report

Harvey, D. (1999) *The Limits to Capital*. London and New York: Verso.

Hopewell, K. (2018) 'What Is "Made in China 2025" and Why Is It a Threat to Trump's Trade Goals?', *The Washington Post*, Monkey Cage Analysis, 3 May.

Hung, Ho-fung. (2008) 'Rise of China and the Global Overaccumulation Crisis', *Review of International Political Economy*, 15(2): 149–179.

Hung, Ho-fung. (2009) 'America's Head Servant? The PRC's Dilemma in the Global Crisis', *New Left Review*, 60(6): 5–25.

Ikenberry, G.J. (2009) 'Liberal Internationalism 3.0: America and the Dilemmas of Liberal World Order'. *Perspectives on Politics*, 7(1): 71–87.

Jahn, B. (2018) 'Liberal Internationalism: Historical Trajectory and Current Prospects', *International Affairs*, 94(1): 43–61.

Krippner, G.R. (2005) 'The Financialization of the American Economy', *Socio-Economic Review*, 3(2): 173–208.

Laskai, L. (2018) 'Why Does Everyone Hate Made in China 2025?' Council on Foreign Affairs, Blog Post, 28 March.

Mann, M. (1997) 'Has Globalization Ended the Rise and Rise of the Nation-State?', *Review of International Political Economy*, 4(3): 472–496.

Montgomerie, J. (2008) 'Bridging the Critical Divide: Global Finance, Financialisation and Contemporary Capitalism', *Contemporary Politics*, 14(3): 233–252.

Pettis, M. (2019) 'Why Trade Wars Are Inevitable?' *Foreign Policy*, 19 October.

Popielarz, P.A. and Neal, Z.P. (2007) 'The Niche as a Theoretical Tool', *Annual Review of Sociology*, 33(1): 65–84.

Setser, B.W. (2020) 'Lessons from Phase One of the Trade War with China', Council on Foreign Affairs, Blog Post, 31 January.

State Council (2015) 'Made in China 2025'. Available at: www.gov.cn/zhengce/content/2015-05/19/content_9784.htm

Tinbergen, J. (1961) 'Do Communist and Free Economies Show a Converging Pattern?', *Soviet Studies*, 12(4): 333–341.

Wang, Y. (2015) 'The Rise of the "Shareholding State": Financialization of Economic Management in China', *Socio-Economic Review*, 13(3): 603–625.

Wen, J. (2007) Speech at the National People's Congress, 5 March. Available at: www.gov.cn/gongbao/content/2007/content_595132.htm (accessed 14 May 2020).

Xinhua (2018) 'There is a Doorway behind the Buy-Buy-Buy – Visiting the Major Delegations of the China Import Expo', 22 October. Available at: www.xinhuanet.com/world/2018-10/22/c_1123595395.htm

Yu, Y. (2012) 'Rebalancing the Chinese Economy', *Oxford Review of Economic Policy*, 28(3): 551–568.

Zhang, X. (2017) 'Chinese Capitalism and the Maritime Silk Road: A World-Systems Perspective', *Geopolitics*, 22(2): 310–331.

Zhang, Y. (2019) 'Zhongmei Maiyizhan de 600 tian [The 600 days of the China-US trade war]', *The Initium*, 2 December. Available at: https://theinitium.com/article/20191202-mainland-economic-data-trade-war/

13

INDIA IN THE 'ASIAN CENTURY'

Thinking like a hegemon?

Ravi Dutt Bajpai and Swati Parashar

Introduction

The rise of some of the Asian states in the global order has prompted the call for the current century to be labelled as 'The Asian Century'. This chapter explores the concept of hegemony in this emerging global order, especially focusing on the role of India in this new configuration. India witnessed colonial rule under the British imperial project. The Indian independence movement was, in fact, an assortment of several contradictory yet complementary counter-hegemonic struggles of the historically oppressed classes and social groups. The postcolonial state of India has faced a different dynamic of multiple hegemonies and struggles of counter-hegemonies often intersecting with one another, both in contestation and collaboration. India offers a distinct case study to explore how the hegemonic contestations among various elite groups and counter-hegemonic resistance can be explained by being attentive to both the colonial legacies and the intricacies of postcolonial state formation.

The emerging global order is often referred to as 'the rise of the rest' and provides openings to institute alternatives to the existing Eurocentric ways of thinking and doing international relations. To this end, this chapter aims to investigate the opportunities this emerging global order provides to the postcolonial state of India. We explore India's track record in the global community in challenging the existing hegemonic order and then situate how India with its specific experiences with multiple hegemonies could participate in imagining an alternative framing of the global order.

This chapter is organised in three parts. The first section argues that the legacy of colonial rule and the histories of counter-hegemonic movements continue to hold an enduring influence on the conduct of domestic politics in postcolonial societies. In the case of India, its independence movement incorporated numerous counter-

DOI: 10.4324/9781003037231-13

hegemonic struggles under the aegis of the overarching objective of political independence (Guha 1983; Amin 1995). However, the advent of the independent nation-state did not meet the aspirations of several of these counter-hegemonic struggles; instead, the postcolonial state reinforced certain types of inherited hegemonies. The ongoing struggle of these counter-hegemonic movements continues to shape India's domestic politics. This section offers an insight into multiple forms of hegemonies in the postcolonial state-building project of India.

The second section highlights the role of colonial histories in the identity construction of postcolonial states. Several theoretical debates in IR have dealt with the construction of the state's identity, the composition of the state's interests and the conduct of its foreign policies. David Campbell (1998) argued that states' identities and foreign policy are mutually constitutive, implying that the constitution, production and maintenance of states' identities and their foreign policies cannot exist without the other. This section explores how its historical interactions with hegemonic structures during the colonial rule and since its advent as a postcolonial political entity, tend to shape the identity construction of the Indian state. The third section discusses how the rise of China and India in the global order may open new possibilities and approaches for the conduct of international relations. The international order has long been identified as an anarchical and unequal system, a system that is acquiescent to hegemonic control. This section investigates whether the dawn of the 'Asian Century' would inspire India to challenge the prevalent hegemonic ordering of global politics, and whether India would offer an effective alternative to organise global politics.

The counter-hegemonic descriptive of the postcolonial state

The discipline of International Relations (IR) as an academic endeavour draws most of its theoretical foundations from realism, still a dominant perspective to understand international politics. Realism asserted that international politics, with its systemic condition of anarchy, was different from domestic politics and thus, imposed a clear demarcation between the international and domestic (Morgenthau 1978; Waltz 1979; Jervis 1997). IR's fixation with systemic analysis while ignoring the internal dynamics of the agents (states) has been challenged, and domestic factors are recognised as vital analytical tools to explain how a state has practised international relations (Moravcsik 1997; Milner 1997). The all-embracing march of the processes of globalisation and the subsequent blowback against it by domestic interest groups have highlighted 'the conditions under which domestic and systemic factors moderate or reinforce one another' (Chaudoin, Milner and Pang 2015, 280).

The arguments about the primacy of domestic factors on the state's conduct of its international relations may be long-drawn. However, few would dispute the role that history or rather histories play in shaping the identity, interests and international relations of any modern nation-state (Wodak et al. 2009). In the case of postcolonial societies, the notion of the social and political collective as the 'self', the concept of nationhood and political ambitions for independent statehood, stem from claiming 'otherness' from colonial powers and their practices. In the case of India during colonial times, that 'otherness' was constructed as the binary opposite to the hegemonic colonial power of the British. Thus, resistance to hegemony is one of the foundational elements in the construction of India's national identity. However, before delving further into India's counter-hegemonic narratives, it is imperative to locate how we propose to understand hegemony.

IR offers several accounts of hegemony; most scholars see it as the power to dominate others. In order to emerge as a hegemon, a state needs to possess sufficient power and the will to exercise that power. Hegemonic power is seen as an actor powerful enough to establish an international rule; it ensures they are followed, and has the resolve to do so (Keohane 1989). However, the maintenance of hegemonic practices for a state, an organisation or an idea involves a complex interplay of various material, institutional and social capabilities. The prevalent hegemonic liberal order is built upon the assumption that the US as the 'owner and operator' would maintain the rules and institutions of the order and enjoy special rights and privileges. Most importantly 'the order is built on strategic understandings and hegemonic bargains' (Ikenberry 2011, 2). This chapter adopts the Gramscian approach to explain the concept of hegemony.

The Gramscian approach classifies two types of political control: domination based on coercion, and hegemony based on consent. Hegemony is seen as a way of transforming ideas into dominant discourses so that gradually these ideas become 'common sense'. In the Gramscian school of thought in IR, a state is understood as the leading group/ruling class of society. According to Gramsci (1971), hegemony is the dominance of the ruling class in terms of control over interests, preferences and ways of conducting tasks of everyday life of other groups. In other words, the ruling class presents its interests and modes of achieving them in such a way that it appears as 'common sense'. To maintain this 'common sense', either consent or coercion or a mix of both is deployed. As long as the consensual aspect of power is at the forefront, hegemony prevails, while coercion – though always palpable – is manifested in marginal, deviant cases. In case the ruling classes lose the consent of the subordinate class, the state is in crisis as the ruling group is no longer leading, but only dominating.

The prevalent hegemony can be challenged, if a new ruling class reaches consent with other classes and overthrows the existing hegemon. Unlike realism, which identifies hegemony only through coercive power, the Gramscian approach to hegemony is a combination of coercion and consent. Furthermore, while realism treats the state as a unitary actor, in Gramscian thought, the state comprises ruling classes of a society. For a social class to emerge as the ruling class, it must achieve consent among other subordinate classes (Gramsci 1971, 244). This is achieved by presenting the preferences, ideas and values of the ruling class as aspirational or universal (Carnoy 1984, 66). To create their version of the 'common sense', the ruling class must rely on the discursive construction of social reality. Thus, in the Gramscian approach to hegemony, cultural leadership through discursive practices is an important aspect. It means that, unlike realism, Gramscian hegemony relies on both the hard power of material capabilities and the soft power of attractive culture, ideology, values and institutions (Fontana 2008, 92).

The Indian nationalists in the quest for political independence recognised the dominance of the colonial rule over material and military power. The nationalists also realised that to contest the soft power dimension of colonialism, they needed to challenge the dominant discourse. Therefore, they proceeded to imagine 'the world of social institutions and practices as two domains – the material and the spiritual' (Chatterjee 1993, 6). The economy, statecraft, science and technology were regarded as material domains and thus, were in firm control of the colonial powers. On the contrary, the Indian nationalists claimed sovereignty on spiritual spheres focusing on cultural identity. Mahatma Gandhi's *Hind Swaraj* promulgated a manifesto for the colonised people to imagine themselves belonging to a higher civilisation and culturally different from the British colonisers (Gandhi 1933, 93–4). It was an idea that found resonance with other anti-colonial thinkers in Asia and Africa, such as Frantz Fanon, who identified the conceptual core of the anti-colonial struggle as 'cultural nationalism' (Fanon 1963). Thus, anti-colonial nationalists tend to trace their national histories before the colonial interventions and envision their nationalist foundations beyond the largely territorial and material dimensions fabricated during the colonial era.

The Indian elites associated with the anti-colonial movement then mobilised various socially and economically marginalised groups to amalgamate their specific counter-hegemonic aspirations into the larger political movement for national independence. It is significant to highlight that the Indian independence movement embraced other counter-hegemonic struggles, based on gender, caste, class within itself. However, the overlaying political struggle for independence – while drawing strengths from them – could not obliterate the individual aspirations of these different counter-hegemonic struggles.

Counter-hegemonic struggles in India have traditionally relied on political violence, as practised by the British Raj in India, as embodied by the postcolonial Indian state in its quest for dominance and sovereignty, and as embedded in subaltern politics, in acts of resistance by non-state actors and marginalised subject populations. There are more continuities than ruptures in the configuration of structural violence between the colonial rulers and their postcolonial successors (Parashar 2019, 338). Hegemony is critical to the violent contestations in the postcolonial state where the dominance of powerful groups relies more on coercion than on gaining consent of the ruled. Resistance by subaltern groups involves a challenge to the statist status quo as well as an aspiration to belong to the inherently hegemonic architecture of the modern nation-state system, which perpetuates violence and exclusions from the global, national to individual levels. The subaltern studies scholarship endeavoured to reclaim the history of the subjugated people from their perspective and not from the elite or colonial perspectives. Therefore, it is important to revisit the subaltern studies scholarship that has tried to make sense of the colonial and postcolonial politics of dominance and resistance.

While subalternity and resistance are well theorised in subaltern studies, hegemony and forms of dominance are less developed. The most attention to the concept of hegemony was given in *Dominance without Hegemony: History and Power in Colonial India* by Ranajit Guha published in 1998, in which he built a case for 'dominance without hegemony' in colonial and postcolonial India.

> We take the enigma of that oversight common to both of those rival ideologies (colonialist and nationalist) as our point of departure and go on to suggest that the colonial state in South Asia was very unlike and indeed fundamentally different from the metropolitan bourgeois state which had sired it. The difference consisted in the fact that the metropolitan state was hegemonic in character with its claim to dominance based on a power relation in which the moment of persuasion outweighed that of coercion, whereas the colonial state was non-hegemonic with persuasion outweighed by coercion in its structure of dominance. (Guha 1998, xii)

Guha argues that the South Asian colonial state was 'a historical paradox', since 'the metropolitan bourgeoisie professed and practiced democracy at home, but were quite happy to conduct the government of their Indian empire as an autocracy' (Guha 1998, 4). Guha claims that the colonial state was non-hegemonic since it could not 'assimilate the civil society of the colonized to itself', therefore, the colonial state represented 'a dominance without hegemony' (Guha 1998, xii). Furthermore, the indigenous bourgeoisie 'spawned and nurtured by colonialism' (Guha 1998, 5) failed 'to assimilate the class interests of peasants and workers effectively into a bourgeois hegemony' (Guha 1998, 133). The Indian bourgeoisie could not integrate 'vast areas in the life and consciousness of the people' into their hegemony (Guha 1998, xii) and the postcolonial state thus, continues with its 'dominance without hegemony' over the population.

Consequently, the lack of a hegemonic ruling culture ensured a heterogeneous political domain where civil society remained active and separate from the state (the consequences of which can be witnessed today in the form of numerous resistance movements). This 'dominance without hegemony', Guha argues, was reproduced under the postcolonial state because the leadership of the Indian bourgeoisie shaped the form and trajectory of the Indian freedom struggle (Guha 1998, 20). Central to this narrative is the story of the power contest between two dominant elite groups: one representing the bourgeois colonial rulers, who gained political dominance in India by coercion, and the other, the Indian elite bourgeois nationalists, who hoped to displace colonial domination to perpetuate their own, in the same language and idioms as the colonial masters (Guha 1998, 4). Neither was hegemonic for Guha in the strict Gramscian sense; their dominance had neither moral persuasion nor consent.

The organic class consciousness of the Indian masses who constituted an autonomous domain of anti-colonial and anti-bourgeois politics of their own, parallel to the domain of the elitist power contest, has been missing in the colonial story

(Amin 1995; Chaturvedi 2007). These masses, organised themselves into various interest groups, offering violent resistance to both the colonial state and the elite nationalist movement in order to realise their political 'hegemony'. In Guha's work, hegemony is arguably conceived of in a way that, on the one hand, points to the significance of subaltern agency in the construction of hegemonic formations, and, on the other hand, emphasises the element of consent over coercion.

Moreover, Gramsci argued that hegemony evolved through a continuous process of interactions between dominant and subordinate groups and always had an element of coercion in it. This is visible in India when some subaltern groups are incorporated into the hegemonic state whereas others have been dealt with more brutally through violence (Parashar 2019, 343). Understanding hegemony as a contested process in which consent and coercion are closely intertwined is particularly apt to highlight the character of India's neoliberal turn and subsequent counter-hegemonic struggles of various subaltern groups against elite interests.

The hegemonic contestations among various elite groups and counter-hegemonic resistance in India can be explained by investigating both the colonial legacies and the intricacies of postcolonial state formation. The elite groups will continue to wage the battle for cultural and political hegemony, and against this backdrop, subaltern groups will continue to reinvent their strategies for struggle and survival. The histories of anti-colonial struggles during its independence along with the contemporary counter-hegemonic movements have had a profound impact on how the postcolonial state of India perceives itself in the international community of nations.

The counter-hegemonic narrative of the postcolonial state

In this section, we discuss some of the key constituents and key arguments that inform India's identity construction as a postcolonial state. India has exalted its anti-colonial movement as an anti-hegemonic struggle; consequently, India has deployed its postcolonial statehood as a benchmark against the hegemonic order and practices. The postcolonial state may be considered a temporal aftermath while postcolonial conditions represent 'critical aftermath – cultures, discourses and critiques that lie beyond, but remain closely influenced by colonialism' (Blunt and McEwan 2003, 3). The self-perception of India as an ancient and rich civilisation and its subjugation by the colonial power, continue to be the key elements of the Indian state's identity construction. The constitution, production and maintenance of the Indian states' identity and its conduct in the international arena could not be imagined in the absence of either.

For a long time IR's theoretical space was dominated by the two rationalist perspectives of Realism and Liberalism; both explored how individual states' material capabilities are deployed to navigate the anarchical international system. The end of the Cold War allowed alternative perspectives to emerge such as constructivism which considered that 'human interaction is shaped primarily by ideational factors, not simply material ones' (Finnemore and Sikkink 2001, 1). It is important to remember that while constructivist perspectives existed before the end of the Cold War, it was 'the rise of identity politics' that gave constructivism an unexpected relevance to scholars in the field' (Onuf 2018, xiv). In recent times, the concept of identity has emerged as one of the key organising principles in IR theory. In contrast to the state as a rational actor, post-positivists claim that 'identities are the most proximate causes of choices, preferences, and actions' (Hopf 1998, 4).

Poststructuralists argue that foreign policies are not only discursive practices but more significantly they play a crucial role in the co-constitutive processes of states' identities and interests. Recognising states' foreign policy and their identity as discursive practices implies, 'that they stand, in social science terminology, in a constitutive, rather than causal, relationship' (Hansen 2006, xiv). Thus, states' identity reflects the self-perception of the state about itself and regulates how this self-perception guides and informs foreign and domestic policies. Although the states' identity is exalted through public discourse and promoted through bureaucratic processes, it is neither unitary nor an exclusive property of the state. Instead, the state's identity is discursive, relational, political and of a social nature. As discursive practices, identity is constructed through discourses, and just as one singular and stable discourse is not possible, a singular and immutable identity is unachievable. It is often argued that 'absolute fixity or absolute non-fixity is not possible with discourses' (Laclau and Mouffe 2001, 111). Likewise, absolute fixity or non-fixity of any identity is a chimaera, though specific constructions of identity tend to be dominant over a period of time.

In the light of the brief theoretical discussion above, we turn our attention to explain how the Indian state's identity as a postcolonial entity is propagated through its discourses on counter-hegemonic struggles. To start with, we claim that well before its independence in 1947, the idea of India as a nation was in existence as a discursive practice both by the die-hard Indian nationalists and the hard-nosed British imperialists. The legendary imperialist and British prime minister Winston Churchill disparaged the idea of the nation-state of India and asserted that 'India is merely a geographical expression. It is no more a single country than the Equator' (cited in Tharoor 1998, 128). On the other hand, one of the most renowned anti-colonialist and independent India's first prime minister, Jawaharlal Nehru, claimed that 'India is a geographical and economic entity, cultural unity amidst diversity, a bundle of contradictions held together by strong but invisible threads' (Nehru 1946, 562).

The tumultuous and violent partition of India by the departing colonial administration traumatised its successor postcolonial state to such an extent that, India 'has cartographic anxiety inscribed into its very genetic code' (Krishna 1994, 509). Therefore, it should come as no surprise that the Indian state holds the concepts of sovereignty, territorial integrity, and autonomy as some of its most sanctimonious ideals. Krishna (1994) described this phenomenon of boundary building to achieve national identity construction as another part of 'cartographic anxiety' where cultural, ethnic and social affinities transgress the territorial boundaries. In this case,

identity construction itself becomes a hegemonic process where the national identity subsumes or often obliterates other forms of identities.

David Campbell proposed that identity construction was 'achieved through the
inscription of boundaries that serve to demarcate an "inside" from an "outside", a
"self" from an "other", a "domestic" from a "foreign"' (Campbell 1998, 8). Using
Campbell's notion of demarcation of 'the others' in the identity construction of the
'self', we can argue that India has imagined itself 'in counterpoise to a colonial and
imperial west' (Krishna 1999, xxxiii). At one end it was colonialism that symbolised
domination, discrimination, and exploitation by foreign hegemons; in contrast to it
the Indian identity was posited as one struggling to overthrow colonial rule. The
state's identity construction through the dichotomy of colonial powers versus
colonised subalterns, allows the colonised countries to be recognised as a victim
while identifying 'others' as the victimisers (Miller 2013).

Colonial occupation and subjugation are considered the most distressing experiences of postcolonial societies and the fact that this collective trauma continues to
haunt India's quest for status and identity, is not an anomaly. Mahatma Gandhi's
idea of nonviolence and passive resistance in India's anti-colonial movement was
significant in constructing the Indian identity, a vision guided by higher moral
principles than merely material gains and realpolitik. Thus, invoking colonialism as
the other not only constitutes meanings and identities in opposition to India's own
self-identity but also 'unites all Indians: their common opposition to foreign
oppression, dictates, discrimination, interferences and exploitation' (Wojczewski
2019, 188).

It is often argued that deploying a counter-hegemonic identity against the
colonial power was a necessity to create a pan-Indian identity, given the scale of
internal divisions within Indian society. The nationalist elites leading the Indian
independence struggle had already recognised the difficulties in sustaining the discourse of national identity based merely upon the counter-hegemonic contest
against the colonial empire. Therefore, to provide a much longer temporal
dimension, India was imagined as a cultural unit; a timeless civilisation with abundant glories was included as a critical component to the mix of identity
construction.

It is worth noting that the civilisational legacies continue to be the core constituents for national identities of China and India, as both countries frame their
national identities in terms of civilisational entitlement and colonial occupation
(Malik 2011; Ollapally 2014). Civilisational entitlement is a sense of considering
oneself (as a state) as the natural and worthy inheritor of the ancient civilisational
glory, and framing their policies to regain the power and status befitting of their
size, population, geographic position and historical heritage' (Malik 2011, 28).
This sense of entitlement is further entrenched in the national identity construction, as the foreign occupation is held responsible for the loss of the glorious
ancient civilisational status. In the context of the 'Asian Century', it is important
to underline that the idea of victimhood is an essential part of national identity
construction in both China and India, referred to as 'the century of national

humiliation' in China and 'a century of rule by an alien race and culture' in India (Garver 2011, 103).

The idea of an ancient and peaceful civilisation has allowed India to project itself as 'domestically tolerant and pluralistic, and externally non-aggressive and non-interventionist' (Ollapally 2014). Indeed, in the formative years of the new nation-state, the understanding of the Indian civilisational links with the outside world also shaped the framework of its international relations. India's first prime minister, Nehru believed that the Indian civilisation was benign, peaceful and dynamic during the periods it was in contact with the outside world, while the lack of outside interactions made the Indian civilisation stagnant and backward (Chacko 2011). However, Indian foreign policy fixation with its civilisational exceptionalism has dismayed other states. To those outside, the Indian civilisational narrative, as propagated by the Indian leaders, 'proclaimed a special destiny or mission for India in Asia and the world, based on the greatness of its civilization, its strategic location, and its distinctive view of the world' (Cohen 2001, 46). In a way, the construction of the tolerant, peaceful and non-interfering nature of India's civilisational heritage is construed as a hegemonic discourse in itself.

Despite attaining political independence, India continues to agonise over 'post-colonial anxiety' of a society suspended forever in the space between the 'former colony' and 'not-yet-nation' (Samaddar 1999, p. 108). It implies that postcolonial societies must catch up with their colonising societies to be treated as a worthy member state of the international community. The modern enterprise of nation-building on the basis of the ideals of secularism, democracy, the rule of law and prosperity in socio-economic parameters are taken as global yardsticks to which India must measure up. To implement these ideas of nation-building, scientific growth, security, modernisation and development, the Indian state often resorts to behaving like a hegemon using state violence against those who dissent from this developmental model (Nandy 2003).

It is an acute dilemma for postcolonial states, should they fail to measure up to the hegemonic metrics of the modern developmental index; they are then classified as fragile/failing/failed states. On the other hand, should a state behave like a domestic hegemon, it may yet not achieve the requisite developmental metrics, while the state violence may trigger wider unrest, enabling possibilities of its categorisation as a fragile/failing/failed state. It is a paradox that most postcolonial states continue to struggle with: standing up to hegemonic forces in the international arena and yet behaving like a hegemon within their territories.

The above discussion is primarily focused on how India constructs its state identity through discourses, as a counter-hegemonic force in world politics. Though the Indian state is often fraught with cartographic and postcolonial anxieties, it often follows the policies of its colonial predecessors to overcome these deficiencies. India has managed to connect the discourses of its anti-colonial struggle and its ancient civilisational heritage, thereby, giving its statist identity much more endurance, acceptability and vigour in the eyes of its domestic as well as international audiences. As a counter-hegemonic, anti-colonial force in international politics, India emphasises self-determination as one of the key drivers of its foreign policy and that has been one of the guiding principles of the conduct of India's international relations.

The counter-hegemonic prescriptive of the postcolonial state

It is no surprise, given its anti-colonial history, that the independent Indian nation-state decided to adopt an autonomous foreign policy, instead of becoming a camp follower in the then bipolar world during the Cold War. It was an audacious decision given the precarious state of material and institutional resources of the newly independent state. India's idea of non-alignment and disarmament was primarily based upon its belief that mere political independence of postcolonial societies was inconsequential unless these societies could be free from the immanent hegemonies of the international society and the practices of statecraft and diplomacy that perpetuate colonial hegemonies. In recent times the global shift of power to Asia has offered historical opportunities both to China and India to challenge the existing Eurocentric approaches to international relations. In this section, we examine how India with its experiences in dealing with hegemony would utilise these opportunities in challenging the immanent hegemony of the international order.

In March 1947, even before its independence, India had organised the Asian Relations Conference in New Delhi to revive old regional connections broken by colonialism and to make collective efforts to bring peace and progress in the region. Though the conference did not lead to any significant material or institutional outcomes, it set the tone of anti-colonial, counter-hegemonic identity for several of the Asian states. At the conference, Nehru observed that for too long 'Asia have been petitioners in Western courts and chancelleries' and declared that 'We [Asians] do not intend to be playthings of others' (Asian Relations Organisation 1948, 24). Thus, not being a plaything or supplicant to hegemonic agents (Europeans in this instance) was at the forefront of Nehru's agenda. Therefore, it should come as no surprise that India since its independence has placed a high value on protecting its strategic autonomy and supporting anti-colonial nationalisms in other societies struggling for independence.

In the 1950s, Indian foreign policy under the leadership of Nehru followed an internationalist approach and worked to build a third alternative, moving away from the hegemonic structuring of the bipolar world for newly independent African and Asian nations. The idea of the Non-Aligned Movement was to extrapolate India's nonviolent and peaceful resistance to British colonial power as a moral framework to conduct international relations. At Bandung *Panchsheel* [1] – or the five principles of peaceful co-existence – was asserted as an alternative to Cold War bipolarity. It was the first 'assertion of a specifically Asian approach to international relations at a time when the determination of international affairs remained the preserve of the West' (Percival Wood 2010, 78). *Panchsheel* was seen as the rejection of Western hegemony on the analytical framework for the conduct of international relations. The Asian-African Conference held at Bandung in 1955 led to the formation of the Non-Aligned Movement, through which 'the newly decolonised nations sought to establish an international political, economic and ideological identity, distinct from those of the capitalist West and the communist East' (Young 2006, 12). These two conferences were in continuation of each other: the 'Asian Relations Conference was about independence (from colonial rule), Bandung was about intervention (security from great power or superpower intervention)' (Acharya 2016, 1006).

In the 14-year period from the 1947 Asian Relations Conference, to the formal setup of the Non-Aligned Movement in 1961, India had acquired a leadership role in the international arena. Admittedly, India did not have the requisite material resources to be considered as a powerful state in the traditional sense, yet 'India's position on world issues was informed by a rare moral clarity and courage which won India many admirers, made India the leader of the developing countries' (Sikri 2008, 11). However, the Sino-Indian border clashes in 1962 dashed the high hopes of Asian solidarity, postcolonial comradeship, and most unfortunately dealt a blow to the aspirations of the Non-Aligned Movement.

It is arguable that at the multilateral, regional fora – despite India's genuine efforts to foster anti-hegemonic solidarity – the results have been somewhat mixed. However, it must be underlined that while India had enough moral power to make an exclusive claim to the leadership of postcolonial and non-aligned nations, instead of behaving like a hegemon, India has always preferred to share power with China, the other significant Asian power. It does reflect in some ways how India might behave if it achieves a 'great power' status in the international community.

After defeat in the 1962 Sino-Indian war, India abandoned its policy of disarmament and embraced massive arms procurement. In the aftermath of this war, India adopted a more pragmatic strategic outlook and devised a regional policy that placed South Asia at the heart of India's security policy. Therefore, India assumed the responsibility of settling any domestic conflicts in neighbouring countries, precluding any intervention of outside, or extra-regional powers (Wagner 2012, 4). This change in security outlook then led to Indian interventions in the region. In 1971, India's military intervention in Bangladesh (then East Pakistan) was considered as the declaration to take on the 'hegemonic role in South Asia' (Devotta 2003, 367). India's decisive military action in Bangladesh is interpreted as its emergence as a dominant regional power, with accusations of displaying hegemonic tendencies (Crossette 2008).

Other Indian military interventions too followed; though these were not unilateral interventions, India deployed its military only with the consent of the host countries. In 1987, India dispatched its military to Sri Lanka to resolve the civil war between the Sri Lankan state and the Liberation Tigers of Tamil Eelam (LTTE); and in 1988, India rushed its military to prevent an imminent coup in the Maldives (Bhasin 2008). As part of non-military interventions, India enforced a road blockade on landlocked Nepal not once but twice in 1989 and as late as in 2015 (Singh 2016). Thus, in the South Asian region, India is seen more as a hegemon than a benign leader. It is evident that in South Asia, India's size and other capabilities make it look like a hegemon. However, with growing resistance from its neighbours and with changing geopolitical equations, India has not found it easy to behave like a hegemon in the region.

The first two decades of the twenty-first century have witnessed the ascent of Asian powerhouses, China and India as major strategic and economic powers in the world. In the next few years, China will emerge as the biggest economy on the globe while India may rise to third or fourth in that list. Economic power, though desirable and necessary, is not a sufficient condition to be considered as a major global power; extremely prosperous Japan and Germany are a case in point. Given India's inherent economic, social and geopolitical vulnerabilities, one can argue that even in strictly material terms India has a long and an arduous journey ahead to emerge as an authentic global power. However, assuming that India does rise in a largely misleading global power index, a more critical question to ask is, does India have the will to be a global power? Thus, like hegemony which needs both capabilities and the will to deploy those capabilities, power in the context of world politics is not something you hoard but what you exercise.

The transformation from being a putative or potential power to a practising power in the global order happens once the emergent power is willing to assume additional responsibilities that come with being major stakeholders in the global system, that is from being a mere 'rule-taker' to becoming a robust 'rule-maker'. Existing hegemonies are challenged by the emerging powers by assuming the role of 'rule-maker' in the global system. To apply the Gramscian approach to hegemony, once the authority over the discursive construction of 'common sense' is taken away from the ruling class, a new historical block would emerge. However, the existing hegemon would try different mechanisms including persuasion and coercion to thwart the formation of the alternative figurehead. Thus, it is no surprise that China's rise in the global system is often paraphrased as 'a challenger to rule-based order' or 'a revisionist power'.

The new global order positions China and India as leaders and mandates that India rise to the challenge of taking on extra responsibilities towards global governance. This brings us to the critical question: how far can India go in framing the agenda for global governance with its structural deficiencies? However, a new multilateral arrangement can be imagined along the lines of BRIC[2] although this is not to assume that these very states will form the alternative group. No matter which states become part of this collective, one thing is certain that both China and India would feature among some of the prominent members along with several other postcolonial states as stakeholders.

Such a multilateral group would be very different from the existing American led liberal hegemonic order where the US takes the role of the patron, sets the rules and gets special privileges in the bargain. As a collective of states, this arrangement would not allow a singular leviathan to override other members of the group or even the rest of the global society. The leadership of such a group would not be in a dominant position to impose arbitrary ideas and subjective ideals from their domestic political culture, governance model or the personal preferences of individual leaders. At the beginning alone such an unusual grouping would face several daunting tasks but none more prominent than the dislocation of the prevalent 'common sense' with an alternative narrative and the task to share the responsibilities and material liabilities towards the upkeep of global governance among the leadership group.

Given our understanding of IR and available analytical frameworks, it is hard to imagine such a diverse multilateral coalition of different political systems as one cohesive, synchronised group. One would encounter several theoretical, institutional and logistical challenges even to imagine such a divergent group as a collective. However, as in social science, there are no final answers and while the exact composition, characteristics and charter of such a group may be unknown, it is certain that an alternative arrangement of global order will undoubtedly emerge.

Conclusion

One person's leader is another person's hegemon; there is no denying that, like everything else in social sciences, hegemony is discursive as long as it is based on consent and not on coercion. Material capabilities in terms of military, economy, geography and demography are considered as essential ingredients to achieve hegemony, but hegemony is sustained through discourses, by assuming cultural leadership. In the Gramscian understanding, the concept of hegemony is understood as the framing of dominant discourse by the ruling classes to project their interests and preferences so that it appears as 'common sense'. The efforts to superimpose this 'common sense' over the other classes of society is achieved through consent or coercion or a mix of both. Gramsci believed that hegemony prevails through consensus, while coercion is used only in exceptional cases. If the consensus is lost, then the ruling class is no longer leading but only dominating.

The emerging world order has positioned India as one of the future global powers, and this chapter explored the concept of hegemony with India as a specific case study. The fascination with imagining India as an imminent global power somehow ignores the basic fact that India is indeed a postcolonial society with its share of discriminatory politics, oppression and exploitation of certain sections of population, inherited from the colonial empire. The contemporary Indian nation-state is a product of extractive colonial policies and cartographic (mis)adventurism. The Indian independence struggle was led by the local elites but its success was enabled only through the active participation of the larger society.

We argued that the Indian independence movement incorporated many other counter-hegemonic struggles under its umbrella, with an implicit understanding of addressing those grievances during the anti-colonial struggle and in the post-independence period. Just as the revolution devours its own children, an elite-dominated political movement decimates its own subaltern children. India, after its political independence, sustained the very same systemic inequalities that it promised to uproot, thus reviving the colonial era domestic counter-hegemonic struggles against the state. Postcolonial India is, thus, an example of how multiple forms of hegemonies and challenges to those hegemonies are negotiated on a regular basis.

We also traced the process of identity construction of India as an independent nation-state. Independence dawned on the Indian state but only after the Indian nation was partitioned along communal lines. As a postcolonial construct marred by territorial separation and consumed by the desire to prove itself as equal to the colonial rulers, India adopted the vocabulary and strategies of state-building of the colonial masters. India constructed its national identity on the basis of anti-colonialism and on the notions of being the inheritors of an ancient and glorious civilisation. The early leaders were keen to project the Indian state as a counter-hegemonic force among the community of nations. However, domestically India had to resort to certain hegemonic practices to proclaim successful state-building in a postcolonial context, in order to present itself as a counter-hegemonic force in the international arena.

India's national identity as a counter-hegemonic force and an ardent supporter of the other oppressed nations was on full display in the international arena right from its independence. Even as a poor, third world, postcolonial state, India endeavoured to imagine a world order based on equality, sovereignty, self-respect and self-reliance for all the other states. We highlighted India's role in imagining and institutionalising the third alternative to the Capitalist West and the Communist East, to contest the immanent hegemony of the Cold War driven bipolar world order. We explored the histories of Indian efforts to foster Asian solidarity, third world solidarity and the Non-Aligned Movement. We claim that by propagating the idea of *Panchsheel*, India along with China provided an authentic Asian framework to International Relations, a discipline mainly reflecting Western hegemony on how to manage international relations.

We discussed that India is perceived as a hegemon in the South Asian region in some parts due to its follies, but its size and influence make it susceptible to be called a hegemon. In recent times the rise of China and India in the world order has raised expectations from other states. Contemporary India is indeed better prepared than before to play a more significant role in global affairs, but India alone cannot change the existing hegemonic ordering of the global system. We conclude that India would need to forge a multilateral collective with other states in order to bring in any meaningful change in the prevalent hegemonic global order.

Notes

1 Panchsheel: As adopted in the 1954 Sino-Indian Treaty. The five principles include (1) Mutual respect for each other's territorial integrity and sovereignty (2) Mutual non-aggression (3) Mutual non-interference in each other's internal affairs (4) Equality and mutual benefit (5) Peaceful co-existence.
2 BRICS: An association of five leading developing countries – Brazil, Russia, India, China and South Africa, to challenge the monopoly of Western-dominated Bretton Woods institutions over global governance.

References

Acharya, A. (2016) 'Studying the Bandung Conference from a Global IR Perspective', *Australian Journal of International Affairs*, 70(4), 342–357.

Amin, S. (1995) *Event, Metaphor, Memory: Chauri Chaura, 1922–1992*. Berkeley: University of California Press.

Asian Relations Organisation (1948) *Asian Relations: Being a Report of the Proceedings and Documentation of the First Asian Relations Conference, March–April 1947*. New Delhi: Asian Relations Organisation.

Bhasin, M. (2008) 'India's Role in South Asia: Perceived Hegemony or Reluctant Leadership?' Available at: www.globalindiafoundation.org/MadhaviBhasin.pdf (accessed 30 January 2019).

Blunt, A. and McEwan, C. (2003) *Postcolonial Geographies*. New York: Continuum.

Campbell, D. (1998) *Writing Security: United States Foreign Policy and the Politics of Identity*. Minneapolis: University of Minnesota Press.

Carnoy, M. (1984) *The State and Political Theory*. Princeton, NJ: Princeton University Press.

Chacko, P. (2011) *Indian Foreign Policy: The Politics of Postcolonial Identity from 1947–2004*. New York: Routledge.

Chatterjee, P. (1993) *The Nation and its Fragments: Colonial and Postcolonial Histories*. Princeton, NJ: Princeton University Press.

Chaturvedi, V. (2007) *Peasant Pasts: History and Memory in Western India*. Berkeley and Los Angeles: University of California Press.

Chaudoin, S., Milner, H. and Pang, X. (2015) 'International Systems and Domestic Politics: Linking Complex Interactions with Empirical Models in International Relations', *International Organization*, 69(2), 275–309.

Cohen, S.P. (2001) *India: Emerging Power*. Washington, DC: Brookings Institution Press.

Crossette, B. (2008) 'Indira Gandhi's Legacy: Vying for Mastery in South Asia', *World Policy Journal*, 25(1), 36–44.

Devotta, N. (2003) 'Is India Over-Extended? When Domestic Disorder Precludes Regional Intervention', *Contemporary South Asia*, 12(3), 365–380.

Fanon, F. (1963) *The Wretched of the Earth*. New York: Grove Press.

Finnemore, M. and Sikkink, K. (2001) 'Taking Stock: The Constructivist Research Program in International Relations and Comparative Politics', *Annual Review of Political Science*, 4(1), 391–416.

Fontana, B. (2008) 'Hegemony and Power in Gramsci', in R. Howson and K. Smith (eds), *Hegemony: Studies in Consensus and Coercion*, New York: Routledge, 80–107.

Gandhi, M.K. (1933) *Hind Swaraj or Indian Home Rule*. Varanasi, India: Sarva Seva Sangh Prakashan.

Garver, J. (2011) 'The Unresolved Sino–Indian Border Dispute', *China Report*, 47(2), 99–113.

Gramsci, A. (1971) *Selections from the Prison Notebooks*. New York: International Publishers.

Guha, R. (1998) *Elementary Aspects of Peasant Insurgency in Colonial India*. New Delhi: Oxford University Press.

Hansen, L. (2006) *Security as Practice: Discourse Analysis and the Bosnian War*. London and New York: Routledge.

Hopf, T. (1998) 'The Promise of Constructivism in International Relations Theory', *International Security*, 23(1), 171–200.

Ikenberry, G.J. (2011) *Liberal Leviathan: The Origins, Crisis, and Transformation of the American World Order*. Princeton, NJ: Princeton University Press.

Jervis, R. (1997) *System Effects: Complexity in Political and Social Life*. Princeton, NJ: Princeton University Press.

Keohane, R.O. (1989) *International Institutions and State Power: Essays in International Relations Theory*. Boulder, CO: Westview Press.

Krishna, S. (1994) 'Cartographic Anxiety: Mapping the Body Politic in India', *Alternatives*, 19(4), 507–521.

Krishna, S. (1999) *Postcolonial Insecurities: India, Sri Lanka, and the Question of Nationhood*. Minneapolis: University of Minnesota Press.

Laclau, E. and Mouffe, C. (2001) *Hegemony and Socialist Strategy: Towards a Radical Democratic Politics*. London: Verso.

Malik, M. (2011) *China and India: Great Power Rivals*. Boulder, CO: FirstForumPress.

Miller, M.C. (2013) *Wronged by Empire: Post-Imperial Ideology and Foreign Policy in India and China*. Stanford, CA: Stanford University Press.

Milner, H.V. (1997) *Interests, Institutions, and Information*. Princeton, NJ: Princeton University Press.

Moravcsik, A. (1997) 'Taking Preferences Seriously: A Liberal Theory of International Politics', *International Organization*, 51(4), 513–553.

Morgenthau, H.J. (1978) *Politics among Nations: The Struggle for Power and Peace*. New York: Alfred A. Knopf.

Nandy, A. (2003) *The Romance of the State and the Fate of Dissent in the Tropics*. New Delhi: Oxford University Press.

Nehru, J. (1946) *The Discovery of India*. London: Meridian Books.

Ollapally, D. (2014) 'India's Evolving National Identity Contestation: What Reactions to the "Pivot" Tell Us'. Available at: www.theasanforum.org/indiasevolving-national-identity-contestation-what-reactions-to-the-pivot-tell-us/ (accessed 30 January 2019).

Onuf, N. (2018) 'Preface', in M.E. Bertucci, J. Hayes and P. James (eds), *Constructivism Reconsidered: Past, Present, and Future*, Ann Arbor, MI: University of Michigan Press, xii–xx.

Parashar, S. (2019) 'Colonial Legacies, Armed Revolts and State Violence: The Maoist Movement in India', *Third World Quarterly*, 40(2), 337–354.

Percival Wood, S. (2010) 'Sovereignty and Resistance: India, China and the Asian-African Conference, 1955'. Thesis (PhD), Deakin University, Melbourne.

Samaddar, R. (1999) *The Marginal Nation: Transborder Migration from Bangladesh to West Bengal*. New Delhi: Sage.

Sikri, R. (2008) 'Mahatma Gandhi's Influence on India's Foreign Policy', in I. Ahmed, R. Sikri, D.M. Nachane and P.N. Mukherji (eds), *The Legacy of Gandhi: A 21st Century Perspective*, Singapore: Institute of South Asian Studies, 11–15.

Singh, B. (2016) 'India's Neighbourhood Policy: Geopolitical Fault Line of Its Nepal Policy in the Post-2015 Constitution', *Journal of International and Area Studies*, 23(1), 59–75.

Tharoor, S. (1998) 'E Pluribus, India: Is Indian Modernity Working?', *Foreign Affairs*, 77(1), 128–134.

Wagner, C. (2012) 'Emerging Powers in Regional Architecture'. www.swp-berlin.org/fileadmin/contents/products/arbeitspapiere/WP_FG7_2012_01_August_wgn.pdf (accessed 11 May 2020).

Waltz, K. N. (1979) *Theory of International Politics*. Boston, MA: McGraw-Hill.

Wodak, R., de Cillia, R., Reisigl, M., Liebhart, K., Hirsch, A., Mitten, R. and Unger, J.W. (2009) *The Discursive Construction of National Identity*. Edinburgh: Edinburgh University Press.

Wojczewski, T. (2019) 'Identity and World Order in India's post-Cold War Foreign Policy Discourse', *Third World Quarterly*, 40(1), 180–198.

Young, R.J.C. (2006) 'Postcolonialism: From Bandung to the Tricontinental', *Historein*, 5: 11–21.

14

ON THE POWER OF IMPROVISATION

Why is there no hegemon in Central Asia?

Viktoria Akchurina

Introduction: Power as control and social change

Central Asia represents a case which challenges the conventional understanding of power as control. Since the infamous Mackinder's verse (1904), the region has been portrayed as 'tabula rasa' or the no one's land, which can grant its hegemon the gates to world domination. Some authors approach the region through 'local rules', which the local elites set up within the Great Game (Cooley 2014). While both structural and power-based approaches to hegemony provide a graceful entry to the context of power in the region, they are helpless in understanding the social sources of power in the times of uncertainty, which often lie in improvisation and social resistance.

While Russia has been the so-called 'hegemon by default' (Russo 2018), the history and negotiation patterns within the Eurasian Union demonstrate the fluid and contingent nature of the so-called 'Russian project', with smaller states often portraying bigger influence than the larger states. China, as a 'hegemon by improvisation' (Russo 2018), has been challenged many times in the course of crafting its influence by a number of social protests and social movements across Kazakhstan, Kyrgyzstan and Tajikistan (Laruelle 2018). The United States and its seeming military hegemony in the aftermath of the Soviet Union's collapse have been challenged both by the governments and by the social movements.

Grounded in Raymond Aron's (1965) pragmatic understanding of power – that is the ability to direct social change – this chapter suggests that societal consequences of hegemony-oriented geopolitical, political, economic or military projects today are unintended, random and transcendental, therefore total hegemony cannot be claimed by a single political entity in the region.

The case of Central Asia suggests that hegemony today has become less about dominance on a political *Chessboard*, but rather about projects aiming at change and

DOI: 10.4324/9781003037231-14

development in one way or another, for these projects have potential to create a hegemonic development vision and organisation of economic and social power. In the case of Central Asia, there is a number of connectivity projects. This chapter focuses on two of them, the Central Asia South Asia water-sharing project (CASA-1000) and the Central Asian Regional Economic Cooperation (CAREC), which aim to restore regional economic connectivity and water-sharing, respectively. However, none of these projects fully consider the unintended societal consequences, such as the direction of social change they could trigger and the change of the societal organisation across the involved geographical spaces. It is worth noting that unintended consequences do not necessarily imply a linear causality between the hegemonic projects and their impact. Rather, these consequences may be fostered by the processes which emerge from the neglect of history, local and transnational factors, within and outside Central Asia.

This argument unfolds by first providing a conceptual discussion of the power of improvisation; secondly providing the biographies of CAREC and CASA-1000; and thirdly analysing societal consequences of these two projects. The conclusions discuss how a better understanding of the social sources of power can provide some ground for power as improvisation, without which there can be no hegemony today.

Power as improvisation and its social sources

Max Weber defined power 'as any chance [not a "probability" as it is often translated] within a social relation to impose one's will also against the resistance of the others, regardless of what gives rise to this chance' (Weber 1980 [1921–2], 28 in Guzzini 2013, 4). Along the same lines, Peter Katzenstein (Katzenstein and Seybert 2018, xv) has underlined that 'traditional accounts of control power say little about decentralized, uncoordinated, but highly impactful dynamics'. The concept of 'protean power', which 'emerges in uncertain contexts' was offered by Katzenstein (Katzenstein and Seybert 2018) as the concept and a framework to explain influence under the conditions of 'unknown unknown' (Jervis et al. 1985), which often appears to be the operational reality and the 'weapon of the weak' (Scott 1987). Charles Tilly (2000) sketched the road to understanding power beyond control by offering the metaphor of 'power as improvisation'. While seeming vague, power as improvisation or power as a chance needs to be operationalised and captured analytically. Drawing from Henri Lefevre's theories of state and space, this chapter suggests focusing on the material objects of empowerment, such as railways, grids, dams, roads, social or economic structures, as material manifestations of larger projects of power and hegemony.

By focusing on the societal consequences of these projects, this chapter captures the anthropology of social change thereby showing that none of these projects can result in a full hegemony, unless their stakeholders learn to improvise and follow the rhythms and directions of the societal forces. Furthermore, time and space of the power projects and their societal basis can differ, that is societal relations and practices can reflect historical patterns, which the hegemonic projects do not take into account or a societal organisation can extend far beyond the territorial borders of the state, by plugging into the ideological or financial power networks beyond the control of the state.

CAREC and CASA-1000, as the examples of regionalisation- or connectivity projects related to trade and infrastructure, criss-cross borders of multiple states and institutions of multiple state, private and multilateral actors. Therefore, political authority in this case becomes shared if not dispersed. Whether a grand infrastructure project is an epitome of power of external actors or ruling elites on one hand or whether they are current reincarnations of hegemony or colonialism on the other is arguable. What is clear is that connectivity projects can be seen as techniques of (re)territorialisation and management of social space, as territorialisation is a social construct (Kratochwil 1986; Ruggie 1993), for the territory itself is a 'political technology' or a composition of political, geographical, economic, strategic, legal, and technical relations (Elden 2013). In other words, looking at hegemony through the lens of material objects means looking at the very technology of materialising an idea (for example, that of the neoliberal logic, as in the case of CAREC).

Just like artificial islands, watercourses, checkpoints and fences, railways and power grids represent objects of both geopolitics and geophysics or forms of modern social institutions which influence spatial politics by creating social territorial and social practices 'by which power is constructed and contested' (Peters et al. 2018, 18).

Once in its history, Central Asia went through Soviet state engineering, when power grids, railways and dams had a lasting impact on societies, territories and environment. However, back in the days, this geophysics of power was imposed from Moscow. Today's connectivity projects expose multilayered 'authority', which on one hand should be a perfect fit for the complex societies of the region, but in reality fail to direct changes in societal organisation, identities of resistance and social change in general. Thus, a power grid combined with grassroots change in survival strategies may lead to the change of societal organisation and therefore foster processes, counter-productive to the hegemonic aspirations of a specific project.

CASA-1000: What does water-sharing have to do with anthropology of resistance?

The biography of a hydro-hegemony

Central Asia South Asia water-sharing project (CASA-1000) is part of a regionalisation project implemented by the World Bank, which aims to change the landlocked status of the Central Asian countries and open up their economic space. Since water has been identified as an 'abundant resource' or 'comparative advantage' in Central Asia, CASA-1000 would help to develop exports of water from

Tajikistan and Kyrgyzstan to nearby water-deficit countries, such as Afghanistan and Pakistan. The project aims to recreate interdependence along the Silk Road, allegedly interrupted and suppressed by Soviet rule (USAID 2013). Water-sharing is its first step, which implies the creation of a common resource pool between Tajikistan and Kyrgyzstan, as water suppliers, and Afghanistan and Pakistan as recipient states.

Specifically, its new water-sharing schemes suggest the connection of the power grids of southern Kyrgyzstan (Datka power grid) with northern Tajikistan (Khujand power station) in order to transmit hydro-energy generated by Tajikistan and Kyrgyzstan to Afghanistan and Pakistan, and from there to the countries of South Asia (ADB 2012).

In institutional terms, CASA-1000 is a multilateral framework, initiated by the governments of Tajikistan, Kyrgyzstan, Afghanistan and Pakistan, which puts in place an Inter-Governmental Council, supported by the World Bank group, the Islamic Development Bank, the United States Agency for International Development (USAID), the US State Department, the United Kingdom Department for International Development (DFID), the Australian Agency for International Development (AusAID), and other donor communities (CASA-1000). In other words, this framework comprises international banks, governments and business investors and, therefore, a constellation of conflicting interests and different rationales for being involved in this project.

In practical terms, at its initial stages, it will use power generated by stations such as Santguta I and Santguta II in Tajikistan, whose capacity is currently insufficient for long-term CASA-1000 plans. For this reason, CASA will also require the construction of larger power stations, such as Rogun in Tajikistan and Kambarata (I and II) in Kyrgyzstan. Rogun, on the other hand, has been the Tajik government's pet project, regardless of the acute social and political tensions caused by this idea in the region. In brief, Rogun is located about 110 km away from Dushanbe, on the river Vakhsh, which, after confluence with the river Pyanzh, flows further into Amu-Darya and makes up to 27% of its flow (World Bank 2014b, 7).

Within the CASA-1000 framework, the goal of Rogun is to produce more hydro-energy for water export (Rossi and Khakimov 2014). Construction restarted in 2008, but has continually been interrupted since 2012. In September 2014, Tajikistan received the results of the World Bank's techno-economic and environmental-social assessment proving that the risks of ecological disaster are minimal and could be managed by adapting certain parameters of the dam and construction techniques (Coyne et Bellier 2014). Hence, on 27 March 2014, the project was finally approved with the completion date set for 30 June 2020. The agencies implementing the programme include the National Transmission Companies of the stakeholder states (World Bank 2014a).

On 24 April 2015, Tajikistan, Kyrgyzstan, Afghanistan, and Pakistan signed a number of agreements in Istanbul, initiating the project. Specifically, the International Development Association (IDA) provided a grant of $45 million to Tajikistan for the realisation of the Rogun project (Asia-Plus 2015). This meeting confirmed that 70% of the electricity will be supplied by Tajikistan, and the remaining 30% by Kyrgyzstan. On the recipient side, Afghanistan will consume 300 MW and Pakistan 1,000 MW. Furthermore, Pakistan and Tajikistan agreed to expand transmission lines to Chitral in northern areas of Pakistan in order to mitigate the energy crisis in Islamabad (Express Tribune 2015). On 13 June 2015, the Joint Working Group (JWG) of the CASA-1000 Project met in Almaty, Kazakhstan. Also in attendance were the main donors such as the World Bank, Islamic Development Bank (IsDB), European Bank of Reconstruction and Development (EBRD) and other major international development agencies. On 9 July 2015, tender packages for the supply and installation of Multi Terminal HVDC Converter Stations in Pakistan, Afghanistan, and Tajikistan were opened (World Bank 2014c). Today, the building of the dam is proceeding with intermittent success and with partial violations of safety standards.

CASA-1000 societal consequences: Internal displacement and identity of resistance

Proceeding with CASA-1000 means proceeding with the Rogun project. This plan's societal consequences promise to be dramatic, for it implies the resettlement of the population living in the areas surrounding the river Vakhsh, flooding most of the area: 42, 000 people will be internally displaced or 'resettled' to other areas. Whilst the technical and economic assessment has been conducted, the data on the potential societal consequences of CASA-1000 have not been fully considered, due to the lack of data on the affected communities (Coyne et Bellier 2014). This displacement is reminiscent of the techniques of population displacement during Stalinist times and, therefore, can be seen as a similar social trauma, which will have a lasting effect on people's consciousness and contribute to the development of the identity of resistance to the modern state.

This social trauma is not a mere socio-psychological problem. It has several tangible implications. First, the areas of displacement include power domains of the elites opposed to the ruling elite, which is why the displacement can be seen as a means to destroy the elites' social basis through the destruction of existing social networks and patterns of social interaction, habit and routine. Secondly, this displacement implies the deprivation of the communities from their usual survival strategies. Thirdly, it re-engineers the sense of belonging, as holy sites or sites of cultural heritage, which collectively function as sites of belonging, would be flooded, even if these have been promised to be 'resettled', too. The project neglects the connection between the social and geographical realm, as well as physical objects signifying memories and capturing histories. The Rogun dam is located in the Rasht Valley, which includes seven regions: Faizabad, Rogun, Rasht, Tavildara, Tajikabad and Djirgital. These are the main areas from which people will be displaced to other areas, such as Dangara, Tursunzade and Rudaki. The three last sites compose the domains of the ruling elite, where the Presidential power is under the least amount of risk.

Resettlement measures would be implemented by the Directorate for the Inundation Zone of the Rogun Hydropower Project (HPP), a special unit set up by GoT for this purpose (World Bank 2014a, 7). Out of 42,000 people planned to be resettled, 2000 have already been resettled. The World Bank (2014a, 7) reports the conditions for resettlement as satisfactory, in terms of social services, such as schools and medicine. However, IMF data on the budget share of social services in Khatlon region (which includes Dangara) shows that it has been reduced to 5% in recent years (World Bank 2014b). Hence, with the increased amount of people, these social services might be provided using World Bank resettlement aid. It would go through the same channels as other foreign aid, i.e. the network of banks under the control of the ruling elite. At the local level, the problems of the displaced would be addressed by the leaders of hosting communities or the Jamoats (Rossi and Khakimov 2014). This disruption of existing social networks has also been noted by the World Bank's outsourced Pöyry Consulting report, specifically the loss of land and the loss of access to communities located on different river banks. In particular, the villages on the left bank of Vakhsh would be cut from access to bridges and roads (Zwahlen 2014a, 213). The reason is that most of these roads and bridges will be substituted with new ones, whose location would correspond to the new contours of the Valley after inundation (Zwahlen 2014a, 208). The Human Rights Watch Report (2014) provides evidence of human trauma and distortion of livelihoods during the resettlement process.

This change of infrastructure will include the reconstruction of the M-41 route, one of the world's most important drug trafficking routes (UNODC 2013). According to the Final Report: 'overall, 36 farms, 62 km of roads, of which 3 km make up the National Road M 41 and 59 km of local district roads, will be submerged' (Zwahlen 2014a, 208). The M-41 route has provided logistics for one of the main economic resources of the country, which is drug trafficking (UNODC 2013; ICG 2012). Since part of this route is located within the Garm domain, i.e. beyond the direct control of the central state, its reconstruction may have an impact on restructuring control over drug trafficking, which has been ongoing since the time of the civil war. Finally, since this route connects two least governable [for the ruling elite] domains, Badakhshan and Garm, it may contribute to the extension of the power of the ruling elite to these rebellious areas. Initially, the reconstruction of this road started in 1980, together with the first stages of Rogun construction. According to the Planning and Design Institute, the entity in charge of road planning in the country, the completion of this road will repair the structures built during the Soviet period (Zwahlen 2014a, 208).

CASA and Rogun provide a useful legitimation framework for the ruling elite to destroy the social basis of these domains, through simple social and geographical re-engineering. The areas around the Vakhsh river, including the Rasht Valley (Garm), are associated with the power domains of President Akhmadov. It includes Kamarob Valley, where his rival, Mullo Abdullo, was killed in 2010. The rival elites of these domains have also been eliminated. Today the dam construction represents the exercise of power to change both the geographical and social landscapes, as parameters, such as 'social harmony, avoidance of protest action, food security, diversion of budget from social programmes, the cost of livelihood support for resettled people and the associated problem of identification of land and jobs for them, macroeconomic risks, and the potential financial burden on the people' (World Bank 2014b, 10).

The main social problem here is the loss of agricultural land and the deprivation of the displaced people from the access to land. Instead of land, people would be compensated in cash. However, agriculture and small trade form one of the main pillars of the survival strategies of large parts of Central Asian society. The displaced people are deprived of the agricultural plots, and their access to trade depends on intra-communal social relations which are disrupted by population displacement.

In trying to prove that there is no risk of inter-community conflict, the final assessment reports note that 'host communities do not have to give up land which they cultivated so far and which will now be occupied by the new settlers [and thus] land shortage is not an issue' (Zwahlen 2014a, 214). The same assessment reports the loss of livestock, the lack of sites for livestock husbandry, along with the loss of agricultural land (Zwahlen 2014a, 217). It is not that the lack of land is an issue. It is the way that land and property rights have developed in the post-Soviet period that may clash with new practices of land usage. Whilst addressing the land rights issue, the resettlement bodies make the reference to Article 32 of the Constitution of the Republic of Tajikistan which states in essence that every citizen has a right to land and no one is entitled to deprive them from private property; and Article 13 of the Constitution that land, water, air and other resources belong to the state and that the state guarantees their usage (Constitution of the Republic of Tajikistan). As for compensation for the loss of land, the experts refer to the Land and the Civil Code of the Republic of Tajikistan, which simply states that the rights for the private property of the citizens are guaranteed and citizens therefore have to be compensated (Rossi and Khakimov 2014). There follows a set of legislation regulating the specificities of these potential situations. Cash compensation is envisioned. Yet, whether cash can substitute the social meaning of land is debatable.

Apart from being a part of their survival strategies, land also connects people with their spiritual and cultural practices. For instance, the same WB assessment identifies the importance of the cultural heritage which is to be flooded by Rogun. The list of cultural heritage sites to be destroyed by Rogun includes graveyards, places of worship, fortresses, and other holy sites (see full list in Zwahlen 2014a, 227–9). These holy sites have a special importance for the local populations. According to data from focus groups conducted by the Pöyry Consulting (Zwahlen 2014b) report, most people suggest that visiting holy sites has been a part of the daily routine of these communities. They believe that these places can heal and provide prosperity (Zwahlen 2014b, 117). As Gullette and Heathershaw (2015) have shown, Central Asian people have special relations with their ancestors and connect such ideas as statehood and sovereignty to a moral duty owed to previous generations. This is why they can be considered the means of providing the sense of belonging, which will be uprooted once people are displaced.

The resettlement associated with CASA-1000 will not be limited to Tajikistan, but will also involve Pakistani and Afghanistani communities living along the new transmission lines. For instance, according to both the International Crisis Group (ICG) and the World Bank group, the lines would pass through the Salang Pass in Afghanistan, which represents one of the hardest territories in Afghanistan, both in environmental and social terms. There are also risks of landmines and sabotage, social unrest and protests against this construction have been identified as its main social consequences (ICG 2002, 96).

As the World Bank research group itself notices, there is a huge gap in the data on the households and the communities in the Central Asian borderlands, which hinders prognosis of the concrete societal risks (Kaminski 2012). To ameliorate the risks of social unrest, the World Bank group offers compensation to the displaced people. However, with the revival and strengthening of community-based social orders in the respective borderlands, the loss of property and land signifies more than a mere loss of material wealth. It is the loss of social position within the community, access to resources, legitimacy, and, subsequently, the loss of power that this displacement signifies.

CAREC: connecting societies – disconnecting states?

On the link between non-standard trade and shadow economies

Established in 1997, Central Asian Regional Economic Cooperation (CAREC) is a project sponsored mainly by the Asian Development Bank (ADB) with the goal of encouraging economic cooperation between Central Asian countries. According to the 'CAREC Strategic Framework 2020', its main goal is to 'unlock the land-locked Central Asian economies' and foster development and poverty eradication by supporting non-standard trade (ADB 2012). While not hegemony in a realist understanding – that is with a primacy of a specific powerful actor – CAREC is a project based on the hegemony of the neoliberal idea about how we organise economies and societies.

The CAREC institutional framework comprises three sets of actors: governments, multilateral institutions and private actors. CAREC prioritises four areas: transport, trade facilitation, energy and trade policy. Each of these priority areas comprises national and multilateral institution representatives (ADB 2012).

The triple logic of this framework, through diminishing the accountability mechanism of this type of global governance structure, reflects the 'complex actorship' which is natural for the region and the wider globalised world, where it is difficult to identify a unitary actor with a concrete foreign or national interest (Kavalski 2010). In spite of this diminishing accountability mechanism, this framework does not aim to institutionalise itself in the formal sense, rather it relies on the 'sub-regional or corridor-specific projects' and keeps its own institutional framework 'flexible and informal' too (ADB 2012, 18). Whether the creation of an informal institution over the informal space would make this space more 'legible' and transparent remains to be seen (Scott 1998).

The process of 'unlocking' the region is envisioned by establishing six transport corridors connecting the borderlands and opening their access to the Middle East, South Asia and Europe (through Russia). These transport corridors are meant to expand trade routes. However, Central Asian countries specialise in commodity goods, since their industrial sectors were obliterated economically after the collapse of the Soviet Union. Therefore, whether this type of trade would help the development of Central Asia, or instead revive the extractive demand chains similar to the Soviet ones is debatable. However, the energy pillar of this project, perhaps, envisions Central Asia as the supplier of hydro-energy to the neighbouring regions, which is commonly (and mistakenly) perceived as being an abundant resource in the region.

Besides improvements in logistics, a remarkable feature of the CAREC project is its focus on the development of non-standard trade in the Fergana Valley borderlands (ADB 2012). This project covers the 'cross-border trade activities [that] are not reported in the foreign trade statistics' (ADB 2012, 3). This unreported trade is operated through 'non-standard' channels of the bazaars. This trade concerns mainly domestically produced goods and some goods which are re-exported. According to World Bank surveys, bazaars 'play a major role in the local chains of production and distribution' (Kaminski 2012, 8). The surveys also found that bazaars in Central Asia meet five key requisites of effective markets: 'trusting most of the people most of the time, being secure from having your property expropriated, smooth flow of information about what is available where and at what quality, curtailment of side effects on third parties, and competition at work' (McMillan 2002). Furthermore, 'trust in protecting property rights and among trading partners rests more on the informal device of reputation and special connections than on the formal application of the rule of law through public institutions' (Kaminski 2012, 10).

Indeed, bazaars as part of the social organisation of communities, entail a great degree of intimate interaction between the local people. However, trust is based not on the information-sharing related to protection of property rights. Rather, it emerges from common memories, sentiments, and moral duties dictated by a traditional hierarchy of social relations (Fukuyama 1995). The inter-ethnic tensions in southern Kyrgyzstan in 2010 exemplify how one's property can be burnt overnight if it conflicts with the social order that the politically active part of the population sees as desirable. These inter-ethnic tensions have influenced the distribution of property in such strategically important bazaars as Osh and Kara-Suu.

However, the rationale for the CAREC approach lies in the general idea of decentralisation and bottom-up development, relying on grassroots institutions prone to market competition. In general terms, it is rooted in the neoliberal economic agenda of the IMF and the World Bank, the leading actors involved in restructuring the post-Soviet states from the outset. To dismantle the Soviet system, the Central Asian states were prescribed a path of liberalisation by the IMF and the World Bank (Gleason 2003). Although liberalisation took different modes in these three countries, the newly emerging national economies relied upon its core principles. In practice, these principles comprised the Washington Consensus templates for states 'in transition to democracy' (Gore 2005). The idea was to develop free market competition which would later result in the creation of democratic institutions. Development of the free market and political decentralisation were two guiding principles of the process of liberalisation. Hence, the rationale of neoliberalism was the leading one during the first decade of independence. Market liberalisation did not imply the organising of economies in institutional terms, i.e. it did not allow for (re)institutionalisation or (re)standardisation of the economies that had been previously organised according to the centralised (Soviet) design (Gleason 2003).

The CAREC project represents an example of an attempt at restructuring within this template. In a nutshell, it is a project of informal, decentralised management of informal trade in Central Asia. Political decentralisation has diminished regional states' infrastructural power, preventing them from permeating the grassroots social organisation of their own societies. This is because the indigenous community-based social structures, which are seen to be substituting formal institutions, may foster a social order and framework of management which is efficient and viable, yet different from the one of the modern state. To date, the international community has failed to construct a workable institutional structure to govern societies with these underlying community-based types of social organisation. Instead, international multilateral platforms themselves have become influenced by the non-standard processes (or the so-called informal processes) and have become prone to informalisation of their organisational settings. In other words, decentralisation, as Michael Mann predicted, created a system of 'societal control' (that is, influence) over the formal management frameworks, rather than vice a versa (Mann 1993, 59).

Hence, in order to understand potential societal consequences of this project, it is useful to also consider the territories which are to be connected. As in the CASA-1000 case, Central Asia will be more strongly integrated into the 'Islamic space', i.e. more closely connected with Afghanistan, Pakistan and the Middle East. Considering the socio-cultural context of these regions, Central Asia will be opened up to the area of complex and hardly controllable territories. This is not a warning of potential conflict. On the contrary, it is simply to draw attention to the fact that opening up potential new power networks to bypass those of the states, may result in the outsourcing of the states' ideological power. In practical terms, non-standard trade draws into its orbit other types of cross-border social activities (to be shown in the subsequent section), which is why these policies indirectly contribute to the transnationalisation of societies, which can increase the condition of uncertainty when it comes to social order and social change.

CAREC's societal consequences: Parallel realms of societal organisation

The institution of the bazaar, in the context of Central Asia, represents the operational realm for both legal and illicit activity. The line between them is difficult to draw when the state does not have a fully functional fiscal system which can unravel the operational complexity of the bazaar, since this is the institution which supports non-standard trade and is the forum for the agricultural activity of the local population. Firstly, the bazaar is one of three main institutions (along with mosques and madrassahs) providing recruitment for Islamist movements and the dissemination of the Islamist social agenda. Furthermore, this is the space where religious activities intersect with drug and human trafficking, small-scale entrepreneurship, mafia-like networks, and it is also where politicians try to engage with and expand their electoral base (Engvall 2011; Erica Marat 2006). For instance, Marat's field research on the state-crime nexus demonstrates how the clashes between the mafia networks of key criminals occur 'over the control of bazaars, gas stations, and supermarkets' (Marat 2006, 67). Bazaars were reported as one of the main venues of drug dissemination (Marat 2006, 54). Engvall, in his 'State as investment market' (2011), shows how these networks are connected to formal politics by means of bribery. These networks 'invest' in the protection of their businesses and access to control over drug trafficking and natural resources, such as gold and coal mines. Additionally, there is, reportedly, competition over drug trafficking between the identifiable Russian, Afghan, Azeri, Tajik, Chechen and Kyrgyz drug mafias (Makarenko 2004). An example of this state of affairs is the situation in the southern Kyrgyzstan, in the provinces of Jalal-Abad and Osh, which were 'the major transit points of [both drugs] and human trafficking to the Middle Eastern countries, Europe, and Russia' (Marat 2006, 63). It is also widely reported that the individual who was most famous as 'the charismatic' mayor of Osh was, prior to his election to office as a mayor, part of one of the most powerful organised crime networks 'covering'[1] the Osh and Kara-Suu bazaars. Traditionally, the bazaar is also an institution representing the structure for self-governance of the community.

According to World Bank studies, the bazaar operates mostly according to customary laws and traditional practices. According to estimates of some international organisations (UN, World Bank, etc.), between 40 and 60% of the Central Asian economy is informal. This can be explained because of the multiplication of bazaars, the number of which reached 400 in the 1990s alone (Spector 2006). In the 1990s, shuttle-trade and the bazaars provided employment for different social groups, of varying ages, genders, and professions (Blacher 1996; Kaiser 1997). This informal trade has not only been integrated into international trade flows, but has also changed the structure of the trade system internationally (Thorez 2008). The large bazaars of the Fergana Valley, such as Osh, Aravan, Bazar-Kurgan, Naukat, Suzak, Kara-Suu and Uzgen have been the hubs through which 90% of the re-export from China have flowed. These have also historically been the main bazaars for local agricultural produce. From the hub in Osh, products would be redistributed to markets in Bishkek (especially the biggest one in Central Asia – 'Dordoi' bazaar), from which it would go to Kazakhstan, Russia, Ukraine and beyond. There are a number of official and unofficial routes passing through the Fergana Valley, connecting the Osh hub with Khorog (Pamir province of

Tajikistan, bordering with Afghanistan), and connecting China with Afghanistan, via Kyrgyzstan and Tajikistan (Thorez 2008). Reportedly, in late 2000 the routes connecting the Fergana Valley with heart in Afghanistan have become the busiest of these routes (Thorez 2008; Abdelkhah and Bayart 2006).

Hence, it seems that the integration of the reviving traditional modes of social organisation into non-standard economic processes (bordering with illicit activities) could pose a challenge to any forms of formal governance and territorially-bound social order, dissolving the possibility of domination by a single actor or idea.

Conclusion: On objects of empowerment and social change

Time accelerates. So does social change. While control and domination still remain the prerogative of governments, their monopoly on influence, impact and leadership have been fading. People matter more than ever before. Social developments in and around Central Asia are an example of how hegemonic projects can undermine themselves in complex borderlands.

While approaches to hegemony usually focus on the balance of power among the key international powers at the macro-level, this chapter attempted to understand its microcosm at the societal level. Both CAREC and CASA-1000 could have potentially become infrastructures for hegemonic projects of development, if they managed to direct the social change in the societies they engage in. However, both of these projects contributed to the increasing social resistance potential in the given societies.

Specifically, CAREC's underlying idea to support the non-standard economies was implemented though the support of informal economic institutions, such as bazaars, which are the main units of cross-border trade in the Central Asian borderlands. While being a seemingly classical neoliberal idea of supporting grassroots economic actors, in practice this policy turned into supporting shadow economies in Central Asia, which diminished the role of the state and only increased the gap between the state and societies in the region.

In parallel to the processes of increased informalisation of grassroots political economies, CASA-1000 attempted to install infrastructure to connect power grids of Fergana- and Rasht Valleys to the borderlands of Afghanistan and Pakistan through the turbulent Salang pass. As the installation of this infrastructure has resulted in internal displacement of thousands of people, flooding of agricultural lands and holy sites, this process can be seen not only as the infringement of societal survival strategies but also as re-engineering of societal memories, restructuring of the intricate balance of local elites structures, social trauma and merely creating a political geography bound by the identity of resistance, which is beyond borders as such.

Finally, trade and infrastructure are never just about trade and infrastructure in the context of complex borderlands. Every material object is an embodiment of an idea or a trigger for completing ideas to consolidate. In this case, Islam of resistance has been one of the growing sources of social identity across the given borderlands.

Therefore, connecting material objects, while increasing the gap between states and societies, has only created favourable conditions for the manifestation of alternative identities, which in turn can undermine a hegemonic project, rooted in a neo-liberal ideology.

In general, CAREC and CASA-1000 can be seen as small-scale connectivity projects, similar to those of the Belt and Road Initiative.[2] Their societal consequences suggest which risks and challenges such projects imply for hegemonies in complex borderlands.

Notes

1 Protecting by means of racketeering.
2 In fact, CAREC has lately been integrated into the BRI in Central Asia.

References

Abdelkhah, F. and Bayart, J. (2006) 'Le Réveil du Khorasan – La Recomposition d'un Espace de Circulation'. Anthropologie Du Voyage et Migrations Internationale: Publication du Fonds d'analyse des sociétés politiques (FASOPO). Available at: www.fasopo.org/sites/default/files/anthropologievoyage_avpro_1206.pdf (accessed 10 May 2020).

ADB (2012) *Carec-2020: A Strategic Framework for Central Asian Regional Economic Cooperation*. Manila: Asian Development Bank.

Akchurina, V. (2018) 'Borders and Waters: Compartmentalized Security in the Eurasian Heartland', in P. Dutkiewicz and R. Sakwa (eds), *Eurasia on the Edge: Managing Complexity*, Lanham, MD: Lexington Books.

Akchurina, V. and Lavorgna, A. (2014) 'Islamist Movements in the Fergana Valley: A New Threat Assessment Approach', *Global Crime*, Special Issue: 'Transnational Organized Crime and Terrorism: Different Peas, Same Pod?', 15(3–4): 320–336.

Alden Willy, L. (2003) 'Land Rights in Crisis: Restoring Tenure Security in Afghanistan', Afghanistan Research and Evaluation Unit, Issues Paper Series. Available at: www.rmportal.net/framelib/ltpr/052709/wily-land-rights-in-crisis-afghanistan.pdf (accessed 30 December 2018).

Aron, R. (1965) 'Catégories dirigeante ou classe dirigeante?', *Revue française de science politique*, 15(1): 7–27.

Asia-Plus (2015) 'A Tender on Highway Engineering along the Rogun HPS Flood Zone has been Announced', 14 August. Available at: www.asiaplus.tj/en/news/tender-highway-engineering-along-rogun-hps-flood-zone-has-been-announced (accessed 7 September 2015).

Bartlett, D. (2001) 'Economic Recentralization in Uzbekistan', *Post-Soviet Geography and Economics*, 42(2): 105–121.

Berman, S. (2003) 'Islamism, Revolution, and Civil Society', *Perspectives on Politics*, 1(2): 257–272.

Blacher, P. (1996) 'Les "Shop-Turisty" De Tsargrad Ou Les Nouveaux Russophones D'istanbul', *Turcica*, 28: 11–50.

Cooley, A. (2014) *Great Game, Local Rules: The New Power Contest in Central Asia*. New York: Oxford University Press.

Cooley, A. and Heathershaw J. (2017) *Dictators without Borders: Power and Money in Central Asia*. New Haven, CT: Yale University Press.

Coyne et Bellier (2014) *Techno-Economic Assessment Study for Rogun Hydroelectric Construction Project*, 3 vols. World Bank. Available at: www.fasopo.org/sites/default/files/anthropolo gievoyage_avpro_1206.pdf (accessed 10 May 2020).

Crutzen, P. (2002), 'Geology of Mankind', *Nature*, 415(6867): 23.

Dadabaev, T. (2013) 'Community Life, Memory, and Changing Mahalla Identity in Uzbekistan', *Journal of Eurasian Studies*, 4: 181–196.

Dorian, J., Wigdortz B. and Gladney D. (1997) 'Central Asia and Xinjiang, China: Emerging Energy, Economic and Ethnic Relations', *Central Asian Survey*, 16(4): 461–487.

Elden, S. (2013) *The Birth of Territory*. Chicago: University of Chicago Press.

Engvall, J. (2011) 'The State as Investment Market: An Analytical Framework for Interpreting Politics and Bureaucracy in Kyrgyzstan'. Thesis, Uppsala University, Uppsala.

Eriksson, C. (2006) *Changing Land Rights, Changing Land Use: Privatisation Drives Landscape Change in Post-Soviet Kyrgyzstan*. Uppsala: Swedish University of Agricultural Sciences.

Express Tribune Pakistan (2015) 'From Central to South Asia: Energy Ministers Strike Transmission Line Accord'. 26 November 2015. Available at: http://tribune.com.pk/story/998516/from-central-to-south-asia-energy-ministers-strike-transmission-line-accord/ (accessed 7 September 2015).

Foucault, M. (1990) *The History of Sexuality*, Vol. 1: An Introduction. New York: Vintage Books.

Fukuyama, F. (1995) *Trust: The Social Virtues and the Creation of Prosperity*. New York: Free Press.

Gleason, G. (2003) *Markets and Politics in Central Asia*. London: Routledge.

Gore, C. (2005) *The Rise and Fall of the Washington Consensus as a Paradigm for Developing Countries*. Washington, DC: World Bank Publications.

Gullette, D. and Heathershaw, J. (2015) 'The Affective Politics of Sovereignty: Reflecting on the 2010 Conflict in Kyrgyzstan', *Nationalities Papers*, 43(1): 122–139.

Guzzini, S. (2013) *Power, Realism, and Constructivism*. New York: Routledge.

Hibou, B. (2011) *The Force of Obedience: The Political Economy of Repression in Tunisia*. Cambridge: Polity Press.

Human Rights Watch (2014) '"We Suffered When We Came Here": Rights Violations Linked to Resettlements for Tajikistan's Rogun Dam'. Available at: www.hrw.org/report/2014/06/25/we-suffered-when-we-came-here/rights-violations-linked-resettlements-tajikistans (accessed 22 July 2019).

International Crisis Group (2002) *Kyrgyzstan's Political Crisis: An Exit Strategy*. International Crisis Group. Available at: https://www.crisisgroup.org/europe-central-asia/central-asia/kyrgyzstan/kyrgyzstans-political-crisis-exit-strategy (accessed 16 May 2020).

International Crisis Group (2012) *Kyrgyzstan: Widening Ethnic Divisions in the South*. International Crisis Group. Available at: https://www.crisisgroup.org/europe-central-asia/central-asia/kyrgyzstan/kyrgyzstan-widening-ethnic-divisions-south (accessed 16 May 2020).

Jervis, R., Richard, N. and Stein, J. (1985) *Psychology and Deterrence*. Baltimore, MD: Johns Hopkins University Press.

Kaiser, M. (1997) 'Informal Sector Trade in Uzbekistan', Université de Bielefeld, Sociology of Development Research Centre, Working Paper, 281 (50). Available at: https://www.ssoar.info/ssoar/handle/document/42283 (accessed 16 May 2020).

Kaminski, B. and Mitra, S. (2012) *Borderless Bazaars and Regional Integration in Central Asia: Emerging Patterns of Trade and Cross-Border Cooperation*. Washington, DC: World Bank Publications.

Katzenstein, P. and Seybert, L. (eds) (2018) *Protean Power: Exploring the Uncertain and Unexpected in World Politics*. Cambridge: Cambridge University Press.

Kavalski, E. (2010), *Stable Outside, Fragile Inside? Post-Soviet Statehood in Central Asia*. Farnham: Ashgate.

Kratochwil, F. (1986) 'Of Systems, Boundaries, and Territoriality: An Inquiry into the Formation of the State System', *World Politics*, 39 (October): 27–52.

Laruelle, M. (ed.) (2018) *China's Belt and Road Initiative and Its Impact in Central Asia*. Washington, DC: The George Washington University, Central Asia Program.

Laruelle, M. and Peyrouse, S. (2013) *Globalizing Central Asia: Geopolitics and the Challenges of Economic Development*. Armonk, NY: M.E. Sharpe.

Lefebvre, H. (2009) *State, Space, World: Selected Essays*. Minneapolis: Minnesota University Press.

Lenczowski, G. (1978) *Iran under the Pahlavis*. Stanford, CA: Hoover Institution Press.

Lerman, Z. and Sedik, D. (2014) *Agricultural Cooperatives in Eurasia*. FAO Regional Office for Europe and Central Asia. Available at: www.fao.org/3/a-au856e.pdf (accessed 16 May 2020).

Liu, M. (2012) *Under Solomon's Throne: Uzbek Vision of Renewal in Osh*. Pittsburgh, PA: University of Pittsburgh Press.

Mackinder, H. (1904) 'The Geographical Pivot of History', *The Geographical Society*, 23(4): 421–437.

McMillan, J. (2002) *Reinventing the Bazaar: A Natural History of Markets*. New York: W. W. Norton.

Makarenko, T. (2004) 'The Crime-Terror Continuum: Tracing the Interplay between Transnational Organised Crime and Terrorism', *Global Crime*, 1(1): 129–145.

Mann, M. (1986) *The Sources of Social Power*, Vol. 1: *A History of Power from the Beginning to AD 1760*. Cambridge: Cambridge University Press.

Mann, M. (1993) *The Sources of Social Power*, Vol. 2: *The Rise of Classes and Nation States, 1760–1914*. Cambridge: Cambridge University Press.

Marat, E. (2006) *The State-Crime Nexus in Central Asia: State Weakness, Organized Crime, and Corruption in Kyrgyzstan and Tajikistan*. Washington, DC: Silk Road Studies Program.

Megoran, N. (2012) 'Rethinking the Study of International Boundaries: A Biography of the Kyrgyzstan–Uzbekistan Boundary', *Annals of the Association of American Geographers*, 102(2): 464–481.

Moses, N. (2013) *The End of Power: From Boardrooms to Battlefields. Why Being in Charge in Not What It Used to Be?* New York: Basic Books.

Nasritdinov, E. (2006) 'Regional Change in Kyrgyzstan: Bazaars, Open-Air Markets and Social Networks'. PhD Dissertation, The University of Melbourne, Melbourne.

Peters, K., Steinberg, P. and Stratford, E. (eds) (2018) *Territory beyond Terra*. Lanham, MD: Rowman & Littlefield.

Peyrouse, S. (2012) 'The Kazakh Neopatrimonial Regime: Balancing Uncertainties among the "Family", Oligarchs and Technocrats', *Demokratizatsiya: The Journal of Post-Soviet Democratization*, 20(4): 345–370.

Raballand, G. and Andrésy, A. (2007) 'Why Should Trade between Central Asia and China Continue to Expand?', *Asia Europe Journal*, 5(2): 235–252.

Rastogi, C. and Arvis, J.F. (2014) *The Eurasian Connection: Supply Chain Efficiency along the Modern Silk Route through Central Asia*. Washington, DC: World Bank.

Reeves, M. (2014) *Border Work: Spatial Lives of the State in Rural Central Asia*. Ithaca, NY: Cornell University Press.

Rossi, E. and Khakimov, P. (2014) *Audit Pereselenia Na UrovneDomohozyaistv* [Resettlement. Intermediary Audit Report. Level of Households]. Duhanbe: BarkiTochik.

Ruggie, J. (1993) 'Territoriality and Beyond: Problematising Modernity in International Relations', *International Organization*, 47(1): 139–174.

Russo, A. (2018) *Regions in Transition in the Former Soviet Area: Ideas and Institutions in the Making*. Basingstoke: Palgrave Macmillan.

Scott, J. (1987) *Weapons of the Weak: Everyday Forms of Peasant Resistance*. New Haven, CT: Yale University Press.

Scott, J. (1998) *Seeing Like a State: How Certain Schemes to Improve the Human Condition Have Failed*. New Haven, CT: Yale University Press.

Spector, R. (2006) 'Who Governs the Marketplace? The Politics of Bazaars in Kyrgyzstan, Bishkek', Institute for Public Policy. Available at: http://ipp.kg/en/analysis/341/ (accessed 2 October 2015).

Thorez, J. (2005) 'Flux et Dynamiques Spatiales en Asie Centrale – Géographie de La Transformation Post-Soviétique'. Thèse de doctorat Université de Paris 10 – Nanterre.

Thorez, J. (2008) 'Bazars et Routes Commerciales en Asie Centrale: Transformation Post-Soviétique Et Mondialisation Par Le Bas', *Revue Européenne Des Migrations Internationales*, 24(3), 167–189.

Tilly, C. (1975) *The Formation of National States in Western Europe*. Princeton, NJ: Princeton University Press.

Tilly, C. (2000) 'How Do Relations Store Histories?' *Annual Review of Sociology*, 26: 721–723.

Trofimov, D. (2001) 'Tashkent MezhduAnkaroj I Tegeranom: Uroki 90-H Godov I Perspektivy [Tashkent between Ankara and Tehran: Lessons of the 1990s and the Perspectives]', *Central'naya Aziya i Kavkaz* [Central Asia and the Caucasus], 5(17): 123–134.

UNODC (2013) *World Drug Report*. Available at: www.unodc.org/unodc/secured/wdr/wdr2013/World_Drug_Report_2013.pdf (accessed 7 December 2015).

USAID (2013) *Conflicts on Irrigation Water in the South of the Kyrgyz Republic*. United States Agency for International Development. Available at: www.cawater-info.net/bk/iwrm/pdf/conflicts-kg_e.pdf (accessed 16 May 2020).

Weber, M. (1980 [1921–1922]) *Wirtschaft und Gesellschaft. Grundriss der verstehenden Soziologie*. Tübingen: J. C. B. Mohr (Paul Siebeck).

Wolf, E. (1966) 'Kinship, Friendship, and Patron-Client Relations in Complex Societies', in M. Banton (ed.), *The Social Anthropology of Complex Societies*, London: Routledge, 1–22.

World Bank (2014a) *Final Report: Engineering and Dam Safety*. Panel of Experts for Rogun Hydropower Project. Washington, DC: World Bank. Available at: www.worldbank.org/content/dam/Worldbank/document/eca/central-asia/EDS%20PoE%20Report_FINAL_eng.pdf (accessed 26 January 2015).

World Bank (2014b) *Final Report of the Environmental and Social Panel of Experts*. Washington, DC: World Bank.

World Bank (2014c) 'Supply and Installation of Multi-Terminal Hvdc Converter Stations in Pakistan, Afghanistan, and Tajikistan'. Available at: www.worldbank.org/projects/procurement/noticeoverview?id=OP00029815&lang=en (accessed 3 November 2014).

Zhang, W. (2018) *Opening Remarks at the CAREC High Level Session on New Opportunities for Regional Cooperation*. Asian Development Bank. Available at: www.adb.org/news/speeches/carec-new-opportunities-regional-cooperation-wencai-zhang (accessed 20 November 2018).

Zwahlen, R. (2014a) *Environmental and Social Impact Assessment Report*, Vol. 1. Zurich: Pöyry Energy AG. Available at: http://pubdocs.worldbank.org/en/219381488268265345/ESIA-Vol-I-Final-eng.pdf (accessed 18 February 2020).

Zwahlen, R. (2014b) *Environmental and Social Impact Assessment Report*, Vol. 2. Zurich: Pöyry Energy AG. Available at: http://pubdocs.worldbank.org/en/125961488268270391/ESIA-Vol-III-ESMP-Final-eng.pdf (accessed 18 February 2020).

CONCLUSIONS

Hegemony and world order

Piotr Dutkiewicz, Tom Casier and Jan Aart Scholte

Hegemony and World Order: Reimagining Power in Global Politics explores one of the central issues of our time: how is world order sustained, is it shifting, is it being reinvented, or are we on the cusp of global *disorder*? A key lens used to examine these questions through the chapters of this book is that of 'hegemony'.

We present the overall conclusions of our study in the following way. We start with a brief review of the volume structure. Then we highlight how this book has reshaped understandings of hegemony, why we have decided to rethink it, and what is novel in the book's differentiated theoretical approach. Then we discuss the issue of whether hegemonies are a matter of choice or a 'matter of systemic inevitability', noting a likely future scenario of increased processes of re-hegemonisation of regional and global regulatory arrangements. We finish with a summary of potential policy consequences and suggested directions of future research.

Our present moment faces many simultaneous crises. This situation results from multiple processes and challenges that current economic and political systems struggle to handle. That in turn creates systemic fears that generate a complex hegemonisation of the world order.

The book in summary

The three sections of this volume respectively discuss: (a) how hegemony is conceptualised; (b) what kinds of resources are mobilised (material, discursive, institutional and performative) to maintain hegemony; and (c) the current status and prospects of various regional incarnations of hegemony in world politics.

The first group of chapters ('Hegemony as conceptual map') explores past notions of hegemony and how we can rethink the concept to better reflect its complexity. The book meets this challenge by offering a refreshing diversity of theoretical approaches. The chapter by Schmidt develops realist conceptions of

DOI: 10.4324/9781003037231-15

hegemony. Silver and Payne carry forward earlier work in a world-systems vein. Casier and Safranchuk take broadly neo-Gramscian routes. Finally, Scholte proposes a new 'metatheoretical premise' of a complex hegemony (that guided some other chapters in this volume and outlines future directions of research).

The second part of the book ('Practices of hegemony') examines concrete hegemonic strategies and answers the question how hegemony is built, maintained and defended. States remain important vectors of hegemony, but a complex hegemony consists of multilayered systems of which states (even the leading ones) are themselves members and participants, simultaneously objects and subjects of a complex web of relations. The chapters show that old-style Western hegemony, led by the United States, was underpinned by legitimisation discourses (Chebankova), patterns of governance (Pal), and financial/economic practices (Germain). Other chapters discussed hegemonic strategies in migration politics (Geiger) and ways that states use hybrid warfare to maintain or achieve hegemony at the regional level (Sloan). The currently unfolding reinvention of hegemonies brings new ideas (and accompanying institutions) about society, state, new actors and economy.

The final tranche of chapters ('Hegemony in action') explores various regional incarnations of hegemonies: in India (Bajpai and Parashar), Central Asia (Akchurina), the US and China (Zhang and Wang). These chapters argue that new configurations of hegemony are different from old ones. Today's emergent hegemonies do not have the same basis in military power, although security is still important. They do not have the same basis in ideological dominance, although ideas and norms are still important. They do not have the same basis in brute economic dominance, although trade and exchange are still crucial. Hegemonies of the future are therefore likely to be more subtle and possibly more flexible, more focused on multilayered primacy, and involving new sources of power beyond material power alone.

In this concluding chapter we draw together these various threads by first discussing notion(s) of hegemony. Then we offer an account of the roots of contemporary hegemonic change. We finish with thoughts for fascinating policy debates that may follow this book, as well as indicate possible avenues for further research.

What is hegemony and why focus on it?

We live in an age of multiple crises. Social, economic, political and environmental disruptions across local, national, regional and global levels are the new normal. The scale of challenges requires unprecedented amounts of global cooperation; however, a high level of volatility and a low level of trust among key global and regional players generates a new level of competition, trade conflicts, and social and political tensions. Some go so far as to suggest that 'the policy objective today is the prevention of hell on Earth rather than the creation of Paradise' (Barabanov et al. 2018, 1).

Our volume provides some answers to central questions about the trajectories of current world politics, focusing specifically on what hegemony is today, what new incarnations it takes, and how strategies are developed to gain (or at least not lose) it. As Jan Aart Scholte underlines in Chapter 5, a starting point of our collective

effort is that contemporary world politics and global governance require fundamental rethinking of hegemony. As the meaning of terms shapes our understanding
of the processes we describe, let us offer a brief explanation of how we in this
volume understand hegemony, why we have decided to rethink it, and what is
novel in this book's approach.

While our contributors have used different theoretical approaches to illuminate
different aspects and locations of systemic shifts, we agreed, as per our introductory
chapter, to define hegemony broadly as 'legitimated rule by dominant power'
where 'superior forces in world politics deploy their concentrations of resources to
sponsor ordering arrangements for world society'. Those 'ordering arrangements',
encompass multiple and complex processes, including the creation of rules and
institutions, legitimisation exercises, multiple strategies to gain and maintain power,
changing boundaries of sovereignty, and imposing dominant discourses.

Those actors (both state and non-state) who participate in hegemonic ordering
are often tempted to adjust their positions or to turn to counter-hegemonic struggle. Our volume discusses cases of states in relation to the US, China, India and
Russia. As examples of non-state actor involvements in hegemony we have
examined the T-20 global policy group, the institutionalisation of migration flows,
and water management and energy projects in Central Asia.

This book seeks to move beyond some of the more conventional perspectives
on hegemony. A first is related to 'hegemonic stability theory' (HST), popular
among certain International Relations scholars. This approach posits that 'international economic openness and stability is most likely maintained when there is a
single dominant state' (Webb and Krasner 1989). According to John Ikenberry
(2011), 'the core idea of this post world war II international order was that the
United States would need to actively shape its security environment, creating a
stable, open, and friendly geopolitical space across Europe and Asia. This required
making commitments, establishing institutions, forging partnerships, acquiring clients, and providing liberal hegemonic leadership (Ikenberry 2011; Stewart 2009).
HST suggests that non-hegemonic systems are 'inherently unstable' and that global
stability thus depends on the capacity of the hegemon to make the order stable.
HST is further split into two camps. One sees hegemony as delivering a 'collective
good' by creating a certain level of international stability and economic liberalisation that benefits most participants in global trade (Kindleberger 1981, 247 and
249–50). The other camp sees hegemony as a guarantor of national security (and
thus, by default, a provider of stability) rather than a public good (Gilpin 1975,
104).

Moreover, a group of HST sceptics have questioned the rationality behind
hegemony, asking whether it still serves American interests (Layne 2014; Mearsheimer 2018). As Brian Schmidt writes in this volume,

> [f]or those who no longer believe that hegemony serves American interests,
> the policy of primacy or 'deep engagement' is preventing the United States
> from achieving its core national interest. Moreover, with the onset of relative

decline and the rise of peer-competitors such as China, realist scholars such as Christopher Layne and John Mearsheimer have argued that a fundamentally different foreign policy is necessary today. Most realists are in basic agreement that a policy of offshore balancing, which before the cold war was the traditional policy that the United States adhered to, would better serve American interests today. (Schmidt, Chapter 2)

Meanwhile, scholars writing from a postcolonial perspective underline the far-reaching consequences of hegemonic subordination for actors other than the hegemon. These critics highlight the curtailment of development opportunities that results when imposing a certain rationality that mostly serves the economic interest of the centre (Bajpai and Parashar: Chapter 13; see also Staniszkis 2003).[1]

The notion of a 'complex hegemony' elaborated in this book by Scholte (Introduction and Chapter 5) provides an alternative approach that helps to systematize the debates in this volume. It also guides several chapters in avoiding reductionist diagnoses of hegemony. 'In particular', Scholte writes, 'a complexity approach reacts against the reductionism and linearity that have dominated modern science. Instead, complexity conceives of reality – including the realities of hegemony in world politics – in terms of systems with multiple co-constituting forces'. Our introductory chapter further proposes a fourfold typology of material, discursive, institutional and performative techniques that are overlapping in concrete actions leading to hegemonic domination (Scholte, Casier, Dutkiewicz, Introduction). This book's position is that

> [w]hether hegemony lies with state, capital, knowledge, empire, or whatever, it establishes and sustains itself through a mix of material, discursive, institutional, and performative techniques. None of the four is sufficient by itself. For example, to control the rule-making institutions, a hegemonic force needs command of resources, narratives, and rituals. Likewise, deployment of discursive techniques requires economic means, institutional frameworks, and ceremonial presentations. (Scholte, Chapter 5)

Combined, this approach allowed us to look at hegemony from multiple theoretical and policy lenses, adding to the complexity of the current debate, or in the words of Scholte, 'the notion that hegemony operates in complicated and substantially unpredictable ways through a co-constitution of multiple forces ... and its "complexity" involves not a precise explanatory theory, but a general meta-theoretical orientation' (Scholte, Chapter 5). Combined, the chapters in this volume contribute to drawing and understanding a complex picture of hegemony as part and parcel of the changing world order.

Crisis and change?

Is the future of hegemonic orders fixed or alterable? Our authors suggest that hegemonic arrangements are likely to be 're-imagined' and 're-invented' in the period ahead. Beverly Silver and Corey Payne suggest a change from "'catching up" with core locations' to another reconfiguration of the hierarchy of wealth among non-core locations. Similarly, Piotr Dutkiewicz suggests that a new multi-hegemonic and multi-centric international system is on the horizon (Dutkiewicz 2019; the argument is elaborated in Dutkiewicz 2017).

Let us offer a tentative explanation of the roots of the current potential moment of hegemonic change. The current chaotic world order is a consequence of unresolved structural contradictions that – while providing dynamism to the system – are increasingly quickly mutating. The consequence of these contradictions is systemic fear: a fear that we are no longer subjects of most processes of governance.

Rather than acting as an expedient but ad hoc political *tool*, fear has become the de facto essence of politics. Fear now provides an impetus and reason for politics, replacing – in part – other sources of legitimisation of power. Zygmunt Bauman proposed that states (small and big) have limited capacity to govern because we are in a state of 'inter-regnum', in which 'the inherited means of having things done no longer work, yet the new and more adequate ways have not been invented, let alone deployed' (Bauman and Della Sala 2013). The condition of inter-regnum has resulted from the progressive separation and divorce of power (an ability to have things done) and politics (ability to decide which things are to be done), and the resulting disparity between the task in hand and tools available to the state. On one hand, power is increasingly free of state control, but also the state increasingly suffers from a deficit of power. The result is that we (as people) fear that the gap between the scope of tasks to make our life more secure/stable and the ability of institutions to deal with them is an abysmal and ever-widening gap. Power is shifting its focus from state to capital (Nitzan and Bichler 2009), in the hands of very few and moving beyond public control (Hardoon 2017). That adds to a sense of inevitability about new lines of confrontations (for example, around trade and social inequality) as well as declining trust.

In line with certain scholars of ontological security, it could be argued that globalisation has caused 'a state of disruption', 'where the individual or collectives of individuals have lost their stabilising anchor (their sense of security) and their ability to sustain a linear narrative and answer questions about doing, acting and being'(Kinnvall and Mitzen 2017, 7). Thus, a feeling predominates among many that we are no longer able to act conclusively in protecting individual and group interests. We thereby lose our stake in the system and become deprived of the future (Dutkiewicz and Kazarinova 2018). Thus, fear is no longer merely an expedient ad hoc political tool, but has become the essence of politics. Fear provides the main impetus and reason for politics, replacing legitimating discourses around democracy, justice and the common good. Yet *fear as politics* may also have a *transformational capacity* vis-à-vis norms and institutions as an enabler for a multiplicity of the hegemonic arrangements as a tempting solution to re-gain (or gain) influence, manageability, control, domination and primacy.[2]

Thus the analyses in our volume generate an expectation of a wave of new hegemonic arrangements. The 'complex hegemony' approach proposed in this book (involving multiple, non-reducible and interrelated forces) suggests that future hegemony will work in substantially indeterminate and largely uncontrollable ways. Creation and maintenance of this complex hegemony will require substantial power and a broad menu of hegemonic practices. In this environment of high uncertainty, state and non-state actors alike will demand more stability and predictability, which can drive them to first rethink and then reinvent local, national, regional and global hegemonies in an effort to provide at least some control over domestic and external affairs.

Insights on hegemony

As stressed in the introduction, this book represents a diversity of approaches. This diversity has produced a plethora of insights on hegemony, sometimes conflicting, often overlapping. Some of the key insights on different hegemony related issues are revisited here.

Most chapters recognise the relevance of both state and non-state actors for hegemony. Some have focused on the role of the former, in particular the role of the current hegemon, the United States, and rising powers that may or may not challenge its dominance, in particular China, Russia and India. Others have studied in particular non-state actors and inter-state actors, acting as 'quasi-hegemonic' actors (Geiger) or local societal actors obstructing hegemonic efforts (Akchurina). Several contributions go beyond this binary view of state and non-state actors. Scholte stresses the complexity of hegemony and sees transnational elite networks at work. In a similar vein, Pal speaks of 'neural networks' of diverse actors (consisting of governments, international organisations, think tanks, NGOs, universities, political parties and media) who continuously constitute hegemonic order through their articulations and practices.

But all chapters go beyond the question of actors and recognise the importance of forces sustaining hegemony. The key question at the heart of several chapters is the role of material versus ideational factors. Whereas Schmidt puts the emphasis on material preponderance and leadership, others recognise the distribution of ideas as an equally crucial pillar of hegemony (Pal, Casier). These ideas do not form 'a single coherent ideological system of beliefs, but a synaptic flaring of ideas and concepts that create a conceptual justificatory space' (Pal). Chebankova goes beyond this, arguing that the ideational factors play a crucial role in hegemony and attributing the crisis of Western hegemony to the crisis of liberalism, as its underpinning ideology. Safranchuk sees a historical first in today's world: a mismatch between global material power and non-universal consent on its application, in a context where universally shared ideas are in decline.

Several chapters, inspired by neo-Gramscianism, recognise the importance of both coercion and consent in sustaining hegemony. Ideational and material factors are complemented by a third pillar: institutions, that serve as a setting to reproduce ideas and to give the unequal distribution of benefits both stability and legitimacy.

In a different way Scholte sees hegemony as 'a complex of interweaving forces', which cannot be reduced to causal factors in their own right but are interrelated and co-constitute hegemony. This co-constitution of forces is what renders hegemony a degree of consistency and stability. Drawing on Giddens, Scholte refers to this interrelatedness of leading states, elite networks, capitalism, technicism and disciplining discourses as structuration in Internet governance.

Germain sees the consistency and durability in a 'deep multilayered structure'. In Casier's approach, building on Robert Cox, stability results from the configuration of three forces (material capabilities, ideas and institutions) that reinforce each other. Together they form relatively stable structures that obtain an aura of universality.

The complexity of hegemony is reflected in the wide variety of practices studied throughout the book, dealing with diverse issues such as the hegemonic position of the US dollar (not only backed up by its material position, but also by a *mentalité* – Germain), hybrid warfare (as an instrument to maintain or achieve hegemony – Sloan), financialisation (Zhang), trade (Wang), Internet governance (Scholte), migration politics (Geiger) and regional connectivity projects (Akchurina).

Contestation and counter-hegemonic efforts are covered widely, be it driven by states (China, Russia and to a lesser degree India) or driven by social forces (global civil society or local social structures).

Many chapters bring in their own original perspectives, such as the role of perceptions and domestic needs in counter-hegemonic policies (Wang) or the role of incomplete statehood and the power of improvisation in the failure to establish hegemony (Akchurina). Many authors acknowledge the co-existence of multiple hegemonies. Bajpai and Parashar highlight ambiguities in India's attitude, simultaneously contesting and reinforcing hegemonies.

On the question to what extent the current hegemonic order is in crisis, the answers provided in this book diverge more strongly. Several authors see a deep crisis of the hegemonic liberal order, reflected in global social protests (Silver and Payne), in the contradictions and dilemmas produced by liberalism (Chebankova) or the mismatch between material power and non-universal consent (Safranchuk). Several authors see a relative decline of the leading state, the US. Schmidt confronts Realist and Liberal views on the future of US leadership.

On the other side of the spectrum, some authors claim that the current hegemonic order may turn out to be more resilient than expected. This is because it forms a relatively stable structure of forces, in contrast to rapidly shifting power relations (Casier). In this case a hegemonic order may survive the decline of the hegemon as long as consent on core ideas – such as free trade in a relatively open global economy – persist. Germain comes to a similar conclusion in the case of the hegemonic position of the US dollar, as deeply entrenched structure.

Inevitably this opens different perspectives on the future of hegemonic order. But the choice does not need to be simply one between collapse or survival of hegemonies. Many authors recognise the possibility of co-existence of multiple hegemonic orders, whether organised geographically, ideologically or along rather contingent lines. These views connect with recent debates and concepts formulated by Flockhart, Acharya et al. Wang sees the current trade and technology war between Washington and Beijing as a restructuring of world order, whereby the US and China will eventually co-exist as leading powers. This seems supportive of the idea of Buzan and Lawson of the possibility of either inter-capitalist competition or a concert of capitalist powers, whereby the deeper structures would not necessarily change fundamentally.

Further questions, further debates

Many insights advanced in this volume raise questions about policy implications. Indeed, some of our authors have reflected on practical consequences in policy briefs that are collected in a separate Report (Dutkiewicz et al. 2019). Several themes come out of this exercise, providing food for a fascinating policy debate and indicating possible avenues for further research.

Deep change versus reorganisation

Do shifts in material power relations entail a transformation of world order? Are rising powers like China successful in promoting alternative ideas and institutions of world order? Are we witnessing a reconfiguration of core principles (such as free trade) or are we at the edge of overhauling them? What lessons for policy can be drawn from those two distinctive pictures?

Our authors agree that world order is currently undergoing substantial change. Power relations are shifting, and hierarchies underpinning world order are being contested. Yet, views differ regarding what to expect. Are we on the cusp of the new order? Or do currently unfolding changes not call into question fundamental principles of the global order? As hegemonically generated rules and regulatory institutions (e.g. the World Bank or the International Monetary Fund) still enjoy substantial legitimacy, it may be premature to announce a change in the international order, despite profound changes in power relations.

China, the world's most important rising power, has been cautious in challenging the established world order, primarily in order not to jeopardise its access to an open global economy. Our contributors differ on whether the future order will be determined by 'inter-capitalist competition' or whether it will be deeply restructured beyond capitalism. An interesting question at the heart of the debate is how far the maintenance of hegemony continues to serve American interests and whether American hegemony is in decline.

Another policy question is whether the changing world order offers new opportunities for countries that have been traditionally subjected to hegemonic subordination (such as India). Since the new global order is arguably moving away from unilateral hegemony towards a plural hegemonic configuration – the emerging new order could well eventually include prominent states who share the goal of changing the rulebook of the prevailing system (Bajpai and Parashar Chapter 13). The big question is whether these 'rising powers' will be willing to cooperate within existing power structures or rather will try to recreate their own regional or sub-regional hegemonic orders.

The nature of the new world order

Due to the legitimacy that it entails, hegemony cannot be disconnected from beliefs. If one believes, as liberal theory asserts, that hegemony is beneficial for the hegemon and provides public goods for others (see the case of the US discussed in our volume), then one might wish to preserve it. Conversely, if one concludes that hegemony does not serve American interests, which is the position of defensive realists, then the US should accept or even promote hegemonic decline. The proposition of 'complex hegemony' rejects this binary approach, but further research of hegemony in terms of systems with multiple co-constituting forces could be fruitful. As Scholte notes (Chapter 5), 'the overall promise of complexity thinking is thus far underdeveloped. In particular, the approach has little entered the study of hegemony in world politics, apart from previously noted partial steps in respect of world-systems theory and intersectionality. The moment can be ripe to push these explorations further'.

Locus of power

Power is omnipresent in our book. With a complexity perspective, the key focus of our contributors was on the interrelations and mutual effects of these forces. Power in this volume has many incarnations and locations: material, institutional, ideational, processual, discursive, normative, imaginary or a combination of all above. Power produces hegemony, as it also feeds the sources of its contestation. The tempting question then arises as to which power sources are most important in securing international hegemony? Our book has provided a significant contribution to this question by showing that hegemony cannot be located in one principal force, but many fascinating research questions remain as to how these forces are intertwined and applied.

We have located power in states and non-state actors, institutions, ideas, social and economic processes. As power is changing locations and no single actor today possesses the exclusive monopoly on the multiple sources of power, further work will be required on whether those who control them will be able to coordinate or will clash, and – as a result – whether different hegemonic forces will be able to co-exist peacefully.

Contesting hegemony

That a certain degree of consensus exists on the normative networks (for instance around free trade or health) does not mean that the current hegemonic world order is not contested. But it is contested in the first place for the way it sustains hierarchies and for the way it benefits dominant powers, while constraining the rise of others. Here we find a number of interesting paradoxes. One has to do with which potentially rising powers benefit most from the current system. The steepest riser, China, has greater potential to challenge current hegemonic structures but needs to maintain some fundamental pillars of this order to protect its current position. Russia, the relatively weaker player, is the most vocal contender but has limited means to back up its protests. A second paradox has to do with the internal contradictions within counter-hegemonic movements. We discussed how the legacy of colonial rule and the histories of counter-hegemonic movements continue to have an enduring influence on the conduct of domestic politics in post-colonial societies. We discussed – for instance – how anti-colonial movements incorporated numerous counter-hegemonic struggles under the aegis of the over-arching objective of political independence. However, the advent of the independent nation-state did not meet the aspirations of several of these counter-hegemonic struggles. On the contrary, in many cases, the postcolonial state reinforced certain types of inherited hegemonies. Further inquiry on how counter-hegemonic forces in postcolonial societies (internationally) combine re-production of past hegemonies domestically may add significantly to our debates on counter-hegemony.

Finally, our book – pointing to the complexity of processes discussed – proposed a scenario of accelerated processes of re-hegemonisation (reconfiguration of power in different forms and shades) of the regional/global regulatory and institutional arrangements. We contend this is a result of multiple processes and challenges the current economic and political systems are unable to react to in a meaningful way. The most fascinating aspect of studying hegemony, in all its configurations and reconfigurations, remains that it is a topic that can never be fully exhausted and will never stop to invite new research or to provoke new debates. Taking complexity and diversity as a starting point, this book has attempted to contribute to the various ways in which power and hegemony can be re-imagined to reflect the volatility and profound changes of these times.

Notes

1 'Improper sequence of liberalization and the global logics ability to inject institutions and procedures that are rational, from its own perspective, but not from the perspective of the level of development (historical time) of peripheries lead to un-steerability [...] This leads to a situation within which – even when all the institutional networks are based upon the economic rationality of the market – there is one logic for the local, 'young' market (whose overriding directive is the accumulation of capital, and whose institutional infrastructure is poorly developed) and another logic for the mature market, one poised for expansion' (Staniszkis 2003, 275).

2 One can argue that key policy areas such as migration (Huysmans 2006), safety and security (Furedi 2008), the labour market (Blanchflower and Shadforth 2009), development (Oxfam 2018), race (Ioanide 2015), democracy (Sleeper 2016), international relations (Taras 2015), the environment (Ritter & Borenstein 2016), and health and well-being are now fear-driven – either through attempts to address fear or by using it to legitimise further empowerment of elites or other actors.

References

Barabanov, O.*et al.* (2018) *War and Peace in the 21st Century: International Stability and Balance of the New Type.* Valdai Discussion Club Report. Available at: https://valdaiclub.com/files/9635/ (accessed 18 February 2020).

Bauman, Z. and Della Sala, V. (2013) 'Re-create the Social State', in P. Dutkiewicz and R. Sakwa (eds), *22 Ideas to Fix the World*, New York: New York University Press, 186–201.

Blanchflower, D.G. and Shadforth, C. (2009) 'Fear, Unemployment and Migration', *The Economic Journal*, 119(535), F136–F182.

Dutkiewicz, P. (2017) 'Conclusions', in V. Popov and P. Dutkiewicz (eds) *Mapping a New World Order: The Rest beyond the West*, Cheltenham: Edward Elgar, 196–206.

Dutkiewicz, P. (2019) 'Chaos, Fear, and Hegemony: Equality and Efficiency in the International Order'. DOC Expert Comment. Available at: https://doc-research.org/2019/07/equality-efficiency-international-order/ (accessed 18 February 2020).

Dutkiewicz, P. and Kazarinova, D.B. (2018) 'Fear as Politics', *Polis. Political Studies*, 4: 8–21.

Dutkiewicz, P.*et al.* (2019) *(Re)Imagining Hegemonies: Key Policy Outcomes.* DOC Special Report. Available at: https://doc-research.org/2019/11/reimagining-hegemonies-key-policy/ (accessed 18 February 2020).

Furedi, F. (2008) 'Fear and Security: A Vulnerability-led Policy Response', *Social Policy & Administration*, 42(6), 645–661.

Gilpin, R. (1975) *U.S. Power and the Multinational Corporation: The Political Economy of Foreign Direct Investment.* London: Macmillan.

Hardoon, D. (2017) 'An Economy for the 99%', Oxfam Briefing Paper, January 2017. Available at: www.oxfam.org/en/research/economy-99 (accessed 18 February 2020).

Huysmans, J. (2006) *The Politics of Insecurity: Fear, Migration and Asylum in the EU.* Abingdon: Routledge.

Ikenberry, J. (2011) *Liberal Leviathan: The Origins, Crisis, and Transformation of the American World Order.* Princeton, NJ: Princeton University Press.

Ioanide, P. (2015) *The Emotional Politics of Racism.* Stanford, CA: Stanford University Press.

Kindleberger, C.P. (1981) 'Dominance and Leadership in the International Economy: Exploitation, Public Goods, and Free Rides', *International Studies Quarterly*, 25(2), 242–254.

Kinnvall, C. and Mitzen, J. (2017). 'An Introduction to the Special Issue: Ontological Securities in World Politics', *Cooperation and Conflict*, 52(1), 3–11.

Layne, C. (2014) 'This Time It's Real: The End of Unipolarity and the Pax Americana', *International Studies Quarterly*, 55(1), 1–11.

Mearsheimer, J. (2018) *The Great Delusion: Liberal Dreams and International Realities.* New Haven, CT: Yale University Press.

Nitzan, J. and Bichler, S. (2009) *Capital as Power: A Study of Order and Creorder.* London: Routledge.

Oxfam International (2018) 'Richest 1 Percent Bagged 82 Percent of Wealth Created Last Year - Poorest Half of Humanity Got Nothing', Oxfam Press release. Available at: www.oxfam.org/en/pressroom/pressreleases/2018-01-22/richest-1-percent-bagged-82-percent-wealth-created-last-year (accessed 18 February 2020).

Ritter, K. and Borenstein, S. (2016) 'Environmental Activists Fear "Climate Progress is Dead" after Trump Takes U.S. Election', *National Post*. Available at: https://nationalpost.com/news/environmental-activists-fear-climate-progress-is-dead-after-trump-takes-u-s-election (accessed 18 February 2020).

Sleeper, J. (2016) 'A History of Unwarranted Fears of Tyranny', *The New York Times*. Available at: www.nytimes.com/roomfordebate/2016/05/12/is-tyranny-around-the-corner/a-history-of-unwarranted-fears-of-tyranny (accessed 18 February 2020).

Staniszkis, J. (2003) 'The Asymmetry of Rationalities (Power of Globalization)', *Polish Sociological Review*, 3(143), 275–288.

Stewart, P. (2009) *The Best Laid Plans: The Origins of American Multilateralism and the Dawn of the Cold War*. Lanham, MD: Rowman & Littlefield.

Taras, R. (2015) *Fear and the Making of Foreign Policy*. Edinburgh: Edinburgh University Press.

Webb, M. and Krasner, S. (1989) 'Hegemonic Stability Theory: An Empirical Assessment', *Review of International Studies*, 15(2), 183–198.

INDEX

Note: Page locators in **bold** refer to tables and in *italic* refer to figures.

Printed in the United States
by Baker & Taylor Publisher Services